Alfred Wilhelm LEIBNIZ

THE MONADOLOGY

AND

OTHER PHILOSOPHICAL WRITINGS

TRANSLATED

WITH INTRODUCTION AND NOTES

BY

ROBERT LATTA, M.A., D.PHIL. (EDIN.)

LECTURER IN LOGIC AND METAPHYSICS AT THE
UNIVERSITY OF ST. ANDREWS

Oxford
AT THE CLARENDON PRESS
1898

Oxford
PRINTED AT THE CLARENDON PRESS
BY HORACE HART, M.A.
PRINTER TO THE UNIVERSITY

PREFACE

----·----

In this country Leibniz has received less attention than any other of the great philosophers. Mr. Merz has given, in a small volume, a general outline of Leibniz's thought and work, Professor Sorley has written for the *Encyclopaedia Britannica* a remarkably clear, but brief, account of his philosophy, and there are American translations of the *Nouveaux Essais* and of some of his philosophical papers. That is very nearly the whole of English writing about him. Yet few philosophical systems stand so much in need of exposition as that of Leibniz. His theories have to be extracted from seven large volumes of correspondence, criticism, magazine articles, and other discursive writings, and it is only in recent years that this material has been made fully available by the publication of Gerhardt's edition. No complete and detailed account of Leibniz's philosophy has hitherto been published in English, and accordingly I have written a very full Introduction to this book, with illustrative foot-notes, consisting mainly of translations from Leibniz himself.

The endeavour of the book is to make the *Monadology* clear to students. I cannot agree with Dillmann in treating it as of little importance.

Leibniz himself expressly intended it to be a compact and ordered statement of the views he had expounded in many scattered papers and in his somewhat desultory *Théodicée*, the only book he published. There is evidence of this in his correspondence and in the fact that he annotated the *Monadology* with references to passages in the *Théodicée*. My original intention was to publish a translation of these passages along with the *Monadology*, but on re-consideration it seemed better to translate several short papers illustrating different parts of Leibniz's system and explaining its growth. Thus the *Monadology*, as being the centre of the book, is printed first of the translations (although in date it is last), while the other writings follow in chronological order. The only disadvantage of this arrangement is that it places the *Principles of Nature and of Grace*, which is most akin to the *Monadology*, farthest away from it.

If I might venture to suggest to the student the way in which the book should be read, I would recommend him first to read Part I of the Introduction, then the *Monadology* (without the notes), afterwards Parts II and III of the Introduction, the *Monadology* again (with the notes), the other translations, and finally Part IV of the Introduction, in which I have endeavoured to 'place' the philosophy of Leibniz in relation to the systems which came before and after his.

My indebtedness to authors is so great and varied that I cannot acknowledge it in detail; but I may mention as specially helpful to me the works of Boutroux, Dillmann, Nourisson, Nolen, and Stein. My thanks are due to Professor Jones, of Glasgow, who read the Introduction in manuscript, for much valuable suggestion and criticism; and I am more than grateful to Professor Ritchie, of St. Andrews, who read the whole book, both in manuscript and in proof, and to whom it owes numerous improvements as well in form as in matter.

I have adopted the spelling 'Leibniz' in place of the traditional 'Leibnitz,' because the former was invariably used by Leibniz in signing his own name.

It ought perhaps also to be mentioned that Parts II and III of the Introduction were accepted by the University of Edinburgh as a thesis for the degree of Doctor of Philosophy.

ROBERT LATTA.

UNIVERSITY OF ST. ANDREWS,
    June, 1898.

TABLE OF CONTENTS

CONTENTS

ABBREVIATIONS

—◆—

E. *God. Guil. Leibnitii opera philosophica quae extant latina, gallica, germanica omnia*, ed. J. E. Erdmann. Berlin, 1840.

G. *Die philosophischen Schriften von G. W. Leibniz*, herausgegeben von C. J. Gerhardt. Berlin, 1875–90.

G. Math. *Leibnizens mathematische Schriften*, herausgegeben von C. J. Gerhardt. · Berlin and Halle, 1850–63.

Dutens. *G. G. Leibnitii opera omnia, nunc primum collecta*, studio Ludovici Dutens. Geneva, 1768.

Klopp. *Die Werke von Leibniz*, herausgegeben von Onno Klopp. Hanover, 1864–77.

Foucher de Careil. *Œuvres de Leibniz, publiées pour la première fois d'après les manuscrits originaux*, par A. Foucher de Careil. Paris, 1859–75.

Mollat. *Rechtsphilosophisches aus Leibnizens ungedruckten Schriften*, von Dr. Georg Mollat. Leipzig, 1885.

INTRODUCTION

———•———

PART I.

THE LIFE AND WORKS OF LEIBNIZ.

His Boyhood.

On June 21, 1646, two years before the close of
the Thirty Years' War, Gottfried Wilhelm Leibniz was
born at Leipzig. His family was of Bohemian origin;
but his ancestors for several generations had lived in
Saxony and Prussia, and his father was a Professor of
Philosophy in the University of Leipzig. Leibniz was
only six years of age when his father died; and, though
in his early years ·he had the training of a pious mother,
she also passed away before he had completed his University studies. The boys of Leipzig in Leibniz's time
appear to have been brought up on 'the picture-book of
Comenius and the little Catechism' (Luther's); but the
soul of Leibniz already sought stronger meat, and having
found in the house an illustrated copy of Livy, of which
he could not thoroughly understand a single line, he
managed to get a tolerable idea of its contents, supple-
menting his scanty Latin by a study of the pictures and
some judicious guessing. As an indirect result of this
precocity, his father's library was thrown open to him,
and he wandered at will from volume to volume, finding
(as was ever characteristic of him) some good in all[1].

[1] 'It is characteristic of me to hold opposition (*Widerlegen*) as of

B

Providence or Fortune seemed to say to him, *Tolle, lege ;* and it is significant for the philosophy to come that he turned first to the Ancients, to Cicero, Quintilian, Seneca, Pliny, Herodotus, Xenophon, Plato, the historians of the Roman Empire, and the Fathers of the Church. Of these he tells us that 'he understood at first nothing, then gradually something, and finally enough'; but unconsciously his mind was coloured by their style and thought, 'as men walking in the sun have their faces browned without knowing it,' and under their inspiration he made it the rule of his life ever to seek clearness in speaking and a useful purpose in acting (*in verbis claritas, in rebus usus*). Thus at fourteen years of age he was counted by his fellows a prodigy of learning and ability, and already his reading of Logic and intense determination towards clearness of thought and speech had led him to ideas which were afterwards developed into the suggestion of a logical Calculus and an 'Alphabet of Concepts' as means to the discovery of truth [1].

University Life.

At fifteen years of age Leibniz became a student at the University of Leipzig, and about the same time he became

little account, exposition (*Darlegen*) as of much account, and when a new book comes into my hands I look for what I can learn from it, not for what I can criticize in it.' *Schreiben an G. Wagner* (1696) (E. 425 b ; G. vii. 526).

[1] 'Before I reached the school-class in which Logic was taught, I was deep in the historians and poets ; for I had begun to read the historians almost as soon as I was able to read at all, and in verse I found great pleasure and ease ; but as soon as I began to learn Logic I found myself greatly excited by the division and order of thoughts which I perceived therein. I immediately began to notice, so far as a boy of thirteen could, that there must be a great deal in it. I took the greatest pleasure in the Predicaments' (i. e. the Categories) 'which came before me as a muster-roll of all the things in the world, and I turned to "Logics" of all sorts to find the best and most detailed form of this list. I often asked myself and my schoolfellows to which Predicament and also to which sub-class this or that thing might belong.' *Schreiben an G. Wagner* (E. 420 a ; G. vii. 516).

acquainted with the works of some of the modern philosophers, beginning with Bacon's *De Augmentis Scientiarum.* At this time also, as he himself tells us, he read with interest the works of Cardan and Campanella and the suggestions of a better philosophy in Kepler, Galileo, and Descartes. But he was no 'reading-machine, all wound up and going.' He thought for himself : he read in order to ' weigh and consider.' And thus in after-years he recalls how, when he was fifteen years of age, he walked alone in a wood near Leipzig, called the Rosenthal, to consider whether or not he should retain in his philosophy the 'Substantial Forms' of the Scholastics'. Although his favourite teacher at Leipzig was Jacob Thomasius, a Professor of Philosophy, deeply versed in ancient and scholastic learning, the private reading of Leibniz at first prevailed in his thought and he turned from the older philosophies to ' mechanism ' and mathematics. The 'Substantial Forms' were for the time set aside, to reappear, transmuted, in later years. His scholastic studies, however, bore fruit in the earliest of his published writings, a graduation thesis with the significant title *De principio individui,* in which he defended the Nominalist position. Intending to devote himself to the profession of law, he went for a year (in 1663) to Jena, where the mathematician, Erhard Weigel, was lecturing on 'the Law of Nature,' or what we should now call Jurisprudence in general. Doubtless the influence of Weigel tended to confirm Leibniz's mathematical bent, and he still continued his study of history. In 1666 the University of Leipzig, ostensibly on the ground of his youth, refused to give him the Doctorate in Law; but his thesis, *De casibus perplexis in jure,* was immediately accepted by the University of Altdorf (near Nürnberg), where he declined the offer of a professorship. Thus ended his connexion with Leipzig.

[1] *Lettre à M. Remond* (1714) (E. 702 a ; G. iii. 606).

Boineburg and the Elector of Mainz.

In Nürnberg, at that time the capital of a small republic, which had suffered less than many other German States from the Thirty Years' War, Leibniz spent a year, in the course of which his extensive curiosity led him to become a member of a secret society of the Rosicrucians, who were trying to find the philosopher's stone. Fontenelle tells us that Leibniz's method of gaining admission to the society was to collect from books on alchemy all the most obscure phrases he could find and to make of them an unintelligible letter, which he produced as evidence of his fitness for membership. The society was so impressed that it immediately appointed him to be its secretary. The chief gain to Leibniz appears to have been that through this society he became acquainted with Baron von Boineburg, 'one of the most celebrated diplomatists of his age,' who had formerly been minister to the Elector and Archbishop of Mainz, the most powerful man in the Empire. With Boineburg Leibniz went to Frankfort, where he wrote and published a paper on legal education, which was the means of introducing him to the archbishop, in whose service he remained for some time. This was the beginning of his career as a diplomatist. The long war had left Germany in ruins, and, ere there was time to rebuild, the whole empire was threatened by the immense power of Louis XIV, who was dreaming of world-wide sway. The Elector of Mainz, says Leibniz, 'had seen the miseries of Germany, whose ruins were still smoking : he was one of those who had laboured most to bring back rest to the land, from which life seemed almost to have gone. The country was (as one might hardly say) "peopled" with little children, and if war were to break out again (as might be expected when Sweden was irritated and France threatening) there was every reason to fear that this seed of a new population would be destroyed and a great part of poor Germany left almost without inhabitant[1].' The treaty of Westphalia had secured peace and some measure of political unity, but it pointed also to an ecclesiastical reunion, yet to be realized, which to men like the Elector of Mainz and Boineburg seemed the best means of restoring power and happiness to the country. Negotiations for the reunion of Roman Catholics and Protestants had already been begun, and thus early in his diplomatic career Leibniz took part in the work of conciliation which in various ways he continued throughout his life. At the suggestion of Boineburg he made a special study of the doctrine of transubstantiation, with the result (expressed in a letter to Arnauld in 1671) that he found it impossible to reconcile the Cartesian view of material substance as pure extension either with the Roman Catholic or with the Lutheran doctrine. He accordingly formed the purpose of discovering a theory of substance which should satisfy both, and should thus become a philosophical basis for the reconciliation of the Churches.

Paris and London.

Presently events occurred which led him away from Mainz and gave him new opportunities of study and of intercourse with learned men. Leibniz and his friends felt strongly the necessity of drawing into safe channels the military ambitions of Louis XIV, and accordingly Leibniz prepared a most elaborate work in which he suggested to the King of France the advantages that would arise from a conquest of Egypt, and tried to convince him that it was more worthy of a Christian king to fight the unchristian Turks than to harass a poor little people like the Dutch[2]. This book was never

---

[1] From a letter of Leibniz, quoted by Foucher de Careil, vol. iv. Introduction, p. xx.

[2] This *Projet de Conquête de l'Égypte* was published by Foucher de Careil, vol. v. It shows a most remarkable knowledge regarding the state of the country and its possibilities, and so clever are the

actually presented to King Louis, but Leibniz in 1672 went by invitation to Paris to explain his project. His advice was not taken ; but he remained in Paris for four years, during which he devoted himself to the study of the higher mathematics[1] and to the discussion of the Cartesian philosophy. He had already corresponded with Arnauld, and he now met also Huygens and Malebranche. At this time, says Leibniz himself, 'law and history were my forte[2].' But intercourse with Huygens and the study of the mathematical works of Pascal introduced him to the problems of modern mathematics. Huygens, he tells us[3], 'had no taste for metaphysics,' but Leibniz learned from him mathematical methods and principles which influenced the growth of his philosophy, and which set him on the way to the discovery of the Differential Calculus. At this time also Leibniz invented a calculating machine, superior to that of Pascal, which could only add and subtract, while his own machine could also multiply, divide, and extract roots. And in other ways the residence of Leibniz in Paris greatly affected his life-work. For instance, it probably led to his writing so much in French. He had already, in his essay on the philosophical style of Nizolius (1670), advocated the use of the German language for philosophical and other works. But in the time of Louis XIV Paris was the intellectual centre of Europe, and to write for the world was to write in French. While, therefore,

plans which it suggests that Napoleon was at one time supposed to have borrowed its ideas for his campaign. Though this has been shown to be a mistake, the coincidence between the suggested expedition of Louis XIV and the actual expedition of Napoleon is sufficiently noteworthy.

[1] 'The merit of an author in mathematics cannot be disputed, as it can in other subjects. This is the reason why I remained some time in France, in order to perfect myself in mathematics, and I gave my time to these sciences not on their own account, but in order to make them contribute to the advancement of piety.' *Lettre au Duc Jean Frédéric* (undated) (Klopp, iv. 450).

[2] *Lettre à la Comtesse de Kilmansegg* (1716) (Dutens, iii. 456).

[3] E. 702 b ; G. iii. 607.

Leibniz has rightly been called 'the father of German philosophy,' he is only to a very small extent a German author.

The four years' residence of Leibniz in Paris was broken by a brief visit to England in the early months of 1673. Leibniz had already sought the favour of English learning by dedicating one of his publications to the Royal Society, and he had also been greatly interested in the philosophy of Hobbes, with which to a great extent he found himself in agreement, especially as regards questions of physics, although he was strongly opposed to his political theories. In 1670 he wrote a letter to Hobbes, to which he received no answer, and afterwards he began another letter, but left it unfinished. It has recently been maintained that, up to the year 1670, Leibniz was 'more deeply affected by Hobbes than by any other of the leading spirits of the new time [1].' When Leibniz visited London, Hobbes was still living there, but he was eighty-five years of age, and some years earlier Leibniz had heard from his countryman Oldenburg, who was secretary of the Royal Society, that Hobbes was in his dotage. Accordingly it is not surprising that they did not meet. Apart from Oldenburg, the man with whom Leibniz seems to have had most intercourse during this visit to London was Robert Boyle, the famous physicist; but there is no reason to suppose that Leibniz gained much from his stay in England, except an additional stimulus to the study of the higher mathematics, which he carried on more systematically after his return to Paris. As a fitting conclusion of his Parisian period came the discovery of the Differential Calculus, which was practically accomplished by Leibniz

[1] See Tönnies in *Philos. Monatshefte*, vol. xxiii. pp. 557-573. Cf. Leibniz's *Letter to Hobbes* (1670) (G. i. 85): 'I constantly maintain among my friends, and, with the help of God, I will always publicly maintain also, that I know no writer who has philosophized more accurately, more clearly, and more elegantly than you, not even excepting a man of such excellent genius as Descartes himself.'

in 1676. There can be no doubt that Newton was in possession of a similar method as early as 1665. He at first made known only some of the results of the method, and not the method itself. Hence an attempt has been made to show that Leibniz got hints of the method during his first visit to England, and that he was thus more or less a plagiarist of Newton. But there is nothing to confirm this, and a full consideration makes it much more likely that each discovered the method independently. Leibniz published his account of the method in 1684: Newton's was first published in 1693. To Newton belongs the glory of priority, whatever that may be worth; while the form which Leibniz gave to the Calculus, the names and the signs which he used, have come to be universally employed in preference to those of Newton [1].

Visit to Spinoza.

Shortly before Leibniz went to London, Boineburg died; and the visit to London was unexpectedly brought to an end in March, 1673, by the death of the Archbishop of Mainz. Leibniz was now without an official position, and during the next few years he made various unsuccessful attempts to obtain a diplomatic appointment. At last, in 1676, he somewhat reluctantly accepted the post of librarian to the Duke of Brunswick at Hanover, which was to be his home during the remainder of his life. During the earlier years of his residence in Paris, Leibniz had given much attention to the philosophy of Descartes and the Cartesians, with the result that he became more and more convinced of its insufficiency [2]. In his en-

---

[1] See Merz, *Leibniz* (Blackwood's Philosophical Classics), ch. iii. and v. Cf. Guhrauer's *Leibnitz*, i. 170 sqq.

[2] A few years after (in 1679) Leibniz writes to Philipp: 'As to the philosophy of Descartes I have no hesitation in saying absolutely that it leads to atheism' (G. iv. 281). And in the same year he writes to Malebranche that, while in many respects he admires Descartes, he is 'convinced that his mechanics is full of

deavour after a more satisfactory metaphysic he afterwards made a considerable study of Plato, and in 1676
he translated the *Phaedo* and the *Theaetetus*. Towards
the end of 1675 Leibniz became acquainted with the
young Bohemian nobleman, Tschirnhausen, Spinoza's
acute critic and correspondent, who was at that time in
Paris, and who had earlier in the same year written
some of the remarkable letters on account of which his
name will always be associated with that of Spinoza[1].
Leibniz had already (in 1671) written to Spinoza from
Frankfort about a question of optics; but now Tschirnhausen seems to have aroused in him the hope that
a solution of the difficulties of Cartesianism might be
found in the unpublished system of Spinoza. In
November, 1675, a medical friend of Spinoza in Amsterdam (G. H. Schuller) wrote to him: 'Von Tschirnhausen
further mentions that he has found at Paris a man called
Leibniz, remarkably learned and most skilled in various
sciences, as also free from the vulgar prejudices of
theology. With him he has formed an intimate acquaintance, founded on the fact that Leibniz labours with him
to pursue the perfection of the intellect, and, in fact,
reckons nothing better or more useful. Von Tschirnhausen
says that he is most practised in ethics, and speaks without any impulse derived from the passions, but by the
sole dictate of reason. He adds that he is most skilled in
physics, and also in metaphysical studies concerning God
and the soul. Finally, he concludes that he is most
worthy of having communicated to him the master's
writings, if you will first give your permission, for he
believes that the author will thence gain a great advantage, as he promises to show at length, if the master
be so pleased. But if not, do not doubt in the least that

errors, his physics is too hasty, his geometry is too limited, and
his metaphysics has all these faults combined' (G. i. 328).
    [1] Letters, 57 sqq. Van Vloten and Land, vol. ii. p. 204; Bruder,
vol. ii. p. 321 (Letters, 61 sqq.).

he will honourably keep them concealed as he has
promised, as in fact he has not made the slightest mention of them. Leibniz also highly values the *Theologico-
Political Treatise*, on the subject of which he once wrote
the master a letter, if he is not mistaken [1].' Spinoza, in
reply, recollects having some correspondence with Leibniz,
but Leibniz was at that time a counsellor at Frankfort,
and Spinoza would like to know, before entrusting his
writings to him, what he is doing in France, and he
would also like to have Tschirnhausen's opinion of
Leibniz, after a longer and more intimate acquaintance.
Spinoza's shyness had probably no other effect than to
whet the curiosity of Leibniz, and accordingly, when he
left Paris in October, 1676, he went for a week to
London (where he met for the first time Newton's friend
Collins) and then crossed to Amsterdam, where he stayed
four weeks with Schuller, eagerly reading and criticizing
every writing of Spinoza's which Schuller could give
him. At last, in November, Leibniz obtained an inter-
view with Spinoza at the Hague, where he seems to have
spent some time. They had many conversations together
regarding philosophical matters, of which Leibniz has
left hardly any record except the remark that 'Spinoza
did not quite clearly see the defects of Descartes'
laws of motion : he was surprised when I began to show
him that they were inconsistent with the equality of
cause and effect[2].' The persistence of Leibniz ultimately
induced Spinoza to show him the MS. of the *Ethics*
(or at least a portion of it), and he seems even to
have had permission to make a copy of the leading
definitions, axioms, and propositions[3]. What at this time
most dissatisfied Leibniz was Spinoza's treatment of
Final Causes. His recent study of Plato had impressed

---

[1] Letter 70, Van Vloten and Land, vol. ii. p. 235.
[2] Foucher de Careil, *Réfutation inédite de Spinoza*, p. lxiv.
[3] Spinoza died in the following year, and soon afterwards the
Ethics was published.

Leibniz with the value of teleological considerations, and he was already seeking in that direction an escape from the imperfections of the mechanical view of things. But his general hostility to Spinoza's system did not show itself until ten years later, when he had settled the essential points of his own doctrine of substance. At this time Leibniz was still seeking light in every quarter.

Residence in Hanover. Correspondence and Growth of his System.

Leibniz arrived at Hanover in the last days of 1676. Efforts had already been made to convert him to the Roman Catholic faith, and he had begun a correspondence with Pellisson (a distinguished convert from Protestantism) in the hope of finding some means of Church reunion. This correspondence led to others, of which the most important was one with Bossuet. But, though Leibniz was more or less occupied with these discussions throughout the rest of his life, nothing practical came of them. Bossuet's attitude in the discussion was only too well expressed in his exclamation regarding Leibniz: *Utinam ex nostris esset!* 'Would that he were one of us!' And Leibniz was too much of a scientific inquirer to unite two opposed religious communions. He might draw up a statement of dogma to which both sides could assent [1], but inevitably it would express the real belief of neither. The endeavour to convert Leibniz was not given up for a very long time, and a brief visit of his to Rome in 1689 seems to have caused a flutter of excitement. He was offered the librarianship of the Vatican and other posts with a vista of preferment; but conversion was so far from his mind that we hear of him bringing from the Catacombs a piece of glass, reddened with the blood of martyrs, in order to submit it to chemical analysis !

[1] He actually attempted this, in what has been grandiloquently called the *Systema Theologicum*, written in 1686.

It was during the early years of his residence in Hanover that Leibniz worked out the leading ideas of his system. Disappointed in his hope of finding in Spinoza a saviour from the errors of Descartes, and being the rather confirmed, by Spinoza's conclusions, in his conviction of the insufficiency of any merely mechanical interpretation of things, he turned with renewed interest to Plato[1], with the result that towards 1680 he had reached the conception of substance as essentially *active force*. It is possible also that, in spite of his general dissatisfaction with Spinoza's position, some of Spinoza's ideas (such as that of the *conatus* or self-preserving tendency of things) may have contributed to the development of his new view of substance. One further step was needed to complete the theory, namely, the recognition that the force constituting a substance is not a universal world-principle, but something individual— that there are *substances* which are *forces*. To this position he seems to have attained about 1684 or a little later, through a return to the consideration of Aristotle and the Peripatetic Schools, whose views he had set aside in his boyhood, nearly twenty-five years before. The main ideas of his philosophy (such as his conception of 'simple substance' and his pre-established harmony) were first stated in the correspondence with Arnauld, which took place between 1686 and 1690. This correspondence, however, was not published as a whole until 1846 ; and the learned world was first made aware that Leibniz had worked out a philosophical system of his own by two papers which he published in 1695 — one (the *Specimen Dynamicum*) in the Leipzig *Acta Eruditorum*, and the other (the *Système Nouveau*) in the French *Journal des Savants*. Leibniz uses the term 'monad' for the first time in 1697.

---

[1] 'Of all the ancient philosophers I find Plato the most satisfactory in regard to metaphysics.' *Lettre à M. Bourguet* (1714) (E. 723 a ; G. iii. 568).

The ' Nouveaux Essais ' and the ' Théodicée.'

Having thus definitely fixed his philosophical system[1], and having published its leading principles, Leibniz gradually expounded it in detail, for the most part by means of correspondence and criticism. Hitherto he had given most attention to ontological or purely metaphysical problems. But now he began to consider more carefully the theory of knowledge and the psychological questions that are connected with it. Locke's *Essay* was published in 1690, and a few years afterwards Leibniz read it, writing (as was his custom) notes and comments as he read. Some of these criticisms were in 1697 sent to Locke, who treated them with contempt, and made no reply[2]. In 1703 Leibniz wrote the *Nouveaux Essais sur l'Entendement humain*, a long dialogue, in which the views of Locke and of himself are set in contrast throughout a discussion dealing with the subjects of Locke's *Essay* chapter by chapter. This book was evidently intended to call forth a rejoinder from Locke. But before it was ready for publication Locke died (in 1704); and Leibniz, saying that he 'greatly disliked publishing refutations of dead authors,' and that he now 'preferred to publish his thoughts independently of another person's,' allowed the *Nouveaux Essais* to remain in manuscript, so that the book was first published by Raspe in 1765, nearly fifty years after Leibniz's death.

After writing some other papers on psychological and

[1] In 1697 he writes to Thomas Burnet of Kemnay: 'I have changed and changed again, according as new light came to me; and it is only about twelve years since I found what satisfies me, and arrived at demonstrations regarding matters which did not seem capable of demonstration.' (G. iii. 205.)

[2] Leibniz (in 1714) says that he was not surprised at Locke's disdain. 'The difference between our principles was somewhat too great, and what I maintained seemed to him to be paradox.' He adds that Locke 'had subtlety and dexterity, and he had a kind of superficial metaphysics which he knew how to make the most of; but he did not know the method of mathematicians.' *Lettre à Remond* (E. 703 b; G. iii. 612).

epistemological subjects, Leibniz, in 1710, published his *Théodicée*, the one great work of his which was printed in his lifetime. It was written, not continuously, but at intervals, in a very diffuse and discursive style, and its purpose was to develop the principles of its author's philosophy in maintaining, against the arguments of Pierre Bayle, the harmony of faith and reason, and to 'vindicate the ways of God to man.' The writing of the *Théodicée* was suggested to Leibniz as the result of conversations with Queen Sophia Charlotte of Prussia, who also induced him to write various other philosophical papers, and who encouraged him in his plans for the founding of an Academy at Berlin. Besides the exposition of his system which he gives in such elaborate works as the *Nouveaux Essais* and the *Théodicée*, Leibniz met the objections of critics and suggested new applications of his principles in the course of a varied correspondence. On questions of mathematics and physics in their connexion with metaphysics, he corresponded with John Bernouilli for more than twenty years (from 1694 to 1716), and for ten years (1706-1716) he discussed with Des Bosses the possibility of combining his philosophy of substance with the presuppositions of the doctrine of transubstantiation. Further, among many other epistolary discussions, mention may be made of Leibniz's correspondence, during the last two years of his life, with Bourguet on the chief doctrines of his philosophy, with special reference to biological questions, and with Clarke on space and time and the Divine attributes.

Founding of Academies.   Closing Years.

The amazing intellectual activity of Leibniz found expression in many other writings. During the greater part of his residence at Hanover he worked at a history of the house of Brunswick, in connexion with which he travelled much and ransacked the libraries of Germany and Italy. He suggested the development of mining in the Harz Mountains, and in connexion with this he studied and wrote on geological subjects and on the currency. But, above all, the interest of Leibniz in these later years lay in the endeavour to extend science and civilization throughout Europe. With this end in view, he, who (according to Frederick the Great) was an Academy in himself, succeeded after much effort in obtaining the foundation of an Academy at Berlin, of which he himself was appointed the first president (1700). Afterwards he made long-continued but unsuccessful attempts to induce the King of Poland, the Czar, and the Emperor to found similar Academies at Dresden, St. Petersburg, and Vienna. He had interviews with Peter the Great, whom he expected to become 'the Solon of Russia,' and he lived for some time in Vienna, where he tried to bring about an alliance between the Czar and the Emperor. Charles VI favoured his projects for the founding of learned societies. and he was also strongly supported by Prince Eugene of Savoy, for whom in 1714 he wrote the *Monadologie* (or, as Gerhardt maintains, the *Principes de la Nature et de la Grâce*). But Europe was full of wars and rumours of wars, and the peaceful plans of Leibniz were set aside. The Berlin Academy had a struggling existence, and no other was founded until long after Leibniz's death.

The happiest years of the life of Leibniz were now over. The Duke of Brunswick[1] died in 1698, and Leibniz seems gradually to have lost favour with his son and successor, our George I. After the death of his friends, 'the two Electresses,' Sophia and Sophia Charlotte (the mother and the sister of George I), Leibniz's position became intolerable. George I succeeded to the English crown in 1714, and his prejudices against Leibniz, shown in his displeasure on account of the latter's residence in Vienna, were encouraged by some of Newton's friends,

[1] Successor of the duke who had originally appointed Leibniz to the librarianship at Hanover.

whom he met in England.   Leibniz thought of leaving
Hanover; but in later years his health had been somewhat broken, and on November 14, 1716, he died during
an attack of gout.   His secretary, Eckhart, invited all
the people of the Court to his funeral, but not one of
them came, and Eckhart alone followed his master's body
to the grave.   An acquaintance of Leibniz, John Ker of
Kersland [1], who had come to Hanover on the very day
of Leibniz's death, says that he was buried 'more like
a robber than, what he really was, the ornament of his
country.'   No minister of religion was present; for
Leibniz was *parcus deorum cultor et infrequens,* and his
absence from church was counted to him for irreligion,
so that from priests and people he got the nickname
Lövenix (the Low German for *Glaubet nichts,* believer in
nothing).   The Berlin Academy and the Royal Society
of London took no notice of his death; but a year
afterwards Fontenelle commemorated it in a fine oration,
delivered before the Parisian Academy.

Personal Characteristics.

As to the personal characteristics of Leibniz, Eckhart
tells us that he was of middle height, with a somewhat
large head, dark-brown hair, and small but very sharp
eyes.   He was near-sighted, but had no difficulty in
reading, and himself wrote a very small hand.   His lungs
were not strong, and he had a thin but clear voice, with
a difficulty in pronouncing gutturals.   He was broad-
shouldered and always walked with his head bent forward, so that he looked like a man with a humped back.
In figure he was slim rather than stout, and his legs

---

[1] A leader of the Scottish Cameronians. He lived on political
intrigue, and when his resources in England were failing him he
presented to the Emperor, through Leibniz, a project for privateer-
ing and buccaneering against the Spaniards in the Pacific.   In
the *Political Memoir* containing Ker's proposals there is a curious
medley of religious considerations and the hope of gain. Cf. Foucher
de Careil, iv. 272 sqq.

were crooked. His household arrangements (if they can be called 'arrangements') were very irregular. He had no fixed hours for meals, but, when a convenient opportunity came in the course of his studies, he sent out for something to eat. He once made a proposal of marriage (when he was fifty years of age), but the lady took time to consider, and (Fontenelle says) 'this gave Leibniz also time to consider, and he never married.' He slept little, but well: he often spent the night in his chair, and sometimes he would remain in it for several days at a time. This enabled him to do a great deal of work ; but it led to illness, for which, disliking physicians, he employed remedies more 'heroic' than wise. He enjoyed intercourse with all sorts and conditions of men, believing that he could always learn something even from the most ignorant. '*Cum Socrate semper ad discendum paratus sum.*' 'He spoke well of everybody,' says Eckhart, 'and made the best of everything' (*er kehrte alles zum Besten*). He often congratulates himself on being self-taught (αὐτοδίδακτος), and thus able to avoid acquiescence in superficial, ready-made knowledge and to strike out paths of his own. For he is ever (he tells us) 'eager to penetrate into all things more deeply than is usually done and to find something new.'

'When,' says Diderot, 'one considers oneself and compares one's talents with those of a Leibniz, one is tempted to throw books away and seek some hidden corner of the world where one may die in peace. This man's mind was a foe of disorder : the most entangled things fell into order when they entered it. He combined two great qualities which are almost incompatible with one another—the spirit of discovery and that of method ; and the most determined and varied study, through which he accumulated knowledge of the most widely differing kinds, weakened neither the one quality nor the other. In the fullest meaning these words can bear, he was a philosopher and a mathematician[1].'

[1] *Encyclopédie, Œuvres* (Assézat's ed.), vol. xv. p. 440.

The Works of Leibniz.

Many of the most important philosophical works of
Leibniz were not published till after his death. Large
quantities of manuscript were preserved in the Royal
Library at Hanover, and successive editors have continually drawn upon it for publication. The chief editions
of the philosophical works are that of Erdmann (1840)
and that of Gerhardt (1875-90), the latter being the
most complete. In 1866 Janet published an edition in
French, containing the principal works as they are given
in Erdmann, with the addition of the correspondence
between Leibniz and Arnauld, which had not been published when Erdmann's edition appeared. The mathematical works were published by Gerhardt in seven
volumes (1850-63). Of the historical and political works
Onno Klopp published ten volumes (1864-77). Foucher
de Careil also published in seven volumes (1859-75)
some of Leibniz's political works, along with his correspondence on the reunion of Christendom and his writings
in connexion with the founding of academies. In addition
to these may be mentioned the old edition of Dutens in
six volumes (1768), which contains some things not included in any of the others, and the booklet of Mollat
(1885), containing some papers of Leibniz on ethics and
jurisprudence.

The following are the principal philosophical works of
Leibniz, with the dates at which they were written or
published. The letters J. S. indicate those which appeared
in the *Journal des Savants*, and the letters A. E. those
which appeared in the *Acta Eruditorum*. Those marked
with an asterisk were published in Leibniz's lifetime.

Correspondence with Philipp and others regarding the Philosophy of Descartes,
1679 80. (In French.) G. iv. 281 sqq.
*Meditationes de Cognitione, Veritate et Ideis, A. E. 1684. G. iv. 422; E. 79.
Correspondence with Arnauld, 1686-90. (In French.) G. ii. 1. Published by Grotefend, 1846.

*Extrait d'une Lettre à M. Bayle. Published in the *Nouvelles de la République des Lettres*, 1687. G. iii. 51 ; E. 104.

De Vera Methodo Philosophiae et Theologiae, 1690. G. vii. 323 ; E. 109.

Si l'Essence du Corps consiste dans l'Étendue, J. S. 1691 and 1693. G. iv. 464 ; E. 112.

Animadversiones in partem generalem Principiorum Cartesianorum, 1692. Published by Guhrauer, 1844. G. iv. 350. Mentioned by Leibniz in a letter to Bernouilli, 1697.

*De Notionibus Juris et Justitiae, preface to *Codex Juris Gentium Diplomaticus*, published in 1693. E. 118.

*De Primae Philosophiae Emendatione et de Notione Substantiae, A. E. 1694. G. iv. 468 ; E. 121.

*Système Nouveau de la Nature et de la Communication des Substances, J. S. 1695. G. iv. 471 ; E. 124. Also three *Éclaircissements du Nouveau Système*, J. S. 1696.

Schreiben an Gabriel Wagner vom Nützen der Vernunftkunst oder Logik, 1696. Published by Guhrauer, 1838. G. vii 514 ; E. 418.

De Rerum Originatione radicali, 1697. G. vii. 302 ; E. 147. Published by Erdmann, 1840.

*De ipsa Natura, sive de Vi insita Actionibusque Creaturarum, A. E. 1698. G. iv 504 ; E. 154.

Various papers (without titles) on Cartesianism, written between 1700 and 1702. G. iv. 393 sqq. ; E 177.

Considérations sur la Doctrine d'un Esprit Universel unique, 1702. G. vi. 529 ; E. 178. Published by Erdmann, 1840.

Sur ce qui passe les Sens et la Matière (Letter to Queen Sophia Charlotte of Prussia), 1702. G. vi. 488.

Nouveaux Essais sur l'Entendement humain, 1704. G. v. 41 ; E. 194. Published by Raspe, 1765.

*Considérations sur les Principes de Vie et sur les Natures plastiques (*Histoire des Ouvrages des Savants*, 1705). G. vi. 539 ; E. 429.

Ad rev. Patrem des Bosses Epistolae 71, 1706–16. G. ii. 291 ; E. 434, &c. E. gives 29 only. Dutens gives 70.

De Modo distinguendi Phaenomena realia ab imaginariis. G. vii. 319 ; E. 443.

Animadversiones ad Joh. G. Wachteri Librum de recondita Hebraeorum philosophia, c. 1708 (including the 'Refutation of Spinoza'). Published by Foucher de Careil, 1854.

Commentatio de Anima Brutorum, 1710. G. vii. 328 ; E. 463. Published by Kortholt, 1735.

Essais de Théodicée sur la Bonté de Dieu, la Liberté de l'Homme et l'Origine du Mal, 1710. G. vi. 1 ; E. 468.

Von der Glückseligkeit, 1710 (?). G. vii. 86 ; E. 671. Published by Guhrauer, 1838.

Principes de la Nature et de la Grâce, fondés en Raison, 1714.   G. vi. 598 ;
     E. 714. First published in *L'Europe Savante*, Nov. 1718.

La Monadologie, 1714.   G. vi. 607 ; E. 705.   Germ. trans. Köhler
     (Jena), 1720.   Lat. trans. A. E. 1721.   Original French in E.
     1840.

Correspondence with Nicholas Remond, 1713-16.   (In French.)   G. iii.
     599 ; E. 701, &c.

Correspondence with Bourguet, 1709-16.   (In French.)   G. iii. 539 ;
     E. 718, &c.

Correspondence with Clarke, 1715-16.   (In French.)   G. vii. 347 ;
     E. 746.

PART II.

Statement of Leibniz's Problem: How can that which is continuous consist of indivisible Elements?

In the preface to his *Théodicée*[1] Leibniz declares that 'there are two famous labyrinths, in which our reason often goes astray : the one relates to the great question of *liberty* and *necessity*, especially in regard to the production and origin of *evil* ; the other consists in the discussion of *continuity* and of the *indivisible points* which appear to be its elements, and this question involves the consideration of the *infinite*. The former of these perplexes almost all the human race, the latter claims the attention of philosophers alone.' Accordingly, while a right understanding of the principle of continuity is of the utmost speculative importance, the practical value of a true knowledge of necessity is equally great. Thus, Leibniz makes his *Théodicée* an investigation of the meaning of liberty and necessity, while in others of his writings he offers a solution of the problem which he describes as the special perplexity of philosophers.

It is this latter problem with which we are here mainly concerned. The philosophical work of Leibniz was an endeavour to reconcile the notion of substance as *continuous* with the contrary notion of substance as consisting of *indivisible elements*. The opposition of these two notions

[1] E. 470 a; G. vi. 29.

seemed to him to arise from an inadequate conception of substance, and the task he set himself was that of deepening the current notion of substance, or, as he himself would have put it, finding a better hypothesis than that which had satisfied his Cartesian predecessors.

Stated in another way the problem is: How are we to interpret the relation of whole and parts so that the continuity or complete unity of the whole shall not be in conflict with the definiteness or .real diversity of the parts? To say that the whole is continuous or really one seems to mean that, if it is divisible at all, it is infinitely divisible. If it were not infinitely divisible, it would consist of insoluble ultimate elements, and would thus be discontinuous. Accordingly, if the whole be really continuous there seem to be no fixed boundaries or lines of division within it, that is to say, no real, but only arbitrary parts [1].

On the other hand, if the whole consists of real parts and not merely possible subdivisions, these parts must be definite, bounded, separate from one another, and consequently the whole which they constitute must be, not a real continuous unity, but a mere collection or arbitrary unity. Nevertheless, we cannot hold either that the whole is real and the parts unreal, or that the parts are real and the whole unreal.

Quantitative or extensive Notion of Substance held by Descartes and Spinoza, on the one hand, and by the Atomists on the other.

The philosophy of Spinoza, with its cardinal principle that 'Determination is negation,' practically amounted to an assertion of the unity and continuity of the whole at the expense of the reality of the parts. According to

---

[1] For instance, the spectrum is continuous. There is no limit to the number of varieties of colour that may be discriminated in the rainbow : the usual division into seven colours is an arbitrary arrangement made by observers. It probably originated in a suggested analogy with the musical scale.

Spinoza, 'substance' is 'that which is in itself and is conceived through itself; in other words, that, the conception of which does not need the conception of another thing from which it must be formed [1].' That is to say, substance is the unconditioned, or that which is not conditioned or determined by anything other than itself. There is ambiguity in the statement. It may mean either that substance is self-conditioned or that it is absolutely unconditioned, to the exclusion of all determination. In the one case substance would be a real system of reciprocal determinations; in the other, it would be unbroken being, to which every determination is foreign. The latter is the dominant aspect of substance in the philosophy of Spinoza. That aspect alone is consistent with the principle that 'Determination is negation.' Consequently his position amounts to saying that substance can have no real parts. For the very meaning of a part implies that it must be determined or conditioned by other parts [2].

In contrary opposition to this, there is the theory of atoms and the void, which Leibniz tells us at one time charmed his imagination [3]. To affirm the real existence of indivisible material atoms is to deny the infinite divisibility of matter. Accordingly, if the atoms constitute the ultimate reality of the world, its unity is destroyed, its continuity becomes an illusion. However numerous the atoms may be, they can together constitute no true unity, 'but only a collection or heaping up of parts ad infinitum [4].' Atomism thus endeavours to establish the reality of the parts at the expense of the whole.

It is necessary, then, to lay bare the presuppositions of these contrary theories in order to find the elements of truth in each and to reconcile them in a more comprehensive view. The doctrine of Spinoza is the consistent

[1] *Ethics*, Part i. def. 3, Hale White's Tr.
[2] Ibid. Part i. prop. 12 and 13.
[3] *New System*, § 3.
[4] *Loc. cit.*

logical development of the principles involved in the
position of Descartes[1]. In this connexion it is Descartes's
special theories that Leibniz has mostly in view, although
his arguments are equally applicable to the more thorough
metaphysic of Spinoza. 'Spinoza,' he tells us, 'has done
nothing but cultivate certain seeds of the philosophy of
M. Descartes[2].' Descartes endeavoured to reach absolute
metaphysical certainty by a method which was afterwards more clearly and fully applied by Spinoza, who
defined it in his great principle that 'Determination is
negation.' The essence of Descartes's method of doubt
is the endeavour to attain certainty by stripping from
experience (as it is given in common consciousness) all
specific qualities or determinations, on the ground that
no contradiction in terms is involved in regarding each of
these qualities by itself as non-existent or other than it
is. The result of the method is to give, as the residual
ultimate certainty, nothing but the instrument by which
the process of stripping has been carried out, viz. the

---

[1] '*Cartesianae disciplinae intemperantia Spinozae doctrinam parit; in
hac sententia totum reperire est Leibnitium*' (Lemoine, *Quid sit materia
apud Leibnitium*, p. 52). 'The philosophy of Descartes . . . seems to
lead straight to the opinions of Spinoza, who dared to say what
Descartes carefully avoided.' (G. iv. 346.)

[2] *Lettre à l'Abbé Nicaise* (1697) (E. 139 b; G. ii. 563). Leibniz,
especially in his earlier days, recognized that his philosophy had
much in common with that of Spinoza, although, as time went on,
it became more and more evident to him that they were fundamentally at variance. Thus, in an early letter (February, 1678), we
find Leibniz writing: 'I find in it' [the *Ethics*] 'plenty of fine
thoughts agreeing with mine, as is known to some of my friends
who are also friends of Spinoza. But there are also paradoxes
which seem to me unreal and not even plausible. As, for example,
that there is only one substance, namely God; that created things
are modes or accidents of God; that our mind has no wider outlook
[*nihil amplius percipere*] after this life; that God Himself thinks
indeed, but nevertheless neither understands nor wills, that all
things happen by a certain necessity of fate; that God acts not for
an end but by a certain necessity of nature, which is verbally to
retain, but really to give up, providence and immortality. I regard
this book as a dangerous one for people who will give themselves
the trouble to go deeply into it, for others do not care to understand it.' *Archiv für Geschichte d. Philosophie*, vol. iii. p. 75.

thinking Ego, without any specific thought. If we challenge the reality of this instrument, we do so by means of the instrument itself, and so involve ourselves in self-contradiction. The thinking Ego cannot be thought non-existent : to think its non-existence would be a contradiction in terms. Spinoza's advance upon this was merely to pass from Descartes's practical method of attaining truth (namely, the discarding of specific determinations) to the general metaphysical principle which the method implied, the principle, namely, that the essence or reality of a thing is that which remains after the differences in its states and qualities have been thought away, or that which is common to all its forms and manifestations, and consequently that the ultimate reality or substance is that which is free from all specific determinations, that which includes or is common to everything because it is not (specially) anything.

Now when we rigorously apply this principle, that the reality of substance is that which remains after all specific or differential qualities have been removed, we are left with nothing but quantity—either, as in the case of Spinoza, quantity of substance in general[1]; or, as in the case of Descartes, quantity of a specific substance, that is to say quantity of one quality. Thus Descartes's position is that in addition to the one true and perfect substance, God, whose existence is externally unconditioned, there are two created substances, whose existence is not conditioned by anything finite, but by infinite

---

[1] It is true that Spinoza regards substance as indivisible, in the sense that it has no real parts; and this may seem inconsistent with the contention that Spinoza's substance is merely quantitative. But the contradiction is Spinoza's : it is a fragment of the great fissure of inconsistency that traverses his whole system, namely, the confounding of a substance possessing infinite attributes with a substance whose reality is reached by the exclusion of all specific determinations. If we hold strictly to the second of these views of substance, then substance can be said to be indivisible only on the ground that there is nothing to divide. Cf. Spinoza, *Ethics*, Part i. prop. 12 and 13, with *Tractatus de Intellectus Emendatione*, 108, ii. iii.

substance alone. These are bodily substance and thinking substance. They are mutually opposite: the one is
what the other is not. Neither is conditioned by the
other nor dependent upon it. The essential attribute
of bodily substance is extension, that of thinking substance is thought. All the specific qualities of created
things are reducible to one or other of these as a common
quality; and consequently the essence or reality of
created substance comes to be either extension without
specific contents or thought without a specific object.
In other words, bodily substance is quantity of one
determination, namely extension; while thinking substance is quantity of one other determination, namely
thought. Thus the presupposition of the Cartesian
systems is a purely quantitative relation of whole and
parts [1].

The same presupposition in another form underlies
the Atomist philosophy. The atoms are material particles, and the whole consists of their aggregation. If
the theory is self-consistent they must be regarded as

---

[1] Cf. Descartes, *Principia*, Part ii. § 8: 'Quantity and number
differ only in thought [*ratione*] from that which has quantity and
is numbered.' § 11: 'It will be easy to discern that it is the same
extension which constitutes the nature of body as of space, and
that these two things are mutually diverse only as the nature of
the genus and species differs from that of the individual, provided
we reflect on the idea we have of any body, taking a stone for
example, and reject all that is not essential to the nature of body.
In the first place, then, hardness may be rejected, because if the
stone were liquefied or reduced to powder it would no longer
possess hardness, and yet would not cease to be a body; colour also
may be thrown out of account, because we have frequently seen
stones so transparent as to have no colour; again, we may reject
weight, because we have the case of fire, which, though very light,
is still a body; and finally, we may reject cold, heat, and all the
other qualities of this sort, either because they are not considered
as in the stone, or because, with the change of these qualities, the
stone is not supposed to have lost the nature of body. After this
examination we shall find that nothing remains in the idea of
body, except that it is something extended in length, breadth, and
depth; and this something is comprised in our idea of space, not
only of that which is full of body, but even of what is called void
space' (Veitch's Tr.). Cf. *Principia*, Part i. §§ 51-53, 63-65.

homogeneous, and the specific qualities of things must arise from the variety of their combinations. They could not all really exist and be different from one another without some of them being complex. And in any case the very essence of the theory is that the whole should be taken as a sum or totality, a quantity of parts.

Leibniz's non-quantitative or intensive Notion of Substance, developed through criticism of Cartesian and Atomist views regarding material Substance.

Accordingly, the essence of Leibniz's argument is that a quantitative conception of the relation of whole and parts affords an inadequate theory of substance. The common element in the contrary positions of the Cartesians and the Atomists is the explicit or implicit reduction of qualitative to quantitative differences[1]. And it appears to Leibniz that the solution of the dilemma is to be found in the opposite hypothesis, namely, that the essence of substance is non-quantitative, and that the relation of whole and parts must be conceived as *intensive* rather than *extensive*. Thus a 'simple substance' has no parts, i. e. no quantitative elements[2], and yet it must comprehend a manifold in unity[3]; that is to say, it must be real, it must be *something*, it must be qualitative, specifically determined.

While the general principle of Leibniz's argument may be stated in this way, he actually develops it through criticism of Descartes's theory of material substance. To regard matter as ultimately pure extension is to make it essentially a substance with nothing more than a shadow of quality. An extended *nothing* is meaningless. An extended *something* must have quality. And to call

---

[1] The mechanical view of things 'has two forms: *Cartesianism* and *Atomism*. . . . The one, which makes matter continuous, may be called *geometrical* mechanism; the other, which makes it discontinuous, may be called *arithmetical* mechanism.' E. Boutroux, *La Monadologie de Leibnitz*, &c., p. 36.

[2] *Monadology*, § 1.   [3] Ibid. § 12.

that quality extension itself is merely to cover up the difficulty with a name : an extended extension is much the same as a shaded shadow of nothing. 'In my opinion corporeal substance consists in something quite other than being extended and occupying a place : we must, in fact, ask ourselves *what* it is that occupies the place[1].' 'Those who hold that the extended is itself a substance transpose the order of the words as well as of the thoughts. Besides extension there must be an object which is extended, that is to say a substance which can be repeated or continued. For extension means nothing but a repetition or a continued multiplicity of that which is spread out, a *plurality, continuity*, and *coexistence of parts*; and consequently it [extension] is not sufficient to explain the very nature of extended or repeated substance, the notion of which is anterior to that of its repetition[2].'

Again, it cannot be said that pure extension has any real parts. There can be no real unit of mere extension[3]. It would be an erroneous conception to regard mathematical surfaces as made up of real lines, and these lines as made up of real points. The line is the limit of the surface, and the point is the limit of the line. A mathe-

---

[1] *Epistola ad Schulenburgium* (1698) (G. Math. vii. 242).

[2] *Extrait d'une lettre* (1693) (E. 114 b; G. iv. 467). Cf. Lotze, *Microcosmus*, bk. iii. ch. 4, § 2 (Eng. Trans. vol. i. p. 356). Cf. also *Examen des principes du R. P. Malebranche* (c. 1711) (E. 691 a; G. vi. 580) : '*Ariste*. But do you not think that the destruction of extension, which carries with it that of body, proves that body consists only in extension? *Philarète*. It proves only that extension enters into the essence or nature of body; but not that it constitutes its whole essence. Similarly, magnitude enters into the essence of extension, but is not equivalent to it; for number, time, motion have also magnitude, and yet they are not extension.' Also (E. 692 b; G. vi. 584) : 'Extension is nothing but an abstraction and requires something which is extended. . . . It presupposes some quality, some attribute, some nature in the thing, which quality extends or diffuses itself along with the thing, continues itself.'

[3] 'You are right in saying that all magnitudes [*grandeurs*] may be divided *ad infinitum*. None of them is so small that we cannot conceive in it an infinity of divisions which will never be exhausted.' *Lettre à Foucher* (1692) (E. 115 a; G. i. 403).

matical point may, then, be regarded as indivisible, but only because there is nothing in it to divide. It cannot be a real unit, for there is nothing to determine its unity. We should have to conceive it as the unit of that whose sole characteristic is to consist of units, to be a quantity. For such is, strictly speaking, the nature of Descartes's 'extension.' Thus, as Leibniz puts it, 'mathematical points are exact' [i. e. indivisible]; 'but they are only modalities[1],' that is to say abstractions and not real existences[2].

Now, while Leibniz regards the parts of Cartesian extension as thus indivisible without being real, he maintains on the other hand that the parts to which Atomism reduces material substance are real only if they are not indivisible. Their claim to be indivisible rests upon the supposition that they are infinitely hard. But hardness is a relative term. There is no absolute hardness, as there is no absolute motion or rest. And thus infinite hardness is a self-contradictory conception. 'By an atom,' says Leibniz, 'I understand a corpuscle,

---

[1] *New System*, § 11.

[2] Cf. *Epistola ad Bernoullium* (1698) (G. Math. iii. 535): 'Indeed many years ago I proved that a number or sum of all numbers involves a contradiction, if it be taken as one whole. And the same is true of an absolutely greatest number and an absolutely least number or an absolutely smallest fraction. . . . Now, just as there is no (given) numerical element or smallest part of unity or least among numbers, so there is no (given) least line or lineal element ; for a line, as a unity, can be cut into parts or fractions. . . . Suppose that in a line there are actually $\frac{1}{2}$, $\frac{1}{4}$, $\frac{1}{8}$, $\frac{1}{16}$, $\frac{1}{32}$, &c., and that all the terms of this series actually exist. You infer from this that there is also an absolutely infinite term, but I think nothing else follows from it than that there actually exists any assignable finite fraction, however small. . . . And indeed I conceive points, not as elements of a line, but as limits, or negations of further progress, or as ends [*termini*] of a line.' Cf. *Lettre à Foucher* (1693) (E. 118 a; G. i. 416). 'As to indivisible points in the sense of the mere extremities of a time or a line, we cannot conceive in them new extremities, nor parts, whether actual or potential. Thus points are neither large nor small, and no leap is needed to pass them. Yet the continuous, though it has everywhere such indivisible points, is not composed of them.' Cf. *Explanation of the New System*, 1, note.

mentally divisible indeed, but which actually neither is
nor has been divided.   Not that it cannot be actually
divided ; for such atoms do not occur, since they would
demand perfect hardness.   But it suffices for my definition that there should be corpuscles, whose particles have
never been separated, from the foundation of the world
to the present day[1].'   Every material atom must be at
least ideally divisible, if it be real.   ' The atoms of matter
. . . are still composed of parts, since the invincible
attachment of one part to another (if one could rationally
conceive or suppose it) would in no way destroy their
diversity[2].'

How the Relation of Whole and Parts is to be conceived. The real and indivisible Unit of Substance (Monad). ' Perception' and ' Appetition.'

Leibniz's problem thus takes the form of an attempt
to find a unit of substance which shall avoid the imperfections of both the Cartesian and Atomist theory.   This
unit must be at once real and indivisible.   Its reality
must be of such a kind that it does not conflict with its
indivisibility, and it must be indivisible in a sense which
is consistent with the continuity of the whole.   The basis
of its reality cannot be quantity, for no quantity is
indivisible.   And its indivisibility cannot be exclusive
particularity in space or time, for indivisible points in
space or time may form an aggregate but cannot become
a *continuum*.   The unit of substance must then be intensive rather than extensive, and the continuity of the
whole must be not a mere empty homogeneity, but a

---

[1] *Epistola ad Bernoullium* (1697) (G. Math. iii. 443).
[2] *New System*, § 11.   Cf. *Lettre à Hartsoeker* (1710) (G. iii. 507):
'Nothing is large or small, except by comparison, so that such
a particle as an atom is as considerable in itself, and in relation to
others proportionately less (and consequently, in the sight of God),
as our visible system is considerable in relation to it.   Atoms are
the effect of the weakness of our imagination, which likes to rest
and to hasten to an end in subdividing or analyzing.   It is not so
in nature, which comes from infinity and goes to infinity.'

continuity through infinite degrees of intension. The word 'intension,' however, does not help us much. It must be more precisely defined.

The antinomy between whole and parts, which was the issue of the quantitative or extensive view of substance, had its roots in the conception of whole and parts as inevitably exclusive of one another, the whole being regarded as prior to the parts or the parts as prior to the whole. That is to say, either, as in the view of Spinoza, the parts are to be deduced, in a purely analytic way, from the whole as self-evidently given, or, as in the Atomist doctrine, the whole is a secondary construction, of a purely synthetic kind, from the primary parts. In contrast with this the intensive doctrine of substance which regards determination as primary or essential amounts to a declaration that whole and part are inseparable. All specific determinations, states, or functions are determinations, states, or functions of the whole, not in the sense that they are ultimately reducible to one vague determination which is common to everything, but in the sense that the whole is expressed, symbolized, and therefore in some way included in each, however specific, individual, limited it may be. Thus the parts are not determined or characterized without reference to the whole, and the whole is not a mere vague aggregate of independent parts. In some sense each part must contain the whole within itself, each unit must include an infinite manifold. The whole stands not merely in a mechanical, but in a dynamic relation to the part. The whole is not merely other than the part, but in some way passes into it and expresses itself through it. That, in general, is the conception of substance as essentially intensive rather than extensive.

There is here an approach to the modern conception of organism as more adequate to the expression of substance than are merely mechanical conceptions[1]. But the special

[1] Leibniz does hold that all real substances are organic (cf. p. 108).

angle at which Leibniz regards his problem prevents him
from developing this. His early imaginative liking for
'atoms and the void,' when first he 'freed himself from
the yoke of Aristotle¹,' the love of historical system and
of well-grounded hypothesis which set his whole intellectual character in revolt against Spinoza's abstract unity
and his purely *a priori* deductions, probably also the
influence of his Scholastic training with its suggestions
of an infinite multiplicity of 'substantial forms'—all
resulted in a tendency to emphasize rather the elements
of reality than its wholeness. That there can be no real
whole without real units, is Leibniz's guiding thought²,
and accordingly his question does not primarily take the
form: 'What must be the nature of a whole which
expresses itself in each of its parts?' It rather is:
'What must be the nature of a part or unit which can in
some way contain or express the whole within itself?'

Now the part cannot contain the whole within itself
actually and fully, in all its realized completeness; for
thus the distinction between whole and part would
vanish. The part must, therefore, contain the whole
potentially and ideally or by means of representation.

The relation of whole and parts is not to be conceived
as one of greater and less, of thing containing and things

But the notion of organism, as he uses it, is much more vague than
it has since become. According to Leibniz anything is an organism
if it has a 'soul' or principle of unity, that is to say, if it is other
than a mere aggregate of independent elements.

¹ *New System*, § 3.
² Cf. *Lettre à Arnauld* (1687) (G. ii. 97): 'Every machine presupposes some substance in the pieces from which it is made, and
there is no manifold without real units. In short, I take as
axiomatic this identical proposition, in which the difference is
entirely a matter of accent, namely, that what is not really *one*
[*un*] being is not really a [*un*] *being*. It has always been thought
that unity [*l'un*] and being are reciprocal things. "Being" is one
thing, "beings" is another; but the plural presupposes the
singular, and where there is not one being there will still less be
several beings.' 'Being and unity are convertible terms [*ens et
unum convertuntur*].' *Epist. ad des Bosses* (1706) (E. 435 b ; G. ii. 304).
The phrase is used by Nicholas of Cusa, *De docta ignorantia* (1440), ii. 7.

contained, but rather as a relation of symbolized and symbols, sign and thing signified. That is to say, the part must be a representation of the whole from some particular point of view, a symbol or expression of the whole, and the part must contain the whole in such a way that the whole might be unfolded entirely from within it [1].

Thus the part must have a certain spontaneity or power of acting from within itself, and in virtue of this Leibniz describes the individual substance as essentially a 'force' rather than a quantity. This intensive essence or force in the part (or individual substance) appears in two ways. As representative or symbolic of the whole, the part, in Leibniz's terminology, has 'Perception,' while, in so far as in the part the potential whole tends to realize itself, the part is said to have 'Appetition.' Both of these characteristics must belong to it, for, if it had perception alone, the part would merely represent one aspect of the whole, like an unchanging picture. It is in virtue of its appetition that the part is able to realize the life of the whole, to unfold spontaneously from within itself all the variations of that which it represents [2].

This new atom or unit of substance (the 'simple substance' in his own phrase) Leibniz calls a Monad [3].

[1] Although, as a matter of fact, it never is so unfolded. *Praedicatum inest subjecto*; but, in the case of any actual thing, to develop the predicate out of the subject would involve an infinite analysis. We here touch a fundamental inconsistency in Leibniz's thought.

[2] Cf. *De Anima Brutorum*, 12 (E. 464 b; G. vii. 330): 'Not only is the variety of the object represented in that which has perception; but there is also variation in the representation itself, since that which is to be represented varies.'

[3] Cf. *Epistola ad R. C. Wagnerum* (1710) (E. 466 a; G. vii. 529): '. . . Monads, and, so to speak, metaphysical atoms, without parts.' Also *Réplique aux Réflexions de Bayle* (1702) (E. 186 b; G. iv. 561): 'In fact, I regard souls, or rather Monads, as *atoms of substance*, since, in my opinion, there are no *atoms of matter* in nature and the smallest portion of matter has still parts.' See also *New System*, §§ 3 and 11. Leibniz says that he applies the term 'Monad' to the simple substance, because it is *unum per se*. *De ipsa natura* (1698) (E. 158 a; G. iv. 511). But 'Monads are not to be confounded with atoms. Atoms (as people imagine them) have shapes; Monads no

The word is almost as old as European philosophy, and has varied greatly in meaning and application. Shortly before the time of Leibniz the term was used by Giordano Bruno, whose Monads were ultimate spherical points, regarded as possessing both spiritual and material characteristics. There are some parts of the philosophy of Bruno with which the doctrine of Leibniz has affinity, as, for instance, Bruno's contention that there is nothing, however little or valueless, that does not contain in it life or soul. But Leibniz repeatedly attacks the doctrine of a world-soul, which is Bruno's central conception. Thus, in adopting the term 'Monad,' Leibniz may be said to have taken from Bruno little more than the name[1].

The Monad, then, has perception, but not necessarily in the sense of consciousness. For consciousness is not the essence of perception, but merely an additional determination belonging to certain kinds or degrees of perception. Conscious perception is called by Leibniz 'Apperception.' But the essence of perception in general is that in it we have a unity variously modified or a unity which appears in a multiplicity of relations. 'I have many ideas [*Vorstellungen*], wealth of thoughts is in me; and yet I remain, in spite of this variety, one[2].' But it is not necessarily because I am conscious of many thoughts or many objects that I 'perceive' and thus exhibit a multiplicity in unity. All representation is

more have a shape than souls have. They are not parts of bodies, but presuppositions of them.' *Epistola ad Bierlingium* (1712) (G. vii. 503).

[1] Professor Ludwig Stein, in his *Leibniz und Spinoza*, has shown that the term 'Monad' was actually suggested to Leibniz, not by the writings of Bruno, but by Leibniz's contemporary, François Mercure Van Helmont (1618–1699), with whom he had much intercourse and considerable correspondence. ἡ μονάς to the Greek meant simply the unit in arithmetic. Leibniz himself attributes the term to Pythagoras. In the sense of a numerical unit it occurs in Plato (*Philebus*, 15 B; *Phaedo*, 105 C, 101 E). But Leibniz's chief forerunner in the use of the term was Bruno. It is also used by Nicholas of Cusa.

[2] Hegel, *Geschichte der Philosophie*, iii. 412.

perception [1]. Similarly, the Monad has appetition, but not necessarily in the sense of conscious desire or will. As the essence of perception is multiplicity in unity, so the essence of appetition is change within the identity or permanence of a simple substance. Appetition is 'the action of the internal principle which produces change or passage from one perception to another [2].' As the Monads alone are real, every change in nature must be change within a Monad. This change, as we have seen, must be the unfolding of the whole which the Monad potentially contains or represents. That is to say, it must be the passing from one perception (or state of representation, whether conscious or unconscious) to another. And thus, wherever there is change there is appetition. It is simply another name for the spontaneity of the Monad, its power of unfolding its whole nature and experience from within itself. The Monad as perceptive is thus a universal within, rather than exclusive of, the particular, while as appetitive it is dynamic and not static [3].

---

[1] Cf. p. 135. Also *Epistola ad R. C. Wagnerum* (1710) (E. 466 a ; G. vii. 529): 'This correlation of the internal and external, or representation of the external in the internal, of the compound in the simple, of multiplicity in unity, really constitutes perception. In a letter to Arnauld (1687) (G. ii. 112) Leibniz says that 'expression is a genus of which natural perception, animal feeling, and intellectual knowledge are species. In natural perception and feeling, it is enough that what is divisible and material, and is actually dispersed among several beings, be expressed or represented in a single indivisible being or in substance which has a genuine unity.'

[2] *Monadology*, § 15.

[3] 'We could not say in what the perception of plants consists, and even that of animals is not well conceived by us. Yet, according to the general sense I give to these words, in order that there may be a perception, it is enough that there should be a variety in unity; and in order that there may be appetition it is enough that there should be a tendency to new perceptions.' *Lettre à Bourguet* (1715) (E. 732 b ; G. iii. 581). 'The soul has perceptions and appetitions, and its nature consists in these. And as in body there are understood to be ἀντιτυπία and figure of some kind, although we do not know what are the figures of imperceptible bodies; so in the soul there are understood to be

As the Monads are purely intensive centres or units, each must be absolutely exclusive of all others. Not being quantitative, they are simple, in the sense of having no parts[1]; and thus no one Monad can include another. Further, no Monad can really influence another or produce any change in it. For that would mean a transference of quality from one to the other. But as the quality of a substance, being its very essence, is inseparable from it, such a transference is impossible[2]. The Monads are also real ultimate elements, because, being entirely non-quantitative, they cannot have been formed out of any combination of simpler elements, nor is it possible in any way to dissolve them, as they are without parts[3]. The point which is at once real and indivisible has thus (Leibniz thinks) been found in the Monad, as contrasted, on the one hand, with the mathematical point of Descartes, which is indivisible only when it ceases to be real, and, on the other hand, with the physical point of the Atomists, which, if it is real, must always be divisible[4].

The Identity of Indiscernibles and the Law of Continuity.

The indivisible having thus been established, there remains the question of continuity and the infinite. As we have seen, a quantitative *continuum* cannot have indivisible parts. But, as the actual indivisible elements of reality are essentially perceptive, real continuity must also be a continuity of perception. As each Monad is a part or element of the universe, in the sense that each represents it or reflects it as in a mirror from some particular angle, in some special aspect, the whole must

perception and appetition, although we do not distinctly know the imperceptible elements of the confused perceptions, by which the imperceptible elements of bodies are expressed.' *Epistola ad Bierlingium* (1711) (E. 678 a ; G. vii. 501).

[1] *Monadology*, § 1. [2] Ibid. § 7.
[3] Ibid. §§ 3-6.
[4] As to the contrast between Leibniz's view of substance and that of Locke, see Locke's *Essay*, Fraser's ed.. vol. i. pp. 399 sqq.

be the infinite totality of Monads, representing the
universe from every possible point of view. And thus,
while the Monads are entirely separate from one another,
each must represent the universe in a way which differs
to the least possible extent from the representation given
by some other. No two Monads (and *a fortiori* no two
things, which are all aggregates of Monads) can be exactly
the same: no thing can have a merely numerical difference from another. The Monads are essentially non-
quantitative, and number by itself is merely a measure
of quantity. The Monads differ from one another in
quality or intension alone, so that two Monads not
differing in quality are impossible. This is the doctrine
of Leibniz which is usually called the 'Identity of Indiscernibles[1].' It is simply his law of continuity in a
negative form. The number of Monads must be infinite[2]: otherwise the universe would not be represented
from every possible point of view, and would thus be
imperfect. But if the number of Monads is infinite, and
if every Monad differs in quality from every other, then
the Monads must be such that they might be considered
as a series, each term or member of which differs from
the next by an infinitely small degree of quality, i. e. by
a degree of quality less than any which can be assigned.

Leibniz explains his principle of continuity in a letter
quoted by his biographer, Guhrauer[3]. 'I think, then,'

---

[1] 'There are no two indiscernible individuals. A clever gentle-
man of my acquaintance, talking with me in presence of Mme. the
Electress, in the garden of Herrenhausen, was of opinion that he
could quite well find two leaves entirely alike. Mme. the Electress
would not believe it, and he spent a long time vainly seeking them.
Two drops of water or of milk, looked at through a microscope, will
be found discernible. This is an argument against atoms, to which,
no less than to the void, the principles of true metaphysic are
opposed ... To suppose two indiscernible things is to suppose the
same thing under two names.' *IV*^me *Lettre à Clarke*, §§ 4 and 6
(E. 755 b, 756 a; G. vii. 372). Cf. *Nouveaux Essais*, bk. ii. ch. 27, § 3
(E. 277 b; G. v. 214).

[2] Du Bois-Reymond compares the infinite series of Monads to
the ordinates of a curve, which grow from nothing to infinity.

[3] *G. W. F. von Leibnitz, eine Biographie*, vol. i., Anmerkungen, p. 32.

he says, 'that I have good reasons for believing that all
the different classes of beings, the totality of which forms
the universe, are, in the ideas of God, who knows
distinctly their essential gradations, merely like so many
ordinates of one and the same curve, the relations of
which do not allow of others being put between any two
of them, because that would indicate disorder and imperfection. Accordingly men are linked with animals, these
with plants, and these again with fossils, which in their
turn are connected with those bodies which sense and
imagination represent to us as completely dead and inorganic [*informes*]. But the law of continuity requires that,
*when the essential determinations of any being approximate to
those of another, all the properties of the former must gradually
approximate to those of the latter.*] Therefore all the orders
of natural beings must necessarily form only one chain,
in which the different classes, like so many links, are so
closely connected with one another that it is impossible
for sense or imagination to determine exactly the point
where any one of them begins or ends] all the species
which border upon or which occupy, so to speak, dis-
putable territory [*régions d'inflexion et de rebroussement* [1]]
being necessarily ambiguous and endowed with characteristics which may equally be ascribed to neighbouring
species. Thus, for instance, the existence of zoophytes,
or, as Buddeus [2] calls them, *Plant-animals*, does not imply
monstrosity, but it is indeed agreeable to the order of
nature that they should exist. And so strongly do I hold

The Academy of Berlin declared this letter to be spurious; but
there seems no good reason to doubt its genuineness. All they
proved was that the letter had not been addressed to the person to
whom it was said to have been addressed. See also *Introduction*,
Part iii, p. 83 note, and *New Essays, Introduction*, p. 376. Cf. Locke,
Essay, bk. iii. ch. 6, § 12, Fraser's ed., vol. i. p. 67; cf. note on
p. 380.

[1] Literally, places where the curve or chain turns back upon
itself.

[2] Probably Johannes Franciscus Buddaeus (1667–1729), Professor
of Philosophy at Halle, and afterwards of Theology at Jena. He
published many books, mostly on moral philosophy.

to the principle of continuity that not only should I not
be astonished to learn that there had been found beings
which, as regards several properties—for instance, those
of feeding or multiplying themselves—might pass for
vegetables as well as for animals, and which upset the
common rules, founded upon the supposition of a complete
and absolute separation of the different orders of beings
which together fill the universe: I say, I should be so
little astonished at it that I am even convinced that there
must be such beings, and that natural history will perhaps
some day come to know them, when it has further studied
that infinity of living beings whose smallness conceals
them from ordinary observation, and which lie hid in the
bowels of the earth and in the depths of the waters [1] . . .'

The pre-established Harmony between Substances.

There is, then, in the system of the Monads a perfectly
continuous and infinite gradation of intension, that is to
say, of perception or representation, combined with appetition or spontaneous change. And thus the universe is
at once continuous and not only infinitely divisible, but
infinitely divided, consisting of an infinity of real elements [2]. But we still have to consider how the principle
of continuity, as thus interpreted, is consistent with the
changes which take place in real things. In the system
of Monads the principle of continuity corresponds to the

---

[1] · M. Malpighi, founding upon very considerable analogies in
anatomy, is much inclined to think that plants may be included
in the same genus as animals, and that they are imperfect animals.'
Lettre à Arnauld (1687) (G. ii. 122).

[2] Cf. *Lettre à Foucher* (1693) (G. i. 416): 'I hold by the *actual
infinite* to such an extent that, in place of admitting that nature
abhors it, as is commonly said, I maintain that nature affects it
everywhere, so as the better to indicate the perfections of its
Author. Thus I think that there is no part of matter which is
not, I do not say merely divisible, but actually divided; and
consequently the smallest particle must be regarded as a world
filled with an infinity of different creatures.' Also *Lettre à Arnauld*
(1686) (G. ii. 77): 'Not only is the continuous infinitely divisible;
but every part of matter is actually divided into other parts.' See
Monadology, § 65 note.

'void' in the older Atomism. Each is the necessary correlative of the indivisible and impenetrable elements. The conception of continuity, however, by implying a *plenum*, escapes the contradictions that are involved in the idea of a void. But it has still to be shown how change is possible within a *plenum*, or how change can take place without disturbing the continuity of the infinite series of Monads. Any change within a *plenum* affects every part of it. This is the principle involved in the scientific point of view regarding the universe, which became current with the rise of modern philosophy. Everything in the world acts and reacts upon everything else. However separate things may be, no change can take place in any one without affecting every other. The influence may in some cases be imperceptible, infinitely small; but it exists. If, however, the universe be a quantitative *plenum*, it is impossible to understand how any change could originate within it. It must receive its motion from outside, and must thus be regarded as finite, which again is inconsistent with its reality as a *plenum*. Leibniz overcomes this difficulty by regarding the universe, not as an infinite mass occupying all that there is to occupy, but as a continuity or infinite gradation of qualitative differences, each containing within itself the principle of its own changes. He substitutes for an extensive *plenum* of mass an intensive *continuum* of force or life.

But if the universe consists of an infinity of Monads, each independent of the rest, impenetrable and unaffected by them, and each containing within itself the principle of all its changes, how is it possible for a change to take place in any one of them without destroying the continuity of the series[1]? Each Monad contains within

---

[1] How the perfect independence of the Monads is to be reconciled with the continuity of their series is a question which Leibniz does not answer. For him the ideal unity of the Monads (as each representing the same universe) does not make their mutual independence any the less complete. To give up the independence of the

itself a representation of the whole universe from one
particular point of view, which differs to an infinitely
small degree from the representations contained in some
other Monad. If, then, any change, however slight,
takes place in the perception or representation of one
Monad, the continuity of the series will be broken and
we shall have two indiscernible Monads. But it is of
the very essence of the Monads to be 'living mirrors,'
'forces' (as distinct from masses), centres of appetition,
spontaneously unfolding a sequence of perceptions. Accordingly this change within the Monad does take place :
it is essential to its nature. The continuous order or
system of the Monads must therefore be destroyed, unless
we can say that any change within one Monad produces,
or is invariably accompanied by, correlative changes in
other Monads, of such a kind that the equilibrium of the
whole system is maintained. In other words, there must
be something of the nature of mutual influence, action
and reaction, between the various elements in the system.
If the system were a *plenum* of mass, this interaction
would be intelligible without further explanation. But,
as the Monads form a qualitative *continuum* of such a
kind that no part can really act upon another, a further
hypothesis is required to complete the theory.

This hypothesis is Leibniz's system of the pre-established harmony between substances. Though no true
substance can really act upon another, everything in the
universe takes place as if this mutual interaction were
real. Substances form a system, not of physical relations,
but of harmony or mutual compatibility. In the creation
of the world, the inner development of each Monad has
been so prearranged that all its changes are accompanied
by corresponding changes in others. The succession of

Monads would for him have meant to fall into Spinoza's pantheism,
while, on the other hand, to give up the continuity of their series
would have meant having recourse to Atomism. And these he
regarded as equally irrational alternatives. Cf. this *Introduction*,
Part iv. p. 188.

changes in each Monad is different from that in every other, and yet all are in harmony, the perfections of one being accompanied by counterbalancing imperfections in others. One Monad influences another ideally [1], that is to say, not *ab extra*, but through an inner pre-established conformity [2].

Relation of the System of pre-established Harmony to Scholastic and Occasionalist Theories.

Like most of the other doctrines of Leibniz, this system of the pre-established harmony is a new hypothesis devised to remedy the imperfections of previous theories. The general problem which it is meant to solve appeared at first for Leibniz in a particular form, that of the relations between soul and body. The usual pre-Cartesian solution of this special problem was the theory of an *influxus physicus* or actual passage of elements from the one substance to the other. Descartes's complete separation of soul from body, of thinking substance from extended substance, was in total opposition to the earlier theory [3].

[1] *Monadology*, § 51.

[2] Cf. *Nouveaux Essais*, bk. iv. ch. 10, § 10 (E. 376 a; G. v. 421): 'As each of these souls expresses in its own way what takes place outside of it, and is unable to have any influence upon other particular beings, or rather, as each must draw this expression entirely from within its own nature, each soul must necessarily have received this nature (or this internal ground of its expressions of what is external) from a Universal Cause, upon which these beings are all dependent, and which makes each of them to be perfectly in agreement and in correlation with every other. This implies the use of infinite knowledge and power and great ingenuity, especially with reference to the spontaneous agreement of a mechanism with the activities of the rational soul.' Also *Monadology*, §§ 51 sqq. and 81; *New System*, §§ 14 and 15.

[3] Cf. *Théodicée*, Part i. § 59 (E. 519 b; G. vi. 135) :—'The scholastic philosophers believed that there is a reciprocal physical interaction between body and soul; but since a thorough investigation has shown that thought and extended mass have no connexion with one another, and that they are created things which differ *toto genere*, several modern writers have recognized that there is no physical communication between soul and body, although there always remains the metaphysical communication, which makes of soul and body one and the same agent, or what is called one person.'

The problem itself is left by him without any satisfactory solution; but his followers made a definite attempt to solve it by the theory of 'Occasionalism,' in which they developed a suggestion that had been made by Descartes when he spoke of thinking and extended substance as alike dependent on nothing but the 'ordinary co-operation' (*concours ordinaire*) or 'assistance' of God. The Occasionalist theories varied to some extent, but in its most consistent form the hypothesis is that God is the sole real Cause, that finite substance has no power or activity of its own, and consequently that the changes which take place in soul and body are both directly produced by God. Consequently on the occasion of the appearing of a phenomenon in the one substance God produces a corresponding phenomenon in the other. The two phenomena are quite independent, except for the fact of their contemporaneous production by God, the one real Cause.

Leibniz's pre-established harmony has sometimes been regarded as merely another variety of Occasionalism, in spite of his frequent criticisms of the Occasionalist theory. And he has been accused of borrowing (without acknowledgement) from the Occasionalist Geulincx the well-known illustration of the two clocks which he uses in explaining his pre-established harmony. But Dr. Edmund Pfleiderer has clearly shown[1] that Leibniz, who

---

[1] *Leibniz und Geulincx mit besonderer Beziehung auf ihr beiderseitiges Uhrengleichniss* (Tübingen, 1884). Zeller comes to the same conclusion. The illustration appears in a note to Geulincx's *Ethica*, *Tract.* i. cap. ii. § 2, note 19; Land's ed., vol. iii. p. 211. Cf. *Third Explanation of the New System*, note 3. The notes are not in the first edition of the *Ethica*, and they do not seem to have been known to Leibniz. He received the illustration from Foucher, who probably arrived at it independently, not knowing that it was used by Geulincx. Cf. E. 130 a; G. iv. 488.

L. Stein holds that Leibniz was unaware of the source of the illustration, and may have considered it superfluous to assign any special source for it, inasmuch as it was a universally used simile, characteristic of the Cartesian school (a *Schulbeispiel*). With other references the illustration is used both by Descartes and by Cordemoy. See *Archiv für Geschichte d. Philosophie*, i. 59.

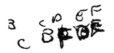

never mentions Geulincx in his writings, must have been quite unaware of Geulincx's use of the illustration. And in any case there is this essential difference between the Occasionalist theory and that of pre-established harmony, that the former regards finite things as empty of all activity except that which is immediately communicated to them by God, while the latter is founded on the conception of finite things as in reality forces, Monads with spontaneous activity[1]. Thus, the Occasionalist theory is open to the criticism which Leibniz repeatedly brings against it, namely, that it involves the supposition of perpetual miracle, or, in other words, that, if it be true, the connexion between soul and body must be a purely arbitrary one, there being nothing in the nature of either which can serve as a reason why *this* phenomenon of soul should accompany *that* phenomenon of body and not some other. The Monads, on the other hand, have at least this in common, that it is of the essence of each to represent the same world from a particular point of view, and that each unfolds the series of its perceptions or representations in an intelligible order. The whole is potentially present and seeks its realization in each of the parts. Consequently, the pre-established harmony is not arbitrary, but rational: no *Deus ex machina* is invoked. Thus it is impossible to regard Leibniz's theory as the completion of the Occasionalist doctrine, unless in the sense

---

[1] 'When I speak of the force and action of created beings, I mean that each created being is pregnant with its future state, and that it naturally follows a certain course, if nothing hinders it; and that the Monads, which are the true and only substances, cannot be naturally hindered in their inner determinations, since they include the representation of everything external [to them]. But, nevertheless, I do not say that the future state of the created being follows from its present state without the co-operation [*concours*] of God, and I am rather of opinion that preservation is a continual creation with an orderly change. Thus Father Malebranche might perhaps approve the pre-established harmony without giving up his own hypothesis, to the effect that God is the sole Agent [*acteur*]; though it is true that otherwise it [his hypothesis] does not appear to me well founded.' *Lettre à Bourguet* (1714) (E. 722 a; G. iii. 566).

that it is an hypothesis which seeks to reconcile the contrary views of Scholastics and Cartesians [1].

The scholastic theory of an *influxus physicus* connected soul and body in a way which ultimately confounded them, making it impossible to draw any clear line between them. The Cartesian or Occasionalist view, on the other hand, separated them so absolutely that nothing but a purely arbitrary connexion could be supposed—a connexion external to the nature of both. The Scholastics seemed to Leibniz to be right in holding that the connexion is a real one, grounded in the nature of the substances ; the Cartesians seemed right in maintaining that the substances are mutually exclusive. And the antinomy is solved for Leibniz by the supposition of a mutual '*ideal influence*,' a relationship of perception or representation, between independent self-active Monads, the harmony of whose inner developments has been established before their creation [2].

Leibniz's Illustrations of the pre-established Harmony— the Clocks and the Choirs.

The simile of the clocks, by means of which Leibniz illustrates his theory in relation to the Scholastic and Cartesian views, is given in the *Third Explanation* of his *New System.* Two clocks may be made to keep perfect time with one another in three different ways. They may be actually connected together, for instance by a piece of wood, in such a way that there is a mutual transference of vibrations between them, resulting in a perfect agreement of the motions of the pendulums [3]. Or,

---

[1] Cf. H. C. W. Sigwart, *Die Leibnizsche Lehre von der prästablirten Harmonie in ihrem Zusammenhange mit früheren Philosophemen betrachtet* (Tübingen, 1822), pp. 107 sqq.

[2] For an application of the doctrine of pre-established harmony to a particular case, see Appendix A, p. 200.

[3] This was suggested to Leibniz by an experiment of Huygens, who hung two pendulums on a bar of wood, and found that, though they were set swinging out of time with one another, the vibrations which each gave to the bar of wood caused them ultimately to swing in harmony. Cf. *Third Explanation of the New System*, p. 332.

in the second place, they may be supposed to be kept in time with one another from moment to moment by a skilled workman. Or, finally, they may have been so perfectly constructed that they keep time of themselves, without any mutual influence or assistance. If we compare soul and body to the two clocks, the first of these ways of connexion corresponds to the doctrine of an *influxus physicus*, the second to the Occasionalist view, and the third to the pre-established harmony.

It is, however, misleading to suppose, as has too often been done, that this is Leibniz's favourite simile for explaining his system of pre-established harmony[1]. He uses the illustration, not so much to explain his own theory as to make clear the relation in which it stands to previous hypotheses. He accepts for the moment the limited problem which these hypotheses endeavour to solve. But his own problem is larger and his own hypothesis is therefore more comprehensive than those of his predecessors. Body, for Leibniz, is nothing but a collection of Monads (or phenomena of Monads), and consequently the question of the connexion between soul and body is only a confused and imperfect form of the question as to the relation between any one Monad and another. The larger problem thus deals with the relations of body to body and soul to soul as well as the relations of soul and body, with which alone the earlier theories were concerned.

Leibniz would maintain that, as substances (Monads) are not physical but metaphysical, it is impossible for us to realize the true relations between them by conceptions of sense or imagination. These relations are metaphysical or ideal, and are therefore only intellectually apprehended.

---

[1] The somewhat misleading prominence which has been given to this illustration is to be attributed to Wolff and his school, who represented the metaphysics of Leibniz in a very imperfect way. Too many historians and teachers have been content with a Wolffian Leibniz; though for this there was doubtless some excuse in the imperfection of the editions of his writings. For instance, the *Correspondence with Arnauld*, in which the illustration of the choirs occurs, was first completely published by Grotefend in 1846.

But he elsewhere uses a simile for the pre-established harmony more adequate than that of the two clocks, when he compares the Monads to completely independent bands of musicians playing in perfect harmony. 'In short, to use an illustration, I will say that this concomitance, which I maintain, is comparable to several different bands of musicians or choirs, playing their parts separately, and so placed that they do not see or even hear one another, which can nevertheless keep perfectly together by each following their own notes, in such a way that he who hears them all finds in them a harmony that is wonderful and much more surprising than if there had been any connexion between them. It would even be possible that some one, being beside one of two such choirs, should by means of the one judge what the other is doing, and should even acquire such a habit of doing this (particularly if we suppose that he could hear his own without seeing it, and see the other without hearing it) that, with the help of his imagination, he should no longer think of the choir beside which he is, but of the other, or should take his own merely for an echo of the other [1],' &c. The analogy must not be pressed to an extreme ; but the simile is much better than that of the clocks. The clocks are too much alike to represent the Monads, and the harmony of their movement is too empty and almost meaningless. But in the case of the bands there is a real harmony formed out of the complementary movements of several self-acting units, and there is also the spontaneous development from the written notes of the score to the system of sounds which they signify. This development from the written signs to the sounds signified might be said to correspond to the passage from unconscious to conscious perception in the Monad [2]. An unconscious perception is, for Leibniz, a symbol of the corresponding conscious perception.

We have now considered the three chief conceptions of

[1] *Lettre à Arnauld* (1687) (G. ii. 95).   [2] Cf. G. ii. 74.

the metaphysic of Leibniz, and we have seen how they arise as the solution of his problem in the form which is given to it by its historical setting. In the first place, intension, force, or life, in the form of perception and appetition, is the essence of real, individual substance. In the second place, the principle of continuity or the identity of indiscernibles is the hypothesis by which Leibniz endeavours to explain the system or inter-relation of strictly individual substances. And, in the third place, the pre-established harmony is introduced to account for the possibility of change in elementary substances without prejudice to the whole.

Clear and confused Perception and Degrees of Appetition.

We must now consider more fully the varieties of perception and appetition which constitute the differences amongst Monads. In regard to perception Leibniz adopts the Cartesian distinction among ideas, with considerable modifications. Descartes divided ideas into those which are obscure, those which are clear, and those which are distinct as well as clear. 'I call that clear,' he says, 'which is present and manifest to the attentive mind, as we say we see an object clearly when it is present to the eye looking on, and when it makes on the sense of sight an impression sufficiently strong and definite; but I call that distinct which is clear and at the same time so definitely distinguished from everything else that its essence is evident to him who properly considers it[1].' And 'all the things which we clearly and distinctly conceive are true[2].' Leibniz follows Descartes in regarding clearness and distinctness as the marks of perfection in ideas or perceptions[3]; but he does not limit the dis-

---

[1] *Principia*, i. 45.   [2] *Method*, Part iv.
[3] Leibniz, however, interprets clearness and distinctness somewhat differently from Descartes. The distinction of one idea from all others is emphasized by Descartes, while Leibniz rather lays stress upon the internal distinctness of the idea, the distinctness of its elements. Cf. *Meditationes de Cognitione, Veritate et Ideis* (1684)

tinction between distinct and confused ideas to the ideas
which we consciously possess, nor does he draw a sharp
line between ideas which are perfectly clear and distinct,
and all others, which are confused or obscure. Confused
perceptions are not for Leibniz, as for Descartes, mere
mistakes and illusions ; but they belong to the real order
of things, which without them could not be what it is.
And there is no question, as in Descartes, regarding the
correspondence of perceptions to reality, clear and distinct
ideas representing their objects with perfect truth, while
obscure and confused ideas are 'of no avail in affording
us the knowledge of anything out of ourselves, but serve
rather to impede it [1].' According to Leibniz all perceptions
are more or less perfect representations of objects ; but
they vary infinitely in their degrees of distinctness or
confusedness. Confusedness is simply a low degree of
distinctness : the more perfect any perception or representation is, the more distinct is it, while the less perfect it
is, the more is it confused. Thus the differences among the
Monads consist entirely in the various degrees of perfection or distinctness with which they perceive or represent

(E. 79 a ; G. iv. 422): 'A notion is obscure when it does not suffice
for the recognition of the thing represented, as for instance when
I remember some flower or animal formerly seen, but not so well
as to be able to recognize it when it appears and to distinguish it
from some other near it, or when I think of some scholastic term
insufficiently explained, like the "entelechy" of Aristotle, or
"cause" in so far as the name is applied indifferently to material,
formal, efficient, and final causes. . . . Thus knowledge is clear
when it enables us to recognize the thing represented, and clear
knowledge again is either confused or distinct. It is confused
when I cannot separately enumerate the marks which are sufficient
for distinguishing the thing from others, although the thing really
has such marks and essential elements, into which its notion may
be analyzed. . . . So we see painters and other artists knowing
rightly what is well and what is badly done, but often unable to
give a reason for their opinion and saying that the thing they
dislike is lacking in something, *they know not what.* But a distinct
notion is such an one as the assayers have regarding gold, namely
one acquired through marks and tests sufficient for the discerning
of the thing from all other similar bodies.' For Locke's views, cf.
Essay, bk. ii. ch. 29, §§ 1 sqq. (Fraser's ed., vol. i. p. 486).

[1] *Principia,* Part iv. § 203.

E

the universe. But as each Monad actually represents the whole universe, however confusedly or imperfectly, and as each is essentially a force or living principle, proceeding, by its own spontaneous activity, from one perception to another, the distinct and the confused are not essentially separate from one another, but it is possible for the confused perception to unfold into distinctness. Each Monad contains the whole more or less confusedly within itself[1], and by its appetition may rise to a more perfect state. Each Monad contains as it were enfolded within itself all that it is to be. It is 'big with the future.' It is like an exceedingly condensed algebraical statement which can be indefinitely expounded : somewhat like the symbol π in the problem of determining the relation between the lengths of the diameter and circumference of a circle, with this very important difference, that the Monad 'reads *itself* off.' An omniscient Being could see the reality and history of the whole universe within the lowest Monad.

Three Classes of created Monads—(1) unconscious, (2) conscious, (3) self-conscious.

While there is thus a perfect continuity in the degrees of perfection with which the Monads represent the universe, Leibniz has roughly distinguished created Monads into three main classes—(1) unconscious or bare Monads (*monades nues*), (2) conscious Monads, and (3) rational or self-conscious Monads. As we have seen, every Monad or simple substance has a certain degree of perfection or completeness, inasmuch as it ideally or potentially contains the whole within itself. Thus the Aristotelian name of Entelechies might be given to all Monads, since they have each 'a certain perfection' (ἔχουσι τὸ ἐντελές), and 'a certain self-sufficiency (αὐτάρκεια) which makes them the sources of their internal actions,

---

[1] 'The world is entirely in each of its parts, but more distinctly in some than in others.' *Lettre à la Princesse Sophie* (1696) (G. vii. 544).

and, so to speak, incorporeal automata [1].' That is to say, each is, in its own way, complete in itself as representing the universe and complete in itself as an active living being or force. On the other hand, every Monad might be called a 'soul,' inasmuch as it has both perception and appetition, in the general sense of these words which has been already explained. Nevertheless, in spite of this essential unity of nature in the Monads, it is possible to draw broad lines of division among them. Conscious sensation or feeling, accompanied by the simpler forms of memory, clearly marks off certain Monads from those which have merely unconscious or confused perception. To the former class the name 'souls' may be specially applied, while for the latter the general name of Entelechies or Monads will suffice. And as there are still higher Monads which have self-consciousness and reason or thought proper, in addition to unconscious and conscious perception and memory, we may call these 'rational souls' or 'spirits' (intelligences, esprits) [2]. The class of rational souls or spirits includes men and higher intelligences. The intermediate 'soul'-class is that of animals, and the class of Entelechies or bare Monads includes all real beings that have not reached the stage of consciousness.

The differences of appetition in the three classes of created Monads (corresponding to the three grades of perception which characterize them) may be expressed as mere impulse, animal instinct or blind desire governed by mere feeling, and self-conscious desire or will.

Each of the two higher classes possesses, in addition to its own specific qualities, the characteristics of the

---

[1] *Monadology*, § 18.

[2] Cf. *De Anima Brutorum* (1710), §§ 10 and 13 (E. 464 b; G. vii. 330): 'Sense is perception which contains something distinct and is combined with attention and memory. . . . Besides the lowest degree of perception, which also occurs in those who are stunned, and the intermediate degree, which we call sense . . . there is a certain higher degree which we call thought. Now thought is perception combined with reason.'

inferior Monads.   Thus both animals and men have
unconscious as well as conscious perceptions, for example, when they fall into a faint or have a profound
and dreamless sleep[1].   In such a case they are not
entirely destitute of perceptions, for the Monad is indestructible (being indivisible) and it cannot exist without
perception of some kind.   The changes of the Monad
are entirely from within, so that when the man or
animal awakes out of a sleep or trance his conscious
perceptions must have unfolded themselves out of immediately preceding perceptions of an unconscious kind[2].
Again, men share with the animals both sense-perception
and the empirical sequence of memory and imagination,
which bears a resemblance to the concatenation of rational
thought, but may be sufficiently distinguished from it[3].
Indeed, in most of our actions and beliefs we are empirics, as for instance when we expect the dawn, not
because we know the cause of it, but because it has
happened regularly in the past[4].

Self-consciousness in the Philosophy of Leibniz and in that of Descartes.

The significance of this may be brought out by a
reference to the position of Descartes, which Leibniz
probably had in view. According to Descartes, the
rational soul is the mind and its reality comes only from
its conscious certainty of itself. Thus without self-consciousness there is no mind or soul. Animals have no
self-consciousness and therefore they have no souls—they
are mere machines. But animals have sensations and
impulses, and consequently sensation and impulse are
not functions of self-consciousness, acts of the soul, but
are purely physical and mechanical processes, whether
they occur in man or in the lower animals. It is in

[1] *Monadology,* § 20.   [2] Ibid. §§ 22 and 23.
[3] Ibid. §§ 26 sqq. Cf. *Nouveaux Essais,* bk. ii. ch. 11 (E. 237;
G. v. 129). and Fraser's ed. of Locke's *Essay,* vol. i. p. 208.
[4] *Monadology,* § 28.

self-consciousness alone that we have immediate self-certainty, from which we may proceed outward to the certainty of other things. Thus for Descartes the line between consciousness and unconsciousness on the one side and self-consciousness on the other must be very sharply drawn : the complete independence of self-consciousness is the root of the Cartesian dualism.

Now, Leibniz desires to preserve the independence of self-consciousness or the self-certainty and self-sufficiency of the mind. The validity of thinking must not be made to depend on reference to a reality external to it[1]. But, on the other hand, the mechanical dualism of Descartes must be avoided. The independence of self-consciousness is preserved through the conception of the Monads as a plurality of real, independent substances. Mind is not merely a modification of substance, an attribute (as Spinoza made it) ; it is an independent substance, in its various forms one or other of the infinite number. But, on the other hand, mind must not be regarded as identical with self-consciousness alone : self-consciousness must not be taken as entirely exclusive of mere consciousness or of unconsciousness. Otherwise we have returned to the Cartesian dualism. There must somehow be an unconscious activity of mind, and the opposition between mind and body becomes a difference, not of kind but of degree.

---

[1] Cf. *Remarques sur le sentiment du P. Malebranche* (1708) (E. 452 b ; G. vi. 578): 'The truth is that we see all things in ourselves and in our souls, and that the knowledge we have of the soul is very real and correct, provided we have given some attention to it. And further, it is through the knowledge which we have of the soul that we know being, substance, God Himself, and it is through reflexion upon our thoughts that we know extension and bodies. Yet it is true that God gives us all that is positive in this, and all the perfection involved in it, through an immediate and continual emanation, in virtue of the dependence of all created beings upon Him. In this way it is possible to give a good meaning to the phrase that God is the object of our souls and that we see all things in Him.' Cf. also Part iii. of this Introduction, p. 136.

Self-consciousness in the philosophy of Leibniz is, however, a very different thing from self-consciousness in the philosophy of Descartes. The latter arrives at the self-conscious Ego as the result of a rigorous analysis, whose instrument is doubt[1]. It is an ultimate fact, the fact of a subject thinking, without regard to any specific object of its thought. Self-consciousness is the bare witness of consciousness to itself, its empty self-consistency. In the certainty of self-consciousness Descartes (justifiably or not) finds involved the certainty of God, the Perfect Being, and from this he proceeds to the certainty of the external world and to the principle that clear and distinct ideas are characteristic of self-consciousness and are a sufficient warrant for the reality of their objects. For Leibniz, on the other hand, the Ego is not a pure subject, whose essence is immediate self-consciousness. No Monad can be a pure subject. 'Not only is it immediately clear to me that *I think*, but it is quite

---

[1] Leibniz seems strangely to have missed the significance of Descartes's method of doubt, probably because his interest lay more in Descartes's doctrines than in his way of reaching them. 'M. Descartes,' he says, ' has acted like the quacks [*charlatans*] who, in order to attract people and get a sale for their remedies, set up open theatres in which they show farces and other extraordinary, but not very necessary, things. Thus all that he says about the necessity of doubting everything and of treating doubtful things as false has had no other use than to get him a hearing, to raise a commotion, to draw the crowd by its novelty, and even to get himself contradicted, that he may be the more famous. But he has taken care to reserve for himself a way of rationally explaining his paradoxes.' Foucher de Careil, *Nouvelles Lettres et Opuscules inédits*, p. 12. Leibniz elsewhere speaks of Descartes's *Cogito, ergo sum* and his method of doubt as 'trappings to appeal to the people' (*phaleras ad populum*), and he pictures Descartes as 'throwing balls to plebeian minds to play with,' so that 'they seem to have got something great, like boys with a nut or a bean' (G. iv. 327). We must, of course, remember how different is the problem of Descartes from that of Leibniz. Descartes lays special stress upon self-consciousness because he regards himself as having found a principle by means of which to distinguish absolutely the true from the false or doubtful. On the other hand, for Leibniz as for Spinoza, the problem of philosophy is not primarily a problem of knowledge. Leibniz's theory of knowledge follows from his answer to the question—'What in reality is substance?'

as clear to me that *I have different thoughts;* that now
I think of A, now *of B,* &c.[1]' An Ego is one of an
infinite number of substances, and its self-consciousness
is thus not the ground of its existence, but a difference
in degree of quality between it and others[2]. The self-
conscious Monad is merely one which has developed its
representative or perceptive nature more fully than those
which we describe as animal souls or bare Monads. In
other words, we *are* 'Egos' before we think of ourselves,
realize ourselves, or reflect upon ourselves as Egos. We
are 'raised to the knowledge of ourselves and of God[3].'

The difference between the self-conscious Monad and
others consists in the greater clearness and distinctness
of its perceptions and ideas. But, as clearness and distinctness are relative terms (every Monad having perceptions in some degree clear and distinct), the specific
perceptions of a self-conscious being must be further
defined. Leibniz, as we have seen, cannot accept the
Cartesian view which totally rejects confused and obscure
ideas and makes clearness and distinctness the sole criteria
of truth[4]. In addition to being clear and distinct, the

---

[1] *Nouveaux Essais,* bk. iv. ch. 2, § 1 (E. 341 a ; G. v. 348). Cf. G.
iv. 327: 'These two things I regard as mutually independent of
one another and as equally original.' Also *Lettre à Foucher* (1676)
(G. i. 370) : 'There are two absolute general truths, that is to say,
general truths which speak of the actual existence of things: the
one is that we think, the other that there is a great variety in our
thoughts. From the first it follows that we are, from the second
it follows that there is something other than ourselves, that is to
say something other than that which thinks, something which is
the cause of the variety in what appears to us. Now the one of
these truths is as unquestionable, as independent as the other, and
M. Descartes, having in the order of his meditations taken account
only of the first of them, has failed to reach the perfection he set
before himself.'

[2] 'To say, *I think, therefore I am* [exist] is not strictly to prove
existence by thought, since to think and to be thinking are the
same thing; and to say *I am thinking* is already to say *I am.'*
Nouveaux Essais, bk. iv. ch. 7, § 7 (E. 362 a ; G. v. 391).

[3] *Monadology,* § 29.

[4] Cf. *Meditationes de Cognitione, Veritate et Ideis* (1684) (E. 80 b ; G. iv.
425), translated in Appendix to Baynes's ed. of *Port-Royal Logic:*
'And I also see that the men of our time abuse that vaunted

ideas which are characteristic of a rational being must be analyzed, so that their grounds or premises may be as fully exhibited as possible. And thus the specific quality of a rational soul or self-conscious Monad is 'the knowledge of necessary and eternal truths,' that is to say, of the ultimate grounds or premises of all knowledge. The self-conscious Monad represents or perceives the universe in an articulate way. It has carried the internal evolution or realization of the universe so far that its underlying principles have clearly revealed themselves. 'It is by the knowledge of necessary truths and by their abstract expression [*leurs abstractions*] that we are raised to acts of reflexion which make us think of what is called "I," and observe that this or that is within us : and thus, in thinking of ourselves, we think of being, of substance, of the simple and the compound, of the immaterial and of God Himself, conceiving that what is limited in us is in Him without limits. And these acts of reflexion furnish the chief objects of our reasonings [1].'

This at once suggests Descartes, but Descartes with a difference. For Leibniz, as for Descartes, the idea of

principle : *whatever I clearly and distinctly perceive regarding anything, that is true or (rightly) predicable* [*enuntiabile*] *of it.* For often things which are really obscure and confused seem clear and distinct to men judging hastily. The axiom, therefore, is useless, unless there be added such criteria of the clear and distinct as we have given, and unless there is certainty [*constet*] regarding the truth of the ideas. For the rest, the rules of common Logic, which are also used in Geometry, are not to be despised as criteria of true statements, such rules, for instance, as that nothing should be admitted as certain unless it has been proved by accurate observation [*experientia*] or by strict demonstration. But strict demonstration is that which keeps to the form prescribed by Logic, not necessarily always in syllogisms set out in order according to the custom of the schools . . . but at least in such a way that the conclusion of the argument follows from its very form. Any right calculation might be taken as an example of an argument of this kind, conceived in due form. Therefore no necessary premise must be left out, and all the premises must first have been either proved or assumed by way of hypothesis, in which case the conclusion also is hypothetical. Those who will diligently observe these things will easily guard themselves against deceptive ideas.'

[1] *Monadology,* § 30.

God or the most Perfect Being is involved in that of
an imperfect self-conscious being. Yet Leibniz regards
the idea of God as contained, not in the self-conscious
being alone, but, in one way or another, in every real
being. Thus it is of less consequence for Leibniz than
for Descartes that the idea of God is pre-supposed in the
consciousness of self. That which is of most importance
to Leibniz is that self-consciousness pre-supposes a knowledge of necessary truths in *general*. Thus, for Leibniz,
God is not merely the eternally necessary Being whose
very idea (or essence) involves existence and who is in
that way the ground of existence to all other things : He
is also the greatest of beings, the highest of Monads
(*Monas monadum* [1]), whose own existence is one among
many necessary and eternal truths. 'We must not
imagine, as some do, that eternal truths, being dependent
on God, are arbitrary and depend on His will, as Descartes, and afterwards Monsieur Poiret, appear to have
held [2].' There are truths or facts which are dependent
on the will of God, but these are not necessary and
eternal.

The Kinds of Truth according to Leibniz. Necessary and eternal Truths and contingent Truths.

Accordingly as, on Leibniz's view, the self-conscious
being has not a primary and independent reality, based
on a complete difference in kind between itself and other
beings, so the special kind of knowledge (that of eternal
and necessary truths) which belongs to a self-conscious
being is not to be regarded as the only absolutely certain
truth, to the form of which all other real knowledge
must be reduced. 'There are two kinds of truths, those
of *reasoning* and those of *fact* [3].' The former are the
eternal and necessary truths, the latter are contingent.

---

[1] Giordano Bruno, as well as Leibniz, speaks of God as *Monas
monadum.*

[2] *Monadology,* § 46.   [3] Ibid. § 33.

And the difference between them is that the truths of reasoning are either ultimate self-evident principles or truths which are reducible to such first principles by a process of strict logical analysis, while any attempt to analyze truths of fact into their ultimate grounds leads to an infinite process, and they must finally be referred to God as their ground *eminenter*[1].

Logical Principles of the Philosophy of Leibniz. (a) *Principle of Identity or Contradiction.*

With this division of human knowledge into two great kinds we come in sight of the guiding principles of Leibniz's philosophy, its logical pre-suppositions as distinct from its specific metaphysical doctrines. The logic underlying the philosophies of Descartes and Spinoza was a logic of abstract self-consistency[2]. In their view all real knowledge must be ultimately of one kind. All apparent knowledge that is not of that kind must be regarded as entirely unreal and illusory. This was necessarily involved in the position that there is no appeal beyond the witness of consciousness to itself. 'The order and connexion of ideas is the same as the order and connexion of things[3].' And, as all things must be regarded as ultimately referable to one ground or cause, so all ideas must ultimately be referable to one standard; that is, must be linked together by one principle. The standard must be that of self-evidence or absence of self-

---

[1] Cf. *Monadology*, §§ 35-38.

[2] Not that this was perfectly evident to themselves. Descartes, for instance, regards his method of doubt as superior to a logical deduction, based on the principle of contradiction. 'Here, if I am not wrong,' says Eudoxus, 'you must be beginning to see that he who can make a proper use of doubt will be able to deduce from it very certain truths, nay rather, more certain and more useful truths than those which we derive from the great principle we usually lay down as the basis or centre to which all other principles may be referred, "*it is impossible that one and the same thing can both be and not be.*"' *Recherche de la Vérité par les lumières naturelles, Œuvres de Descartes* (Cousin), vol. xi. p. 366.

[3] Spinoza, *Ethics*, Part ii. Prop. 7.

contradiction in the ideas, which is simply another way
of describing the immediate witness of consciousness to
itself. True ideas must be clear and distinct in order
that it may be manifest that they are free from self-
contradiction. All real knowledge must either be immediately recognizable as eternal and necessary truth, or
must be deducible from such truth by a formally or
mathematically conclusive process. Thus the philosophies
of Descartes and Spinoza were ruled by the principle of
contradiction, that A cannot both be A and not A, or
that necessary truths are 'identical propositions, whose
opposite involves an express contradiction[1].' In other
words, they held that self-consciousness is self-consistent,
that it never absolutely contradicts itself.

Now this is, so far as it goes, a perfectly sound doctrine.
Its fault is that it does not go far enough. Self-consciousness is much more than merely self-consistent. Its
self-consistency is not immediate and on the surface. It
is not a mere negative self-identity of parts, without
regard to their specific content. To be self-consistent,
according to the principle of contradiction, is for a thing
to be itself, that is, to be 'not anything else.' But a
thing whose ultimate essence is to be 'not anything else'
is nothing. 'Nothing' is immediately self-consistent
quite as much as 'something[2].' In other words, all real
(not merely formal) self-consistency must be mediate, it
must have grounds. It must spring from the specific
nature of the self-consistent thing[3]. And thus, as Leibniz
contended, even axioms may require proof[4]. Their self-

---

[1] *Monadology*, § 35. *Cf.* ibid. § 31. The principle of contradiction is that 'in virtue of which we judge *false* that which
involves a contradiction, and *true* that which is opposed or contradictory to the false.'

[2] Cf. Locke's *Essay*, bk. iv. ch. 8, § 3; Fraser's ed., vol. ii. p. 293.

[3] Cf. *Nouveaux Essais*, bk. iv. ch. 7, § 9 (E. 362 a; G. v. 392): 'In
the natural' [i. e. logical] 'order, the statement that a thing is what
it is, is prior to the statement that it is not another thing.'

[4] Cf. *Nouveaux Essais*, bk. i. ch. 3, § 24 (E. 222 a; G. v. 98): 'It
is one of my great maxims, that it is good to work out proofs of

evidence requires elucidation : the basis of it must be made manifest[1]. Self-consciousness, then, is really self-consistent only in virtue of its being a definite system, a self-revealing process or development, which contains within itself the ground or reason of its self-consistency, and the ground or reason of existence. Accordingly, to treat it in philosophical investigation as if it were merely superficially self-consistent, as if the law which expresses its whole nature were the law of contradiction, would be to arrive at an empty and abstract result.

Leibniz, however, while recognizing the inadequacy of the principle of contradiction as thus interpreted, did not clearly enough perceive the reason for this inadequacy. He regarded the principle of contradiction, not as an imperfect interpretation of the one principle of all truth, to be made perfect by further definition, but as an independent principle, adequate to a certain kind of truth, yet requiring to be supplemented by another co-ordinate principle, which should be the standard of another kind of truth. If the principle of contradiction be the sole principle of knowledge, whatever is not self-contradictory is true ; and nothing is true unless it can be shown that it is not self-contradictory. But how are we to determine what is or is not self-contradictory ? According to the Cartesians this is to be done by analytically reducing the doubtful statement to one or more self-evident propositions, or, in other words, by showing that the statement is ultimately involved in one or more propositions, of such a kind that their predicate is manifestly contained in their subject[2]. But Leibniz maintains that there are

the axioms themselves.' Cf. Fraser's ed. of Locke's *Essay*, vol. ii. p. 267, note.

[1] Cf. *Nouveaux Essais*, bk. iv. ch. 11, § 14 (E. 379 b ; G. v. 428) : 'As to eternal truths, it is to be noted that at bottom they are all conditional and say in effect : such a thing being supposed, such another thing is.'

[2] According to Leibniz, all true propositions must be such that their predicate is really contained in their subject, although this may not be self-evident. This is simply expressing in another

many statements to which it is impossible satisfactorily
to apply this test. Their very nature is such that the
process of analysis cannot in their case be brought to an
end, and consequently we remain unable to say whether
they are really self-contradictory or not. At any rate,
their self-contradiction, or the absence of it, cannot be
made self-evident. For instance, the statement that
'I took a long walk yesterday' may be perfectly true,
but by no amount of analysis is it possible for us to test
its truth by reducing it to self-evident propositions. It is
not necessarily but contingently true. Its truth is not
directly grounded in the eternal nature of things, but is
determined by a multitude of other truths, which may
each in their turn demand an infinite analysis[1]. These

form his view that 'in the notion of each individual substance all
its events are contained, along with all their circumstances and
the whole sequence of external things.' *Lettre au Prince Ernest*
(1686) (G. ii. 12). 'Always in every true affirmative proposition,
whether necessary or contingent, universal or singular, the notion
of the predicate is in some way comprehended in that of the
subject, *praedicatum inest subjecto;* otherwise I know not what truth
is. But I require no more connexion here than that which exists
a parte rei between the terms of a true proposition, and it is only in
this sense that I say that the notion of the individual substance
includes all its events and all its characteristics, even those that
are commonly called extrinsic (that is to say, those which belong
to it only in virtue of the general connexion of things and on
account of its expressing the whole universe in its own way).
'' For there must always be some foundation for the connexion of
the terms of a proposition, and this is to be found in their notions.''
That is my great principle, as to which I think all philosophers
should be at one, and of which one of the corollaries is the common
axiom that nothing happens without it being possible to give a
reason why things should have gone thus rather than otherwise,
although this reason often inclines without necessitating, a perfect
indifference being a chimerical or incomplete supposition.' *Lettre
à Arnauld* (1686) (G. ii. 56).
[1] Cf. *De Scientia Universali seu Calculo Philosophico* (E. 83 b ; G. vii.
200) : 'The difference between necessary and contingent truths is
indeed the same as that between commensurable and incommen-
surable numbers. For the reduction of commensurable numbers
to a common measure is analogous to the demonstration of necessary
truths, or their reduction to identical truths. But, as in the case
of surd ratios the reduction involves an infinite process and yet
approaches a common measure so that a definite but unending
series is obtained, thus also contingent truths require an infinite

contingent truths, however (if they are to be truths at
all, and not merely false or doubtful statements), must
have some ground or reason[1]. If the truth is such that
it is impossible to find for it an absolute and eternal
reason in the first principles of things, there must at
least be some satisfactory or sufficient reason why it
should be so and not otherwise.

*Logical Principles of the Philosophy of Leibniz. (b) Principle
of Sufficient Reason.*

Thus Leibniz supplements the principle of contradiction by the addition of the principle of sufficient
reason. The name has a makeshift sound—as if one
should say, 'We must be content with a sufficient reason
in cases where a perfect reason is not to be found.' But
in the philosophy of Leibniz it is much more than a
makeshift. This principle is essential to his system and,
indeed, gives it the greater part of its value. In the
Monadology, Leibniz defines this principle as that 'in
virtue of which we hold that no fact can be found real or
existing, no statement true, unless there be a sufficient
reason why it should be so and not otherwise, although
these reasons very often cannot be known by us[2].' As
thus defined, the principle of sufficient reason might
almost be regarded as including the principle of contradiction, inasmuch as the self-consistency of necessary
truths is their sufficient reason. Self-consistency or

analysis, which God alone can accomplish. Accordingly it is by
Him alone that these truths are known *a priori* and with certainty.
For, although the reason of any succeeding state might be found in
that which precedes it, yet a reason for this preceding state can
again be given, and so we never come to the final reason in the
series. But this infinite process itself takes the place of a reason,
because in its own special way it might from the beginning have
been immediately understood outside of the series, in God, the
Author of things, on whom both antecedent and consequent states
are dependent, even more than they are dependent upon one
another.'

[1] *Monadology*, §§ 36. 37.
[2] Ibid. § 32. In the *Théodicée*, § 44 (E. 515; G. vi. 127), he calls
it '*Determining* [deciding] *Reason*.'

absence of self-contradiction is one test of the sufficiency
of the reason. But, on the other hand, the principle of
contradiction has an independent and, in some sense,
superior position, for in the case of necessary truths the
reason can always be given, that is, can be made explicit,
while in the case of contingent truths we often can only
say that there must be a sufficient reason, without knowing fully what the reason is.

The Possible and the Compossible. The best of all possible Worlds.

The value and importance of the principle of sufficient
reason become more manifest when we inquire further—
'In what does the sufficiency of the reason consist?'
We have seen that the grounds of any contingent truth
or fact are to be sought in other contingent truths or
facts, and that an attempt to analyze a contingent truth
or fact into its grounds thus leads to an infinite process.
Accordingly it seems to Leibniz that the final reason of
contingent truths must be sought in something outside
of the system of contingent things, viz. in an eternal and
necessary Substance or God, who is their source. But
this requires some further explanation. In the case of
the principle of contradiction, what may be called the
sufficiency of the reason consisted in the absence of
self-contradiction in the thing or proposition. But to
say that a thing is in itself free from contradiction is the
same as to say that, by itself and without reference to
other things, it is possible [1]. Accordingly, to say that
everything which is not self-contradictory is true or real
is to say that everything possible is true or real. 'I call
possible everything which is perfectly conceivable and
which has consequently an essence, an idea, without
considering whether the remainder of things allows it to
become existent [2].' But the opposite of every particular

---

[1] Cf. *Meditationes de Cognitione*, &c. (1684) (E. 80 b; G. iv. 425;
Baynes, *Port-Royal Logic*, 428).
[2] *Lettre à Bourguet* (1714) (E. 720 a; G. iii. 573).

event or contingent truth is possible in this sense : it does not necessarily imply a self-contradiction. The opposite of the axiom, 'Things that are equal to the same thing are equal to one another,' is not possible, for it involves an immediate self-contradiction. The opposite of the truth, 'I am sitting here at this moment,' is possible, for it does not involve a direct self-contradiction. Accordingly, the truth of contingent things is not grounded in their possibility[1]. It is not in virtue of their very essence or idea that they, and not their opposites, are true or real. Their sufficient reason lies beyond themselves, in their relation to other things. In themselves, the contingent truths and their opposites are alike possible : considered in relation to other things, the truths alone are possible. For instance, if we consider the truth that 'I am sitting here at this moment,' not in itself alone, but in relation to an indefinite number of other truths regarding (say) my habits, character, work, the hour of the day, &c., we shall see that the truth alone is possible, that in this connexion its opposite is impossible. The opposites of contingent truths, though not self-contradictory, are in contradiction with the general system. Each is possible, but they are not jointly possible, mutually compatible, or, in Leibniz's phrase, 'compossible.' Accordingly, 'compossibility,' or conformity with the actual system of things, is the true test of reality, the sufficient reason. Everything which is possible has an essence or meaning, but only that which is also compossible has existence[2].

[1] Descartes did not admit that everything which is possible is realized, but assigned the choice among possible things to the mere will of God. But this is practically to make the choice arbitrary and consequently to make the contingent (which is the result of choice) fortuitous. Spinoza, on the other hand, by holding that everything possible is realized, made the contingent necessary. Leibniz, however, points out that Descartes in one passage (Principia, iii. 47) says that 'Matter must successively take all the forms of which it is capable,' an approach to Spinoza's view. Réponse aux Réflexions, &c. (1697) (E. 144 a ; G. iv. 340).

[2] Cf. Lettre à Bourguet (1714) (E. 719 b ; G. iii. 572): 'I do not admit that, in order to know whether the romance of Astraea is

But, while the ground of the individual thing's reality is its compossibility with the actual system of things, Leibniz does not admit that mere compossibility with any system whatever implies the existence of the compossible essences. The principle of sufficient reason is not interpreted by him as a general reference to system or as reference to a system which is held to be the only one possible, to an all-inclusive system[1]. There are several possible systems or universes, each of which consists of a collection of compossible elements. Indeed it must be supposed that there is an endless series of such possible universes, of which one only has existence as well as essence. But the principle of sufficient reason

possible, it would be necessary to know its connexion with the rest of the universe. That would be necessary in order to know whether it is *compossible* with it, and, consequently, whether this romance has been, is now. or shall be [realized] in any corner of the universe. For assuredly, without that, there will be no place for it. And it is very true that what does not exist, has never existed, and never shall exist, is not possible, if by possible we mean compossible, as I have just said. . . . But it is another question whether *Astraea* is absolutely possible. I say "yes," because it involves no contradiction. But, in order that it may actually exist, the rest of the universe would have to be quite other than it is, and it is possible that it may be otherwise' L'*Astrée* was the first French pastoral romance, modelled on such works as the *Aminta* of Tasso or the *Pastor Fido* of Guarini. It was written by Honoré d'Urfé (1568–1625) and was published in parts between the years 1610 and 1619. It is a strange medley of historical and imaginary events and characters, and the Court society of Europe for a long time amused itself by trying to ' identify ' the characters of the story. It was translated into almost every European language, many ' keys ' to it were written, plays were founded upon it, and it was read with much appreciation by such writers as La Rochefoucauld, La Fontaine, and Rousseau.

[1] *Remarques sur la lettre de M. Arnauld* (1686) (G. ii. 45) : ' If we were to reject absolutely things which are merely possible, we should do away with the contingent, for. if nothing is possible except what God has actually created, whatever God has created would be necessary—supposing that God has resolved to create anything.' Nolen (*La Critique de Kant et la Métaphysique de Leibniz*, p. 24) remarks that ' the relation between the world of possibles and the world of existences remains one of the obscure points in the philosophy of Leibniz. The correspondence with Arnauld . . . shows that Leibniz was conscious of the insufficiency of his explanations and of the difficulty of the problem.'

still requires that a cause or reason be assigned for the existence of the actual universe rather than any other among those which are possible. The existence of the actual universe is its creation by God, that is to say, its being not merely in the region of ideas, or essences, or possibilities, which is the pure understanding of God, but also in the sphere of final causes, in which the will of God operates [1]. In other words, the actual universe is the result of a free choice of God amongst all possible universes. While the choice of God is free, being unlimited in its application, it is not an arbitrary choice, but a choice according to reason. God chooses as the actual universe that whose compossible elements admit of the greatest amount of perfection or reality, that is to say, the fullest and most complete essence. Thus the actual universe is ' the best of all possible worlds '—of all worlds which are really worlds or systems, that is, in Leibniz's language, of all worlds whose elements are compossible. God makes this choice because, being omnipotent, His choice is unlimited, He may create any possible world ; being omniscient, He contains all possible worlds in His understanding and perceives that which is best ; and, being perfect in goodness of will, He chooses the best. Thus the Divine Nature is ultimately the sufficient reason of all particular things, since it is the ground both of the essence and of the existence of the actual universe [2], which, in its turn, as a system of compossibles, is the immediate ground of its individual elements.

Accordingly, the principle of contradiction and the principle of sufficient reason remain side by side in the

---

[1] According to Leibniz, existence (or the creation which produces existence) involves no change in the essence of a thing. Its essence is the same, whether it be in the actual world or merely in the region of the Divine ideas. Cf. *Monadology*, §§ 43 and 47, notes.

[2] Cf. *Théodicée*, § 7 (E. 506 a ; G. vi. 107): ' His understanding is the source of essences, and His will is the origin of existences.' Also *Monadology*, §§ 53-55, and *Théodicée*, § 201 (E. 565 b ; G. vi. 236).

philosophy of Leibniz, each having its specific function. but neither reducible to the other, while no attempt is made to find a more comprehensive principle which may include both. There are certain eternal and necessary truths which are independent of the will of God, existing in His understanding alone, and these are subject to the principle of contradiction ; but the reality of all individual substances and their changes is dependent on the will as well as the understanding of God, and they are all subject to the principle of sufficient reason. Each principle expresses a certain necessity ; but the necessity of the principle of contradiction differs in kind from that of the principle of sufficient reason, the former being an absolute, compelling, or metaphysical necessity, whose opposite is impossible, involving self-contradiction, while the latter is a relative, inclining, or moral necessity, whose opposite is not impossible, but incompossible. inconsistent not with itself but with the system of which it is a part, inconsistent not so much with the eternally true as with the best possible.

The leading Characteristics of Leibniz's Philosophy as Results of the two great logical Principles.

We are now in a position to see how the main features of the Metaphysics of Leibniz are determined by these great logical principles which underlie it[1]. The principle of contradiction, taken by itself, is a principle of exclusion. A is A (every real thing is identical with itself) at all times, in all circumstances, throughout all changes, in every variety of relations. Strictly speaking, then, A can never *become* B. A is always A, B is always B ; each is for ever exclusive of the other. 'Black is black, *furieusement* black ; white is white, *furieusement* white.' The principle of contradiction, as thus interpreted, is

---

[1] What follows is, of course, not an exposition of Leibniz's explicit doctrine, but an analytic investigation of the way in which his logical principles fix the main lines of his philosophy.

a principle of pure self-identity which asserts permanence to the exclusion of change or, in general, unity to the exclusion of difference.   In other words, it insists on the reality of Terms, making relations subordinate or fictitious.   Consequently a philosophy whose dominant principle is that of contradiction, in this sense, must (consciously or unconsciously) treat whole and parts as exclusive of one another, asserting the reality of the one as against that of the other.   For if the whole be real it must be simple, it must exclude as unreal all relations or differences.   Otherwise it will not be purely self-identical, but may receive a variety of real predicates. And as it is simple it can have no real parts.   Since A cannot be not-A, and since not-A includes B, C, &c., it cannot be true that some A is B or C.   Some A can only be A without further distinction.   On the other hand, if the parts be real and purely self-identical, if the reality of each is self-centred and is determined without regard to its relations to the others, then there is no real whole, but only a numerical collection of individuals which may even be contradictory of one another.   The principle of contradiction, considered as meaning merely that the real is that which is not self-contradictory, yields either a whole, which has no real parts or determinations because it is equally indifferent to all possible determinations, or a bare collection of severally possible, but jointly ' incompossible' parts.

Now, it is the influence of the principle of contradiction, thus abstractly interpreted, that leads Leibniz to the conception of real substance as simple, i. e. as without parts, indecomposable.   And it is the same principle that accounts for the infinite plurality of simple substances and their complete isolation from one another: For Leibniz, in order to give due value to the differences in the universe, holds the principle of contradiction as ensuring reality to the parts, leaving the whole to be otherwise accounted for.   And, on the other hand, the

mutual isolation of simple substances is but another
name for their abstract self-identity. A can never become
B, and, as A and B are simple, no part of A can ever
become B, or a part of B. One Monad can never become
another, and no quality of one Monad can ever become
a quality of another.

The principle of sufficient reason in combination with
the principle of contradiction yields the idea of the
Monad as itself the source of all the differences it contains, the whole variety of its existence [1]. The principle
of contradiction requires that real substance must contain its whole nature within itself in such a way that
it may be analytically deduced. The notion of substance
is self-explicative. Every true proposition must be analytic. Thus the Monad must be self-sufficient. But
now the principle of sufficient reason is added to explain
that the analysis is not necessarily completed in every
case, that, while substance must be self-sufficient and self-
explicative, its self-sufficiency is not necessarily in every
case fully realized. Its self-identity is not static but
dynamic: it is not immediately self-explaining, but pro-
gressively self-revealing. Many true propositions are not
actually but potentially analytic. While the predicate
of every true proposition must in some way be contained
in the subject, it does not follow that in each particular
case the relation can be made perfectly and self-evidently
clear [2]. The predicate must have a sufficient ground or
reason in the subject, but not necessarily a self-evident
one. The Monad must be conceived as sufficiently the
reason of its changes or varieties, though not self-evidently
the reason of each. In other words, the various perceptions which are the variety or change in the Monad,
the manifold [*multitude*] in the simple substance, have

[1] The problem how the *simple* substance can contain *differences* is
the same as the problem how the principles of contradiction and
sufficient reason can be treated as independent and co-ordinate.
Of this Leibniz offers no clear solution.

[2] Cf. this Introduction, Part ii. p. 60, note 2.

reality even though they are not all perfectly clear and distinct. Thus Spinoza, under the guidance of the principle of contradiction, rejected merely empirical knowledge, the contingent sequence of ideas that comes *ab experientia vaga*, as confused and therefore unreal and illusory, a work of imagination. On the other hand, Leibniz (for whom this empirical sequence is the series of perceptions in Monads that have not reached the self-conscious stage) attributes to this sequence a relative reality, inasmuch as it is potentially, though not actually, clear and distinct.

Further, we see the influence of the principle of sufficient reason in the conception of the Monads as each representative of the whole universe from its particular point of view. The Monads are indeed *Terms* or absolute points, centres exclusive of one another; but they are not Terms exclusive of relations. It is a part of their essential reality to contain within themselves a multiplicity of relations. The Monad may be likened to 'a centre or point in which, quite simple though it is, there exists an infinite number of angles, formed by the lines which meet in it[1].' The principle of contradiction requires nothing but a pure simplicity in the individual substance; any kind of simple substance would satisfy it. But the principle of sufficient reason imposes the further condition that the simple substance must have relations to other simple substances and to the whole, and that only those simple (self-consistent) substances are real which are also consistent with the real unity of the whole. For otherwise every real substance would have its ground or reason wholly *in se*, and those things for which we must be content with a ground or reason *in alio* would be entirely illusory. Thus the combination of self-consistency with consistency in relation to the

---

[1] *Principles of Nature and of Grace*, § 2. Cf. *Extrait du Dictionnaire de Bayle*, &c. (1702) (G. iv. 542): 'God has put in each soul *a concentration of the world.*'

whole is what Leibniz means by the character of the Monad as at once exclusively individual and representative or perceptive of the whole universe from its particular point of view.

Again, the appetition of the Monads is due entirely to the principle of sufficient reason. A substance which is real in virtue of its mere possibility can have no tendency to a change of state [1]. If it were really to change it would cease to be itself. But the appetition of the Monads is ruled not by the principle of realizing the self-consistent or the abstractly possible, but by the principle of realizing the best or the full harmony of a system. The pre-established harmony of the universe as a system of 'compossible' substances is the ground or reason of the appetition in each, the principle of its changes. But this, as we have seen, is a consequence of admitting the principle of sufficient reason.

Lastly, a very slight consideration will show that the law of continuity (with its obverse, the identity of indiscernibles) is a particular application of the principle of sufficient reason. A breach in the continuity of the series of simple substances would mean a void in nature. Such a void is not inconsistent with the principle of contradiction : it is not self-evidently impossible. But it is inconsistent with the principle of the best or most fitting which governs the actual system of things, that is to say, it is inconsistent with the principle of sufficient reason. That one possible thing is in itself more perfect than another is no sufficient reason for the *existence* of the former rather than the latter ; the former might perhaps be incompatible, while the latter is compatible, with the rest of the world. But it is inconsistent

---

[1] Cf. Spinoza's *Conatus*, the 'effort by which each thing endeavours to persevere in its own being,' and which is 'nothing but the actual essence of the thing itself.' *Ethics*, Part iii. Prop. 7. Leibniz might say that, on Spinoza's principles, to call this an 'effort' is to beg the question, because effort implies tendency towards something.

with the principle of sufficient reason that nothing
should exist where something is possible; for the principle of sufficient reason requires the existence of a
complete world, that is to say, of that entire system of
compossible things which contains the fullest reality or
the greatest amount of essence [1]. Consequently the law
of continuity derives its force from the principle of
sufficient reason. And thus, in general, Leibniz's solution of his main problem is accomplished by the combination of the principles of contradiction and sufficient
reason, giving, on the one hand, real units of substance,
even more thoroughly impenetrable and indivisible than
physical atoms; and, on the other hand, in consistency
with these, a real whole, which is not a mere aggregate
of independent and perhaps mutually contradictory ele-

[1] Cf. IVme Lettre à Clarke (1716), Apostille (E. 758 b; G. vii. 378)
(Clarke's translation): 'In like manner, to admit a vacuum in
nature is ascribing to God a very imperfect work; 'tis violating
the grand principle of the necessity of a *sufficient reason*; which
many have talked of, without understanding its true meaning. . . .
To omit many other arguments against a *vacuum* and *atoms*, I shall
here mention those which I ground upon God's perfection and
upon the necessity of a sufficient reason. I lay it down as a principle that every perfection which God could impart to things
without derogating from their other perfections has actually been
imparted to them. Now let us fancy a space wholly empty. God
could have placed some matter in it, without derogating in any
respect from all other things; therefore He hath actually placed
some matter in that space: therefore there is no space wholly
empty: therefore all is full. . . . I shall add another argument,
grounded upon the necessity of a *sufficient reason*. 'Tis impossible
there should be any principle to determine what proportion of
matter there ought to be, out of all the possible degrees from
a *plenum* to a *vacuum*, or from a *vacuum* to a *plenum*.' [? The proportion of either *plenum* to *vacuum* or of *vacuum* to *plenum*.] 'Perhaps
it will be said that the one should be equal to the other; but,
because matter is more perfect than a *vacuum*, reason requires that
a geometrical proportion should be observed, and that there should
be as much more matter than *vacuum* as the former deserves to
have the preference before the latter. But then there must be no
vacuum at all; for the perfection of matter is to that of a *vacuum* as
something to nothing.' Cf. also the beginning of Leibniz's second
letter (E. 748 b; G. vii. 356): 'The more matter there is, the more
opportunity is there for God to exercise His wisdom and His power;
and for this reason, among others, I hold that there is absolutely
no void.'

ments, but the most perfect system of mutually consistent or compossible substances, in each of which the whole is in some way ideally contained [1].

[1] Further consideration of the relation between these two great principles in the philosophy of Leibniz is given in the Fourth Part of this Introduction, p. 174.

PART III.

DETAILED STATEMENT OF THE PHILOSOPHY OF LEIBNIZ.

PASSING from the general consideration of the doctrines of Leibniz, we now come to their more specific development. We shall, in the first place, examine the relation between his philosophical principles and the ruling conceptions of his Mathematics, and we shall afterwards endeavour to trace the principles of the Monadology in the various departments of knowledge which are concerned with Matter, with Organism, and with Self-consciousness. This review of human knowledge, proceeding from the most abstract or simple to the most concrete or complex of the sciences[1], will reveal to us the interpretation which Leibniz's conception of Substance requires us to give to the judgments of common consciousness. From another point of view, we may consider ourselves as inquiring:—'What are the answers which Leibniz would make to objections against his system, based upon facts, hypotheses, or common beliefs in mathematical and physical, biological and mental science?'

A. LEIBNIZ'S MATHEMATICS IN RELATION TO HIS PHILOSOPHY.

It was partly through Mathematics that Leibniz arrived at the notion of Substance which is the core of his philosophy. Dissatisfaction with the Mathematics of Descartes and with its consequences in Physics led him to reject the Cartesian theory of matter and motion

[1] The consideration of Leibniz's Theology or Philosophy of Religion is beyond the scope of the present volume.

and to substitute for it a more adequate theory of Force and a higher Mathematics. Both the Mathematics and the Physics of the time appeared to Leibniz to be too abstract, and the great object of his speculations was to bring them more into touch with concrete reality.

The Transition from Synthetic to Analytic Geometry.

Early in the seventeenth century a considerable advance was made in the science of Mathematics, mainly through the work of Kepler, Cavalieri, and Descartes. The Geometry of the Greeks was synthetic or synoptic. "It dealt with ideal figures as discrete wholes, not taking into consideration the possibility of their being analyzed into elements, of which they are combinations or functions." Thus the relations of the figures to one another are considered as external. Each is what it is: no one is regarded as having in it the possibility of passing into another. A rectilineal figure is one thing; a curvilinear figure is another. The barriers between them are regarded as insurmountable, at least by the methods of exact or demonstrative science. Thus a curve is still a curve, however small may be its curvature. A polygon is still a polygon, however numerous may be its sides. And the kinds of curves are each independent of the others. An ellipse is still an ellipse, however distant one focus may be from the other.

Kepler's introduction of the notion and the name of infinity into Geometry was the beginning of a great change in mathematical methods. The geometrical figures of the Greeks were all finite, and therefore capable of representation to the eye, or, in other words, capable of being pictured. Every curve must have a definite curvature. Every polygon must have a definite number of sides. Kepler, in order to attain to greater exactness in the statement of mathematical relations, suggested that finite (or definite) figures might be regarded as consisting of an infinite (or indefinite) number of elements. Thus he considered a circle to be composed of an infinite number of triangles, having their common vertex at the centre and forming the circumference by their bases[1]. Such an analytic conception of the figure is, of course, not capable of being pictured. But it at once suggests the possibility of representing the figure, not by a rough drawing or image, but by an infinite numerical series the terms of which are so related to one another that their sum is finite. Accordingly, in thus considering the finite as made up of an infinite number of elements, we have promise of a connexion between Geometry and Algebra, of such a kind that geometrical relations may be symbolized algebraically and the knowledge of them may be extended and generalized by calculation. Such a connexion would mean the reduction of the discontinuous concepts of Synthetic Geometry to the comparative continuity of Algebraic Concepts or Numbers. It would thus lessen the abstractness of Geometry, and make it more adequate to the continuity of nature, or, looking at the same thing from the opposite point of view, it would enable the continuous system of space-relations to be more completely brought within the range of mathematical demonstration. For instance, problems which the Greeks had to solve by the indirect and unsuggestive method of *reductio ad absurdum* would now be capable of a direct demonstrative solution, and there would arise many new problems which the old methods could not touch.

[1] In a similar way Cavalieri afterwards suggested that the area of a triangle might be conceived as made up of an infinite number of straight lines, each parallel with the base. The lengths of these lines he regarded as forming an infinite series in arithmetical progression, of which the first term is zero. The sum of this series is equal to half the product of the last term (i.e. the length of the base of the triangle) and the number of terms (i.e. the altitude of the triangle). As against this it was pointed out that, since a line has no breadth, no number of straight lines can ever make up a

The Basis of Analytical Geometry.

This connexion between Algebra and Geometry was definitely established by Descartes in the Analytical Geometry, of which he was the inventor. The basis of the Analytical Geometry is the finding of a definite proportion between the space-relations or ratios investigated by Geometry and certain numerical ratios. But the space-relations of Geometry are not merely quantitative as are the relations of number. To take the simplest of instances, the square upon a line may be represented by the square of a number. But the square of a number n is simply n times n, that is to say, it is the sum of n n's added together. The square of n is a quantity of n's or a simple series of homogeneous units, which may be interchanged within the series without in any way affecting the result. On the other hand, the relation of a geometrical square to the line upon which it is constructed (i.e. to any one of its sides) is not purely quantitative. The square is not a sum of lengths. It is a figure with special characteristics. The line cannot intelligibly be regarded as its unit. It is its *side*, and as the side of a square it has properties other than those which it would have as a mere line. It is, in fact, part of a unity which is more than merely quantitative. And yet a quantitative ratio can express the relation between the square and its side, in such a way that the properties of the square may be algebraically calculated without direct reference to the geometrical figure. Thus

plane area. Pascal, however, showed that Cavalieri's method really implied that the infinite series of straight lines is an 'indefinite' number of 'small' rectangles, which are so small that the minute triangles between them and the sides of the given triangle may be neglected in the computation. This 'indefinite' of Pascal is the 'infinite' of later mathematicians, and his 'small' is manifestly their 'infinitely little.' Thus we have here the transition from the ancient to the modern methods. Pascal vindicated Cavalieri's method on the ground that it differed only in manner of expression from the method of exhaustions, used in the Greek mathematics.

relations of quantity (that is to say, of mere aggregation) may become signs or symbols of relations which are more than quantitative, relations in which the part is not indifferent to the whole but characteristic of it. All the processes of Algebra, however complex and elaborate, are forms of the addition and the subtraction (or separation) of abstract units. Thus the abstract number 1 remains the same, into whatever algebraic combination it may enter as a part. But the conception of a straight line, for instance, varies (the line has various functions) according to the nature of the whole into which it enters as a part, and according to the special way in which it is related to the whole. Thus in relation to different kinds of figures (rectilineal, curved, &c.), or on account of the various forms of its relation to one and the same figure, a straight line is a side, a tangent, a radius, a directrix, an axis, a sine, &c. There is a closer, more real unity between the part and the whole than in the relation of mere quantity, where the part is indifferent to the special character of the whole.

Relations of purely quantitative Unity and geometrical Unity. Infinite Series and the infinitely little.

But there is no absolute gulf fixed between quantitative unity and geometrical unity. The difference is, that geometrical unity, while abstract in comparison with organic unity or with the real concrete unity of all existence, is less abstract than merely quantitative unity[1]. And the bridge between the unity which is expressed in the Algebra of finite quantities and that which is expressed in the Geometry of finite space-relations is to be found in the analysis of a finite quantity into an infinite series. No finite quantity can be resolved into an infinite series

---

[1] Strictly speaking, a merely quantitative unity is a contradiction in terms, for mere quantity is pure difference, the absence of unity. But what I mean here is unity of the lowest degree, unity on the point of vanishing, or the most indeterminate unity.

formed by an addition of independent integers, such as $1 + 1 + 1$, &c., or even $1 + 2 + 3$, &c., that is to say, by an addition not conditioned by any special law.   But there are certain numerical series in which the terms are not mutually indifferent (nor immediately reducible to a set of mutually indifferent terms), but are arranged, or rather proceed from one another, according to a definite law, which law is of such a kind that, although it never brings the series actually to an end, it results in the sum of the series approaching more and more nearly to some finite quantity.   Accordingly it is held that, if the series be regarded as consisting of an infinite number of terms, the difference between the sum of its terms and the finite quantity will be infinitely little, and therefore practically negligible.

This 'practically negligible' is the keystone of the bridge between algebraic quantity and geometrical, physical, or any other kind of relation. Strictly speaking, if the series be regarded as a pure sum, and therefore ultimately analyzable into an addition of homogeneous units ($1 + 1 + 1$, &c., or $n + n + n$, &c.), the finitude of its sum is incompatible with its having an infinite number of terms.   It is only inasmuch as the series is regarded, not as a merely quantitative unity, but as a unity determined by a characteristic law or principle, that we are entitled to disregard the 'infinitely little' difference between the sum of its terms and the finite quantity. There can be no absolute 'infinitely little' in mere quantity.   The 'infinitely little' here considered is 'infinitely little' as determined by the law or character of the particular series.   That is to say, we are certain that the law of the series holds unchangeably, however far the process of analysis may be carried ; and we have thus inferential certainty regarding the result of the analysis (the equation of the sum of the terms to the whole finite quantity), even although we may be unable actually to count each one of the terms.   It is the law or principle of the series which enables us to say that the 'infinitely little' difference may be neglected because the character of the series is not affected by it.

But in neglecting this 'infinitely little' difference, because of the special character or law of the series, we have virtually passed from the unity of mere quantity to a unity of character, a unity in which the parts are not entirely indifferent to the whole and to one another, but are connected in accordance with some special principle. We have thus given an indefinite increase of elasticity to the formulae of Algebra and have prepared the way for an algebraic representation and calculus not merely of the elementary space-unities (figures) of the Greek Geometry, but also of more comprehensive geometrical unities of which these are elements, and further of physical unities and indeed of any unity the elements of which are in themselves capable of a sufficiently accurate quantitative expression. For instance, the phenomena with which Physics deals are differences of a unity, elements in a whole. But the unity, the whole, is not one of quantity merely. And yet its elements are capable of quantitative expression with a degree of accuracy such that its difference from *absolute* accuracy may be neglected so far as physical science is concerned. Consequently it becomes possible to state and to work out problems of physical science in terms of Algebra.

The Infinitesimal Calculus and the Principle of Becoming or System.

The practical development of this possibility is the function of the Infinitesimal Calculus of Leibniz and Newton[1]. As we have already seen, the Analytical

---

[1] A succinct account of the famous controversy regarding the discovery of this method, and of the different forms in which Leibniz and Newton expressed it, will be found in Dr. Williamson's article 'Infinitesimal Calculus' in the 9th ed. of the *Encyclopaedia Britannica*. Cf. Merz, *History of European Thought in the Nineteenth Century*, i. 100–103.

Geometry reduces the discontinuity of Synthetic Geometry to the relative continuity of number, or quantity of homogeneous units. But number as a sum of finite units (even though it may take the form of an infinite series) is still to some extent discontinuous. It may, however, be made continuous by regarding its elements not as finite units, but as 'infinitesimals' or infinitely little quantities. In other words, any numerical unit we may choose to employ may be subdivided infinitely, and thus every finite number may be regarded as the sum of an infinite series of infinitely small terms. This is the basis of the Infinitesimal Calculus as originally conceived by Leibniz. It may be otherwise expressed by saying that the series of finite numbers or quantities is ultimately to be expressed, not as a series of terms which grow by finite increments (like $1 + (1 + 1) + (1 + 1 + 1)$ &c.), but as a series whose terms flow into one another, their differences being infinitely small. That is to say, any variable magnitude must be regarded as increasing or diminishing by infinitely small increments or decrements. The work of the Calculus is to determine the relations between unknown quantities or magnitudes, not by considering them merely as fixed wholes and directly finding equations between them, but indirectly, by treating the quantities as variables or as growing, and in the first place finding equations between their elements or differences[1].

---

[1] From one point of view it may be regarded as the solving of the problem of Achilles and the tortoise. Cf. *Lettre à M. Foucher* (1693) (E. 118 a; G. i. 416): 'As to *indivisibles*, in the sense of the mere extremities of a time or of a line, we cannot conceive new extremities, nor actual nor potential parts in them. Thus points are neither large nor small, and no leap is needed to pass them. Yet the continuous, although it everywhere has such indivisibles, is not composed of them, as the objections of sceptics seem to suppose. There is, in my opinion, nothing insurmountable in these objections, as will be found if they are put into strict form. Father Gregory of St. Vincent has excellently shown, by the Calculus of infinite divisibility, the place where Achilles should overtake the tortoise which starts before him, according to the proportion of their velocities. Thus Geometry dissipates these apparent difficulties.'

Accordingly, for instance, Newton regarded all geometrical magnitudes as capable of generation by continuous motion. Lines may be regarded as generated by the motion of points, surfaces by that of lines, and solids by that of surfaces. That is to say, these figures are distinct from one another, not absolutely, but merely in the degree in which they possess certain characteristics. The difference between the point and the line is an infinitely small degree of length, the difference between the line and the surface is an infinitely small degree of breadth, the difference between the surface and the solid is an infinitely small degree of depth. 'Motion,' in Newton's way of putting it, is in this connexion merely a metaphor for continuity. Again, in physical science we have to deal with phenomena which not merely are variable but are continually varying, and the Infinitesimal Calculus is of the utmost value in enabling us to state the laws of these variations, that is to say, to establish proportions between different sets of constantly changing phenomena.

The value of the Infinitesimal Calculus in the interpretation of nature rests ultimately on this, that the conception of 'infinitesimals' which it employs is a virtual recognition of System in knowledge or of the principle of Becoming as distinct from that of abstract Being. When we say that a thing (a geometrical figure, for instance) has a certain quality or characteristic in an infinitely small amount, we mean that it both has and has not that quality or characteristic, or (to use another metaphor made familiar by Psycho-physics) that it is on the 'threshold' of having it. The identity of the thing is not merely superficial, of such a kind that when a quality seems to pass away from it the thing ceases to exist and another thing appears ; the identity of the thing is maintained through an indefinite amount of difference. Thus, as we have seen, the point, the line, the surface, and the solid are all recognized as differences or relations within one system. So in general, when we have shown that the difference between

one thing and another is infinitely little, we have not
converted each into the other, but have explained them
both by referring them to a common ground. We can express each in terms of the other, provided we state explicitly their relations to one another within some system.
A parabola is not an ellipse ; but a parabola is an ellipse
with one of its foci at an infinite distance from the other.

Continuity and the Logical Calculus.

Now it cannot be said that all this was fully manifest
to Leibniz himself ; but the truth of it underlies his
thinking. The Infinitesimal Calculus in his mathematics
is an expression of the same tendency of thought which
makes the principle of sufficient reason so important an
influence in his philosophy—the tendency to a less
abstract, less dogmatic, more intensive way of looking at
things, in contrast with the *a priori* deductive methods
of the Cartesians. The influence of the mathematics of
Leibniz upon his philosophy appears chiefly in connexion
with his law of continuity and his prolonged efforts to
establish a Logical Calculus. As to the law of continuity
it is unnecessary to say more. It is the law of the endless relativity of things, the principle of system, of infinite multiplicity in unity, and we have seen that the
Infinitesimal Calculus is an application of it[1]. On the

---

[1] Cf. *Lettre à M. Bayle* (1687) (G. iii. 51 ; E. 104 a) : ' I have seen
the reply of Father Malebranche to the remark I made on some laws
of nature which he laid down in the *Recherche de la Vérité*. He
appears somewhat disposed to give them up himself, and his in-
genuousness is most laudable ; but he gives reasons for it and makes
restrictions which would bring us back into the obscurity from
which I think I have delivered this subject, and which conflict
with a certain *principle of general order* that I have observed. I hope,
therefore, that he will kindly allow me to take this opportunity of
explaining this principle, which is of great use in reasoning, and
which does not yet appear to be sufficiently employed nor known
in all its scope. It has its origin in the conception of the *Infinite* ;
it is absolutely necessary in Geometry, and it also holds good in
Physics, inasmuch as the Supreme Wisdom, which is the source
of all things, acts as a perfect geometrician, and according to a
harmony which cannot be bettered. . . . The principle may be stated
thus : *When the difference between two cases can be diminished below any*

other hand, the endeavour to find a Logical Calculus (implying a universal philosophical language or system of signs) is an attempt to apply in theological and philosophical investigations an analytic method analogous to that which had proved so successful in Geometry and Physics [1]. It seemed to Leibniz that if all the complex

given magnitude in datis *or in the antecedents* [ce qui est posé] *it will necessarily also be diminished below every given magnitude* in quaesitis *or in the consequents* [ce qui en résulte]. Or, to put it more simply : *when the cases (or what is given) continually approach and are finally lost in one another, the consequences or results (or what is required) must do the same.* This again depends upon a more general principle, to wit : *datis ordinatis etiam quaesita sunt ordinata.* [If there is order in the grounds there will also be order in the consequents.] But, for the understanding of this, instances are necessary. It is known that the case or supposition of an ellipse may be made to approximate, as much as we like, to the case of a parabola, so that the difference between the ellipse and the parabola may become less than any given difference, provided that one of the foci of the ellipse be made sufficiently distant from the other, for then the *radii vectores* proceeding from this distant focus will differ from parallel *radii vectores* as little as we like. Consequently all the geometrical theorems which may be proved of the ellipse in general can be applied to the parabola by considering it as an ellipse one of whose foci is at an infinite distance, or (to avoid this expression) as a figure which differs from some ellipse by less than any given difference. The same principle holds in Physics. For instance, rest may be regarded as an infinitely small velocity or as an infinite slowness. Accordingly, whatever is true of slowness or velocity in general ought also to be true of rest, thus understood ; so that the law of rest should be regarded as a particular case of the law of motion. Otherwise, if this does not hold, it will be a sure sign that these laws are ill-constructed. In the same way equality may be regarded as an infinitely small inequality, and inequality may be made to approximate to equality as much as we like.' See also *New Essays*, Introduction, p. 376, and *Nouveaux Essais*, bk. iv. ch. 16, § 12 (E. 392 a ; G. v. 455) : ' But the beauty of nature ... requires the appearance of discontinuity [sauts] and, so to speak, musical cadences among phenomena.' In the letter to Bayle above quoted, Leibniz also remarks (E. 106 a ; G. iii. 54) : ' It is true that in compound things a small change may sometimes produce a great effect. For instance, a spark falling upon a large mass of gunpowder might overthrow a whole town ; but that is not contrary to our principle, and might indeed be explained on general principles. But in the case of elements or simple things nothing like this could happen ; otherwise nature would not be the result of infinite wisdom.'

[1] As to the analogy between Symbolic Thought and Algebra, &c., cf. Locke, *Essay*, bk. ii. ch. 29, § 9 (Fraser's ed. vol. i. p. 490). See also Fraser, vol. ii. pp. 12 and 124, where further references will be found.

and apparently disconnected ideas which make up our knowledge could be analyzed into their simple elements, and if these elements could each be represented by a definite sign, we should have a kind of 'alphabet of human thoughts.' By the combination of these signs (letters of the alphabet of thought) a system of true knowledge would be built up, in which reality would be more and more adequately represented or symbolized. For, according to Leibniz, the progress of knowledge consists in passing from obscure to clear ideas, from clear to distinct, from distinct to adequate. Ideas are obscure when analysis has not proceeded so far as to enable us definitely to distinguish them from others. They are clear when we can so distinguish them, but are not yet able to enumerate their particular elements or qualities. They are distinct when we can enumerate their qualities, and they are adequate only when the analysis is complete, that is to say, when all the elements of the clear and distinct idea are themselves clear and distinct. In many cases the analysis may result in an infinite series of elements ; but the principles of the Infinitesimal Calculus in mathematics have shown that this does not necessarily render calculation impossible or inaccurate [1]. Thus it seemed to Leibniz that a synthetic calculus, based upon a thorough analysis, would be the most effective instrument of knowledge that could be devised. 'I feel,' he says, 'that controversies can never be finished, nor silence imposed upon the *Sects*, unless we give up complicated reasonings in favour of simple *calculations*, words of vague and uncertain meaning in favour of fixed symbols [*characteres*][2].' Thus it will appear that 'every paralogism is nothing but *an error of calculation.*' 'When controversies arise, there will be no more necessity for disputation between two philosophers than between two accountants. Nothing will be needed but that they should take pen in hand, sit

[1] Cf. this Introduction, Part ii. p. 61 note.
[2] *De Scientia Universali seu Calculo Philosophico* (E. 83 b ; G. vii. 200).

down with their counting-tables, and (having summoned a friend, if they like) say to one another: *Let us calculate.*' This sounds like the ungrudging optimism of youth; but Leibniz was optimist enough to cherish the hope of it to his life's end.

This project of the Logical Calculus or philosophical language connects the mathematics of Leibniz with his theory of knowledge, while the Calculus of Infinitesimals finds immediate application in his revision of Descartes's theories regarding matter and motion. Descartes treated motion and rest synthetically as constant quantitative wholes. Leibniz regards them analytically as consisting of an infinite series of degrees of one constant force. Accordingly Leibniz admits that the Cartesian laws of motion have a certain validity in relation to 'abstract' motion, but denies that they are adequate to the 'concrete' physical phenomena.

B. MATTER.

Descartes's Theory of Matter and Motion.

As we have already seen, Leibniz's view of matter can be understood only as it appears in contrast with that of Descartes. In accordance with his interpretation of the principle of contradiction, viz. that the essence of a thing consists in that only which is common to all its manifestations, or (otherwise expressed) in that only which remains after all varieties or specific determinations have been excluded, Descartes maintained that matter is essentially extension. Bodily substance and magnitude or spatial extent are identical. And all the changes in matter or extension are ultimately reducible to motion. Motion is regarded by Descartes as being 'the transference of a portion of matter or a body from the neighbourhood of those bodies which are in direct contact with it, and which we consider as at rest, to the neighbourhood of other bodies or portions of matter[1].' Matter is infinitely

---

[1] *Principia*, Part ii. 25. Descartes adds: 'By a body, or rather

divisible. Its division is due to motion. Its forms arise solely from the combinations and separations of its parts, which also are due to motion. 'All the variety of matter, or the diversity of its forms, depends on motion [1].' 'I frankly avow that I acknowledge in corporeal things no other matter than that which can be divided, shaped [*figurées*], and moved in all kinds of ways, that is to say, that which mathematicians call quantity, and which they take as the object of their demonstrations; and in this matter I consider only its divisions, shapes [*figures*], and motions; and, in short, regarding this I will accept nothing as true which is not deduced from it with as much certainty as belongs to a mathematical demonstration. And inasmuch as by this means all the phenomena of nature may be explained . . . it seems to me that in Physics no other principles ought to be accepted, or even desired, than those which are here expounded [2].'

Conservation of Motion (or Momentum), its Direction being left out of account.

Again, according to Descartes, the quantity of motion in the world (or in any material system complete in itself and apart from all external influences) is constant. The motion (or *momentum*), whose quantity is thus constant, is in each particular case directly proportional to the mass and the velocity of the moving body, and it may

a portion of matter, I mean the whole of what is transferred together, although this may be composed of several parts which themselves have other motions. And I say that motion is the transference and not the force or activity which transfers, in order to show that motion is always in the moving object and not in that which moves it; for it seems to me that these two things are not usually distinguished with sufficient care. Further, I mean that motion is a property of the moving thing and not a substance; just as form is a property of the thing which has a form, and rest is a property of that which is at rest.'

[1] *Principia*, Part ii. 23 (Veitch's tr.).

[2] Ibid. Part ii. 64 (tr. from Abbé Picot's French). Descartes's object is to show that all the motion in the world is *one*, and thus to get rid of the later Scholastic theories which referred each particular motion to some unexplained principle in the moving body.

be expressed by the formula *mv*. Now no new motion
can come to any body from itself; no material body is
self-moved, because its essence is pure extension, and the
idea of extension does not necessarily involve the transference of parts. To any quantity of matter, whether
large or small, motion comes entirely from without. Thus
at the creation of the world the whole material universe
received a certain fixed quantity of motion, which is conserved by the 'ordinary co-operation' [*concours ordinaire*]
of God. Motion is thus a positive thing and not merely
relative to rest. Motion is not opposed to motion, but
to rest. Motions do not cancel one another; they are
quantities which can merely be combined and separated.
And, on the other hand, each individual portion of matter
must remain in the state in which it is, unless it receives
motion from outside itself. The motion of any one body
is increased only by a corresponding decrease in the motion
of some other; and the motion of any body is decreased
only by a part of it passing into some other. Motion is
diffused, but never destroyed [1].

[1] Cf. *Principia*, ii. 36 (Veitch's tr.): 'With respect to the general
cause of motion, it seems manifest to me that it is none other than
God Himself, who in the beginning created matter along with
motion and rest, and now by His ordinary 'concourse' alone preserves in the whole the same amount of motion and rest that He
then placed in it. For, although motion is nothing in the matter
moved but its mode, it has yet a certain and determinate quantity,
which we easily understand may remain always the same in the
whole universe, although it changes in each of the parts of it. So
that, in truth, we may hold when a part of matter is moved with
double the quickness of another, and that other is twice the size of
the former, that there is just precisely as much motion, but no
more, in the less body as in the greater; and that, in proportion as
the motion of any one part is reduced, so is that of some other and
equal portion accelerated. We also know that there is perfection
in God, not only because He is in Himself immutable, but because
He operates in the most constant and immutable manner possible;
so that, with the exception of those mutations which manifest
experience or Divine revelation renders certain, and which we perceive or believe are brought about without any change in the
Creator, we ought to suppose no other in His works, lest there
should thence arise ground for concluding inconstancy in God
Himself. Whence it follows, as most consonant to reason, that
merely because God diversely moved the parts of matter when He

Now it follows from this, that, while the quantity of motion in the world, or in any isolated system of bodies, is constant, its direction is variable. For, as all space is body and is therefore a *plenum*, moving bodies must continually impinge upon others ; and if a moving body be supposed to impinge upon a body at rest, of such mass that the moving body is unable to overcome the resistance of the other and to make it move, then the direction of the moving body is changed ; it rebounds in the direction from which it came or is deflected in some other way. But, as the moving body has been unable to impart any of its motion to the body at rest, the quantity of its motion remains unchanged, while its direction changes—it being, of course, understood that the action of all other bodies, except the two in question, is left out of account [1].

Leibniz's Theory of Motion.   Conservation of Force.

Now, according to Leibniz, motion is simply change of position. It is not a positive quality belonging, for the time being, to the moving body ; but motion and rest are entirely relative to one another. If the relative position of any two bodies changes, we may regard either as moving and the other as at rest [2]. And, in general, rest is merely an infinitely small degree of motion ; nothing

first created them, and now preserves all that matter, manifestly in the same way and on the same principle on which He first created it, He also always preserves the same quantity of motion in the matter itself.'

[1] Cf. *Principia*, ii. 41 : ' Each thing, whatever it is, always continues to be as it is in itself simply, and not as it is in relation to other things, until it is compelled to change its state by contact with some other thing. From this it necessarily follows that a moving body, which meets on its course another body so firm and impenetrable that it cannot move it in any way, entirely loses the determination it had of moving in this particular direction, and the cause of this is evident, namely, the resistance of the body which prevents it from going further ; but it does not necessarily on this account lose any of its motion, since it is not deprived of its motion by the resisting body or by any other cause, and since motion is not contrary to motion.'

[2] Cf. *Animadversiones ad Cartesii Principia* (1692 ?), Part ii. § 25 (G. iv. 369 ; Duncan's tr. p. 60).

in the world is absolutely at rest. Accordingly no body
begins to move from a state of absolute rest, but from
a state which is to be conceived as already one of motion,
however small in amount. Actual motion is not something added to a body which, to begin with, is bare mass;
it is always gradual growth or increment of a motion
which is already there. Actual motion always pre-supposes potential motion or a force which, though it may
not be observed, tends to appear as actual motion.
Descartes, then, was right in interpreting actual motion
as change of position, but wrong in overlooking potential
motion and thus in regarding the total quantity of actual
apparent motion in the universe, or in any independent
system, as constant. He was right also in holding that
each body tends to continue in the state in which it is;
but he was wrong in thinking that a body can ever be in
a state of absolute rest, and thus in supposing that one
motion cannot oppose another, but can only be opposed
by rest. As a matter of fact everything tends to move,
and would move, were it not for counteracting tendencies
to motion in other things [1]. That which is conserved, then,
is not actual motion, as an extrinsic property of material
substance, but this intrinsic tendency or potentiality of
motion, which Leibniz calls force. As mere change of
position does not enable us to attribute motion to *one* of
the two bodies whose position changes, and *not* to the
other, the body which we call the moving body (as distinct from the body at rest) is so, not in virtue of its
motion (in the sense of change of position), but because it

---

[1] Cf. *Lettre à M. Pelisson* (1691) (Foucher de Careil, i. 208; Dutens,
i. 733): 'It must be observed that every body makes an effort to
act on outside things, and would perceptibly act if the contrary
efforts of surrounding bodies did not prevent it. This has not been
sufficiently noticed by our moderns. They imagine that a body
might be perfectly at rest, without any effort. But this is due to
their failure to understand what bodily substance really is; for *in
my opinion substance cannot* (at any rate naturally) *be without action.*
This also disproves the inaction which Socinians attribute to disembodied souls.'

contains within itself the *cause* of the change, the force or activity which produces the motion. 'The notion of force,' says Leibniz, 'is as clear as that of activity and of passivity, for it is that from which activity follows, when nothing prevents it. It is effort, *conatus*; and while motion is a successive thing, which consequently never exists, any more than time, because all its parts never exist together—while, I say, that is so, force or effort, on the other hand, exists quite completely at every instant and must be something genuine and real. And, as nature has to do rather with the real than with that which does not completely exist except in our mind, it appears (in consequence of what I have shown) that it is the same quantity of force, and not (as Descartes believed) the same quantity of motion, that is preserved in nature[1].'

This force, then, which is constant, is not only an actual but a potential reality. It is not mere capacity for motion, mere passive movableness, nor is it actual manifest motion or activity in general. It is something between the two, an undeveloped or restrained tendency to act, which in appropriate circumstances is the producer of action[2]. This force is to be measured by the quantity of effect it produces. Descartes rightly insisted on the quantity of effect as the thing to be measured; but he

---

[1] *Lettre à M. Pelisson* (no date, probably 1691) (Dutens, i. 719; Foucher de Careil, i. 157). 'The relative velocity of two bodies' [i. e. their apparent motion] 'may remain the same, although the real velocities and absolute forces of the bodies change in an infinity of ways, so that conservation of relative velocity has nothing to do with what is absolute in the bodies.' *Essai de dynamique* (G. Math. vi. 216). Cf. Appendix I, p. 351.

[2] Cf. *De Primae Philosophiae Emendatione*, &c. (1694) (E. 122 b; G. iv 469) : 'Active force differs from the bare potency commonly recognized in the Schools. For the active potency of the Scholastics, or faculty, is nothing but a mere possibility of acting, which nevertheless requires an outer excitation or stimulus, that it may be turned into activity. But active force contains a certain activity [*actus*] and is a mean between the faculty of acting and action itself. It includes effort and thus passes into operation by itself, requiring no aids, but only the removal of hindrance. This may be illustrated by the example of a heavy hanging body stretching the rope which holds it up, or by that of a drawn bow.'

conceived the effect in too narrow a way, regarding it
merely as actual motion (i. e. the *momentum* acquired by a
body) rather than the work done by the force, the kinetic
energy it produces (i.e. the *vis viva* which the body
acquires, and which Leibniz calls *action motrice*). The
formula for this *action motrice* is not *mv* but *mv²*. In the
uniform motions of one and the same body, (1) the *action* [1]
of traversing two leagues in two hours is double the *action*
of traversing one league in one hour (for the first *action*
contains the second exactly twice) ; (2) the *action* of traversing one league in one hour is double the *action* of
traversing one league in two hours (or, *actions* which
produce one and the same effect are proportional to their
velocities) : therefore (3) the *action* of traversing two
leagues in two hours is four times (quadruple) the *action*
of traversing one league in two hours. This demonstration
shows that a moving body which receives a double or
triple velocity, in order that it may produce a double or
triple effect in one and the same time, receives a quadruple
or nonuple *action*. Thus *actions* are proportional to the
squares of the velocities. But most fortunately this
happens to agree with my calculation of force, drawn
both from experiments and from the pre-supposition that
there is no mechanical perpetual motion. For, according
to my calculation, forces are proportional to the heights
by descending from which heavy bodies might have
obtained their velocities, that is to say, as the squares of
the velocities. And, as there is always conserved the total
force for re-ascending to the same height or for producing
some other effect, it follows that there is conserved also
the same quantity of motive " force " [*action motrice*] in the
world ; that is to say, to put it definitely, that in any one
hour there is as much *action motrice* in the universe as
there is in any other hour. But at every moment [2] the

---

[1] I. e. the work done or *vis viva*. For a full explanation of the
whole matter, see Stallo, *Concepts of Modern Physics*, ch. vi, especially
pp. 71 sqq.

[2] 'A momentary state of a body in motion cannot contain motion,

same quantity of force is conserved. And in fact *action* is nothing but the exercise of force, and amounts to the product of the force into the time[1]. Accordingly this motive force or *vis viva*, the amount of which is constant, includes direction, as well as quantity, of motion. For the measure of it is height, or position relatively to the surface of the earth. Descartes's 'quantity of motion' (mv) is the effect of a given force regarded merely as acting during a given time. Leibniz's *vis viva* (mv^2) is the effect of a given force regarded also as acting through a given distance. And Descartes did not take account of the direction of motion, because he did not take into consideration the distance through which the force acts.

Leibniz's Theory of Matter.

(1) *Materia prima.*

This doctrine of the conservation of force, as Leibniz conceives it, involves the rejection of the theory that material substance is nothing but extension[2]. Extension

for motion requires time, but it none the less involves force.' *Lettre à Des Maizeaux* (1711) (E. 676 a; G. vii. 534).

[1] *Lettre à Bayle* (undated) (E. 192 a; G. iii. 60), cf. G. Math. vi. 117. Of course, from one point of view, Leibniz's statement is not quite accurate, since there are many forms of energy of which it takes no account. It is, however, on right lines. And indeed (as Du Bois-Reymond and Stallo have pointed out) Leibniz in one passage anticipates the modern theory of the transformation of energy (the apparent loss of molar motion being represented by increase of molecular motion), although the idea was not worked out until a much more recent time. 'I had maintained,' says Leibniz, ' that *active forces* are conserved in the world. It is objected that two soft, or non-elastic bodies, when they collide, lose some of their *force*. I answer, No. It is true that the "wholes" lose force in respect of their total motion ; but the parts received it, being agitated within the whole by the force of the collision. Thus it is only apparently that the loss occurs. The forces are not destroyed, but dissipated among the particles. That is not losing them but doing as is done by those who turn large money into small change.' *Cinquième Lettre à Clarke,* 99 (E. 775 a; G. vii. 414).

[2] *Projet d'une Lettre à Arnauld* (1686) (G. ii. 72) : 'Extension is an attribute which cannot constitute a concrete [*accompli*] being. We cannot draw from it any activity or change. It expresses only a present state, and not at all the future and the past, which the notion of a substance ought to express. When two triangles are

is mere capacity for receiving motion, bare movableness, while motion is complete activity and is entirely extrinsic to that which is moved. Force, on the other hand, is, as we have seen, something between the two, viz. a potentiality of motion or action that is always passing into actual action when it is not prevented by a similar tendency in another body. This force, then, shows itself not merely in actual, positive motion, but in hindrance or resistance. And if this force were not of the essence of material bodies there would be no resistance among bodies and the absurdity of perpetual motion would be true. For if material bodies consist solely of extension, and if one such body moving should come into contact with another at rest (i. e. destitute of motion), then the former must carry the latter along with it. For, *ex hypothesi*, there is nothing but space to resist the progress of the moving body, and, if motion is possible at all, it must be motion *through* space, i. e. motion which mere space cannot resist[1].

Accordingly, in addition to extension (however it may be interpreted), every material body must have resistance or impenetrability. This mere passive resistance Leibniz on various occasions calls ἀντιτυπία. The ἀντιτυπία of a body is simply its need of space. The body is not mere

found joined together, we cannot infer from them how the joining has taken place. For it may have happened in various ways; but nothing which can have several causes is ever a concrete [*accompli*] being.'

[1] *Epistola ad Des Bosses* (1706) (G. ii. 295): 'If, with the Cartesians, we were to admit a *plenum* and the uniformity of matter, adding only motion, it would follow that there would never be anything in the world but a substitution of equivalents, as if the whole universe were to reduce itself to the motion of a perfectly uniform wheel about its axis or to the revolutions of concentric circles of perfectly homogeneous matter. In that case, it would not be possible, even for an angel, to distinguish the state of the world at one moment from its state at another moment. For there could not be any variety in the phenomena. That is why, in addition to figure, size, and movement, there must be admitted forms from which there arises in matter a variety of appearances; and I do not see whence we can draw these forms, if they are to be intelligible, except from Entelechies.' Cf. *De Ipsa Natura* (1693), § 13 (E. 158 b; G. iv. 512).

place: but it cannot be a body unless it has a place of its own.   And its ἀντιτυπία consists in its maintaining its place, staying where it is.   Resistance is thus a passive force.   'Matter taken by itself or bare matter consists of ἀντιτυπία and extension.   By ἀντιτυπία I mean that attribute in virtue of which matter is in space.   Extension is continuation through space, or continuous diffusion throughout a place[1].   'Matter is that which consists in ἀντιτυπία or which resists penetration; and thus bare matter is merely passive[2].'   In so far, then, as a material body is extended and occupies a place which cannot be occupied by any other body at the same time (for this is the meaning of ἀντιτυπία or impenetrability), it consists of bare matter.   Bare or abstract matter, as thus defined (ἀντιτυπία + extension), Leibniz usually calls *materia prima*.

(2) *Materia secunda.*

But we must beware of supposing that this *materia prima* is by itself anything actual.   As the mathematical point is nothing actual, but is the indivisible limit of extension, so *materia prima* is the indivisible limit of matter.   No portion of matter, no material body, consists of *materia prima* alone, just as no portion of extension is a mere mathematical point.   For *materia prima* is simply body considered as if it were purely passive: it is the abstract passivity of body.   But, as we have seen, there is, according to Leibniz, no such thing as absolute passivity.   Passive resistance, impenetrability, inertia, always involve a real force, a tendency to action, though that tendency may actually be prevented by counteracting forces from realizing itself at this or that particular moment.   Passivity is the limit of activity, as rest is the limit of motion.   Every material body, then, is ultimately something more than ἀντιτυπία + extension.   It is essentially force or energy, activity of some kind.   And

[1] *De Anima Brutorum* (1710), § 1 (E. 462 a ; G. vii. 328).
[2] *Epistola ad Bierlingium* (1710) (E. 678 a ; G. vii. 501).

inasmuch as this force is a potential activity, a force which tends to realize itself, it is automatic or spontaneous, it contains within itself the principle of its future conditions, it is an Entelechy. Thus every actual material body is *materia secunda*, from which *materia prima* is merely a mental abstraction [1]. Every complete substance is *materia prima* + Entelechy, i.e. passivity + activity.

Now while *materia prima*, being abstract passivity, is not to be regarded as real substance, *materia secunda*, inasmuch as it is matter and is therefore extended and infinitely divisible, is, on the other hand, not to be confounded with individual substance. *Materia secunda* must contain an entelechy, but is not identical with it. *Materia secunda* is an aggregate of things: it is to be conceived as quantitative, consisting of *partes extra partes*, and is thus quite distinct from substance, which must be conceived as striving force, i.e. under the relation of means to end [2].

[1] Cf. *Epistola ad R. C. Wagnerum* (1710) (E. 466 a ; G. vii. 529) : 'The active principle is not attributed by me to bare matter or *materia prima*, which is merely passive and consists solely in ἀντιτυπία and extension ; but to body or clothed matter or *materia secunda*, which contains in addition a primary entelechy or active principle. . . . The resistance of bare matter is not activity, but mere passivity, inasmuch as it has ἀντιτυπία or impenetrability, by which indeed it resists that which would penetrate it, but does not re-act unless it has in addition an elastic force. This elastic force must be derived from motion, and thus also from an active force superadded to matter.' Also *De Ipsa Natura* (1698), § 12 (E. 158 b ; G. iv. 512) : 'Matter is understood as either *materia secunda* or *materia prima* ; *materia secunda* is indeed a complete substance, but not a merely passive one ; *materia prima* is merely passive, but is not a complete substance ; and there must further be added to it a soul, or form analogous to a soul, ἐντελέχεια ἡ πρώτη, that is a certain effort or primary force of acting, which itself is an indwelling law, imprinted by Divine decree.' It should be noted that the expression 'substance,' as here applied to *materia secunda*, is not to be taken too strictly. *Materia secunda* is not so much *substantia* as *substantiata*. This is more clearly brought out in Leibniz's later writings. See *Monadology*, note 2, and this Introduction, Part iii. p. 98 note.

[2] Cf. *Lettre à Remond* (1715) (E. 736 a ; G. iii. 657) : 'Strictly speaking, *materia prima* is not a substance, but something incomplete. And *materia secunda* (as, for instance, the organic body) is not a substance, but for another reason : namely, because it is

In short, as *materia prima* is abstract passivity, the limit
of activity, and is thus in reality merely the finitude or
imperfection of a Monad, so *materia secunda* is mere
abstract quantity, the limit of intension, and is thus a
mere phenomenon of that which is essentially one and
indivisible, of the 'soul' which the body 'contains[1].'
Accordingly every created Monad or simple substance
has *materia prima* in so far as it is not entirely active ; or,
in other words (since activity and passivity are relative
terms), every created Monad must have *materia prima*,
because its activity is not entirely realized, but is in part
potential, because it is not *actus purus*, activity without
passivity.   '*Materia prima* is essential to every entelechy
and can never be separated from it, since it completes it,
and is itself the passive potentiality of the whole complete
substance. . . . God . . . cannot deprive a substance of
materia prima; for He would thus make it wholly pure
activity [*purus actus*] which He Himself alone is[2].'
Materia secunda, on the other hand, is not necessarily
attached to any specific entelechy or individual substance.
It is a relationship of Monads imperfectly conceived by us
as a group of things which may vary from time to time,
and which, as a matter of fact, is constantly varying.
Leibniz compares it to a river[3].   'God, by His absolute
power, may be able to deprive substance of *materia
secunda*[4].'   In fact, it is not by itself anything real, but is
merely the relation of certain Monads, regarded abstractly
as a temporary aggregation or collocation.   The *only* real
existences are the Monads, which are purely spiritual,
non-spatial existences, but in relatively confused or

a collection of several substances, like a pond full of fish, or a flock
of sheep ; and consequently it is what is called *unum per accidens* : in
a word, a phenomenon. A real substance (such as an animal) is
composed of an immaterial soul and an organic body ; and it is the
combination of these two that is called *unum per se.*'

[1] Cf. this Introduction, Part iii. pp. 78 sqq.
[2] *Epistola ad Des Bosses* (1706) (E. 440 b ; G. ii. 324).
[3] Ibid. (1706) (E. 436 b ; G. ii. 306). Cf. p. 114 and *Monadology*, § 71.
[4] Ibid. (1706) (E. 440 b ; G. ii. 325).

abstract and imperfect thought (i.e. in 'sense' or 'imagination' as distinct from thought proper) we are presented with the phenomena of things variously grouped in space, and these groups, *qua* groups, are *materia secunda* [1].

Phenomena bene fundata.

As *materia secunda* is always a mere aggregate, while yet every aggregate pre-supposes as its reality an indivisible simple substance or soul, such aggregates or groups of things, together with their powers, acts, and affections, are sometimes described by Leibniz as well-founded phenomena (*phenomena bene fundata*). They are

[1] Cf. *Lettre à Arnauld* (1686) (G. ii. 75, 76) : ' In my opinion, our body in itself (setting aside the soul), or the *Cadaver*, can be called *one* substance only by a wrong use of terms, like a machine or a heap of stones, which are only beings by aggregation ; for regular or irregular arrangement has nothing to do with unity of substance. . . . I hold that a marble pavement is probably only like a heap of stones, and thus cannot pass for only one substance, but is a collection of several. For suppose there are two stones—for example, the diamond of the Grand Duke and that of the Great Mogul—we might give them both, in respect of their value, one and the same collective name, and we might say that they are one pair of diamonds, although they are actually far distant from one another. But it will not be said that these diamonds compose one substance. Now more or less make no difference here. Accordingly, if we bring them nearer one another, and even make them touch one another, they will be none the more united in substance ; and although, after they had been brought into contact, we were to join to them some other body in such a way as to prevent them separating again—for instance, if we were to set them in one ring—all *that* would make of them only what is called *unum per accidens*. For it is as by accident that they are compelled to share in the same motion. I hold then that a marble pavement is not one concrete [*accomplie*] substance, any more than would be the water of a pond with all the fish it holds, even although all the water and the fish were frozen together ; or than a flock of sheep, in which the sheep should be supposed to be so bound together that they could only walk in step, and that one could not be touched without all the others crying out. There would be as much difference between a substance and such a being as between a man and a community, like a people, army, society or college, which are moral beings and in which there is something imaginary and created by our mind. Unity of substance requires an indivisible and naturally indestructible concrete [*accomplie*] being, since the notion of such a being includes all that is ever to happen to it.'

bene fundata in contrast with the phenomena of dreams or visions, which are phenomena pure and simple, not having any proper bond or connexion. *Phenomena bene fundata* may be distinguished from the phenomena of dreams, inasmuch as the former are vivid, multiplex (i.e. varied in their relations and capable of a variety of tests or observations', and congruous or consistent both with themselves and with the general course of life or experience, which we find in other phenomena. The last of these tests is the most satisfactory, especially when it is supported by the testimony of other people who have also applied it. 'But the most powerful proof of the reality of phenomena (a proof which is, indeed, sufficient by itself) is success in· predicting future phenomena from those which are past and present, whether the prediction be founded upon the success, so far, of a reason or hypothesis, or upon custom so far observed[1].' In short, *phenomena bene fundata* are distinguished from illusions, inasmuch as they are not merely separate and disconnected, but held together in a system so that their antecedents may be traced and their consequents deduced[2]. And Leibniz goes so far as to add:—'Although this entire life were said to be nothing but a dream, and the visible world nothing but a phantasm, I should call this dream or phantasm real enough, if we were never deceived by it, when we use our reason rightly[3].' On

[1] *De Modo distinguendi phenomena realia ab imaginariis* (E. 444 a; G. vii. 320).
[2] Can this be reconciled with the view that *materia secunda* is a mere aggregate or collection?
[3] *Loc. cit.* Of course it must be remembered that the 'reality' attributed by Leibniz to *phenomena bene fundata* is entirely relative to the illusoriness of 'pure' phenomena, such as we have in dreams, and is not to be confounded with the reality of substance. Cf. *Nouveaux Essais*, bk. iv. ch. 2, § 14 (E. 344 b; G. v. 355): 'The truth of the things of sense consists only in the connexion of the phenomena, which must have its reason [ground], and that is what distinguishes them from dreams; but the truth of our existence and of the cause of phenomena is of another kind, because it establishes substances. . . . The connexion of the phenomena which establishes *truths of fact* in regard to sense-objects

several occasions Leibniz uses the rainbow as a simile by
which to illustrate what he means by a *phenomenon bene
fundatum*[1]. He simply mentions it without explanation;
but we may suppose him to have meant that the rainbow
is the type of a *phenomenon bene fundatum*, inasmuch as,
being merely colour, it exists as a rainbow only for those
who actually behold it, and is thus a mere appearance,
while, being an appearance which results from certain
physical conditions of light and moisture, it has a ground
or cause, it is the phenomenon of something and is therefore *bene fundatum* and not a pure phantasm or illusion.

Thus, in general, the qualities of matter, whether
secondary, as colour, smell, sound, &c., or primary, as
extension, figure, and motion, are *phenomena bene fundata*.
Taken by themselves, as qualities of a matter which has
no 'soul,' they are not real but merely subjective. But
their order or connexion implies a principle of order (i. e.
a soul), and accordingly they are confused (i. e. not fully
analyzed) representations, perceptions, or symbols of
that which, expressed distinctly, is real substance.
Ultimately ('metaphysically' as Leibniz would say) they
are reducible to non-spatial perceptions or appetitions of
Monads; but in the form in which they are given to us

outside of us is verified by means of *truths of reason*; as the phenomena of optics are explained by geometry. Yet it must be
admitted that this certitude is not of the highest degree. . . . For it
is not impossible, metaphysically speaking, that there is a consecu-
tive dream lasting as long as the life of a man; but that is a thing
as contrary to reason as would be the fiction that a book could
be formed by chance through throwing down type in confusion.'
Cf. Locke, *Essay*, bk. iv. ch. 2, § 14; Fraser's ed., vol. ii. pp. 185
sqq., with Prof. Fraser's *Notes*, and also his *Notes* on pp. 332 and 333.

[1] Cf. *Epistola ad Des Bosses* (1715) (E. 728 b; G. ii. 504): 'I prefer
to say that not substances but species[1] [i. e. sense-qualities]
'remain, and that these are not illusory, like a dream or like
a sword pointing towards us out of a concave mirror, or as
Dr. Faustus ate a cartful of hay, but true phenomena, that is, in
the sense in which a rainbow or a mock sun is a species, indeed
as, according to the Cartesians and in truth, colours are species.'
Also *Epistola ad De Volder* (1706) (G. ii. 281, note): 'Extension itself,
mass and motion, are no more things than the image in a mirror
or the rainbow in a cloud. . . . They exist νόμῳ rather than φύσει, to
use the expression of Democritus' (p. 282, note).

by our senses or imagination (which perceive things confusedly) they are mere connected or orderly phenomena, abstractions or incomplete things, which presuppose souls or Monads.

Space and Time.

In one of the *Letters to Arnauld*[1], Leibniz speaks of space and time as *phenomena bene fundata*. Probably, however, he did not intend this statement to be very rigidly interpreted, and there is much value in the view of Erdmann that space and time are to be regarded as purely ideal, *entia mentalia*[2], while extended bodies and actual events in time are *entia semimentalia*[3] or *phenomena bene fundata*. In any case, what Leibniz desires specially to maintain is that space and time are not real substances nor attributes of real substances. They are nothing but orders or arrangements of co-existing and successive things or phenomena. Individual substances or Monads, which are the sole realities, are not to be conceived as *partes extra partes*: the central thought of Leibniz's philosophy is that this quantitative aspect of things should be treated as subordinate, as not belonging to the essence of real things. Hence space is to be regarded, not as the mutual exclusiveness of real substances, but as simply the order of co-existence pre-supposed in the aggregation or grouping of phenomenal things, while time is the order of sequence of phenomena. 'Time, extension, motion, and the continuous in general, in the way in which they are considered in mathematics, are only ideal things; that is to say, things which express possibilities, just as numbers do. Hobbes has even defined space as *phantasma existentis*. But, to speak more exactly, extension is the order of *possible co-existences*, as time is the order of *possibilities* which are inconsistent, but which have nevertheless some connexion. Thus

---

[1] G. ii. 118.   [2] *Hist. of Philosophy* (Eng. tr.), vol. ii. p. 185.
[3] Cf. *Epistola ad Des Bosses* (1706) (E. 436 b ; G. ii. 306).

extension relates to simultaneous things or things which exist together, time to those which are incompatible and which are nevertheless all conceived as existing, and it is this that makes them successive. But space and time taken together constitute the order of the possibilities of a whole universe, so that these orders (that is space and time) square not only with what actually exists but also with whatever might be put in its place, as numbers are indifferent to whatever can be *res numerata* [1].' Thus space does not mean any *particular* situation of bodies, nor time any *particular* succession of phenomena. Space is simply the indefinitely applicable relation of co-existence, while time is the indefinitely applicable relation of succession or order of successive positions. In each case the things or phenomena related might have been other than they are, and thus the orders are orders of *possibilities*. But in neither case is the order actual apart from *some* ordered or related things. There is no actual empty space or empty time. These are abstractions, harmless or possibly useful when recognized as abstractions, but hurtful if they are regarded as actual things.

Leibniz's disproof of the independent reality of space and time is directly based by him upon the principle of sufficient reason. 'I say, then, that if space was an

---

[1] *Réplique uux Réflexions de Bayle* (1702) (E. 189 b; G. iv. 568). The translation is from Gerhardt's text. Cf. *IIIme Lettre à Clarke*, 4 (Clarke's tr.) (E. 752 a; G. vii. 363): 'I hold space to be something *merely relative*, as time is: I hold it to be an *order of co-existences*, as time is an *order of succession*. For space denotes, in terms of possibility, an order of things which exist at the same time, considered as existing together; without inquiring into their particular manner of existing. And when many things are seen together one perceives that order of things among themselves.' The correspondence between Leibniz and Clarke is mainly devoted to this question of the meaning of space and time. Clarke endeavoured to defend the view of Newton that infinite space is real, and is to be regarded as a kind of sensorium of God or as His omnipresent perception of things. Leibniz attacks not merely this particular view, but all other theories which make space real, as, for instance, those which confound infinite space with the Immensity of God or with any other of His attributes. Cf. Fraser's ed. of Locke's *Essay*, vol. i. pp. 259, 260. See also *Explanation of the New System*, 1, note.

absolute being there would something happen for which
it is impossible there should be a sufficient reason, which
is against my axiom.   And I prove it thus.   Space is
something absolutely uniform ; and, without the things
placed in it, one point of space does not absolutely differ
in any respect whatsoever from another point of space.
Now from hence it follows (supposing space to be something in itself, besides the order of bodies among themselves) that 'tis impossible there should be a reason why
God, preserving the same situations of bodies among
themselves, should have placed them in space after one
certain particular manner, and not otherwise ; why everything was not placed the quite contrary way : for instance,
by changing east into west.   But if space is nothing else
but that order of relation, and is nothing at all without
bodies but the possibility of placing them, then those two
states, the one such as it now is, the other supposed to
be the quite contrary way, would not at all differ from
one another.   Their difference, therefore, is only to be
found in our chimerical supposition of the reality of space
in itself.   But in truth the one would exactly be the same
thing as the other, they being absolutely indiscernible ;
and consequently there is no room to inquire after a reason
of the preference of the one to the other.   The case is the
same with respect to time.   Supposing any one should
ask why God did not create everything a year sooner, and
the same person should infer from thence that God has
done something concerning which 'tis not possible there
should be a reason why He did it so and not otherwise ;
the answer is, that his inference would be right if time
was anything distinct from things existing in time.   For
it would be impossible there should be any reason why
things should be applied to such particular instants, rather
than to others, their succession continuing the same.   But
then the same argument proves that instants, considered
without the things, are nothing at all, and that they
consist only in the successive order of things ; which

order remaining the same, one of the two states, namely, that of a supposed anticipation, would not at all differ, nor could be discerned from the other which now is [1].'

Accordingly, Leibniz's theory of space and time may be summarized thus. Phenomena are *bene fundata* in proportion as they are connected together. Space and time are orders or systems of connexion between phenomena, the bond being co-existence in the one case, succession in the other. Apart from the phenomena, space and time are mere abstractions. Thus pure space and pure time are at two removes from reality, for the things which are in space and time are not Monads but phenomena. Yet ultimately phenomena are imperfect realities, unanalyzed perceptions. They have a basis in simple substance. Thus there must be something non-spatial and non-temporal, of which space and time are the imperfect expressions. And in a letter to Schulenburg (1698) Leibniz, after defining space and time in his usual way, says that ' in themselves [*per se*] they have no reality beyond the Divine Immensity and Eternity [2].'

---

[1] *IIIme Lettre à Clarke*, 5, 6 (Clarke's tr.) (E. 752 a ; G. vii. 364). In answer to this, Clarke, while professedly admitting the principle of sufficient reason, really denies its validity by maintaining that the mere will of God is to be counted as a sufficient reason, and that therefore Leibniz's application of the principle does not prove his case. Cf. *IVme Lettre à Clarke*, 18 (E. 756 b ; G. vii. 374): ' Space being uniform, there can be neither any external nor internal reason by which to distinguish its parts and to make any choice among them. For any external reason to discern between them can only be grounded upon some internal one. Otherwise we should discern what is indiscernible, or choose without discerning. A will without reason would be the ' chance' of the Epicureans. A God, who should act by such a will, would be a God only in name.'

With regard to the general question, cf. *Vme Lettre à Clarke*, 62 (E. 771 b ; G. vii. 406) : ' I don't say that matter and space are the same thing. I only say, there is no space where there is no matter, and that space in itself is not an absolute reality. Space and matter differ as time and motion. However these things, though different, are inseparable.'

[2] G. Math. vii. 242. For Leibniz's account of the origin of our idea of space, see Appendix B, p. 202.

Activity and Passivity of the Monads.   Mutual Influence
of Substances.   Cause and Effect.

So far, then, from space being, as Descartes held, the
essence of matter, it is a purely ideal relation which we
mentally construct between things or phenomena whose
ultimate reality or essence is not quantitative, and is
consequently not material[1].   But, as we have seen, every
one of the real substances (the Monads), each of which is
the essence or reality of a portion of matter, contains that
which, taken abstractly, may be described as *materia
prima*.   Every created Monad is both active and passive ;
for there is no such thing as absolute passivity, and pure
activity belongs to God alone.   As passive the Monad
has *materia prima*, as active it is entelechy.   Thus every
soul has a body ; there is no such thing as an absolutely
disembodied spirit, unless it be the Spirit of God.   And,
on the other hand, mere soulless body has no real existence : it is an abstraction.   The world is active, living
through and through, even in its infinitesimal parts.   It
is compact of souls.

Now this activity and passivity of the Monads do not
mean that any Monad exerts a real influence outside of
itself or receives any real impression from a substance
external to it.   The relations between the Monads are
purely ideal, and their activity and passivity are altogether
internal.   As we have seen, a Monad is in itself passive in
so far as its perceptions are relatively obscure or confused,
active in so far as they are relatively clear and distinct.
And similarly, as each Monad perceives or represents the
whole universe from its own point of view, one Monad is
said to be passive in relation to another in so far as certain
perceptions in the former are obscure or confused in comparison with the corresponding perceptions in the latter ;

[1] In spite, however, of this reduction of space, matter, &c., to
confused perception, Leibniz continues to use the language of
those who speak of them as real, comparing himself to a Copernican
who speaks of sunrise.   Cp. *Théodicée*, § 65 (E. 521 a ; G. vi. 138).

while, on the other hand, the Monad whose perceptions are clearer and more distinct is said to be so far active in relation to the other or (ideally, of course) to act upon it [1]. Thus, as we have already seen, the pre-established harmony is the basis of the inter-relation of the Monads and of their mutual changes [2]. Further, as clear and distinct perceptions are simply the unfolding (explication) or explanation of the corresponding more confused perceptions, the action of one substance upon another is to be regarded as meaning that the active substance, in so far as it is active, contains within itself (or, simply, *is*) the explanation of the passive substance, in so far as it is passive. Substances acting upon others are, accordingly, those in which the reason of the changes in the others may be read more distinctly than in those in which the changes actually occur [3]. Thus the connexion between cause and effect in different substances is a purely ideal relation, a harmony of internal changes and operations, implying no physical influence of one substance upon another. And, further, the cause of any change is not its obscure antecedent nor any power or activity prior in

---

[1] Cf. Spinoza's views of action and passion in *Ethics*, Part iii, especially Defs. 1 and 2, and Props. 1, 2, and 3. Also *Ethics*, Part v. Prop. 40, Corollary.

[2] Cf. p. 40; see also *Lettre à Arnauld* (1690) (G. ii. 135; E. 107 b), in which Leibniz gives a summary of his position: 'There must be everywhere in body substances indivisible, unborn and imperishable, having something corresponding to souls. ... Each of these substances contains in its own nature "*legem continuationis seriei suarum operationum*" [the principle of succession of the series of its own operations] and all that has happened and shall happen to it. All its actions come from its own inner being [*fonds*], except its dependence upon God. Each substance expresses the entire universe, but one does so more distinctly than another, and each expresses it more especially with regard to certain things and according to its own point of view. The union of soul with body, and indeed the operation of one substance upon another, consists only in the perfect mutual accord of substances, definitely established through the order of their first creation, in virtue of which each substance, following its own laws, agrees with the rest, meeting their demands; and the operations of the one thus follow or accompany the operations or change of the other.'

[3] Cf. *Monadology*, §§ 49 sqq.

time to the effect ; the true cause is always the reason or explanation, the distinct as opposed to the confused perception, whatever may be the time-order of the events or phenomena [1].

Mechanical and final Causes.   Soul and Body.

Every substance, as we have seen, consists of soul and body. And the soul, being on the one hand the relatively distinct perception of the substance, and on the other hand its activity, is the final cause of the substance, the end for which it is, the self-development of its nature. It must be conceived under the notion of Becoming, as a thing whose essence it is to move towards an end.   It cannot, therefore, be adequately described by purely mechanical conceptions. It has something more than a static self-identity ; its unity unfolds itself in the series of its changes.   Its reality is thus not determined merely by the principle of contradiction, taken as a principle of pure or abstract self-consistency.   The body of every substance, on the other hand, i.e. its matter, its confused perception, its passivity, is the physical or mechanical cause of the substance.   Being entirely abstract, and in itself a bare possibility, body may by itself be adequately described by mechanical conceptions, under the principle of contradiction.   Thus we may have an abstract science of physics by which the phenomena of abstract matter are explained on purely mechanical principles, that is, as a system of physical or efficient causes.   But if we would explain the concrete reality even of material substance we must employ dynamical rather than mechanical conceptions, or, in other words, we must regard the world as ultimately and essentially a system of final causes, a system which is the expression, not of an indifferent all-powerful Will, but of an all-powerful Will which knows and decrees the best [2].

[1] See Appendix C, p. 204.
[2] Cf. *Epistola ad Bierlingium* (1711) (E. 677 b ; G. vii. 501) : 'You

C.   ORGANISM.

Organic and inorganic Bodies.   Simple and compound
Substances.   Dominant Monad.

The notion of body existing by itself and that of soul
existing by itself are results of confused or imperfect

ask about spiritual, or rather incorporeal things, and you say that
we see the mechanical arrangement of the parts but not the
principles of the mechanism.   True; but, when we see motion also,
we understand from this [what we see] the cause of motion, or
force.   The source of mechanism is primary force [*vis primitiva*].
but the laws of motion, according to which impulses [*impetus*] or
derivative forces arise out of the primary force, issue from the
perception of good and evil, or from that which is most fitting.
Thus it is that efficient causes are dependent upon final causes,
and spiritual things are in their nature prior to material things,
as also they are to us prior in knowledge, because we perceive
more immediately [*interius*] the mind (as it is nearest to us)
than the body; and this indeed Plato and Descartes have
observed.'   Also *Lettre à Remond* (1714) (E. 702 a; G. iii. 607):
'I have found that most of the philosophical sects are right in
a good part of what they maintain, but not to the same extent in
what they deny.   The Formalists. such as the Platonists and
Aristotelians, are right in seeking the source of things in final
and formal causes.   But they err in neglecting efficient and
material causes and in inferring (as did Mr. Henry More in
England, and some other Platonists) that there are phenomena
which cannot be explained on mechanical principles.   But, on
the other hand, the Materialists, or those who hold exclusively
to the mechanical philosophy, err in setting aside metaphysical
considerations and in trying to explain everything by that which
is dependent on the imagination.   I flatter myself that I have
discovered the harmony of the different systems and have seen
that both sides are right, provided they do not clash with one
another; that in the phenomena of nature everything happens
mechanically and at the same time metaphysically, but that the
source of the mechanical is in the metaphysical.'   Also *Lettre à*
Arnauld (1686) (G. ii. 77): 'We are obliged to admit many things
of which our knowledge is not sufficiently clear and distinct.
I hold that the knowledge of extension is very much less so'
[than that of substantial Forms, of which he has been speaking],
'witness the remarkable difficulties as to the composition of the
continuous; and it may even be said that *bodies have no definite and*
precise shape, because of the actual sub-division of their parts [i. e. their
sub-division *ad infinitum*].   So that *bodies would without doubt be*
something merely imaginary and apparent if there were nothing but matter
and its modifications.   Yet it is of no use to mention the unity,
notion, or substantial Form of bodies, when we are explaining the
particular phenomena of nature, as it is of no use for mathe-

perception. The world consists solely of Monads, each
of which is a concrete unity of soul and body, of entelechy
and *materia prima*. Thus nature is throughout living;
there is nothing really inorganic[1]. What, then, is meant
by the common distinction between organic or living and
inorganic or material bodies? In order to answer this
question, we must consider more fully the nature of
compound substance.

While the simple substances alone are real they appear
as phenomena in groups or aggregates, which we call
compound substances. Indeed, although in *reality* they
are secondary, compound substances are prior to simple
substances in the order of *knowledge*. As phenomena
they can be perceived by the senses, while the Monads
cannot be so perceived. For the Monads are not *really*
grouped or combined; the aggregation is purely phenomenal. Now each Monad implied in any such aggregate
perceives or represents all the phenomena constituting its
group, since it perceives the whole universe, of which they
are parts. But as each Monad differs from all the others
in the degree of distinctness of its perceptions there must
in each group be one Monad which represents the group
more distinctly than does any other Monad implied in it.
This Monad of most distinct perception in each compound
substance Leibniz calls the dominant Monad of the
substance[2]. It has a formal superiority over the others

maticians to investigate the difficulties *de compositione continui* when
they are working at the solution of some problem. These things
are none the less important and worthy of consideration in their
own place. All the phenomena of bodies can be explained
mechanically or by the corpuscular philosophy, according to certain
principles of mechanics, which are laid down without taking into
consideration whether there are souls or not; but in an ultimate
analysis of the principles of physics, and even of mechanics, it
appears that we cannot explain these principles by modifications
of extension alone, and the nature of force already requires something else.' See also *Antibarbarus Physicus*, &c. (after 1687) (G. vii.
343). For Leibniz's account of the development of his views, see
Ultimate Origination of Things, Appendix, p. 351.

[1] Cf. *Monadology*, §§ 63 sqq.
[2] Cf. ibid. § 70; *Principles of Nature and of Grace*, § 3.

implied in the group, though all are really independent. Its control or dominance consists solely in the distinctness of its perceptions. Just as cause is not a real influence of one substance upon another, but merely the relation of activity in the one to corresponding passivity in the other, or of distinct to confused perception, so the central Monad of any compound substance has no physical control over the others, but is dominant because of its activity and distinctness. Thus the relation between the dominant Monad and the phenomena (implying other Monads) which, along with it, constitute a compound substance is similar to the relation between the two elements, active and passive (entelechy and *materia prima*), which together constitute simple substance or the individual Monad. The dominant Monad is the entelechy or soul of the compound substance, while its body is a phenomenal aggregate, every portion of which in turn implies a Monad or soul. But this aggregate is *materia secunda*; and thus we have simple substance consisting of *materia prima* and entelechy, and compound substance consisting of *materia secunda* and dominant Monad.

While observing this analogy, we must not forget the essential difference between simple and compound substance. The former alone is really substance : the latter, in so far as it differs from the former, is merely substance by courtesy or common usage. Simple substance is a concrete unity ; compound substance, in so far as it is compound (i. e. apart from its soul or dominant Monad, which is non-quantitative, and therefore cannot be an element in a compound), is merely an aggregate. Thus the *materia prima* or passivity of the individual Monad is a name for its confused, undeveloped or implicit nature taken abstractly : it is confused perception in the substance itself. But the *materia secunda* or body of the compound substance is not confused perception in the substance itself, for the body as compound has no perception of its own, as distinct from the perceptions of the simple substances which it implies. *Materia secunda*, then, is due to the confused perceptions of those who observe the compound substances. Thus to the eye of God there can be no *materia secunda*, no compound substance ; for in Him there is no confused perception.

The aggregates of phenomena which we call things or extended bodies are thus the result of confused perception. And the differences amongst them, which we describe by the names of organic, inorganic, &c., are really differences in their dominant Monads. Without a dominant Monad, body would be mere indeterminate quantity, 'without form' if not 'void,' a chaos of pure difference. The dominant Monad is the unity implied in a specific or definite aggregate, the unity in virtue of which an aggregate or compound is one thing as distinct from other things. If the dominant Monad be a bare Monad, with unconscious perceptions, we call the body inorganic. If the degree of distinctness in the perceptions of the dominant Monad be a little higher, we call the body a plant and so on. The organic and the inorganic pass imperceptibly into one another, and the degree of organic unity possessed by any body is nothing but the degree of distinctness in the perceptions of its dominant Monad. Thus the parts of an organism are more closely connected, more firmly held together, than those of an inorganic mass, because the dominance of the central Monad is greater, more complete (that is to say, its perception is more distinct), in the case of the former than in the case of the latter.

Body without soul, or mere matter considered as inorganic, that is to say, as an aggregate of parts which have no unity other than their aggregation, is unreal. We may regard it either as an abstraction from concrete substance or (more nearly in Leibniz's way of thinking) as an imperfect perception or representation of concrete substance. Nature is organic throughout : no real thing is completely inorganic: what we call 'inorganic' is really organic in a low degree[1].

The body of every created substance is the point of view of its soul. As there is no vacuum in nature, the changes in any one body affect every other. Thus in every body the whole world is represented or expressed. But in each dominant Monad, or soul, the aggregate forming its particular body is more distinctly represented than the rest of the world. Thus each soul perceives or represents the universe through the medium of its own body. While it does represent the whole, it represents it in a form in which its own body is more distinct than any other[2]. The body is like a special lens through which the soul sees the universe. This, of course, follows from the view that body in general is relatively confused perception. For each substance represents the universe 'from its own point of view,' and its point of view is simply the degree of confusedness (or of distinctness, for they are entirely relative) of its perceptions[3].

[1] Cf. *Antibarbarus Physicus*, &c. (G. vii. 344): 'But indeed, although all bodies are not organic, nevertheless in all bodies, including the inorganic, organic bodies lie hid, so that every mass which to outward appearance is formless [*rudis*] and quite undifferentiated [*similaris*] is inwardly not undifferentiated but diversified, and yet its variety is not confused but orderly. Thus there is everywhere organism, nowhere chaos, which would be unbecoming a wise Creator.'

[2] *Monadology*, § 62; cf. Spinoza, *Ethics*, Part ii. Props. 12, 13 (*Scholium*), 16 (Coroll. 1', 26, &c.

[3] Yet it must not be supposed that the soul has *perfect* knowledge of all that takes place in its own body. Cf. *Lettre à Arnauld* (1687) (G. ii. 90): 'It does not follow that the soul must be perfectly conscious [*s'apercevoir*] of what happens in the parts of its body, since there are degrees of relationship between these parts themselves which are not all expressed equally, any more than external things are. The distance of the latter is balanced by the smallness or other disadvantages of the former, and Thales sees the stars when he does not see the ditch before his feet.' Also *Lettre à Arnauld* (1687) (G. ii. 112): 'In natural perception and in feeling, it is enough that what is divisible and material, and is actually divided among several beings, should be expressed or represented in one indivisible being or in substance which possesses a genuine unity. We cannot doubt the possibility of such a representation of several things in one only, since our soul gives us an instance

Changes in compound Substances. Development and Envelopment.

Every compound substance is in constant change. No created Monad, as we have seen, can ever be entirely at rest: each, in virtue of its appetition, is continually either unfolding (developing) itself (i. e. passing from confused to more distinct perception), or enfolding (enveloping) itself (i. e. passing from distinct to more confused perception). And thus, as the dominance of any dominant Monad consists solely in the degree of distinctness of its perception, the relations of formal dominance and subordination, which constitute a compound substance, must be continually varying in particular cases.

of it. But this representation is accompanied in the rational soul by consciousness, and then it is called thought. Now this expression occurs everywhere, because all substances are in sympathy with one another, and each receives some proportional change, corresponding to the least change which happens anywhere in the universe, though this change is more or less observable, according as other bodies or their actions have more or less relation to ours. And I think that M. Descartes himself would have admitted this, for he would doubtless allow that, because of the continuity and divisibility of all matter, the least motion has its effect upon neighbouring bodies, and consequently upon one body after another *ad infinitum*, the effect proportionally diminishing. Thus our body must be in some way affected by the changes in all others. Now to all the motions of our body there correspond certain more or less confused perceptions or thoughts of our soul. Hence the soul also will have some thought of all the motions in the universe, and, in my opinion, every other soul or substance will have some perception or expression of them. It is true that we are not distinctly conscious of all the motions of our body, as, for instance, that of the lymph; but this may be compared with the fact that I must have some perception of the motion of each wave on the shore, in order that I may be conscious [*apercevoir*] of that which results from the totality of them, namely the great noise that I hear when close to the sea. Thus also we experience some confused result of all the motions which take place in us; but being accustomed to this internal motion, we are not distinctly and reflectively conscious of it, except when there is a considerable change in it, as at the beginning of an illness. ... Now since we are conscious of other bodies only through the relation they have to our own, I was right in saying that the soul expresses best what belongs to our own body. Thus we know the satellites of Saturn or of Jupiter, only in consequence of a motion which takes place in our eyes.' Cf. Spinoza, *Ethics*, Part ii. props. 24 and 27.

The phenomena which make up the body of a compound
substance must be continually changing according as the
dominant Monad rises or falls in perceptive rank.   No
dominant Monad has a changeless body ; because of its
own variations its body 'is in a perpetual flux like a
river, and parts are entering into it and passing out of
it continually '.'   And there is endless room for variation ;
because each compound substance is made up of other
compound substances (each with its dominant Monad),
and these again are made up of others *ad infinitum*[2].
Thus some or all of the things which at one time form
an inorganic body may, in new relations, become parts
of an organic body and *vice versa*.   And the size of any
body, belonging to a particular dominant Monad, may
increase or decrease indefinitely.

Metamorphosis.   Birth and Death.

Accordingly the change in compound substance of
every kind is always metamorphosis rather than metempsychosis[3].   The fundamental element in every compound substance is the dominant Monad, and the matter
or body of the substance is continually changing by a
gradual removal and addition of parts.   It is the body
which bit by bit transfers itself from one soul to another.
There is no such thing as the sudden transference of
a soul from one body to another entirely new body.
Such a transference would involve a sudden or discontinuous change in the soul itself, which is impossible.

---

[1] *Monadology*, § 71.   So Lotze compares the life of the parts to
a throng of travellers.   *Microcosmus*, bk. iii. ch. 4, § 4 (Eng. Tr.,
vol. i. p. 368).

[2] Cf. *Epistola ad Bernoullium* (1698) (G. Math. iii. 560) : 'I would
readily allow that there are animals (in the ordinary sense) incomparably greater than ours ; and I have sometimes said in jest
that there may be some system similar to ours, which is the watch
of a very great giant.'   Also *Monadology*, §§ 66 sqq. ; cf. Spinoza, *Ethics*,
Part ii. Lemma vii. Scholium.

[3] Cf. *Epistola ad Bernoullium* (1698) (G. Math. iii. 561) : 'I do not
admit μετεμψύχωσις into a new animal, but μεταμόρφωσις, αὔξησις,
μείωσις of the same animal.'

Though, on the one hand, no soul is limited to any particular phenomenal aggregate as its body, yet on the other hand, no soul can be completely and instantaneously severed from its body and transferred to another. Again, the birth and the death of any organism are simply forms of this metamorphosis [1]. There is no absolute birth, that is to say, no direct and immediate implanting of soul in body, and there is no absolute death, no complete severance of soul from body. All the Monads which constitute the sole reality of a compound substance are alike unborn (*ingénérable*) and imperishable [2]. They proceed directly from God: they are produced by 'fulgurations of His Divinity [3].' None of them comes out of anything else. Thus the phenomena we call 'birth' and 'death' are transformations, changes in the relations between Monads. When we speak of an animal being born, we mean that the body of a microscopic animalcule has enormously increased in size, and that its dominant Monad has undergone a corresponding internal change. The animal was an animal from the first, even in the microscopic, spermatic stage. In being born it has merely become an animal of a higher kind. In every case the process of birth is, in fact, similar to the change which takes place when a caterpillar develops into a butterfly, 'nature being wont to reveal in some particular cases her secrets, which she conceals on other occasions [4].' Birth is thus indistinguishable from growth, increase, development. And on the other hand, when we speak of an animal as dying, we mean that its body has decreased in size or been broken up into new compounds. The animal has not ceased entirely to exist, but has been contracted so that it is no longer perceived. Death is thus the same as decay, decrease, involution [5]. There is no spontaneous

---

[1] *Monadology*, §§ 73 sqq.   [2] Cf. *Principles of Nature and of Grace*, § 6.
[3] *Monadology*, § 47; see the note to that section.
[4] *Lettre à Arnauld* (1686) (G. ii. 75).
[5] *Monadology*, §§ 74 and 75.   Cf. *Théodicée*, § 90 (E. 527 b; G. vi. 152).

generation and no passing from life to absolute lifelessness.   For lifelessness is entirely relative : the very dust
and ashes still have life [1].

Indestructibility and Immortality of Souls.

Accordingly the souls of all living beings are indestructible, while the soul of man is both indestructible
and immortal, since it not merely persists in existence
but continues to have consciousness, memory, and such
other characteristics as constitute personality [2].   It is
apparently, in Leibniz's view, impossible for the mind
of man to degenerate so as to pass into a lower stage of
existence.   The possession of self-consciousness is inalienable.   The rational soul thus differs from all souls
that are beneath it in rank, inasmuch as it does not
experience such wide variations as those to which the
latter are subject.   In a letter to Arnauld (1687), Leibniz
says : 'Others, not being able to explain otherwise the

---

[1] Cf. *Epistola ad Bernoullium* (1698) (G. Math. iii. 553) : ' You argue
entirely to my mind when you say that changes do not take place
per saltum.   And further, I do not laugh at your conjecture, but
I definitely avow that there are in the world animals as much
larger than ours, as ours are larger than microscopic animalcules.
Nor does nature know any limit.   And again it may be, nay it
must be, that in the very smallest grains of dust, and indeed in
the least atoms [*atomulis*] there are worlds not inferior to our own
in beauty and variety ; nor is there anything to prevent what may
appear a still more wonderful thing, that animals at death are
transferred to such worlds ; for I regard death as nothing else than
the contraction of an animal.'

[2] Cf. *Lettre à Des Maizeaux* (1711) (E. 676 a; G. vii. 534) : 'I am
of opinion that the souls of men pre-existed, not as rational souls,
but merely as 'sensitive' [*sensible*] souls, which attained this higher
degree (that is to say, reason) only when the man, whom the soul
is to animate, was conceived.   I grant an existence as old as the
world not only to the souls of the lower animals, but in general to
all Monads or simple substances from which compound phenomena
result ; and I hold that each soul or Monad is always accompanied
by an organic body, which is nevertheless perpetually changing ;
so that the body is not the same, though the soul and the animal
are.   These rules apply also to the human body, but apparently in
a higher degree than to other animals which are known to us ;
since man must continue to be, not merely an animal but also
a person and a citizen of the City of God, which is the most
perfect possible state, under the most perfect Monarch.'

origin of forms, have allowed that they have their beginning in a real creation. While I grant this creation in time only as regards the rational soul, and hold that all forms which do not think were created with the world, they believe that this creation happens every day when the smallest worm is engendered[1].' There is, then, something comparable to a special creation in the case of every mind or rational soul, although this creation is practically no more than the promotion of a Monad to self-consciousness. 'Minds [*esprits*] are not subject to these revolutions [of bodies], or rather these revolutions of bodies are subservient to the Divine economy regarding minds. God creates them when the time comes and detaches them from the body, at least from the earthly [*grossier*] body, by death, since they must always retain their moral qualities and their recollection in order to be perpetual citizens of that universal all-perfect commonwealth, of which God is the Monarch, which can lose none of its members and the laws of which are higher than those of bodies[2].'

[1] G. ii. 117.
[2] *Lettre à Arnauld* (1687) (G. ii. 99). Cf. *Théodicée*, § 91 (E. 527 b; G. vi. 152): 'Thus I should think that the souls which will some day be human souls have, like those of other species, been in the seed and in their ancestors up to Adam, and have consequently existed, since the beginning of things, always in some kind of organic body. . . . It appears to me also for various reasons probable that they then existed only as sensitive or animal souls, endowed with perception and feeling, and devoid of reason ; and that they remained in this state up to the time of the begetting of the man to whom they were to belong, but that then they received reason ; whether we suppose that there is a natural means of raising a sensitive soul to the rank of a rational soul (which I find it difficult to conceive), or that God has given reason to this soul by a special act, or (if you like) by a kind of *transcreation*. This is the more easily admitted, as revelation informs us of many other immediate acts of God upon our souls. . . . And it is much more in harmony with the Divine justice to give to the soul, already *physically* or as an animal corrupted by the sin of Adam, a new perfection, namely reason, than, by creation or otherwise, to put a rational soul into a body in which it is to be *morally* corrupted.' Also *Lettre à Arnauld* (1686) (G. ii. 75): 'The rational soul is created only at the time when its body is formed, being entirely different from the other souls we know, because it is capable of reflexion

The Vinculum Substantiale.

As to organic substance, one other point requires a brief consideration. In a correspondence with Father Des Bosses, Leibniz draws a distinction between a compound substance, strictly speaking, and a mere collection of things, such as a heap of stones, or a flock of sheep, or an army. The compound substance has a certain unity ; it is *substantia composita* [singular number]. It involves something which gives a certain reality to its phenomena (*ens realizans phenomena*), or, in other words, there is a genuine bond of connexion between its phenomena (*vinculum substantiale*). It is *unum per se*. The mere collection, on the other hand, is not *a substance* but *substances* (*substantiae, substantiatum, semi-substantia*). It has no unity of its own. Whether, as in the case of a heap of stones, its unity consists in the contact of its parts or, as in the case of a regiment, it is united by a common purpose, the bond of connexion is entirely in the mind of an observer. In short, when we regard such a thing as a mere collection, we regard it as without a dominant Monad, and therefore as not having a genuine body. It is like the 'corporation' which, according to Sydney Smith, 'has neither a body to be kicked nor a soul to be damned.' It is *unum per accidens*, in contrast with *unum per se* [1].

This distinction, however, is not to be regarded as absolute. It is, in another form, the distinction which we have already considered [2] between *phenomena bene fundata* and the pure phenomena of imagination and dreams. The *vinculum substantiale* is simply the connexion of the phenomena, in virtue of which we describe them as *bene fundata*, since this connexion arises from the

and resembles in miniature the Divine nature.' See *Monadology*, § 82 note.

[1] Cf. this Introduction, Part iii. p. 96, notes 1 and 2.
[2] Cf. this Introduction, Part iii. p. 98.

mutual relations of the Monads which are implied in the
compound substance.   The *vinculum substantiale* is nowhere mentioned by Leibniz except in the correspondence
with Des Bosses.   It is in no way essential to his philosophy; but it is the suggestion of a way in which his
system might possibly be made consistent with the Roman
Catholic dogma of Transubstantiation, which requires
that bodies should be considered as real substances.

Leibniz tells us plainly that he has no great liking for
the *vinculum substantiale*, and that it is better to dispense
with it, unless any would-be disciple of his finds it
necessary as an aid to religious faith [1].   It ought not,
however, to be forgotten that Leibniz was encouraged in
rejecting the Cartesian view that the essence of bodily
substance is extension and motion, by the fact that this

---

[1] Cf. G. ii. 499. A. Lemoine, in his thesis entitled *Quid sit Materia
apud Leibnitium* (Paris, 1850), discusses fully the *Letters to Des Bosses*,
with the object of showing that the *vinculum substantiale* is an excres-
cence upon the philosophy of Leibniz, and that the use he makes
of it involves inconsistency with his general position.   Erdmann,
in his *History of Philosophy* (Eng. Tr., vol. ii. p. 188) holds that it
is not to be regarded merely as a concession to the religious
scruples of Roman Catholics, but that it is really a part of Leibniz's
life-long endeavour to reconcile the Roman Catholic and Lutheran
Churches   Cf. *Lettre au Duc Jean Frédéric* (no date) (Klopp, iv.
444):—'There is also a considerable feature of my philosophy
which will make it somewhat welcome to the Jesuits and other
theologians.   It is this, that I re-establish the substantial forms
which the Atomists and Cartesians claim to have exterminated.
Now it is certain that without these forms and the difference there
is between them and real accidents, it is impossible to maintain
our mysteries; for if the nature of body consists in extension,
as Descartes holds, it undoubtedly involves a contradiction to
maintain that a body exists in many places at once.'   Dillmann
(*Neue Darstellung der Leibnizischen Monadenlehre*, p. 25) has no doubt
that the *vinculum substantiale* is the same as the 'soul' of the
body or its dominant Monad.   Logically, perhaps, it ought to
be so; but it is far from clear that Leibniz meant this.   For he
several times uses the terms 'soul' or 'dominant Monad' in the
same sentence as the term *vinculum substantiale* without identifying
them.   And he speaks of the *vinculum substantiale* being 'abolished,'
'destroyed,' 'supernaturally removed,' &c. But he afterwards admits
that the *vinculum substantiale* cannot come into being or be destroyed.
So that Leibniz's entire treatment of the matter is tentative and
unsatisfactory.

theory is inconsistent both with the Roman Catholic and with the Lutheran doctrine regarding the Real Presence in the Eucharist.

D.   SELF-CONSCIOUSNESS.

By means of the different degrees of clearness and distinctness in the perceptions of their respective souls or dominant Monads, the organic compound substances of which the world is composed may be divided into three main classes, (1) mere living beings, (2) animals, and (3) men. Substances of the first class, including plants and all lower forms of existence, have as their soul a bare Monad, having mere perception or representation, unaccompanied by consciousness. Animals, on the other hand, have a higher degree of perception, which appears as consciousness or feeling (*sentiment*), including memory. The soul of man possesses the characteristics of both of the lower classes, but its perception has a still higher degree of clearness, appearing now as self-consciousness or apperception. The self-conscious soul or spirit does not merely connect its particular perceptions in the empirical sequence of memory; but, having a knowledge of eternal and necessary truths, it can represent things in logical order, that is to say, in their necessary rational relations. This is what is meant by its having reason, or being a rational soul. The possession of reason means the power of reflexion or self-consciousness, because necessary and eternal truths are simply perceptions developed to the highest degree of distinctness, and consequently the knowledge of such truths is a clear and distinct consciousness of what is in ourselves (of the perceptions which constitute our nature), and hence indirectly a clear and distinct knowledge of substance in general [1].

[1] *Monadology*, §§ 18-30 ; *Principles of Nature and of Grace*, §§ 4 and 5. Of course it is not to be supposed that the scale of organic being ends with man. There must be between man and God a continuous succession of other embodied souls, each more perfect than the one beneath it. Otherwise the law of continuity would be broken.

Now, as we saw in considering the meaning of life and death[1], while the self-conscious or rational soul really differs only in degree from the conscious and the unconscious soul, it can never completely lose its rationality. The animal soul may at death lose memory and descend to a lower grade.   But this is not possible in the case of the self-conscious soul.   And on the other hand, while an animal soul may be raised to self-consciousness, Leibniz finds it difficult to conceive that this can take place without a special act or operation of God.   Self-conscious beings have thus a position of peculiar independence, which requires us to devote to them special consideration.   We proceed, then, to consider Leibniz's account (a) of the form in which perception appears in man, and (b) of the form in which appetition appears in him; these being the two essential characteristics of the human soul as well as of every other Monad.

(a) THEORY OF KNOWLEDGE.

Leibniz seeks a Via Media between the Views of Descartes and of Locke.

Human perception or apperception is knowledge, strictly speaking.   Leibniz's theory of apperception is thus a theory of knowledge.   Now apperception is the perception of eternal and necessary truths.   It is clear and distinct knowledge.   But the human soul has also

---

'It is also reasonable to suppose that there are below us substances capable of perception, as there are such substances above us; and that our soul, far from being the last of all, occupies a middle position, from which it is possible to go up or down; otherwise there would be in the order of things a defect, which certain philosophers call *vacuum formarum.*'   *Sur les Principes de Vie* (1705) (E. 431 a; G. vi. 543).   Leibniz calls these higher beings *génies (genii).*   'It is to be believed that there are rational souls more perfect than we, which may be called *génies,* and it is quite possible that some day we shall be of their number.   The order of the universe seems to require it.'   *Lettre à la Princesse Sophie* (1706) (G. vii. 569).

[1] p. 116.

knowledge which is not clear and distinct, knowledge of
contingent things which it cannot reduce to eternal and
necessary truth. This must be so, for otherwise the
human soul would be perfectly clear and distinct in its
perceptions, complete and unrestrained in its activity,
actus purus. But this characteristic of perfect intuitive
knowledge and absolute activity belongs to God alone ;
the perceptions of man are always at best only relatively
clear and distinct. Accordingly it is impossible for
Leibniz to assent to the Cartesian theory of knowledge,
which gave worth only to the absolutely clear and distinct,
drawing a hard and fast line between self-conscious
thinking and all else. Descartes's use of the principle of
contradiction was inconsistent with the possibility of
relative truth. It explains the universal and necessary,
but only by setting aside the contingent as ultimately
inexplicable.

On the other hand, the theory of Leibniz is equally
opposed to the opposite view, expounded in Locke's *Essay
on the Human Understanding.* If distinctively human
knowledge does not consist solely in the perception of
universal and necessary truths, neither is the human mind
altogether destitute of such knowledge and dependent for
its ideas entirely upon the contingency of the senses. As
the human soul is a Monad, its knowledge does not come
to it from outside itself, for it cannot be really influenced
by any other substance. It is not originally a *tabula rasa*
on which externally-produced impressions are made ; for
no Monad can ever be purely passive or absolutely without
perception. The human mind, being spontaneous in all
its activities, must produce its knowledge entirely from
within itself. It is not a vacuum, gradually filled *ab extra*
with independent ideas ; it is a force or life transforming
itself, a growth, a self-revelation [1].

---

[1] Cf. *Nouveaux Essais*, bk. ii. ch. 1, § 2 (E. 222 b; G. v. 99) : 'This
tabula rasa, of which so much is said, is in my opinion nothing but
a fiction, which nature does not allow and which has its grounds

Thus in his theory of knowledge, Leibniz may be regarded as seeking a *via media* between two extreme views, the basis of both of which is mechanical rather than dynamical. Each in its own way fails to do justice to the relations in knowledge, to its unity as a system. Each rests on the absolute (not the relative) validity of

only in the incomplete notions of philosophers, like the void, atoms and absolute or relative rest of two parts of a whole in regard to one another, or like the *materia prima*, which is conceived as absolutely passive [*sans aucunes formes*]. Things which are uniform and contain no variety are never anything but abstractions, like time, space, and the other beings of pure mathematics. There is no body whose parts are at rest, and there is no substance which has nothing to distinguish it from every other. Human souls differ, not only from other souls, but also from one another, although the difference is not of the kind that is called "specific." And I think I can prove that every substantial thing, whether soul or body, has its own special relation to every other; and one must always differ from another by *intrinsic* characters; without mentioning that those who say so much about this *tabula rasa*, after having removed from it the ideas, cannot tell what remains of it, like the Scholastic philosophers who leave nothing in their *materia prima*. Perhaps it may be replied, that this *tabula rasa* of the philosophers means that the soul has originally and by nature nothing but bare faculties. But faculties without any activity, in a word the pure potencies [*puissances*] of the Scholastics, are themselves only fictions, which nature knows not and which are obtained only by making abstractions. For where in the world shall we ever find a faculty which is shut up in mere potency without any activity? There is always a particular disposition to action, and to one action rather than another. And besides the disposition there is a tendency to action, and indeed there is always an infinity of these tendencies at once in every object; and these tendencies are never without some effect. Experience is necessary, I admit, in order that the soul should be determined to such and such thoughts, and in order that it may take notice of the ideas which are in us. But by what means can experience and the senses give ideas? Has the soul windows? Is it like a writing-tablet? Is it like wax? It is plain that all those who think thus of the soul make it at bottom corporeal. There will be brought against me this axiom, accepted among the philosophers, *that nothing is in the soul that does not come from the senses*. But the soul itself and its affections must be excepted. *Nihil est in intellectu, quod non fuerit in sensu;* excipe : *nisi ipse intellectus*. But the soul contains the notions of being, substance, unity, identity, cause, perception, reasoning and many others, which the senses cannot give. This agrees well enough with your author of the *Essay*, who finds the origin of a considerable section of the ideas in the mind's reflexion on its own nature.' Cf. *New Essays*, Introduction, pp. 360, 367 sqq.

certain ideas or impressions ; each is a kind of atomism.
The eternal and necessary truths (or clear and distinct
ideas) of Descartes are unconditionally valid ; they are
a priori atoms, forming the totality of knowledge. The
' simple ideas ' of Locke are equally unconditional in their
validity ; they are *a posteriori* atoms or data of knowledge [1].

But, here as elsewhere, Leibniz would rather reconcile
than overthrow. While the mechanical view of things is
not the truest; it nevertheless has value in its own sphere.
Thus he regards the errors of Descartes and Locke as due
in each case to the over-emphasis of one of the two complementary elements in knowledge, the necessary and the
contingent. Descartes's view might hold if knowledge

---

[1] Locke's opposition to Descartes, great though it was, ought not
to be emphasized to such an extent as to hide the fact that they
have much in common. For instance, we know that Locke's first
attraction to philosophy came from a reading of Descartes, and he
may perhaps owe the suggestion of some of his leading ideas to
such passages as the following extract from an unfinished dialogue
of Descartes, in which the method of doubt is wittily set in contrast with the Scholastic metaphysics. The question is : ' What
is man's first knowledge ? In what part of the soul does it dwell?
And why is it so imperfect at the beginning?' Epistemon, the
representative of Scholastic learning, says : ' That appears to me
to be very clearly explained, if we liken the imagination of infants
to a *tabula rasa* on which our ideas, which are as it were the living
image of objects, are to be painted. Our senses, the dispositions of
our mind, our teachers and our intelligence are the different painters
who can execute this work, and those among them which are least
fitted to succeed, begin it ; namely imperfect senses, blind instinct
and foolish nurses. At last comes the best of all, intelligence ; and
yet is it still necessary that it should serve an apprenticeship of
several years and for some time follow the example of its teachers,
before it dare rectify one of their errors. . . . It is like a clever
artist, called to put the finishing touches to a picture sketched by
learners. Though he use all his art, correcting gradually now one
feature, now another, and putting in all that has been omitted,
there must still remain great defects in it, because the picture was
badly drawn at first, the figures were ill·arranged and little attention was given to proportion.' *Recherche de la Vérité par les lumières
naturelles, Œuvres de Descartes* (ed. Cousin), vol. xi. p. 345 ; cf. ibid.
p. 375 : ' All truths follow from one another and are united by
a common bond ; the whole secret consists in beginning with the
first and most simple, and rising gradually to the most remote and
most complex.' See also Fraser's ed. of Locke's *Essay*, vol. i.
Prolegomena, p. 20.

were entirely necessary ; Locke's might hold if knowledge
were merely contingent. But human knowledge is both ;
it includes both self-evident truths and truths of fact.
A true theory of knowledge must do equal justice to both.
It must have affinity with the views both of Descartes
and of Locke, without altogether accepting either.

Leibniz's Solution of the Question of Innate Ideas and the Tabula Rasa. .

Locke endeavoured to establish his empiricism as
against the position of Descartes by denying that there
are in the human mind any innate ideas. 'If there be
no innate ideas, all our knowledge must reach us *ab
extra*, through the senses. And accordingly the only
true theory of knowledge must explain it *a posteriori*,
entirely from sense-experience. This was the contrary
opposite of the Cartesian view that all our genuine
knowledge comes from pure thought, in complete
independence of the senses (which are bodily, and therefore excluded from the sphere of thinking), and that the
only true theory of knowledge must explain it *a priori*,
as a logical deduction from self-evident innate ideas. To
Leibniz it seems that the conception of the human mind
as a Monad leads to a theory of knowledge which harmonizes the other two, by combining in a new form the
truth they each contain, and at the same time setting
aside their errors. As a Monad the soul of man is not,
as in Locke's view, a purely passive *tabula rasa*, continually
receiving external impressions. It is always an active
force, and it is itself the spontaneous source of all its
ideas, i. e. of the entire sequence of its experience. All
its ideas are therefore innate. But none of its ideas is
from the beginning clear and distinct. When they first
appear they are confused and imperfect. The recognition
of their self-evidence is the result of a process, a development from relative confusion to distinctness. But what
Locke calls sensation is, according to Leibniz, confused

perception, the indistinct representation of things external
to the individual mind. Thus the self-evidence of universal and necessary truths is a result of experience,
though that experience is purely internal. And though
all our ideas are innate, there are many which can never
be reduced to the perfect clearness and distinctness of
self-evident truth, but which we have nevertheless quite
sufficient ground for recognizing as true. Further, though
our experience is entirely internal, it is none the less
objectively real, for it consists in a representation of the
whole universe, in accordance with the pre-established
harmony between substances. Human knowledge is thus
at once *a priori* and *a posteriori*, innate and experiential [1].

Relativity of the Distinction between Perception and Apperception.

The acceptance of this theory involves a change in the
point of view held both by Descartes and by Locke. They
both argue on the assumption that perception and apperception are quite distinct from one another. Descartes's
theory of innate ideas rests on his doctrine that absolute
certainty belongs to self-conscious thought alone, ex-
cluding all other forms of human experience as phenomena of body, which is the contradictory opposite of

[1] 'If all our ideas [*connaissances*] are innate in so far as they are
ideas distinct in themselves, they are all acquired in so far as they
are ideas distinct for us.' Boutroux, ed. of *Nouveaux Essais*, &c.,
Introduction, p. 83. Cf. Lotze, *Streitschrift*, p. 13: 'In earlier times
people made too free a use of the name of innate ideas; but now it
seems to me that they have fallen into an opposite error when they
at once set aside this notion, with a superficial depreciation of its
somewhat inappropriate name. I have never been able to convince
myself that the logical and metaphysical principles regarding the
nature of things, which are necessary to our thought, the aesthetic
feelings and the consciousness of obligation rest upon anything
else than the immediate depth of our spiritual nature, so that they,
under the stimulus of experience, come into our consciousness as
original possessions of our nature, not as complete innate images,
always hovering in our consciousness, but as so grounded in us that
they indeed require the stimulus of experience, but are never given
to us by experience.'

mind. Locke, on the other hand, denies the existence of innate ideas on the ground that children, savages and idiots do not consciously possess them ; an argument which implies that we have an idea only when we are fully aware of it, that is to say, that ideas exist only in self-consciousness or apperception. Thus apperception (in the Leibnitian sense) is regarded by Descartes as containing absolute, innate first principles, from which particular truths may be deduced, while by Locke it is held to give, not first principles, but simple ideas, which are the elements out of which knowledge is built. In both cases it is apperception that is appealed to ; mere perception does not count [1].

Now the great central principle of the philosophy of Leibniz is the idealizing of all substance, by regarding it as throughout perceptive or representative. Apperception, feeling and bare perception (which is not necessarily anything more than the mere possession of real qualities) are not different in kind but merely in

[1] Cf. *Nouveaux Essais*, bk. ii. ch. 1, § 19 (E. 226 a ; G. v. 107): '*Philalethes* [representative of Locke]. "That body is extended without having parts and that a thing thinks without being conscious [*s'apercevoir*] that it thinks, are two assertions which appear equally unintelligible." *Theophilus* [representative of Leibniz]. "Forgive me, sir, but I must tell you that in your contention that there is in the soul nothing of which it is not conscious, there is a *petitio principii*, which has already dominated our first discussion. It was there used for the overthrow of innate ideas and truths. If we were to grant this principle, we should not merely find ourselves in conflict with experience and reason, but we should have without any reason to give up our opinion, which I think I have made sufficiently intelligible. But our opponents, very clever though they are, have never produced any proof of what they so often and so confidently declare regarding this matter, and besides it is easy to prove to them the opposite, that is to say, that it is not possible we should always deliberately reflect on all our thoughts. Otherwise the mind would make a reflexion upon each reflexion *ad infinitum*, without ever being able to pass to a new thought. For instance, in being conscious of some present feeling, I should always have to think that I think of it, and again to think that I think of thinking of it and so *ad infinitum*. But I must surely come to an end of reflecting upon all these reflexions, and there must, in short, be some thought which we allow to pass without thinking of it ; otherwise we should always dwell upon the same thing." '

degree.   One reality pervades them all ; no one of them
is separated from another by any impassable barrier.
Body is confused soul; soul is clear and distinct body.
Self-consciousness is not a unique certainty or reality,
but a high degree of clearness and distinctness in that
which is already real in lower forms.   The self may be
exclusive, self-limited, individual ; but it is so only in
common with every other substance.   There is no substance which is not potentially an Ego, a self-conscious
being.   What Descartes and Locke both ignore is the
internal movement, the becoming, the growth and
development, which is of the essence of every substance.
For them a thing, a mind, an idea, a principle is what
it is, unchangeably ; so that either, as in the case of
Descartes, the variety of real thought is contained, perfect
and entire, within its unity, and is to be set forth by pure
sub-sumption, the lifting out of class from within class, or,
as in the case of Locke, the unity of real thought is a mere
aggregate of its varieties, the elements remaining un-
changeable into whatever groups we may gather them.

*As against Descartes, Leibniz denies the complete Separation
of Matter and Mind.*

Accordingly, Leibniz brings against Descartes's view of
mind essentially the same argument as he used against
Descartes's view of matter.   The Cartesian view of substance as that which is in itself and is conceived through
itself, without need of anything else, resulted in the
complete separation of matter and mind.   Leibniz, on
the other hand, unifies without absolutely identifying
them, through his view of substance as that which is
continually in process of perceiving or representing all
things.   Thus, against Descartes's view of matter as an
independent substance, Leibniz argues that a true
doctrine of substance makes matter by itself an abstraction, for it is really the confused perception which is
potentially clear and distinct perception, apperception or

mind. And similarly, against the view of Descartes that mind is an independent substance, opposed to matter, Leibniz maintains that pure mind belongs to God alone, and that mind as we have it is inseparable from matter and is really nothing but matter raised to a higher power, confused perception that has passed into greater clearness and distinctness. As among created substances there is no body without soul, so there is no soul without body.

In opposition to Locke, he holds that the Mind always thinks.

On the other hand, as against Locke, Leibniz contends that the mind is never without thought. If mind is a *tabula rasa*, receiving all its impressions from outside itself, a mind without thought is a perfectly natural supposition. And *a posteriori* Locke holds that in dreamless sleep the mind exists without thinking. Its existence during such a sleep is, he thinks, assured to us by our recollection afterwards of what took place in the mind before the sleep. Further, Locke maintains that, as body can exist without motion, mind can exist without thought[1]. Now the ground of this contention manifestly is that motion and rest are not relatively but absolutely distinct from one another and, similarly, that clear and distinct consciousness is absolutely and not relatively different from unconsciousness. When a body has no apparent motion, it is absolutely at rest; when a mind has no clear and distinct consciousness or apperception, it is absolutely without consciousness. To this the central principles of the philosophy of Leibniz are in complete opposition[2]. While motion and

[1] Could this be regarded as a strictly logical development of one side of Descartes's philosophy, thus revealing Descartes's inconsistency? Descartes would say that, as thinking is the essence of mind, mind cannot exist without thought and yet it may exist without any specific thought.

[2] Cf. *Nouveaux Essais*, bk. ii. ch. 1, § 10 (E. 223 a; G. v. 101): ' *Philalethes*. "But I cannot conceive it to be more necessary for the soul always to think than for the body to be always in motion, the

rest are apparently absolute opposites, in reality, when we regard them not abstractly but concretely in their relation to the rest of the world, they can be understood only as relatively distinct. For otherwise, the law of continuity, which is the basis of any workable interpretation of the universe, would be broken. In virtue of this law, then, rest must be considered as an infinitely small degree of motion, and every body possesses at least a *tendency* to motion or a *virtual* motion, even if it has no *actual*, apparent, complete motion. In the same way, when mind is considered concretely, as a real substance related (through its representation of them) to all the other substances of which the universe is composed, the distinction between consciousness and unconsciousness is seen to be relative. There can be no total absence of perception, for absence of perception (representation) would mean absence of relation to the rest of the world, and thus a breach of the law of continuity. Unconscious-

perception of ideas being to the soul what motion is to the body." . . . *Theophilus.* "You are right, sir. Activity is no more inseparable from the soul than from the body, a state of the soul without thought and absolute rest in the body appearing to me to be things which are equally contrary to nature and of which there is no instance in the world. A substance which is once in activity will be so always, for all its impressions persist and are merely mixed with other new ones. When we strike a body we arouse in it (or rather determine) an infinite number of vortices as in a liquid, for at bottom every solid has some degree of fluidity, and every fluid has some degree of solidity, and there is no way of ever entirely stopping these internal vortices. Now we may believe that, if the body is never at rest, neither will the soul, which corresponds to it, ever be without perception." . . . *Ph.* "But this proposition— the soul always thinks—is not evident by itself." *Th.* "I don't say it is. It requires a little attention and reasoning to see it. Ordinary people recognize it as little as they recognize the pressure of the atmosphere or the roundness of the earth." *Ph.* "I doubt if I thought last night. This is a question of fact, to be settled by sense-experience." *Th.* "We settle it in the same way in which we prove that there are imperceptible bodies and invisible motions, although some people regard these things as absurd. In the same way there are perceptions without much sharpness, which are not distinct enough for us to be conscious of them or to remember them; but they make themselves known by certain consequences they have."'

ness or apparent absence of perception is then merely an infinitely small degree of perception, and every mind must possess at least *virtual* thought or consciousness, a *tendency* to clear and distinct perception, even although it may actually appear to be empty of all thought [1]. The mind is not like a block of veinless marble, from which the sculptor may take what figure he pleases. It has veins which give the outline of the statue that is to come forth from it [2]. In other words, it is the nature of the mind to 'look before and after.' Leibniz regards his view as expressing the truth that underlies the Platonic doctrine of reminiscence. The present perceptions of the mind may be regarded as recollections of the past, inasmuch as they were already virtually contained in these past perceptions and are developed from them—are, indeed, these past perceptions grown more distinct. And again, the present perceptions of the mind are forecasts or prophecies of the future, since all its future perceptions are confusedly wrapped up in its present states.

The Petites Perceptions.

Thus in the *Monadology* [3], Leibniz maintains the existence of unconscious perceptions, on the ground that perception can only proceed from perception, and accordingly that in the passage from the unconsciousness of a swoon or a deep sleep to full waking consciousness there must be an infinite series of perceptions gradually rising in degree from infinitely little perceptions, which are apparently indistinguishable from absence of perception, upwards to the fuller perceptions of actual waking life. These little perceptions (*petites perceptions*, confused perceptions, or, as we might now call them, sub-conscious thoughts or mental activities) express the continuity of

---

[1] Cf. Locke, *Essay*, Fraser's ed., vol. i. p. 80 note.

[2] *New Essays*, Introduction, p. 367. Cf. Locke, *Essay*, Fraser's ed., vol. i. p. 48 note, and p. 60 note.

[3] §§ 21 and 23.

all souls, from the soul of the pebble to that of the
angel, as Leibniz puts it in his correspondence with
J. Bernouilli[1]. The characteristics of these *petites
perceptions*, which prevent us from being clearly aware of
them, are, he tells us[2], their smallness, their number,
or their individual indistinctness. And by means of
them he explains such psychological phenomena as our
ceasing to be aware of the sound of a mill or a waterfall
when we have become accustomed to it. The perceptions
are still there, but 'having lost the attractions of novelty,
they are not strong enough to claim our attention and
memory, which are directed to more interesting objects.
For all attention requires memory ; and often, when we
are not, so to speak, warned and directed to take notice
of certain of our own present perceptions, we let them
pass without reflexion, and even without observing
them ; but if some one immediately afterwards draws our
attention to them, and speaks to us, for instance, of some
noise that has just been heard, we recall it to ourselves
and perceive that a moment ago we had some consciousness of it. Thus there were perceptions of which we
were not aware at the time, apperception arising in this
case only from our attention having been drawn to them
after some interval, however small[3].' The *petites percep-*

---

[1] G. Math. iii. 560.

[2] *New Essays*, Introduction, p. 370. Cf. bk. ii. ch. 9, § 1 (E. 233 a ;
G. v. 121) : 'We ourselves have also *petites perceptions*, of which we
are not conscious in our present state. It is true that we might
quite well be conscious of them and reflect upon them, were we
not prevented by their multitude, which distracts our mind, or if
they were not effaced or rather obscured by greater ones. . . . I
should prefer to distinguish between *perception* and *apperception*.
For instance, the perception of light and colour, of which we have
apperception [are conscious] is made up of a quantity of *petites
perceptions*, of which we have no apperception [are not conscious];
and a noise, of which we have perception but of which we take
no notice, becomes *apperceptible* by a small addition or increase.
For if what precedes had no effect upon the soul, this little addition
would have none either, and no more would the whole have any.'

[3] *New Essays*, Introduction, p. 371. Cf. *Nouveaux Essais*, bk. ii.
ch. 1, § 11 (E. 224 a ; G. v. 103) : 'We think of a number of things
at once, but we take notice only of the thoughts which are most

tions, accordingly, are merely the confused perceptions of the self-conscious Monad, and their function and value in psychology may be estimated by reference to the importance of confused perception in Leibniz's general doctrine of substance.   However great may be their degree of confusion, and however little we may be conscious of them individually or collectively, they are still perceptions, one in kind with the highest, most distinct apperception or self-consciousness.   The realm of self-consciousness includes the whole of substance; it is by no means limited to man and spirits higher than man. But in the infinite variety of substances, self-consciousness exists in an infinite variety of degrees; and there are many substances in which its degree is infinitely little, that is to say, less than any degree that can be assigned or named.

Leibniz's Theory of Knowledge in relation to the main Principles of his Philosophy.

Thus Leibniz's theory of knowledge is simply the epistemological expression of the main principles of his

distinct : and matters cannot be otherwise, for if we were to take notice of all, we should have to think attentively of an infinity of things at once, all of which we feel and all of which make impression on our senses.   I say even more : something from all our past thoughts remains, and none can ever be entirely effaced. Now when we sleep without dreaming, and when we are stunned by some blow, fall, illness, or other accident, there appears in us an infinite number of little confused feelings, and death itself can produce no other effect on the souls of animals, which must without doubt, sooner or later, regain distinct perceptions, for everything in nature happens in an orderly way. . . . Each soul retains all its preceding impressions, and cannot split itself up. . . . In each substance the future has a perfect connexion with the past.   This is what constitutes the identity of the individual. Yet memory is not necessary nor even always possible, because of the multitude of present and past impressions, which come together in our present thoughts, for I do not believe that there are in man any thoughts which have not at least some confused effect, or which do not leave some vestige to be combined with later thoughts.   We can certainly forget things ; but we might also recollect them after a long interval, if only we were reminded of them in the right way.'

philosophy. All truth is innate, virtually if not actually. But there are two kinds of truth. Eternal and necessary truth has its ground in the principle of contradiction. It is either self-evident or the result of strict demonstration from the self-evident. 'Our mind is the source of necessary truths, and however many particular experiences we may have of a universal truth, we cannot assure ourselves of it for ever by induction without knowing its necessity through reason. . . . The senses may suggest, support, and confirm these truths, but cannot demonstrate their infallible and perpetual certainty [1].' On the other hand, truth of fact or contingent truth, while equally innate, is not demonstrable through the principle of contradiction, but through that of sufficient reason [2]. It is obtained by induction rather than demonstration. It is truth of experience, or perception which we cannot analyze into perfect distinctness and self-evidence, because of the infinite complexity of its relations to the system of

[1] *Nouveaux Essais*, bk. i. ch. 1, § 5 (E. 209 b; G. v. 76, 77).

[2] Thus Leibniz rejects the view of Locke that our real knowledge, as distinct from merely probable knowledge, 'extends as far as the present testimony of our senses, employed about particular objects that do then affect them, and no farther.' (*Essay*, bk. iv. ch. 11, § 9; Fraser's ed., vol. ii. p. 332.) Cf. the corresponding passage in the *Nouveaux Essais* (E. 378 b; G. v. 426): 'Yet I think that we might extend the names of knowledge and certainty to things other than actual sensations, for clearness and plainness [*evidence*] extend further, and I regard them as a kind of certainty : and it would without doubt be an absurdity seriously to doubt whether there are men in the world, when we do not see any. To doubt seriously is to doubt practically, and we might take certainty as a knowledge of truth which we cannot doubt practically without madness ; and sometimes we take certainty in a still more general sense and apply it to cases in which we cannot doubt without deserving to be greatly blamed. But *evidence* would be a luminous certainty, that is to say, a certainty such that, because of the connexion we see between the ideas, we have no doubt whatever. According to this definition of certainty, we are certain that Constantinople is in the world, that Constantine, Alexander the Great, and Julius Caesar have existed. It is true that some peasant of the Ardennes might justly doubt these things, from lack of information ; but a man of letters and of the world could not do so, without great mental derangement.' Cf. also Locke's *Essay*, bk. ii. ch. 21, § 75 (Fraser's ed., vol. i. p. 373).

things.   This infinitely complex mass of relations, which
it is impossible for us to reduce to perfect order and
simplicity, is our confused perception.   Confused perception is, then, the representation in us not of our own
nature, but of the system of things other than ourselves,
that is to say, the other Monads as they are related to us.
But distinct perception is the representation or perception
of our own nature, of that which is in ourselves, and it is
at the same time the evolving of some of our confused
perceptions into clearness ; it is not something quite
separate from our confused perception.   Thus we rise to
a knowledge of ourselves through our knowledge of
external things[1].   Self-consciousness implies the consciousness of objects ; apperception is, indeed, the very
flower of perception, the beauty to produce which perception, in all its degrees, is living and growing.   In
experience or confused thought, rightly interpreted, there
is the basis of distinct, rational knowledge.   Sense,
experience, imagination, must not be derided as fiction-
makers by the intellect which they have nourished[2].

The Meaning which Leibniz attaches to 'Perception' or
   'Representation.'   How does he endeavour to avoid an
   endless Relativity ?

Something remains to be said as to the meaning of this
'perception,' 'representation,' or 'expression,' which is
the key-word to Leibniz's theory of knowledge.   There is
a strong suggestion of *petitio principii* about it.   What
exactly does it mean ?   What is perceived, represented,
expressed ?   And what does the perception, representation,
expression consist in ?   If the essence of every real sub-

---

[1] Cf. *Nouveaux Essais*, bk. ii. ch. 21, § 73 (E. 269 b ; G. v. 197) :
'The senses furnish us with material for reflexion, and we should
never even think of thought, if we did not think of something
else, that is to say, of the particular things with which the senses
furnish us.   And I am persuaded that souls and created spirits are
never without organs and never without sensations, as they cannot
reason without symbols.'

[2] See Appendix D, p. 206.

stance is to perceive, represent, or express every other, we seem to have come upon the doctrine of the relativity of human knowledge in its worst form. It seems as if knowledge must be compared to the life of those unhappy islanders 'who earn a precarious livelihood by taking in one another's washing.'

As to the meaning of the terms, Leibniz says that 'one thing expresses another (in my sense) when there is a constant and regular [réglé] relation between what can be said of the one and what can be said of the other. It is thus that a projection in perspective expresses the original figure[1].' Any two things, then, are related to one another as perceiver and perceived, when the predicates or qualities of the one (whatever these predicates or qualities may be) always vary concomitantly with the predicates or qualities of the other. Perception, representation, or expression is then a relation of harmony (or development according to some law or principle) between the qualities of individual substances. But these qualities are themselves perceptions. What, then, is the ultimate reality of which they are all representations? Leibniz's answer is that the ultimate reality is the nature of God or the ideas of God as an intuitive Knower. God alone has a knowledge which is entirely adequate, perfectly realized; in Him the universe is transparent through and through. There is no reality beyond thought, to which thought must correspond. Thought cannot in any way represent that which is entirely other than itself, that which is separated from it 'by the whole diameter of being' (or by an even greater distance if that were possible). For no sign can be entirely cut off from the thing signified. Sign and thing signified must have some ground of unity in virtue of which this relation between them is possible.

---

[1] *Lettre à Arnauld* (1687) (G. ii. 112): 'Expression is common to all soul-principles [*formes*]. It is a genus, of which natural perception, animal feeling and intellectual knowledge are species.' Cf. this Introduction, Part iii. p. 112, note 3.

Thus pure thought cannot symbolize, represent, or perceive that which is absolutely not-thought. Confused thought is the symbol both of other confused thought and of clear and distinct thought. Accordingly, as between confused thoughts the relation of sign and thing signified is such that that which is now regarded as sign may from another point of view be taken as the thing signified, and vice versa. Nevertheless it is evident that the clearer and more distinct of any two corresponding perceptions will naturally be regarded as the thing signified by the more confused perception, that is to say, the thing which the more confused perception is trying to express, but is unable to express adequately. And thus the ultimate 'thing signified,' the fundamental reality, which all other perceptions in various degrees symbolize or represent, must be perfectly clear and distinct thought, or, in other words, the thought of God. So also God is First Cause as well as Ultimate Reality. For we have already seen [1] that cause is always reason or explanation, the relatively clear and distinct perception as against the corresponding confused perception, which is the effect. Accordingly, as the nature of God is absolutely clear and distinct perception, He must be the Ultimate Cause of all things [2].

(b) ETHICS.

Degrees of Appetition in the Monads—Impulse, Instinctive Desire, Will.

Every Monad has appetition as well as perception. Appetition is the principle of change in the Monad, that

[1] pp. 106, 107.
[2] This seems to imply that God is the ultimate reality of whom all individual created things are modes or manifestations. But Leibniz endeavours to avoid such a conclusion as this, by maintaining that the essences of things are independent ideas in the mind and understanding of God, eternal truths whose nature is not subject to His will. It is hardly necessary to point out how unsatisfactory is this explanation; but it is manifest that the weakness of Leibniz's theory at this point is the inevitable consequence of his attempt to work with two first principles, the mutual relations of which he has not thoroughly thought out.

in virtue of which the Monad passes from one perception to another. Like perception it has an infinite series of degrees ; but three main varieties of it may be noted, corresponding to the three main varieties of perception. Thus the appetition of the lowest class of Monads (the bare Monads) is mere unconscious impulse or tendency, a potential blind force tending to become actual. It is the particular appetition or change of perception (representation) which has its source or ground in unconscious perceptions. This bare impulse may be compared to a watch-spring wound up, which tends to unwind itself [1]; it is a tendency such as that of ' the stone which goes by the most direct but not always the best way towards the centre of the earth [2].' The appetition of animal souls is instinctive appetite or desire, which proceeds from feeling or conscious, yet relatively confused, perceptions. Like the appetition of the bare Monads, it seeks immediate present satisfaction, having nothing to guide it but the consciousness and memory of the animal soul. Finally, the appetition of rational souls is self-conscious desire or will, a principle of change whose basis is apperception or clear and distinct rational knowledge [3]. Appetition, like perception, is one and the same throughout all its degrees and varieties, from bare force to the freest, most rational volition. And in the nature of man we find all degrees of it ; he is not a purely rational will, but has instinctive impulses and passions, which belong to the middle class of appetitions, and physical powers which belong to the

---

[1] *Nouveaux Essais*, bk. ii. ch. 20, § 6 (E. 248 b ; G. v. 152, 153).

[2] Ibid. bk. ii. ch. 21, § 36 (E. 259 a ; G. v. 175).

[3] Cf. ibid. bk. ii. ch. 21, § 42 (E. 261 b ; G. v. 180) : ' There are unfelt [*insensible*] inclinations, of which we have no consciousness [apperception] ; there are felt [*sensible*] inclinations, whose existence and object we know, but which are formed without our being aware of it, and these are confused inclinations, which we attribute to the body, although there is always in the mind something corresponding to them ; and finally, there are distinct inclinations which reason gives us, and of whose force and formation we are aware.'

lowest class. As on the cognitive, so on the practical side
of his nature, the law of continuity holds.

Feeling. Pleasure and Pain. 'Semi-pains' and 'Semi-pleasures.'

The chief features of Leibniz's ethics are fixed by these
general considerations. In applying them it is necessary
for us, who have become familiar with post-Kantian
distinctions, to remember that the usual threefold
division of mental elements into cognition, feeling, and
will, is not of older date than the age of Rousseau [1], and
accordingly that Leibniz still works with the Aristotelian
twofold division of the elements into theoretical and
practical. Thus the 'appetition' of Leibniz covers both
feeling and will (in our sense of the terms), as well as the
lower forms of both, which are conscious and unconscious
forces more or less restrained from full activity, that is
to say, more or less potential or virtual. Accordingly, as
appetition and perception always accompany one another,
Leibniz maintains that there is no perception absolutely
colourless and entirely unchanging or at rest. Every
perception has an element of feeling and activity, although
the degree of it may be infinitely small. If we can be
pardoned the anachronism of using a phrase which Lotze
has made familiar, we may say that every perception has
a 'value' or 'worth'; but it must not be forgotten that
for Leibniz this value is not anything absolute or pre-
eminently real, but merely the unrealized potentiality of
clearness and distinctness in the perception [2].

Speaking then of human nature, which includes all
the varieties of perception and appetition, Leibniz says
that 'there are no perceptions which are entirely indifferent
to us, but when their effect is not observable we can call
them indifferent; for pleasure and pain seem to consist in

---

[1] It is usually attributed to Tetens (*circa* 1750). But it first
comes into prominence through Kant.

[2] Cf. Lotze, *Microcosmus*, bk. iii. ch. 4, § 4 (Eng. Tr., vol. i. p. 366).

an observable help or hindrance[1].' This, he warns us, is not to be taken as a strict definition of pleasure and pain, for he does not think it possible to give such a definition. But his account of these feelings seems to follow directly from his general point of view. Pain is essentially a hindrance or restraining of a Monad's appetition, while pleasure is its free action[2]. They are thus entirely relative to one another. And while we speak of the hindrance or freedom of appetition as pain or pleasure, only when the appetition has reached the degree of consciousness, yet consciousness is separated from unconsciousness by no hard and fast line, and consequently appetitions of a lower degree may be regarded as minutely painful or pleasant, according as they are retarded or advanced. Thus Leibniz speaks of 'semi-pains' and 'semi-pleasures' or 'little imperceptible [*inaperceptibles*] pains and pleasures,' corresponding to the *petites perceptions* in the theory of knowledge. Like the *petites perceptions* these semi-pains and semi-pleasures may, by growing in individual intensity or by combining into one totality, become observable in consciousness as complete pains and pleasures[3]. No soul can ever be absolutely at rest, absolutely without appetition. And no created soul can be purely active, with a perfect freedom. Thus every soul has continual appetition, which is partly free and partly restrained. That is to say, every soul has continually pleasure and pain in some degree.

Accordingly Leibniz takes great interest in the 'uneasiness' in which Locke finds the first movings of

---

[1] *Nouveaux Essais*, bk. ii. ch. 20, § 1 (E. 246 b; G. v. 149). Cf. Locke's *Essay* (corresponding place), with note in Fraser's ed., vol. i. p. 302.

[2] Cf. *Nouveaux Essais*, bk. ii. ch. 21, § 42 (E. 261 b; G. v. 180) : ' I think that fundamentally pleasure is a feeling of perfection, and pain a feeling of imperfection, provided the feeling is sufficiently marked for us to be definitely conscious of it [*s'en apercevoir*].' Cf. *De tribus juris naturae et gentium gradibus* (Mollat, p. 21) : 'Pleasure is nothing else than the sense of increasing perfection.'

[3] See *Nouveaux Essais*, bk. ii. ch. 20, § 6 (E. 248 a; G. v. 151, 152).

desire[1]. This uneasiness is not exactly pleasure or pain, but a vague feeling of discomfort or restlessness, that tends to pass into more definite desire and so to produce action. It is thus for Leibniz the confused perception and undeveloped striving or appetition out of which, by a process of evolution, clear and distinct perception and free volition arise. In so far as this evolution is restrained, we suffer pain: in so far as it proceeds smoothly without impediment, we enjoy pleasure. Thus every soul instinctively seeks its own pleasure: it follows the line of least resistance. This it does in virtue of its own nature, which is to unfold itself spontaneously from within, its present state flowing entirely from its past and holding a prophecy of its future. Soul-activity is pleasure, soul-restraint is pain; and it is of the essence of the soul to be active, for every simple substance is primarily a force.

Freedom, Liberty of Indifference, and the ' Will to will.'

From this Leibniz's view of freedom directly follows. There can be no such thing as a liberty of indifference, an absolutely undetermined choice; for that would imply discontinuity in the life of the soul. An absolutely undetermined choice can only mean that the state of the soul when it makes the choice is not an orderly unfolding of the state of the soul preceding the choice, but is a beginning of action *de novo*. And this is contrary to the

[1] *Nouveaux Essais*, bk. ii. ch. 20, §6 (E. 247; G. v. 150). Cf. ch. 21, §36 (E. 258 b; G. v. 174): 'If you consider your "uneasiness" as a real discomfort [*déplaisir*], I do not admit that in this sense it is the sole goad to action. Most frequently the goad is those little unfelt [*insensible*] perceptions, which we might call imperceptible [*inaperceptible*] pains, were it not that the notion of *pain* implies *apperception*. These little impulses consist in the continual freeing of ourselves from little hindrances, at which our nature works without thinking about it. In this really consists that uneasiness, which we feel without knowing it, which makes us act in passion as well as when we appear most tranquil, for we are never without some activity and motion, which comes merely from this, that nature is always working so as to put herself more at ease.'

very notion of substance. Both in the *Théodicée* and in the *Nouveaux Essais*, Leibniz freely illustrates his view by reference to particular instances, such as the parable of the ass between two equal bundles of hay; and he makes it evident that, as a matter of fact, in every case there is in the state of the soul before the choice is made some determining element of perception. The extreme case, of course, is that of 'willing to will,' resolving to do a thing contrary to our judgment and wishes, merely because we have the power to do it. Leibniz points out that even here our volition is determined by a previous idea, namely that of showing to ourselves or to others that we possess a certain power [1], so that in every case

---

[1] Cf. *Nouveaux Essais*, bk. ii. ch. 21, § 25 (E. 255 b; G. v. 168): 'Men say that, after having known and considered everything, it is still in their power to will, not only what pleases them most, but also the opposite of that, just to show their freedom. But it is to be noticed that this very caprice or obstinacy or, to say the least, this reason which prevents from obeying other reasons, also comes into the balance and makes pleasing to them that which otherwise would not please them at all, and accordingly their choice is always determined by perception. Thus we do not will merely what we will, but what pleases us, although the will may indirectly and, as it were, from afar contribute to make a thing pleasing to us or not.' See also the corresponding passage in Locke's *Essay* (bk. ii. ch. 21, § 24), Fraser's ed., vol. i. p. 327.

A hint of Leibniz's psychology of volition is given in the *Nouveaux Essais*, bk. ii. ch. 21, § 39 (E. 260 b; G. v. 178): 'Several perceptions and inclinations conspire towards complete volition, which is the result of their conflict. There are perceptions and inclinations which are individually imperceptible, but the totality of which produces an uneasiness, which impels us without our seeing the ground of it; several of these perceptions combined together, direct us towards some object or away from it, and then we have desire or fear, also accompanied by an uneasiness, but an uneasiness which does not always amount to pleasure or pain [*déplaisir*]. Finally there are impulses actually accompanied by pleasure and pain, and all these perceptions are either new sensations or images remaining from some past sensation, accompanied or unaccompanied by memory which renews the attractions these same images had in these preceding sensations, and so renews the old impulses in proportion to the vivacity of the imagination. From all these impulses there finally results the *prevailing* effort, which constitutes the full volition. Yet the desires and tendencies of which we are conscious are also frequently called *volitions* (although *less complete*) whether or not they prevail and the will is determined by some reason or perception. The error of abstract indeterminism arises from neglect of sub-conscious perceptions and appetitions. It is thus akin to the error of Descartes and Locke with regard to knowledge, namely that of regarding only self-conscious knowledge or apperception as real knowledge. We have seen[1] that to regard all thought as self-conscious or reflective would make any progress in thought impossible, because it would imply that the mind thinks that it thinks that it thinks *ad infinitum*, and is accordingly never able to go on to any new thought. Similarly, the doctrine of a liberty of indifference, regarding all volition as necessarily developed and conscious, implies a power of willing to will that we will *ad infinitum*. But in fact volition cannot be restricted to deliberate conscious desire or intention. We do and experience many things which ultimately contribute to determine our will, although we

give rise to action. It thus readily follows, that volition can hardly exist without *desire* and *avoidance* [*fuite*] ; for I think we may give this name to the opposite of desire. There is uneasiness not only in the troublesome passions, like hate, cruelty, anger, envy. shame, but also in their opposites, such as love, hope, favour and glory. It may be said that wherever there is desire, there is uneasiness ; but the contrary is not always true, because often we have uneasiness without knowing what we want, and then there is no definite desire. . . . As the final determination [to action] is the result of weighing, I should think it may happen that the most pressing uneasiness does not prevail [in influencing the will] ; for even though it might prevail over each of the opposite tendencies, taken singly, it may be that the others, combined together, overcome it. The mind may even make use of the method of *dichotomy* to make now one and now another set of tendencies prevail, as in an assembly we can make one or another party prevail by a majority of votes, according to the order in which we put the questions. It is true that the mind ought to make provision for this beforehand ; for at the moment of struggle there is no time for these artifices. Everything which strikes us at that moment has a strong influence upon the result and helps to make up a *compound direction*, composed almost as in mechanics, and without some quick turning aside we cannot stop it. *Fertur equis auriga nec audit currus habenas* [The driver is borne on by his horses and the chariot heeds not his guidance'.' The quotation is from Virgil, *Georgics*, i. 514.

[1] Part iii. of this Introduction, p. 127 note.

do not at the time deliberately contemplate that they shall afterwards have this effect [1].

Moral and metaphysical Necessity.

On the other hand, volition is not absolutely necessitated as the system of Spinoza requires. Will is not to be identified with the abstract understanding, whose principle is that of contradiction. Will does not invari-

---

[1] Cf. *Nouveaux Essais*, bk. ii. ch. 21, § 23 (E. 255 b; G. v. 167): 'We do not will to will, but we will to do, and if we willed to will, we should will to will to will and that would go on *ad infinitum*. Yet we must not overlook the fact that by voluntary actions we often contribute indirectly to other voluntary actions, and though we cannot will what we will, as we cannot even judge what we will, we may nevertheless so act beforehand that when the time comes we may judge or will that which we would wish to be able to will or judge to-day. We devote ourselves to the people, the kind of reading, the conditions generally that are favourable to a certain side, we give no heed to what comes from the opposite side, and by these and many other directions which we give to our minds, usually without definite intention and without thinking of it, we succeed in deceiving ourselves or at least in changing ourselves, becoming converts or perverts, according to the experiences we have had.'
There is an interesting suggestion of the views of Leibniz in Montaigne's *Essais*, bk. ii. ch. 14. Leibniz may quite well have read it. 'It is a pleasant fancy,' says Montaigne, 'to think of a mind exactly balanced between two like desires. For it is indubitable that it will never come to a decision, inasmuch as determination and choice imply inequality of value; and if we should be set between the wine and the bacon, with an equal desire to drink and to eat, there is doubtless nothing for it but to die of thirst and hunger. To provide against anything so inconvenient as this, the Stoics, when they were asked how our soul comes to make choice between two indifferent things, so that out of a large number of crowns we take one rather than another, though they are all alike and there is no reason which disposes us to a preference—the Stoics reply that this motion of the soul is extraordinary and exceptional, arising in us from a strange, accidental and fortuitous impulse. It seems to me they might rather have said that nothing comes before us in which there is not some difference, however slight; and that, to sight or to touch, there is always some preference which tempts and draws us, though it be imperceptibly: just as if we suppose a piece of twine equally strong throughout, it is utterly impossible that it should ever break. For in what part of it is the breaking to begin, the flaw to appear? And for it to break in every part at once is against all nature.' Cf. *New Essays*, Introduction, p. 372.

ably act from a reason the opposite of which is self-contradictory: it frequently acts from a sufficient reason, that is to say, from an inclining or probable reason. We do not act merely because we must, because the eternal nature of things makes it absolutely impossible to do otherwise. We act towards an end or ideal which is not a mere fiction of our own imagination, but a recognition of the fitness of things, a more or less clear perception of the best among various possible courses of action. Our will is thus determined by a moral, not a metaphysical necessity, by the inclination which arises from its recognition of the best, however perfect or imperfect that recognition may be. Our will (being our conscious appetition) moves in accordance with our ideals; for these ideals are nothing but our perceptions, the potentialities of our nature, and not merely of our own nature, but of the nature of all things, since our perceptions are representations of the whole universe.

Freedom is Spontaneity + Intelligence.

Accordingly Leibniz, following Aristotle, regards freedom as consisting essentially in spontaneity and intelligence. But intelligence is not to be interpreted merely as the abstract understanding of pure self-consciousness: it includes every degree of perception or representation. There is thus an infinite variety of degrees in freedom, and no actual concrete substance is subject to an absolutely pure necessity, that is, to a necessity which is other than an infinitely small degree of freedom. And as all Monads alike have spontaneity (for they unfold the whole of their life from within themselves), the degree of freedom belonging to any Monad depends on the degree of its intelligence, that is to say, on the degree of clearness and distinctness of its perceptions. Similarly in human beings, an action is free in proportion to the clearness and distinctness of the reasons which determine it. Thus a capricious or wilful action, far from indicating any special freedom of will, is rather lacking in freedom, since its determining reason is so obscure or confused that it is hardly possible to describe it. Its obscurity leads people to overlook it and to fancy that the action is entirely without reason. No human action is undetermined, as none is absolutely necessitated; but the highest freedom accompanies the most perfect knowledge, and God. is the freest of beings, not because He can do whatever He pleases, nor because He always acts spontaneously, from the necessity of His own nature, but because every act of His is determined by infinite wisdom to the best possible ends.

Good and Evil.　The End of Conduct.

So also good and evil are relative terms. Actions are good in so far as they are determined by clear and distinct perceptions, evil in so far as their determining reasons are confused. As error is confused perception and is thus imperfect truth, so sin is the action or appetition which flows from confused perception, and is thus imperfect righteousness. Now since it is of the essence of the soul to be continually active, since its activity is more free the clearer and more distinct are its perceptions, and since pleasure consists in the freedom of its activity, the end of conduct is the highest degree of freedom, which is at once the highest degree of pleasure or felicity and the highest degree of perception or knowledge. Every soul more or less blindly seeks pleasure; but the blinder it is the more does it .tend to seek satisfaction in present, momentary pleasure. Its blindness or confusedness of perception means that it does not think the matter out, that it does not take into account the deeper nature and connexions of things, and thus fails to find the best way to freedom, felicity, wisdom. The soul instinctively tries to take the shortest way to happiness; but the way that is really shortest is apt to appear to purblind souls a roundabout way—an *Umweg*—and so they fail to achieve their end. 'The stone goes by the most direct, but not always the best way towards the centre of the earth, not being able to foresee that it will meet rocks on which it will be broken,' while it would have more nearly attained its end, if it had had the intelligence and the means to turn aside. Even thus, going straight towards present pleasure, we sometimes fall over the precipice of misery[1].' 'We must not abandon those old axioms that the will follows the greatest good it perceives and shuns the greatest evil. That the truest good is so little sought after is mainly due to this, that in matters and on occasions in which the senses have very little influence, most of our thoughts are, so to speak, insensible [*sourdes*] (I call them in Latin, *cogitationes caecae* [blind thoughts]), that is to say, they are void of perception and feeling and consist in the bare use of symbols, like the work of those who make calculations in algebra, without looking from time to time at the geometrical figures. In this respect words usually have the same effect as arithmetical or algebraic symbols. We often reason in words, hardly having the object in mind at all. Now this knowledge cannot move us: something vivid is required that we may be moved. Yet it is thus that men most often think of God, of virtue, of happiness; they speak and reason without definite ideas. Not that they cannot have these ideas ; for they are in their minds. But they do not give themselves the trouble of carrying on the analysis of their ideas[2].'

[1] *Nouveaux Essais*, bk. ii. ch. 21, § 36 (E. 259 a ; G. v. 175).
[2] Ibid. bk. ii. ch. 21, § 35 (E. 257 a ; G. v. 171). As this passage suggests, Leibniz is full of moral optimism. Cf. § 38 of the same chapter (E. 260 a ; G. v. 177): 'When I consider how much ambition and avarice can effect in all those who once set themselves in this line of life, which is almost entirely without sensuous and immediate attractions, I despair of nothing, and I hold that virtue, accompanied as it is by so many substantial blessings, would have infinitely more effect' [than these vices], 'if some happy revolution of the human race were some day to give it vogue and make it fashionable.'

Justice.   Self-love, Love of Man and Love of God.

Self-love, more or less enlightened, is the ground of all
our actions.   And the more enlightened our self-love is,
the higher is the ethical value of our action and the better
are its results.   But as, like all other Monads, our souls
are not mere self-centred atoms but reflect the whole
universe, our self-love is at the same time, according to
its degree, a love for others.   To love others is to desire
their good as we desire our own.   And as it is the
essence of our souls to represent or perceive all other
souls, the more enlightened our own desire of good is,
the more are we seeking the highest good of others and
fulfilling the ends of God.   We can really love others,
and express our love to them only in proportion as we
clearly perceive what is best for them ; and the more
clearly we perceive what is best for ourselves, the more
clearly we perceive what is best for them.   This follows
from the very constitution of our being.   In other words,
we seek our own perfection, however blindly ; and we
are so united to all other men, that in realizing our own
perfection we are also realizing theirs.   Thus the more
enlightened our self-love is the more disinterested does
it become and the more nearly does it approach to a pure
love of God [1].

Accordingly love is the root of law.   Law is not a
merely external arrangement, an arbitrary command, an
expression of bare power.   It is a moral power, and
'moral' means that which is natural to a good man.
'A good man is one who loves all men, so far as reason
allows.   Accordingly,' says Leibniz, 'justice (which is
the ruling virtue of that affection which the Greeks call
φιλανθρωπία) will, if I mistake not, be most fittingly
defined as the *charity of a wise man*, that is to say, charity
in obedience to the dictates of wisdom. . . . Charity is

---

[1] Cf. *On the Notions of Right and Justice*, p. 285 (E. 118 b).

universal benevolence, and benevolence is the habit of loving'.'

Thus the ethical progress of man is an approach to the reality that is in God, a bringing forth of the image of God which is hidden in the soul, through growing enlightenment, that is to say, through the appetition of the soul passing forward to ever clearer and more distinct perceptions. This feature of the philosophy of Leibniz leads Windelband to describe his ethics as expressing 'the philanthropic ideal of morality which was characteristic of the *Aufklärung* period' in Germany. ' "Enlighten thyself, and have a care for the enlightenment of thy fellows : so shall you all be happy ;" that is the philosophy professed by the whole eighteenth century in Germany².'

---

[1] *On the Notions of Right and Justice* (1693), p 283 (E. 118 a). Cf. *Noureaux Essais*, bk. ii. ch. 28, § 5 (E. 286 b; G. v. 232): 'According to this notion' [externally imposed law], 'one and the same action would be at the same time morally good or morally bad, under different legislators, just as our able author' [Locke] 'considered *virtue* as that which is praised, and accordingly one and the same action would be virtuous or not, according to the different opinions of men. Now, as that is not the meaning that is usually given to morally good and virtuous actions, I should prefer for my part to take as the measure of moral good and virtue the invariable rule of reason, which it is the office of God to maintain. So we may be assured that by His means, every moral good becomes also a physical good, or as the ancients said, every honourable act is useful ; in place of which, if we would express the view of our author, we should have to say that moral good or evil is an imposed or *ordained* [*institutif*] good or evil, which he who has command of power endeavours by rewards or penalties to make us do or shun. The good thing is, that what proceeds from the general ordinance of God is conformable to nature or to reason.'

[2] Windelband, *Geschichte der neueren Philosophie*, vol. i. p. 477. Cf. *Von der Glückseligkeit* (E. 673 a ; G. vii. 89) : 'If now a noble [*hohe*] person attains to this, that in the midst of all luxury and honours he yet finds his greatest enjoyment in the activities of his understanding and the practice of virtue, then I hold him doubly noble : in himself, on account of this happiness and true joy of his ; and for others, since it is most certain that this person. on account of his power and insight, can and will also impart light and virtue to many others, for such an imparting means a reflected light upon the giver, and those who have the same common aim can help one another and give new light in the investigation of truth, the increase of human powers, and the promotion of that which is best for all. Thus the exalted [*hohe*] happiness of noble [*hohe*]

and also enlightened persons appears from this that they can do
as much for their happiness as if they had a thousand hands and
a thousand lives, indeed as if they were to live a thousand times
as long as they do.   For our life is to be counted a true life in so
far as we do good in it.   Now he who does much good in a shorter
time is the same as him who lives a thousand times longer; which
is the case with those who can get a thousand and more than a
thousand hands to work along with them, and consequently in
a few years more good can happen for their highest peace and
enjoyment than otherwise many centuries could bring to pass.'

PART IV.

Relation of Leibniz to earlier Thinking, especially to the Peripatetic and Atomist Positions.

No genuine thinker can set himself outside of the philosophic succession. However protestant or revolutionary he may be, his problem is always to a great extent determined for him by the systems of the past. Unless intellect is to be called 'bloodless' these systems may be said to be in his blood ; he could not turn against them if they were not in him, if he had not made them his own. He may cease to seek for truth in the perplexing world, and try to find it in what he takes to be the simplicity and certainty of his own nature ; but, whether he knows it or not, that very nature of his is to a great extent what the tiresome world has made it. He may ignore history or scorn it, but he cannot escape from it.

The conviction of some such truth as this was very strong in Leibniz. He held it against the fashion of his time. The early part of the seventeenth century was a time when the new felt itself to be so very new, the modern so very modern, that, with the infallibility of youth, it could afford to despise what seemed ancient, worn-out, and superseded. When 'our moderns' (as Leibniz frequently calls them) were not contemptuous of older thought they were unconscious of it. In fact, history for them meant a blind tradition, which they had cast off. Descartes, for instance, when he turned from courts and camps to meditation by his own fireside, professed to renounce entirely the methods and results of earlier thinkers, and to draw from his own unaided consciousness a system of truth which no learned sophistry could shake. Descartes was the discoverer of the 'plain man.' Unsophisticated mother-wit will of itself produce absolutely certain knowledge, if only we put the right instrument into its hands, or in other words, if we suggest to it a right method [1]. Thinking thus, Descartes

[1] Cf. *Recherche de la Vérité par les Lumières Naturelles, Œuvres de Descartes* (Cousin), vol. xi. p. 334 : 'My purpose in this work is to bring to light the wealth of our nature, by throwing open to every one the way by which he may find in himself, without borrowing anything from anybody else, the knowledge that is necessary for the conduct of his life, and by which he may afterwards make use of this knowledge to master the most abstruse sciences to which human reason can attain. But lest the magnitude of my plan should at once fill your mind with such amazement that you can no longer find it possible to have any confidence in what I say, I may tell you that what I am undertaking is not so difficult as might be imagined. In fact, the branches of knowledge which are not beyond the reach of the human mind are united together by so wonderful a bond and can be deduced from one another with so complete a necessity, that not much art and skill are required to find them out, provided we begin with the most simple and learn to rise gradually to the most exalted. This I intend to show here, by means of a succession of reasonings so clear and so commonplace that every one will see that, if he has not noticed the same things as I have, it is only because he has not turned his eyes in the right direction nor given his thoughts to the same objects as I have, and that I no more deserve glory for having discovered these things than would a peasant deserve it for having found by chance under his feet a treasure which had long remained hidden, though diligently sought after. . . . I will not inquire into what others have known or have not known. Suffice it to observe that, although all the knowledge we can desire were to be found in books, yet the good they contain is mixed up with so much that is useless and is scattered throughout so many big volumes that life is not long enough to read them, and to recognize what is useful in them would require more ability than to find it out for ourselves. So I hope the reader will not be displeased to find here a shorter way, and that the truths I bring forward will be acceptable to him, although I do not borrow them from Plato or Aristotle but offer them as having value in themselves, like money which has the same worth whether it comes from a peasant's purse or from the treasury.' Cf. *Discourse on Method*, Part vi. (Veitch's Translation, pp. 109 et sqq.). Huet says that 'though Descartes

inevitably turned his back upon the history of thought, counting it little better than 'old wives' fables[1].'

In Leibniz, on the other hand, there is a double reaction—a reaction against the scorn of history, and a reaction against the extremes to which modern philosophy had been carried in its opposition to Scholasticism. The whole bent of Leibniz's thought was against sharp and absolute divisions. Thought does not proceed *per saltum*. In the history of thinking, as in all other history, 'the present is laden with the past and full of the future[2].' Thus, for Leibniz, the Scholastics may have been wrong, but they were not absolutely wrong. And the moderns may be right, but they are not entirely right. Nothing in the past is to be completely set at naught, for out of the past the present has come. The one cannot be

had carefully studied the ancient philosophers and several of the moderns, he yet affected to appear ignorant of them, in order that he might be regarded as the sole discoverer of his doctrine. In this several of his disciples have too thoroughly followed his example; for they have imitated his feigned ignorance by cultivating a real ignorance.' *Traité philosophique de la faiblesse de l'Esprit humain*, bk. iii. ch. 10. Voltaire also gives point to the general opinion regarding Descartes by the satirical suggestion that Descartes had 'never read anything, not even the Gospels.' *Les Systèmes*, line 37; *Œuvres Complètes*, vol. x. p. 169.

[1] It was not only the *fact* of a revolution in thought that gave rise to the Cartesian disregard of history: the very nature of the revolution itself contributed to this end. The substitution of a mechanical for an *a priori* dogmatic way of explaining things was inevitably connected with a fresh interest in the study of mathematics, and this led to a preference of mathematical to historical methods in philosophy. Cf. *Règles pour la Direction de l'Esprit*, *Œuvres de Descartes* (Cousin), vol. xi. p. 211: 'We shall never be mathematicians, even although we were to know by heart all the demonstrations of other people, if we are not capable of solving by ourselves all kinds of problems. In the same way, though we have read all the reasonings of Plato and Aristotle, *that* will not make us philosophers if we cannot bring to any question a steady judgment. In such a case we should, indeed, have learned not a science, but history.' Also, p. 209: 'Regarding the object of our study we must inquire, not what others have thought nor what we ourselves surmise, but what we can see clearly and manifestly [*avec évidence*], or what we can deduce with certainty. This is the only way to obtain real knowledge [*la science*].'

[2] Cf. Wallace, *Logic of Hegel* (2nd ed.); *Prolegomena*, pp. 203 sqq.

understood without the other.   Leibniz from his earliest
days had been a vast reader of books, and his erudition
tempered his imaginative optimism with reverence and
caution. Thus his philosophizing most often takes the form
of hypothesis or suggestion rather than that of dogma or
demonstration.   In the Kantian sense his philosophy is,
of course, 'dogmatic' and not 'critical'; but to some
extent he foreshadows the 'critical spirit[1].' As a thinker,
he counts as foreign to him nothing that men have
thought, and his ideal philosophy would be a philosophy
which says clearly all that all previous thinkers have
stammeringly tried to say.   So people have called him an
'eclectic,' and possibly his fame has suffered from the
imputation.   But there is no lack of originality in the
metaphysical romance[2]' he brings us, for he is to be
called an eclectic mainly in contrast with the Cartesian
extremists, who repudiated all obligation to the past.
While convinced of the value of his own hypotheses,
Leibniz rather glories in his indebtedness, rejoicing to
find himself in the philosophic succession.   'I despise
almost nothing,' he says, 'except judicial astrology and
trickeries of that kind[3].'   'It happens somehow that the
thoughts of other people are usually not displeasing to me,
and I appreciate them all, though in divers degrees[4].'
'There is as much or more reason to beware of those who,
most often through ambition, claim to put forth something
new as to mistrust old impressions.   And after having
devoted a great deal of thought both to the old and the
new, I have come to the conclusion that most of the
received doctrines can be taken in a right sense.   So that

[1] 'In Leibniz the dogmatic philosophy comes in all points so
near to the critical that only one step is needed to rise from the
point of view of the one to that of the other.' K. Fischer, Gesch.
d. neueren Phil., vol. ii. ch. 21, § 1.
[2] Hegel, Gesch. d. Philosophie, vol. iii. p. 408. Kant also speaks of
the universe of Leibniz as 'a kind of enchanted world' [eine Art
von bezauberter Welt]. Rosenkranz, i. 521 ; Hartenstein, iii. 445.
[3] Lettre à Bourguet (1714), (G. iii. 562).
[4] Specimen Dynamicum (1695) (G. Math. vi. 236).

I wish clever men would seek to satisfy their ambition rather by building and making progress than by going back and destroying[1].' 'This system' [Leibniz's own] 'appears to combine Plato with Democritus, Aristotle with Descartes, the Scholastics with the moderns, theology and ethics with reason. It seems to take the best from all sides, and then to go further than any one has yet gone. . . . I see now what Plato meant when he regarded matter as an imperfect and transitory thing ; what Aristotle intended by his entelechy; what is that promise of another life, which Democritus himself made, according to Pliny ; how far the Sceptics were right in crying out against the senses ; how animals are automata, as Descartes says, and have nevertheless souls and feeling, as people think ; how a rational explanation is to be given of the views of those who attribute life and perception to all things—such people as Cardan, Campanella, and (better than these, the late Countess of Conway (a Platonist , and our friend, the late M. François Mercure Van Helmont (though otherwise bristling with unintelligible paradoxes), with his friend, the late Mr. Henry More[2].'

---

[1] *Nouveaux Essais*, bk. i. ch. 2, § 21 (E. 219 a ; G. v. 92).

[2] Ibid. bk. i. ch. 1 (E. 205 a ; G. v. 64). Leibniz might have added the name of Spinoza, who says that 'all individual bodies are animate, though in different degrees.' *Ethics*, Pt. ii. prop. 13, *Scholium.* Cf. *Lettre à Basnage* (1698) (E. 153 b ; G. iv. 523) : ' When we penetrate deeply into things, we observe more reason than would be believed in most of the sects of the philosophers. The lack of reality in the things of sense, according to the Sceptics ; the Pythagorean and Platonist reduction of everything to harmonies, numbers, ideas, and perceptions ; the "One" and even the one Whole of Parmenides and Plotinus, without any Spinozism ; the Stoic connexion, compatible with the spontaneity of others ; the vital philosophy of the Cabbalists and Hermetics, who attribute feeling to everything ; the forms and entelechies of Aristotle and the Scholastics ; and on the other hand the mechanical explanation of all particular phenomena, according to Democritus and the moderns – these are all combined together as in a centre of perspective, viewed from which the object (confused from every other point of view) reveals its regularity and the harmony of its parts. We have failed to accomplish this by our sectarian spirit, limiting ourselves by rejecting others.' The writings of Leibniz are full of similar passages.

Descartes himself 'took a good part of his best thoughts' from the men of old [1]. And thus, Leibniz would say, it is better frankly to own our obligations and to go back to the past that we may, if possible, draw from it neglected truths, by the aid of which our present theories may be improved and thinking may go forward. For the idea of progress on the basis of history controls the mind of Leibniz, to whatever objects he directs his thinking [2]. Accordingly, admitting the value of the modern mechanical philosophy, and yet being conscious of its imperfections and dissatisfied with some of its results, Leibniz turns back to Scholasticism and its roots in the philosophy of Greece, to 'recover the gold from the mire,' and so build up a more perfect system [3]. Thus Dillmann rightly contends that Leibniz can be properly understood only if we recognize that his main endeavour is to reconcile the modern mechanical view of things with the ancient doctrine of 'substantial forms.' Yet it must not be forgotten that Leibniz sought to effect this reconciliation by modifying and reconstructing, and not by merely dovetailing one system into another.

The way of explaining phenomena by reference to 'substantial forms,' which Descartes and Gassendi rejected in favour of a mechanical explanation of nature, was a growth of the Peripatetic philosophy, which in course of time had run to seed. It sprang originally from the sound Aristotelian idea that all events or particular things are to be explained by reference to active principles, not

---

[1] *Lettre à Nicaise* (1692) (E. 120 a ; G. ii. 534). Cf. *De stilo philosophico Nizolii* (1670), § 24 (E. 67 a ; G. iv. 154).

[2] Thus one of his latest (and not least able) expositors, E. Dillmann, offers Leibniz a homage which he himself would at once have condemned. For Dillmann regards the philosophy of Leibniz as final and all-sufficient, if only it be rightly understood. 'The Monadology is the most perfect fruit of philosophical reflexion, the most complete and brilliant system in the history of philosophy.' (*Neue Darstellung*, &c., p. 525.) There is a strange irony in the fact that so able and devoted a disciple has so completely missed his master's spirit.

[3] *Lettre à Remond* (1714) (E. 704 b ; G. iii. 625).

entirely external to the events or things, but appearing in
them.   But the meaning, the spirit of Aristotle's method
was lost sight of.   'Find a principle, a form, of any kind,'
came to be the rule of explanation.   And thus the number
of 'substantial forms' or principles of substance was
multiplied indefinitely, while, in addition, the most
minute changes in substances were each explained by
reference to some 'accidental form' or principle of
accident.   Anything sufficed as an explanation so long
as it was called a form.   Thus when no intelligible
account of a phenomenon could readily be given it was
attributed to some hidden principle (*qualitas occulta*),
which was described by the name of the phenomenon to
be explained.   Thus, for instance, Toletus[1] gives us the
valuable information that 'the substantial form of fire is
an active principle by which fire, with heat as its instrument, produces fire.'   After making this amazing statement he recollects that fire is sometimes produced by
things other than fire, and he proceeds with grave
elaboration to prove that 'fire can result from all the
substantial forms capable of producing it in air, in water,
or in anything else.'

This may be the *reductio ad absurdum* of the Peripatetic
Scholasticism ; for indeed *petitio principii* could no farther
go.   It is almost worse than the *virtus dormitiva* of
Molière's satire.   But the author does not appear to have
seen the humour of it.   Can we wonder, then, that
Descartes turned his back upon history ?   To him it
seemed that an explanation to be an explanation must at
least be intelligible.   There can be truth and certainty, he
thought, only where there is clearness and distinctness.
Accordingly all these hidden principles and inexplicable
forms must be thrown aside as philosophical lumber, a
screen of ignorance and a source of confusion.   In true
explanation there must be no obscurities, fancies, or

[1] Francisco de Toledo (1532–1596), a Spanish cardinal and theo-
logian, author of *Summa Casuum Conscientiae*

guesses; but it must consist in tracing the necessary connexions of things or finding definitely measurable relations between them—connexions and relations which the understanding can clearly grasp. That is, in brief, the mechanical view of what explanation ought to be, as the Cartesians held it in opposition to the Scholastics.

Now Leibniz, as we have seen, is not so exclusively enamoured of the clear and distinct as Descartes was. He thinks Descartes has gone too far in the zeal of his reformation. Doubtless the Scholastics were guilty of gross absurdities, but if we are to be satisfied with no explanation which is not absolutely perfect in its intelligibility, we shall have to do without explanations of most things, and our science will perforce be very abstract and very limited. For to be perfectly intelligible or clear and distinct in the Cartesian sense, an explanation must either be a self-evident truth or must be logically reducible to such a truth. And Leibniz maintains that, while ideas or abstractions ('possible' things) may be capable of such explanation as this, it is impossible so thoroughly to explain any actually existing finite thing or phenomenon. We may 'clearly and distinctly' explain how such a thing is possible; we cannot 'clearly and distinctly' explain why it exists. No absolute reason can be given for its existence; we must be content with a sufficient reason. An examination of the measurable relations or connexions of things does not yield an exhaustive account of their nature, and accordingly, while such an examination is valuable so far as it goes, it requires to be supplemented by other considerations. The infinite complexity of things makes a perfect analysis impossible, and consequently, if we confine ourselves to a strictly mathematical method, our science must remain a science of abstractions and not of actual things as they exist.

Leibniz, then, admits the value of the mechanical view as regards phenomena, considered in abstraction from the realities of which they are the phenomena, but he returns to the older philosophy for an explanation of the realities themselves.   Descartes has done well in clearing away the great mass of forms, which explained nothing, and in accounting for all the changes in nature by regarding them as due to variations in the distribution of one constant quantity of motion.   But motion is not a deep enough principle to explain reality.   It is entirely apparent, phenomenal, on the surface ; and therefore it cannot explain that which is half-hidden, which comes and goes, which passes from potentiality into actuality.   But this is the characteristic of every real thing, every *res completa*. In so far as it exists, and is not merely possible, it has come into being ; it is its nature to pass from potentiality to actuality.   We cannot have a better example of this than the human soul, in which we find continuous process along with unity and self-identity.   Thus it seems to Leibniz that real things or substances are to be conceived as analogous to the human soul, as forms or living principles in a sense deeper than that of the later Scholastics, who had, indeed, almost entirely emptied the term 'form' of signification.   Going back to the source of these views that had so degenerated, Leibniz finds the nearest approach to what he is seeking in Aristotle's 'entelechy,' the principle of a thing in the sense of its implicit perfect realization, what it is *in* the thing to be or become.   Thus Leibniz supplements the Cartesian physics by the idea that mere body or matter is an abstraction, existing nowhere, and that every real existence has a soul or living principle.   And in this way the Monadology restores to philosophy, with new force and meaning, the infinite number of forms which was the chief feature of the Peripatetic philosophy.

Leibniz's relation to Atomist philosophy is for the most part a negative one, and it is hardly necessary to add anything to what has incidentally been said regarding it. He is on the side of modern science in rejecting the idea of an absolute vacuum.   And when he sometimes speaks

of the Monads as atoms his object is probably to show
that the Monadology expresses clearly what the atomists
are groping for.   His leading thought in this connexion
is that a real whole presupposes a real unit, that is to say,
a unit which is essentially connected with the whole,
representative of it, and not in a merely accidental or
indeterminate relation to it.   The atomists are right, he
would say, in insisting upon a real unit, but, on their
view of reality, it is impossible to find any such unit [1].

Leibniz's 'Sufficient Reason' in relation to the 'Cause' of Descartes and Spinoza.

When we look, not at what Leibniz was himself aware
of doing but at what he actually did without clearly
knowing it, we may regard his use of the principle of
sufficient reason as a development of what was implied in
the use which Descartes and Spinoza made of the notion
of ' cause.' Descartes, as we have seen [2], develops his
system under the guidance of the principle of contradiction
alone.   But in order to pass from the subjectivity of the
pure Ego to an objective, external reality, he finds it
necessary to have recourse to the principle that everything
must have an efficient cause which is at least as real as the
effect (and may be more real than it).   This principle he
assumes without any attempt to demonstrate its validity,
and it is the real basis of his proofs, in the first place, of
the existence of God, and in the second place, of the
existence of an external world [3]. The proofs of the
existence of God form the keystone of Descartes's system.
Their function is to make up for the inevitable imperfections of a logic based solely on the principle of contradiction. Clinging, as he does, to the dualism of mind and

---

[1] Cf. this Introduction, Part ii. pp. 27 sqq.
[2] This Introduction, Part ii. pp. 58 sqq.
[3] Cf. *Méditation III* and the mathematically arranged arguments
in the *Réponses aux Deuxièmes Objections*.

matter, of thought and external existence, Descartes could not rest satisfied with the *idea* of a most perfect being. He must get beyond the *idea* to the *reality*; he must justify not one or another idea but thought itself. In the characteristics of 'clearness' and 'distinctness' in ideas he had found a criterion for the consistency of thought with itself. A clear and distinct idea completely satisfied thought, but it still remained to be shown that such an idea has objective validity; that there actually exists that which it represents. Now according to Descartes, it is the truthfulness, the consistency, the goodness of an actually existing God (who would not be perfect had He not these qualities) that assure to us the validity of our clear and distinct ideas. 'Even the principle,' says Descartes, 'which I have already taken for a rule, namely, that all the things which we clearly and distinctly conceive are true, is certain only because God is or exists, and because He is a perfect Being, and because all that we possess is derived from Him. . . . If we did not know that all which we possess of real and true proceeds from a perfect and infinite Being, however clear and distinct our ideas might be, we should have no ground on that account for the assurance that they possessed the perfection of being true [1].' Accordingly, as regards real existence (apart from that of the pure Ego), everything in Descartes's system ultimately turns upon this unexplained principle of cause, by means of which he proves the existence of God, and which he again employs in establishing the reality of the world. God must exist, for otherwise no adequate cause can be assigned for the existence of the idea of God in us. And again, we must postulate the real existence of external

---

[1] *Method*, Part iv. (Veitch's Tr., p. 80). Cf. *Méditation IV*: 'It is impossible that God should ever deceive me; since in all fraud and deceit one meets with some kind of imperfection; and although it may seem that to be able to deceive is a mark of cleverness or of power, the wish to deceive always indicates, without a doubt, feebleness or malice; and accordingly such a wish cannot exist in God.' Cf. Hegel, *Geschichte der Phil.* iii. p. 319.

things as the cause of certain ideas in us, unless we are to suppose that God deceives us [1].

Spinoza takes the one substance, God, as his starting-point of absolute certainty, and accordingly proofs of the existence of God have for him no meaning. Nevertheless, he does not altogether dispense with the notion of cause. Ostensibly he reduces the relation of cause and effect to a logical connexion, like that between a geometrical figure and its properties. But he makes use of the notion of cause to introduce variety into the perfect unity of substance by describing it as cause of itself (*causa sui*). And in his distinction between *natura naturans* and *natura naturata* he endeavours, by a further application of the notion of cause, to bridge the gulf which his logic has set between the infinite (as purely indeterminate) and finite or determinate existence. *Natura naturans* is substance expressed in attributes or ' God as the free cause of all that is.' *Natura naturata* is ' all that follows from the necessity of the Divine nature or from any one of the attributes of God, i. e. all modes of God's attributes, considered as things which exist in God, and without God can neither exist nor be conceived [2].' In short, *causa sui* or substance is analyzed into two moments, cause (*natura naturans*) and effect (*natura naturata*); but both of these are ultimately the same thing. Apart from this distinction without a difference it would be impossible for Spinoza to identify his infinite substance with the actual world. And yet, in spite of it, for Spinoza the finite, as finite, remains unreal.

Now this notion of cause, which Descartes and Spinoza employ without attempting to explain or justify it, is, in a more general form, acknowledged by Leibniz as an independent logical principle, that of sufficient reason. There must be, not merely an adequate cause but a sufficient reason for the existence of each individual thing.

---

[1] Cf. *Méditation VI*, passim.
[2] *Ethics*, Part i. prop. 29, *Scholium*.

And as we have seen [1], the sufficiency of the reason rests
ultimately on the nature of God as perfect in wisdom,
goodness, and power. Manifestly there is here a working-
out of what is more vaguely implied in Descartes's
repeated references to the perfection of the character of
God as our warrant for the reality of things. And the
argument of Spinoza (however inconsistent it may be) is
based on the conviction that every finite thing must find
its place in the one all-embracing system, that is to say,
must follow from the nature of God in whom are all
perfections. Thus the addition of the principle of sufficient reason to that of contradiction is not an entirely
novel suggestion on the part of Leibniz, but is an out-
growth of what was already involved in the reasonings of
his immediate predecessors. It is a step towards the
reconciling of their inconsistencies by bringing into clear
consciousness a principle which they blindly and imperfectly employed.

The Philosophy of Wolff.

The philosophy of Leibniz suffered grievously at the
hands of his immediate disciples [2]. Probably this was
inevitable. Few of his writings were published in his
lifetime, and his philosophical opinions were dispersed
through masses of manuscript which might well be the
despair of his friends. And the philosophical system

---

[1] This Introduction, Part ii. p. 66.

[2] 'It has been with Leibniz as with several philosophers of
antiquity, who might have said : "May God preserve us from our
friends ; as for our enemies, we ourselves shall be able to protect
ourselves from them."' Kant, *Entdeckung nach der alle neue Kritik
der reinen Vernunft durch eine ältere entbehrlich gemacht werden soll.*
Rosenkranz, i. 478 ; Hartenstein, iii. 390. Cf. Wallace, *Logic of
Hegel* (2nd ed.) ; *Prolegomena,* ch. 17. Kant himself in one of his
earlier writings (*Träume eines Geistersehers,* &c.; Rosenkranz, vii. 45 ;
Hartenstein, iii. 58) speaks of 'Leibniz's amusing idea, according
to which we might perhaps swallow in our coffee atoms destined
to become human souls.' And a naturalist of the end of last
century, Otto F. Müller, thought that he had discovered Monads
under the microscope !

itself must have seemed as broken as was the expression of it. The two principles of contradiction and sufficient reason stood side by side, and there was no clear account of the relation between them. A system with two independent principles can have no stability, and this defect must somehow be removed. On the other hand, Newton had triumphed in the long controversy, and his fame had led to Leibniz's discredit. Leibniz's metaphysics seemed in some points incompatible with the Newtonian physics, and must therefore to some extent be modified. This systematizing and modifying of the philosophy of Leibniz were accomplished by Christian Wolff (1679–1754), who himself, however, strongly objected to being called a mere disciple of Leibniz, or an elaborator of the Leibnitian philosophy.

Wolff's position may be regarded as in some respects a return to the Cartesian attitude of mind. His solution of the difficulty arising from the supposition of two co-ordinate first principles is to make the principle of sufficient reason a logical inference from that of contradiction, and thus to make the law of contradiction the one supreme law of thought. He holds that the difference between 'something' and 'nothing' is absolute, 'something' being that of which there is some notion, while 'nothing' is that of which there is no notion[1]. Thus everything must have a sufficient reason, i. e. *some* reason why it exists rather than does not exist, for otherwise something would proceed out of nothing. But *ex nihilo nihil fit* : there is no middle term between 'something' and 'nothing[2].' So in Wolff the antithesis of being and not-being is supreme, to the exclusion of the notion of becoming. 'The impossible is nothing.' And on the other hand, 'the possible is always something[3].' It ought logically to follow that everything possible is actual, and that there is no distinction between essence and existence. But at this point the

---

[1] *Ontologia*, 57, 59.	[2] Ibid. 70.

[3] Ibid. 101, 102.

Leibnitian influence reasserts itself, and Wolff becomes
confused.   His ruthless logic gives way.   'Besides the
possibility of a being, something else is still needed for
its existence.'   'Existence or reality is the complement of
possibility [1].'   As an illustration of what he means he
takes the case of a tree which is potentially in the seed,
but which requires for its actual development (its existence *as* a tree) the co-operation or complement of other
existing things.   Thus Wolff returns to the Leibnitian
distinction between the 'possible' and the 'compossible,'
after he has emptied of all meaning the principle of
sufficient reason, on which the distinction rests.   To put
it otherwise, if the actual existing 'something' is more
than a merely possible 'something' (as Wolff's position
here implies), then there must be a middle term between
the actual 'something' and 'nothing.'   And this, of
course, is flatly contradictory of Wolff's original principle.

Thus while Wolff makes a show of logical completeness
and system, he is really hacking in pieces the philosophy
of Leibniz.   He is fascinated by its individualist element,
the self-sufficiency and mutual exclusiveness of the Monads,
which we have seen to be connected, in the thinking of
Leibniz, with the survival of a narrow interpretation of
the principle of contradiction [2].   Wolff carries to an extreme this tendency (which, after all, is not the supreme
power in Leibniz's thought), and gives us, as the outcome
of the bare principle of contradiction, an abstract indi-
vidualism, just as Spinoza had already from the same
principle developed an abstract universalism or pantheism.
It is because of the essentially dogmatic character of the
principle that such extremes can each be represented as
flowing from it.   As employed by Spinoza and by Wolff
the principle can legitimately yield nothing but the bare
self-identity of the data or assumptions with which each
begins his work.   Accordingly (as in this case) if the

---

[1] *Ontologia*, 173, 174.
[2] This Introduction, Part ii. p. 68.

presuppositions are in complete opposition to one another, we may have two contrary philosophical systems, both apparently flowing from the same first principle.

Wolff, then, rejects the law of continuity and returns to a position which has some analogy with that of Descartes. Ostensibly his philosophy is a Monadology; really it is a kind of combination of Monadology with Atomism [1]. The Cartesian dualism is restored in the form of a distinction between spiritual and physical Monads. The spiritual Monads alone, in Wolff's opinion, deserve the name of Monads. The others are 'elements of things,' *atomi naturae.* These physical atoms or unconscious Monads are no longer regarded as living mirrors, representing or perceiving the whole universe. They are still automata, but they are no longer souls. They have nothing in common with the spiritual Monads except the characteristics of unity, simplicity, and activity. Thus the whole of Leibniz's hypotheses regarding unconscious thinking, *petites perceptions,* &c., are thrown aside, and we have, in place of Descartes's two substances (thought and extension), two sets of independent particular substances, the phenomena of the one set being thoughts and of the other set motions. As an inevitable consequence of this, the system of pre-established harmony, as Leibniz conceived it, disappears also. Wolff retains the name, but he regards the harmony not as a hypothesis by which to explain the relations of each independent particular substance to every other, but merely as an explanation of the connexion between soul and body, between spiritual atoms or Monads and corporeal atoms. According to Leibniz there could be no real interaction between Monads. But Wolff's 'atoms of nature,' being purely physical, do really influence one another. He sees no difficulty in

[1] Cf. Schelling, *Sämmtliche Werke,* vol. vi. p. 116: 'As often happens, the immediate successors of Leibniz set aside the really speculative part of his doctrine, the Monadology. For example the most celebrated of them, Wolff, admits it into his system only in the guise of a hypothesis.'

holding that motion can be transferred from one to another [1]. His difficulty is the original Cartesian problem— How can a purely thinking substance influence an absolutely non-thinking substance, or how can motion pass into thought? And the pre-established harmony is, in Wolff's view, preferable to Occasionalism merely because it means one large and comprehensive initial miracle rather than an endless series of miraculous interventions of God.

The natural, physical world is thus, according to Wolff, entirely subject to mechanical laws. There is, indeed, a realm of final causes, but the ends of things are completely external to the things themselves. The final cause of a physical substance is not, as in the view of Leibniz, to be found in the nature of the substance itself, in its tendency towards self-realization, but in a law imposed upon it from outside. Thus the Wolffian teleology becomes almost childish, and suggests at times the naive explanations of things which are to be found in such writers as Bernardin de St. Pierre, who tells us that the melon is made large in comparison with other fruits to indicate that it ought to be eaten not in solitude but *en famille*, and that the cow with only one calf has four teats because the human race is fond of milk. Wolff hardly rises to this height, but he regards the stars as existing to give us light at night, and he points out that 'the light of day is of great advantage to us; it enables us to carry on comfortably certain works which comparative darkness would make impossible or difficult, and also more expen-

---

[1] Here again Wolff's position is glaringly inconsistent. His physical atoms or Monads are supposed to have a unity like that of the Leibnitian Monads. Yet he denies to them that which, for Leibniz, is the principle of this unity, viz. a soul differing not in kind but in degree from the conscious and rational soul. The *atomi naturae* are, in short, neither atoms nor Monads, but a contradictory jumble of the characteristics of both. Wolff regards the *atomi naturae* as 'in themselves indivisible,' and thus distinguishes them from *atomi materiales*, which are 'in themselves divisible,' but which cannot be actually divided by any natural power. See *Cosmologia*, §§ 182 sqq., 186 sqq. and 232.

sive[1].' This doctrine of final causes is a most essential part of the Wolffian system. For, according to Wolff, although nature is ultimately explicable by purely mechanical laws, we cannot actually reduce it to its ultimate elements, and consequently, in explaining physical phenomena as they are presented to us, we must continually have recourse to final causes. So also, while Wolff, adopting the phrase of Leibniz, speaks of God as freely choosing to create 'the best of all possible worlds,' he takes 'best' as meaning not 'best on the whole,' but rather 'best for mankind.' Thus the optimism of Wolff is as shallow and arbitrary as his teleology, and it is not surprising that Kant, even in the early years when he followed Wolff on most points, deserted him in this matter, and turned back to views more akin to the greater thoughts of Leibniz.

Relation of the Philosophy of Leibniz to that of Kant.

In the earliest writings of Kant (who, through his teacher Knutzen, was bred a Wolffian), questions regarding space are discussed—questions, for instance, as to the reason why our space has three dimensions and as to the possibility and reality of other spaces having more than three dimensions. Kant was evidently already somewhat dissatisfied with the current Wolffian view of space and was beginning the course of inquiry that ultimately led to the doctrine of the Transcendental Aesthetic, a doctrine more in harmony with the view of Leibniz than with that of Wolff[2]. According to Wolff, 'real' space must be distinguished from 'imaginary' space, although

---

[1] *Vernünftige Gedanken von den Absichten der natürlichen Dinge.* Cf. *Ausführliche Nachricht von seinen eigenen Schriften,* §§ 186 sqq.

[2] 'Leibniz's doctrine of sense as confused thought—confused in such a way as to make us represent the world as an order of things in space and time—though Kant explicitly rejects it, is in fact rather elaborated than superseded by his doctrine of space and time as forms of sensibility, under which alone experience is possible, but which prevent what is true of phenomena from being true of things in themselves, and knowledge from reaching the totality which it seeks.' T. H. Green, *Works,* vol. iii. p. 135.

the results obtained from consideration of the notion of
'imaginary' space may justifiably be applied to 'real'
space [1]. 'Real' space is the order of co-existing things [2]
and is inseparable from the things themselves. God
alone can have a perfectly adequate notion of it and can
thus actually perceive its continuity. But we can form
an abstract or 'imaginary' notion of space, by thinking
it as distinct from (or indifferent to) the co-existing things
of which it is an 'order'; and this imaginary space is,
of course, homogeneous and continuous. The space of
mathematics and physics is thus 'imaginary space'; but
it is such that the laws of mathematics and physics are
valid in relation to 'real' space. Manifestly we have here
neither the view of Leibniz nor that of Newton, but a
doctrine which points to a possible reconciliation between
them. On the one hand, space is not merely confused
perception. As space it has reality: it is a real order in
which physical things exist. But, on the other hand,
this real space is not the space of the mathematician.
He deals with a kind of projection or symbol of it, and
thus the Newtonian position also is without Wolff's
assent. It might easily be shown that the Wolffian
doctrine of space is riddled with inconsistencies, of a kind
similar to those which have been noticed in Wolff's
account of individual substances. But the matter of
main interest is that Kant received the problem of space
in the form which Wolff had given it [3], and that through-

---

[1] *Ontologia*, 599.

[2] In analogy with time which is 'the order of successive things
in a continuous series,' space is defined as 'the order of simultaneous things, in so far as they co-exist.' *Ontologia*, 589. Cf.
Cosmologia, 56.

[3] Kant's criticism of Leibniz illustrates this. Cf. *Fortschritte der
Metaphysik seit Leibniz und Wolff* (Rosenkranz, i. 516; Hartenstein,
iii. 441): 'The principle of the identity of indiscernibles (*princi-
pium identitatis indiscernibilium*) is that, if from *A* and *B*, which, in
respect of all their internal characteristics (of quality and of
quantity) are entirely alike, we make a concept as of two different
things, we are in error, and we ought to have taken them for one
and the same thing (*numero eadem*). Leibniz could not admit that

out the writings of his pre-critical period, we find Kant
working towards a view of space in which the Leibnitian
and Newtonian positions shall be reconciled. Although
he does not himself express it in this way, his problem
might fairly be regarded as that of finding a single conception of space which can take the place both of the
'real' and of the 'imaginary' space of Wolff. In what
sense can space be regarded as at once real and ideal?
Not in the Wolffian sense; for that practically involves
a *circulus in definiendo*: 'simultaneous or co-existing'
physical things presuppose space. Nor is the Newtonian
view more satisfactory, for, while it recognizes that space
is prior to actual cases of spatial existence and while it
maintains the reality of space, it implies that the whole
universe is set in space and that the spatial system of
relations has a real existence independent of the things
related. Accordingly, through a course of thinking which
we need not here trace[1], Kant arrives at the position which
he expounds in the *Critique of Pure Reason*, namely, that
space is a form presupposed in the possibility of our
sense-experience. It is not in any way given *ab extra*;
but it is the condition of there being externality for us.
It is not a thing in itself, a real object; but as it is a perfectly pure perception, free from all the contingent detail

we could still distinguish them through their places in space (as it
is possible to perceive quite similar and equal spaces outside of one
another without being able to say that they are one and the same
space, for otherwise we could put the whole of infinite space into
a cubic inch or less). Leibniz could not admit this, for he recognizes no other distinction among things than that which is made
through notions [*Begriffe*], and refuses to allow any way of representation specifically distinct from this, such as intuition [*Anschauung*], and more especially intuition *a priori*. On the contrary
he thought that this must be reduced to pure notions [*Begriffe*] of
co-existence or succession, and thus he set himself against common
sense, which will never be persuaded that the existence of a drop
of water in one place makes it impossible for a perfectly similar
and equal drop to exist in another place.'
[1] For a full account see Caird's *Critical Philosophy of Kant*, vol. i.
Introduction, ch. 5, especially pp. 164-168 and 178-182. Also
bk. i. ch. 2, pp. 304, 305. Cf. Hutchison Stirling, *Text-Book to Kant*,
pp. 34-43 and 366 sqq.

of sense, it satisfies the requirements of Newtonian mathematics even better than if it were an independent entity. On the other hand, while it belongs to perception or direct intuition and is therefore not, as Leibniz and Wolff held, a relation or order among things which are prior to it, yet it is subjective or ideal, it belongs to our minds, and accordingly the difficulties inseparable from the Newtonian view of space (as expounded by Clarke, for instance) are avoided.

But mere sense-perception under the forms of space and time is not, according to Kant, a complete experience. It requires the complement of conception, which is the function of the understanding.   Here Kant believed himself to be in complete opposition to Leibniz, and yet it may well be doubted whether the opposition is really so great as Kant supposed it to be.   In the *Critique of Pure Reason* Kant does draw a much sharper line between perception and conception than Leibniz did.   Kant may be said to regard the difference as one of kind, while for Leibniz it is a difference of degree.   Leibniz, as we have seen, gave to perception an exceedingly wide meaning, a meaning which includes conception and representation of every kind, whether conscious or unconscious.   But Kant's 'perception' is limited to sense-representation. Nevertheless Kant's 'perception' is avowedly abstract, and the confused perception, which is Leibniz's name for sense-knowledge, is abstract also, though in a somewhat different way.   In fact, for Kant the distinction between perception and conception is a distinction between abstract elements in a concrete whole of experience, while the corresponding distinction in Leibniz is a distinction between degrees of perfection in one quality or function. Thus for Kant sense-perception is abstract, because its reality always implies a complementary element, while for Leibniz it is abstract because it is imperfectly developed, because it contains the potentiality of greater perfection.   The weakness of the Kantian position is its

tendency to over-sharpen the distinction between perception and conception by ignoring the idea of development,
while the defect of Leibniz is his inclination to define the
common quality or function ('perception') by its lowest
rather than its highest terms, to interpret it, not as essentially self-consciousness, which is its most perfect development, but as mere representation or multiplicity in unity,
to which consciousness and self-consciousness are added
characteristics [1]. Yet while Kant makes an advance from
the position of Leibniz, they are on similar lines, and we
can read their reconciliation in Hegel [2].

Leibniz does not give any clear account of the relations
between the principle of contradiction and that of sufficient reason, as he uses them in his philosophy ; but it is
evident that he considered them to be, in some way,
ultimately in harmony. The tendency of Kant, on the
other hand, is to emphasize the distinction between them,
while treating each, apart from the other, as abstract.
The course of Kant's pre-critical thinking makes this clear.
He begins with the Wolffian view that the principle of
sufficient reason is reducible to that of contradiction [3], and
accordingly, that the principle of contradiction is the sole
ultimate principle of knowledge. But gradually he comes
to see that the principle of contradiction has to do with
nothing but the form of thought and that it yields merely
a self-consistent system of knowledge, based on dogmatic

---

[1] In this, I think, there is to be found the explanation of the
separation (almost amounting to a distinction of kind) between
rational souls and the other Monads, which Leibniz makes with
such apparent inconsistency. Cf. this Introduction, Part iii. p. 116.

[2] 'The doctrines of Leibniz formed the permanent atmosphere
of Kant's mind. His reading of Hume in middle life no doubt
helped to determine the mode in which he absorbed and transformed them ; but it was upon them, as we find in the *Critique* no
less than in his earlier writings, that his mind constantly worked,
and there would be a better case, at any rate, for describing him
as a corrected and developed Leibniz than for putting him in such
a relation to any one else.' T. H. Green, *Works*, vol. iii. p. 134.

[3] Cf. *Principiorum primorum cognitionis metaphysicae nova dilucidatio*
(1755) (Rosenkranz, i. 4 ; Hartenstein, iii. 4).

presuppositions.   It ensures order and necessary connexion in thought, but it is inadequate to reality.   It gives the logical ground of things (*logische Grund*) but not the ground of their reality (*Real-grund*) [1].   Thus the principle of contradiction is insufficient when treated as the ultimate principle of metaphysics.   Kant develops this position in connexion with the problem of proving the existence of God.   He rejects, as a begging of the question, the Cartesian demonstration which maintains that existence is necessarily involved in the perfection of the most perfect Being.   Existence, Kant says, cannot be a predicate.   That is to say, you cannot take out of any subject more than is contained in it : the principle of contradiction will never entitle you to pass from any mere idea to the reality of that idea.   Pure thought, determined by the principle of contradiction, always presupposes something 'given,' and thus reality must ultimately lie outside of pure thought.   Thus, for example, the real cause of anything is always more than a mere reason : a causal connexion is not a merely logical connexion.   It is this line of thinking that leads Kant to emphasize the distinction between logical understanding and empirical sense, and to lay stress on 'experience' (unrationalized and unexplained) as the ground of *reality*, in a way that recalls the position of Locke.   Thus, while admitting the certainty of mathematics, Kant protests against the use of a purely mathematical method in dealing with metaphysics or with the theory of knowledge, on the ground that such a method is 'merely synthetic,' that is to say, on the ground that it does not analyze actual experience but deduces from (or builds upon) arbi-

---

[1] Cf. *Der einzig mögliche Beweisgrund zu einer Demonstration des Daseins Gottes* (1763) (Rosenkranz, i. 161 ; Hartenstein, vi. 11).   Kant makes advances towards this position in the Essay on *Die falsche Spitzfindigkeit der vier syllogistischen Figuren* (1762) (Rosenkranz, i. 55 ; Hartenstein, i. 1), and in the *Versuch den Begriff der negativen Grössen in die Weltweisheit einzuführen* (1763) (Rosenkranz, i. 113 ; Hartenstein, i. 19).

trary or at least mind-made presuppositions [1]. Finally in the *Critique of Pure Reason* we have Kant's solution of the problem as to the relations between *a priori* and *a posteriori*, thought and experience. And his contention is that the *a priori* is not merely that which is self-evident and can be expressed in an analytic judgment, but that which experience universally and necessarily involves as the condition of its possibility.

This, after all, is but the working out of what is outlined by Leibniz, when he insists on 'compossibility,' or necessity arising from the system of things, as the ground of reality. For Leibniz the real is the 'fitting,' that which has its place in the best possible system or world: for Kant the real is that which is in an orderly experience constituted by principles which are the logical *a priori* conditions of its possibility. In the philosophy of Kant, accordingly, we have a more thorough application of the principle of sufficient reason, which Leibniz had imperfectly applied. Leibniz's explanation of the existence of the actual system of things as the result of a choice among all possible worlds is due to the inconsistency in his position which comes from working with two co-ordinate first principles. The totality of possible worlds is at once a system and not a system. If it were a system, the choice by God of the best possible world would be determined by the nature of the whole system of possibles. The best possible world would be the best world in that system, and thus the problem of Leibniz would not be solved by the 'choice,' but would merely be carried a stage farther back. On the other hand, if the totality of possible worlds were not a system, the choice of God would practically be arbitrary: at least it would be grounded on no

---

[1] Cf. *Untersuchung über die Deutlichkeit der Grundsätze der natürlichen Theologie und der Moral* (1764) (Rosenkranz, i. 75 ; Hartenstein, i. 63). See also Kant's *Inaugural Thesis* on becoming Professor in Königsberg, *De mundi sensibilis atque intelligibilis forma et principiis* (1770), in which the distinction between sense and understanding is brought to the sharpest point. (Rosenkranz, i. 301 ; Hartenstein, iii. 123.)

reason intelligible to us. God would choose the best possible world ; but it would be the best possible for no other reason than that He chose it. Thus the totality of possible ideal worlds has the appearance of being a system, while really it is not. It is this ambiguity that conceals the fundamental inconsistency of Leibniz—the inconsistency of regarding God as both within the system of things and quite outside of it (as the Creator), making Him at once the source of the whole system of mutually exclusive Monads and the highest Monad of the series, without whom the system would itself be incomplete. The principle of sufficient reason, rightly understood, involves the supposition of one all-embracing system ; but though Leibniz had certainly an inkling of the truth of this, his individualistic tendency and his dread of Spinozism prevented him from fully realizing it.

For Kant there is but one system of experience, that which actually exists. The supposition of a choice among possible worlds is no part of his philosophy. But in Kant's doctrine the 'thing-in-itself' performs very much the same function as did the 'choice' in Leibniz's scheme of things. Each is a way of allowing for a possible reality other than the actual system, although the need of this arises from one cause in Leibniz, and from another in Kant. Leibniz wishes to avoid a doctrine of blind necessity : Kant is afraid of a pure relativity. They both feel that the ultimate ground of the system of mutually related things must be sought in some principle outside the system itself[1]. The dogmatism of Leibniz appears in his

---

[1] Cf. *Critique of Pure Reason*, Rosenkranz, ii. 524 ; Hartenstein, ii. 513 (Meiklejohn's Tr., p. 414) : 'The notions of reality, of substance, of causality, of necessary existence itself, have no significance in determining any object, beyond their use in making possible the empirical cognition of a thing. They may thus be used to explain the possibility of things in the world of sense, but they cannot be used to explain the possibility of *the universe itself*; since in this case the ground of explanation must lie outside the world, and can therefore be no object of a possible experience. Now, relatively to the world of sense, I may admit such an incomprehensible being, the object of a mere idea ; though I may not

making this principle a real and independent 'constitutive' ground of the world, and he glosses over the difficulty of explaining its relation to the world by metaphors such as the 'Divine choice' and the producing of created Monads by continual 'fulgurations of Divinity.' The criticism of Kant, on the other hand, leads him to interpret this ultimate principle negatively, as a merely 'regulative' idea, of the absolute nature of which the speculative reason can say nothing. Its reality, however, is assured to us by the practical reason, and in it we must suppose that there is a reconciliation of necessity and freedom, of the kingdom of nature and the kingdom of grace, of mechanism and teleology. We cannot give a completely satisfactory account of the phenomenal world as a system governed by final causes, for we have no speculative knowledge of the ultimate intelligence and the ends it sets before itself. We may guess at final causes; but we cannot understand their producing anything, apart from mechanical causes. And on the other hand, while we cannot help regarding the phenomenal world as a mechanical system, 'absolutely no human reason (in fact no finite reason like ours in quality, however much it may surpass it in degree) can hope to understand the production of even a blade of grass by mere mechanical causes [1].' We must, in certain cases, postulate adaptation to ends. But we can quite conceive an intelligence which can think the world, not discursively from part to part as we do, but immediately and completely, from whole to part, and for such an intelligence, final and efficient cause, freedom and necessity, would be harmonized. For it to know and to create the world would be the

admit its existence in itself. . . . It is only a something in general which I know not in itself, but to which, as a ground of systematic unity in cognition, I attribute characteristics analogous to the notions of the understanding in the empirical sphere.'

[1] Kant, *Critique of Judgment*, Part ii. div. ii. § 77 (Rosenkranz, iv. 301; Hartenstein, vii. 288; Bernard's Tr., p. 326). See the whole passage.

same thing: creation would be its thought.   Thus Leibniz and Kant are at one in placing the ultimate synthesis of things, the sufficient reason of experience, in something that is beyond experience itself, and that is related to experience in a way which stands in need of further explanation.   Leibniz, however, falls into a contradiction which Kant avoids.   For Leibniz regards God as at once the highest of the Monads (the ultimate term in the series) and the Creator of the Monads, i. e. the sufficient reason of the world which they constitute.   But if God is one of the series of Monads, it seems impossible to regard Him as their sufficient reason, as choosing to create the system of which He is an element.   And on the other hand, if the essence of the Monads is to represent the universe, and if He (actus purus) perfectly realizes the universe within Himself, having perfectly clear and distinct perception, what place is there for a system of Monads apart from Him?   Kant avoids the difficulty by the sharp distinction he draws between experience and the thing-in-itself.   He can thus regard God as related to the world in a way which we may attempt to describe as causal, creative, or otherwise, but which it is impossible for us ever with certainty to define [1].   In short, so far as our theoretical knowledge of things is concerned, the account we give of the relation of God to the world is simply a useful hypothesis, by means of which we may give unity to our knowledge, and avoid the fallacies of

[1] Cf. *Critique of Pure Reason* (Hartenstein, ii. 508 sqq.; Rosenkranz, ii. 519 sqq.), Meiklejohn, pp. 410 sqq.: 'The notion of a supreme intelligence is a mere idea, that is to say, its objective reality does not consist in its being immediately referable to an object (for in this sense we cannot establish its objective validity) but it is merely a schema of the notion of a thing in general, a schema constructed according to the conditions of the greatest unity of reason, and serving only to produce the greatest systematic unity in the empirical use of our reason, inasmuch as we deduce this or that object of experience from the imagined object of this idea as the ground or cause of the object of experience.' Cf. also Rosenkranz, ii. 598; Hartenstein, ii. 581; Meiklejohn, p. 471.

dogmatism[1]. Yet, while Kant thus escapes the contradiction in Leibniz's view, he cannot be said to give us a satisfactory solution of the difficulty[2].

The Influence of Leibniz on Fichte.

In the modern idealism which first took shape in the writings of Fichte, there may be traced the influence of certain leading ideas in the philosophy of Leibniz, to which Kant had inevitably done less than justice. The work of Fichte is generally regarded as an endeavour to give systematic unity to the philosophy of Kant by getting rid of the thing-in-itself, regarded as entirely outside of experience. Indeed, until Kant repudiated his interpretation, Fichte regarded himself as an expositor of the true Kantian view, and a defender of the critical philosophy against the misunderstandings of its unintelligent disciples. Fichte's main idea is that experience (in the Kantian sense) has its basis in a self-consciousness (an *Ich-heit*) which is itself the root of the distinction between the empirical ego and the empirical non-ego, between subject and object. Both subject and object are logically involved in the original self-consciousness, out of which all experience, both in its matter and in its form, may be deduced. Thus all reference to a reality beyond experience becomes unmeaning as well as unnecessary. The unity of the universe is maintained with pantheistic

---

[1] D. Nolen (*La Critique de Kant et la Metaphysique de Leibniz*, pp. 331 et sqq.) regards the Monadology as a necessary complement to the 'Criticism' of Kant. It seems to him that the 'thing-in-itself' has, in the philosophy of Kant, a function similar to that of the 'possible thing' or 'essence' in the system of Leibniz. An ingenious attempt has also been make by Otto Riedel (*Die Monadologischen Bestimmungen in Kants Lehre vom Ding an sich*) to show that the things-in-themselves, in so far as they are conceived as positive, have the characteristics of Monads. There is a hint of the same view in Ueberweg's Commentary on the two editions of the *Critique of Pure Reason*.

[2] For Kant's account of his own relation to Leibniz see Appendix E, p. 208.

completeness; and the system of Fichte has well been described as 'Spinoza in terms of Kant[1].'

Now the need of a thing-in-itself, such as Kant postulates, arises from the thoroughness of his separation between perception and conception, between sense and understanding. They are correlative; yet they are treated by him as if quite independent, so that the result of their combination is a merely phenomenal world. Perception cannot evolve from itself the forms of the understanding, through which alone it loses its blindness; and conception cannot produce for itself the matter of sense and experience, without which it is empty. But this dualism indicates, in a negative way, the necessity of a noumenal world, however completely such a world may be beyond the reach of our intellectual comprehension or proof. It is in revulsion from dogmatism that Kant holds this position. And thus he is continually pointing out that the great error of Leibniz is that of regarding experience as a system of concepts, which may constitute an internally self-consistent whole, but which has no certain contact with reality. Such a dogmatism, Kant holds, has no answer to scepticism, and thus to give up the sharp distinction between perception and conception is to lose our grasp of reality and truth.

Accordingly it is not surprising to find that, in setting aside the thing-in-itself (as Kant understood it), Fichte goes back to the doctrine of Leibniz and proceeds to develop, under new conditions, some of its leading ideas[2].

[1] Adamson's *Fichte* (Blackwood's Philosophical Classics), p. 136.
[2] 'The time is come for reviving the philosophy of Leibniz. . . . Nothing is further removed from the thought of Leibniz than the speculative dream of a world of things-in-themselves, which no mind comprehends or knows, but which nevertheless acts upon us and produces all our ideas. The first of his thoughts, that which he makes his starting-point, is, that the representations of external things arise in the soul in virtue of its own laws, as in an isolated world, and as if nothing were present in it except God (the Infinite) and the soul (consciousness of the Infinite). . . . In thus expressing himself Leibniz spoke for philosophers. But now-a-days people will insist on philosophizing, even when philosophy is the last

Leibniz, in antagonism to the dualist position of Descartes, does not lay stress on the distinction of subject and object, but conceives the universe as an infinity of subjects, each self-sufficient and 'in the sea of life enisled.' For Kant, the distinction of subject and object is all in all. Fichte still gives full weight to the distinction, but conceives it as overcome in the unity of self-consciousness, or rather as flowing necessarily from that unity in its most abstract and indefinite form, and being lost in that unity in its highest and most perfect form. Thus, according to Leibniz, the whole succession of a Monad's states, all its perceptions of the universe, proceed spontaneously from within itself, 'as if there were only God and itself in the world[1]'; and every created Monad contains within itself both matter and form, which are in reality degrees of one power or function. Similarly, the ego of Fichte, the primal self-consciousness, is a perfectly spontaneous force, producing from within itself the empirical ego and non-ego, subject and object, making its own external world, projecting that world through the power of imagination, and continually striving towards the ultimate overcoming of this distinction between outer and inner in a pure 'intellectual intuition.' Accordingly Fichte throws down the barriers which Kant had raised between perception and conception, and returns to the position of Leibniz that all knowledge is one great process of development, though, of course, he gives a very different account of this development from that which we find in Leibniz[2].

thing they are fitted for. If any one tells us that no idea [*Vorstellung*] can arise in us from an external action, there is endless astonishment. To be a philosopher one must believe that the Monads have windows, through which things come and go.' (Schelling, *Sämmtliche Werke*, vol. i. 20. *Ideen zu einer Philosophie der Natur*, commended by Fichte, *Werke*, i. 515 note.)

[1] *Lettre à Foucher* (1686), (G. i. 382). Cf. *New System.* § 14.

[2] 'The final notion of Fichte's philosophy, expressed more clearly in the later works than in the *Wissenschaftslehre*, is that of the divine or spiritual order of which finite spirits are the manifestation or realization, and in the light of which human life and its surroundings appear as the continuous progress in ever higher stages towards realization of the final end of reason. Under this

The reality of the world of sense is for Fichte a result of
the activity of imagination. Our mind creates our sensations ; but it creates them unconsciously, and thus our
imagination attributes them to things outside of us,
objectifies them. Yet imagination does not give us mere
illusions, but truths more or less perfectly expressed. 'If
it be shown, as the present system should show, that
upon this activity of imagination rests the possibility of
our consciousness, our life, our being for ourselves, that
is to say, our being as ego [*unseres Seyn als Ich*], this
activity of imagination cannot cease, unless we are to
make abstraction from our ego, which would involve a
contradiction, since that which makes abstraction cannot
make abstraction from itself. This activity of imagination, then, does not deceive us, but gives us truth, the
only possible truth[1].' There are, as it were, two sides
to our knowledge of things. In so far as it is sensation
(that is to say, an idea unconsciously created by the mind)
it is a product of the non-ego, the object ; while in so far
as it is an idea consciously 'projected' by us or referred
to something, it is a product of the ego, the subject.
But the action of ego and non-ego is reciprocal, and they
both have their source in the original self-consciousness
from which they necessarily proceed[2].

It is, of course, beyond the scope of our intention
to consider the many essential differences between the
systems of Leibniz and of Fichte : to have indicated their
connexion is sufficient. And the words of Schelling may

conception, the oppositions of thought which play so important
a part in philosophy—being and thought, mind and nature, soul
and body, freedom and law, natural inclination and moral effort,
mechanism and teleology—are reconciled. They appear in their
due place as different aspects of the several stages in and through
which the spiritual order is realized.' Adamson, *Fichte*, pp. 219,
220.

[1] Fichte, *Sämmtliche Werke*, i. 227.

[2] 'The ego, as understood in common unscientific language,
posits neither the external object nor itself, but both are posited
through general and absolute thinking, and through this the
object is given for the ego, as well as the ego for itself.' Fichte,
Werke, ii. 562.

be taken as showing that this connexion was from the first fully realized. 'Since Leibniz,' he says, 'if we set aside secondary doctrines which do not count, we see that the real, the finite, is generally placed in the region of the ideal. The whole real world has no existence in itself, but only in the representations [*Vorstellungen*] of the soul. . . . Fichte takes up this idealism which is a denial of the independent being of the real, and, in this regard, he does not go beyond Leibniz. The only difference between them is this. Leibniz cannot explain why the soul or the Monad is subject to affections which produce in it finite representations ; or, if he tries to find the cause of this, he is obliged to place it in *God*, in the Infinite, which involves him in inevitable contradictions. Fichte, on the other hand, finds that the finite nature of the soul has its explanation in the absolutely free activity of the soul itself and results from this, that the soul by its *own act* posits *itself for itself* as finite, as separated from the *absolute all*, and consequently imposes on itself the necessity of contemplating no longer this absolute all, but only the negations, limitations, bounds of its infinity [1].' Accordingly it may be said generally that in the philosophy of Leibniz will and intelligence (appetition and perception) are co-ordinate principles of things (the will of God, for instance, not being prior to His understanding nor His understanding to His will), while the philosophy of Fichte is essentially a *practical* idealism, in which will (in however undefined a form) is ultimate and predominant. The 'principle of the best' (the tendency to realize the moral order which is the expression of the infinite good will) is with Leibniz the determining principle of actual, as distinct from merely possible existence, while with Fichte it is the ultimate ground of all reality, of the one system of things [2].

[1] Schelling, *Propaedeutik zur neueren Philosophie*. *Werke*, vol. i. p. 125.

[2] An excellent account of Fichte's historical position is given in

Schopenhauer.

As regards the main principles of his philosophy, Schopenhauer (however unconsciously) follows Fichte [1]. His starting-point is the Kantian distinction between the *intelligible* or noumenal and the *empirical* or phenomenal character of a real subject [2]. As in the philosophy of Fichte, the ultimate reality is will. The 'intelligible character' is a will, which is the source of the 'empirical character'; and in general will is a pure activity which is the source of the system of phenomena. Thus the world is will + idea (i. e. *Vorstellung*, representation, phenomenon). The absolute is the purely practical activity of will, which gives rise to the relative or mutually conditioned, in a way which is beyond explanation, for our understanding cannot pass the limits of the conditioned, the phenomenal world. But this ultimate will is essentially destitute of anything that can fairly be described as ethical character. The world is not a progress towards the realization of the best, but rather an unfortunate episode in the existence of the eternal will, and the highest good is to be attained not by allowing this will or striving (*will to live*) to have free course in us, but by suppressing it as much as possible. The expression, 'the world as will and idea,' recalls the Leibnitian view of substance as essentially appetition + perception. But Schopenhauer, like Fichte, gives to will a metaphysical priority, which is not attributed

Wallace's *Logic of Hegel*, Prolegomena (2nd ed.), ch. 11. See also chs. 12 and 13 for an account of Schelling with suggestive references to Leibniz. In ch. 13 there is a lucid explanation of the various meanings of the term 'Evolution,' as it is used by Leibniz and by later writers. Cf. vol. ii. p. 424.

[1] 'Except his pessimism, which is no necessary consequence of the system, there is absolutely nothing in Schopenhauer's philosophy which is not contained in the later works of Fichte.' Adamson, *Fichte*, p. 219. Though this is the statement of an expert, I venture to think it a little too sweeping.

[2] *Critique of Pure Reason*, Rosenkranz, ii. 422 ; Hartenstein, ii. 420 ; Meiklejohn, p. 333.

to it by Leibniz. Again, Schopenhauer, reducing the categories of Kant to causality (interpreted in a wide sense), gives great importance to the principle of sufficient reason which (in one or other of four different forms) he regards as the governing principle of the phenomenal world. 'All our ideas [*Vorstellungen*] stand to one another in a regular [*gesetzmässig*] connexion, which as to its form is determinable *a priori*, and on account of which nothing self-sufficient and independent, nothing separate and detached, can become an object for us. It is this connexion which the principle of sufficient reason, in its universality, expresses[1].' The principle of contradiction is ostensibly subordinated to that of sufficient reason, it being regarded as one of the general laws of thinking, discovered by induction and used as a judgment 'metalogically true,' which may be the ground or sufficient reason of other judgments[2]. But here there is clearly an inconsistency between Schopenhauer's logical theory and his metaphysic. His absolute, the ultimate will, is (however far he may be from acknowledging it) really determined by the principle of contradiction, in its abstract form, for the will is conceived as that which absolutely *is*, that which is apart from all relation, that which may, in some mysterious way, produce a system of differences, but which has an identity that is perfectly independent of them. Accordingly, while Schopenhauer indicates the deeper and more comprehensive interpretation of the principle of sufficient reason as underlying that of contradiction, he does not allow it to mould his system.

Herbart.

Another thinker who owes something to Leibniz and something more to Kant and to Fichte, is Herbart (1776–1841). He is not content to subordinate the principle of

---

[1] *Ueber die vierfache Wurzel des Satzes vom zureichenden Grunde*, ch. 3, § 16.

[2] Cp. *Ueber die vierfache Wurzel*, &c., ch. 5, § 33.

sufficient reason to that of contradiction, but he practically endeavours to do without the former principle as far as possible. The task of philosophy he regards as that of eliminating the contradictions that appear in common consciousness by transforming the ideas which are given in it[1]. This transformation, for Herbart, practically means abstraction. Every bit of experience, being given, has something real in it[2]. But its reality is that which it is, apart from conditions or relations to other things. The real is always something, a *quale*, a 'this' or 'that' of some kind. But it is absolute *position* (in the Fichtean sense) or affirmation without negation; it has absolute self-identity, so that it is perfectly simple and not, like the Monad of Leibniz, a substance involving in its unity a plurality of qualities; and it is pure quality, without any quantitative element or aspect, so that it is neither a divisible totality nor an unbroken continuum. These 'reals,' like the Monads, are infinite in number, and each is different from every other. But they are absolutely unalterable, they have no characteristic analogous to the perception of Leibniz, and they are not impenetrable, for any number of them may equally be thought as occupying or as not occupying the same point in space. Like the Monads, no one 'real' can act upon another; otherwise they would cease to be absolute. And each 'real' is the immediate cause of one and only one phenomenon of experience, so that the static variety of the world is due to the power of 'self-preservation' (*Selbsterhaltung*) in each 'real.' The actual changes which we find in experience are due to the different aspects in which the 'reals' appear, when they are in different relations to one another, although their true natures remain unchanged (as in the phenomena of colour contrasts). And these different

---

[1] 'Mere uncritical experience or merely empirical knowledge only offers *problems*; it suggests gaps, which indeed further reflexion serves at first only to deepen into contradictions.' Wallace, *Hegel's Philosophy of Mind*, p. lxiii.

[2] 'Wieviel Schein, soviel Hindeutung auf's Sein.'

relations of the 'reals' to one another are, again, due to
the possibility of conceiving the 'reals' as both together
in one point and apart from one another. Accordingly
the soul, being a 'real,' must not be represented as having
in itself powers, faculties, qualities, &c. It is absolutely
simple, and has nothing but 'self-preservation,' which
apparently is little more than a permanent possibility of
relation to other 'reals.' None of the functions and
characteristics of mind belong to it intrinsically. They
are to be ascribed to other things, quite as much as
to the mind or soul itself. They are merely names
for the phenomena or aspects of certain 'reals' (one of
which is the soul) in certain relations to one another.
These phenomenal (of course, not real) interactions of
the 'reals' admit of mathematical calculation, and
accordingly Herbart is the father of those who apply
mathematical methods in empirical psychology[1]. This
is natural in one whose thought is so completely
dominated by the abstract use of the principle of contradiction. And, in short, if we leave out of account the
influence of Fichte upon his psychology, we may regard
Herbart's work as a remodelling of that of Leibniz, on the
supposition that the principle of sufficient reason is to be
dropped.

Hegel's Solution of the Dualism in Leibniz.

In the philosophy of Hegel we have a solution of the
dualism between the principle of contradiction and that
of sufficient reason, as they are used and conceived by
Leibniz. The problem indicated by this dualism underlies the whole course of German speculation from the
time of Leibniz onwards. Wolff, in a negative way, gave

[1] His application of mathematical methods, however, differs
entirely from that which occurs in the psycho-physics of the
Fechner School, and in modern physiological psychology. For
a full explanation, see Wallace, *Hegel's Philosophy of Mind*, pp. lxviii
sqq. It may also be noted that Leibniz's theories regarding unconscious and *petites* perceptions are developed and applied in the
psychology of Herbart.

precision to the problem by suggesting the most superficial possible solution, reducing the principle of sufficient reason to that of contradiction. This (though Wolff perhaps did not realize it) was little better than telling Leibniz that he had discovered a mare's nest. Kant, on the other hand, gives positive precision to the problem by the sharpness of his distinction between the absolute and the relative, while Fichte and Schelling, in different ways, endeavour to make explicit the unity to which the Kantian divisions point. Their re-employment of the principle of development or progressive self-realization, which is so important a feature of Leibniz's thinking, brings us to the verge of Hegel's solution of the problem. Hegel practically reverses the procedure of Wolff, by showing that the principle of contradiction presupposes that of sufficient reason, and that each by itself is an abstract expression of the principle of self-consciousness [1]. The real is not merely *in se* (as it would be if the abstract principle of contradiction were ultimate), nor is it merely *in alio* (as it would be if the abstract principle of sufficient reason were ultimate, which, of course, no one maintains). But the real is that which becomes itself through being *in alio*, through being not itself. There is no such thing as a purely analytic or a purely synthetic judgment; but when we attribute any quality to a subject, we attribute to it not merely a difference from other things but a oneness with that from which we differentiate it [2]. The universe is a system of such perfect unity that the opposites it contains are all contraries and never contradictories. Absolute contradictories or absolute differences are abstractions. To say, as did Leibniz, that no two things are exactly the same implies that no two things (not even the most extreme opposites) are entirely different. A must

[1] See Caird's *Hegel* (Blackwood's Philosophical Classics), chs. 7 and 8. Also Wallace, *Prolegomena* to the *Logic of Hegel* (2nd ed.), ch. 30.

[2] Cf. Caird, *Critical Philosophy of Kant*, vol. ii. pp. 64 sqq.

have something in common with not-A, if their opposition
is to have any meaning.   'The other stands over against
its other[1].'   That is to say, their difference must have
some ground, some underlying unity.   And on the other
hand, every identity, even the identity of a thing with
itself, implies some difference.   There is no pure ground,
no absolute first principle, independent of a sufficient
reason.   Hegel regards the universe as itself one absolute
system.   The world we know is the only world, and it
is not a merely phenomenal system, the expression of
something heterogeneous with it (like the arc electric
light between two opposite points of carbon), nor is it an
inexplicable product of something other than itself, such
as an unconditioned will, nor yet is it the production of
some noumenal absolute.   It hangs upon nothing; it
needs nothing to hang upon.   The universe is one system
of endless mutual determinations, yet not a merely static
system nor a system of cyclical revolutions, endlessly
repeated, which would involve the supposition of an
external absolute as the source or support of all.   It is
rather an evolution of that whose end is in its beginning,
that whose development is free, because, being all-comprehensive, it is perfectly self-determined.

Thus Hegel points out that 'it is the notion which
Leibniz had in his eye when he spoke of sufficient ground
and urged the study of things under its point of view.'   By
the notion Hegel means 'a content objectively and intrinsically determined and hence self-acting.'   This would
sufficiently describe the Monad of Leibniz if we keep out
of view the Monad's absolute particularity, its isolation as
one of an infinite series of independent units, or, in other
words, if we omit from the conception of the Monad all
that is due to the principle of contradiction, interpreted
abstractly as a principle of pure or immediate self-identity.
This isolation, of course, is an essential element in

---

[1] Hegel, *Logic*, § 119 (Wallace's Tr., 2nd ed., p. 222).   See the
whole passage, and also pp. 224 sqq.

Leibniz's conception of the Monad, and the result is that while his speculation points to a view of the universe as one system in which the elements are intrinsically and not externally combined, he does not go far enough to secure this metaphysical position, just as he does not push his logical analysis far enough to reconcile the principles of contradiction and sufficient reason.   The Hegelian 'notion' is thus the completion of what is vaguely shadowed forth in the Monad of Leibniz, and more especially in the *Monas Monadum*, in which all is (however unsatisfactorily) brought to unity.   For the notion implicitly contains all in itself, and all is realized through its logical (not temporal) development.   Like the Monad, the notion is not *in* time any more than it is *in* space; it comprehends both.   The difference is that by Leibniz the development is conceived as a continuous growth or increase in a certain fundamental quality (clearness and distinctness of perception), while by Hegel it is represented as a dialectic movement from that which is relatively abstract, through its correlative abstraction (or its 'negation') to that which, comprehending or uniting both, is relatively concrete.   For Leibniz development is from small to great (witness, for instance, his *petites* perceptions) ; for Hegel development is from fragments to wholes, or rather from the vague and undetermined to the definite and determined.

Accordingly what Leibniz means by saying that the Monad (or its qualities) cannot go out of itself and cannot be entered or influenced from outside, would by Hegel be expressed as the doctrine that thought or self-consciousness is reality, the universe, and that accordingly it can neither go beyond itself nor have anything beyond it.   It may sunder itself ideally, but it cannot really go out of itself, for there is no 'out of itself.'   In the same way the Monad may ideally be sundered into active and passive elements (entelechy and *materia prima*), but it can really give nothing and it can really receive nothing.   The difference at this point between the attitude of Hegel and that of Leibniz is due to the fact that while Leibniz interprets 'perception' as that which it is in its lowest form (mere 'representation' or 'expression'), and regards consciousness and self-consciousness as developments from it by increase or addition, Hegel interprets 'representation' or relation in general as being essentially that which it is in its highest form (self-consciousness), and regards the lower forms as 'abstract' or incomplete foreshadowings, undeveloped expressions of it. For Hegel as for Leibniz the universe is organic throughout. No part of it is actually other than self-determined, for the unity of the whole and its parts is absolutely complete, so that no part can be conceived as having any reality by itself. Leibniz holds that the Monads must be conceived on the 'analogy' of the soul. Hegel insists on a unity which is closer than mere analogy, and which, at the same time, expresses itself in the greatest possible variety; he regards self-consciousness, explicitly or implicitly, as the reality of every part, every member or organ, of the whole. In short, it may be said that in Leibniz's account of simple substance we have the first suggestion of the transition from substance to subject (as the ultimate reality of things), which is brought to completion by Hegel [1].

Lotze's Reconstruction of the Hypotheses of Leibniz.

It seemed to Lotze that the 'bold Monism' of Hegel 'undertook far more than human powers can achieve,' although 'its leading idea by no means loses its value through the great defects in its execution [2].' This 'leading idea' was in Lotze's opinion the 'reconciliation of opposites,' the overcoming of the contradictions in thought by bringing all knowledge to systematic unity. But Lotze's

---

[1] Cf. generally Caird, *Critical Philosophy of Kant*, vol. ii. bk. i. ch. 12, especially pp. 62 sqq. See also *Monadology*, § 30.
[2] Lotze, *Metaphysic*, bk. i. ch. 7, § 88 (Eng. Tr., vol. i. p. 206).

interpretation of 'thought' is very different from that of
Hegel. Although he expressly repudiated the suggestion
that he is to be counted as a follower of Herbart, Lotze's
position as regards thought and the reconciling of its
contradictions is more akin to the view of Herbart than
to that of Hegel. Like Herbart he regards thought as
essentially analytic, as interpreting rather than constituting
reality, and the work of science or philosophy is thus not
that of laying down an absolute all-comprehensive system,
expressing the whole evolution of reality, but that of
unifying our knowledge, resolving the contradictions that
appear in common experience. Thought cannot pierce to
the inner nature of things, cannot understand them so
thoroughly that it could make them. To use a distinction which has become a commonplace among writers on
natural science, thought can *describe* but it cannot *explain*[1].
It can give an account of what happens, can express in the
form of general laws the relations between things, so as to
be able to calculate occurrences, and can possibly reduce
these laws to one general system ; but it cannot tell what
the things themselves really are, how they originally came
into being, and why they are so and not otherwise. In
short, thought is governed solely by the principle of
contradiction ; the principle of sufficient reason (in
Leibniz's sense) is beyond it. 'Reality is infinitely richer
than thought. . . . We know that in fact the nature of
reality yields a result to us unthinkable. It teaches us
that being and not-being are not, as we could not help
thinking them to be, contradictory predicates of every
subject, but that there is an alternative between them,
arising out of a union of the two which we cannot construct
in thought. This explains how the extravagant utterance
could be ventured upon, that it is just contradiction

---

[1] For a fuller account of this distinction, see Merz, *History of
European Thought in the Nineteenth Century,* vol. i. pp. 337, 382, 383, notes.
Venn (*Empirical Logic,* ch. 21) minimizes the distinction, holding
explanation to be generalization.

which constitutes the truth of the real. Those who used it regarded that as contradictory which was in fact superior to logical laws—which does not indeed abrogate them in their legitimate application, but as to which no sort of positive conjecture could possibly be formed as a result of such application [1].'

The revolt of Lotze against the idealism of Fichte, Schelling, and Hegel was due to the bad treatment which the 'Philosophy of Nature' had received at their hands. The self-confidence of a thought which had found itself absolute resulted in a *Naturphilosophie* which despised facts ; and Lotze, as a scientist, felt it necessary to bring down thought from 'the high horse of idealism,' and assign to it the humble work of observation and description. 'The study of medicine, which I had chosen as my life-work, made it necessary for me to acquire a knowledge of natural science, and hence (in brief) I came to see how completely untenable is a great part of the views of Hegel, or rather the whole of them, in the form in which they are put [2].' It was to a large extent through his medical studies that Lotze arrived at one of the chief doctrines of his philosophy, viz. the universality of mechanism as an account of the relations between phenomena. 'The father of modern physiology,' Johannes Müller (1801–1858), had changed the whole aspect of biological science by extending the conception of mechanism to all the phenomena of life [3]. Lotze took a further step in the same direction when he defined mechanism as 'the connexion of all those universal laws, according to which every individual in the created world acts upon every other [4].' The sphere of mechanism is thus extended so as

[1] Lotze, *Metaphysic*, bk. i. ch. 6, § 76 (Eng. Tr., vol. i. pp. 178, 179). See the whole chapter, in which the views of Leibniz and Herbart are discussed.
[2] Lotze, *Streitschrift*, p. 7.
[3] Merz, *History of European Thought in the Nineteenth Century*, vol. i. pp. 216 sqq.; cf. Lotze, *Metaphysic*, bk. ii. ch. 8, §§ 224 sqq. (Eng. Tr., vol. ii. p. 128).
[4] *Streitschrift*, p. 57.

to include the phenomena not merely of inorganic and organic bodies, but also of mind. 'The function of mechanism in the construction of the world is, without an exception, universal in its *extent*[1].' The conception of mechanism governs all science, for the principle of all our thinking is the principle of contradiction, which can only accept what is given in experience and systematize its laws.

But Lotze protests strongly against the view that mechanism gives us a final explanation of the reality of the world. The laws of science are laws of phenomena ; they do not account for the things themselves. We may say that the essence of a thing is to stand in relations to other things. But the thing itself is more than the relations, and mechanism gives us an account of the relations only. Thus while 'the function of mechanism in the construction of the world is universal in its *extent*, it is entirely subordinate in its *importance*[2].' As mere thought is by itself inadequate to reality, so mechanism (the system of laws which it is the work of science to discover and express) is not an eternally necessary system, constituting the very nature of things, but is merely the way in which the ultimate idea, the good, has freely chosen to realize itself[3]. Not thought, but goodness is ultimate, and 'the establishing of mechanism is the first ethical deed of the Absolute. The fact that there is a kingdom of universal laws appears to me to be comprehensible only in a world whose ultimate principle is an ethical one ; another world (if I were to try to form for myself the notion of it, which is for me absurd) might, it

---

Kleine Schriften, iii. 310.

[2] *Loc. cit.*, cf. *Microcosmus*, Introduction (Eng. Tr., vol. i. p. xvi).

[3] 'Mechanism is but the collection of all the instrumental forms in which God has willed that created beings shall act on one another with their unknown natures, and that all their states shall be welded into the endless chain of a world-history. This view explores the sphere of means, not the sphere of ends to which these minister.' *Microcosmus*, bk. iii. Conclusion. (Eng. Tr., vol. i. p. 398.)

appears to me, have arisen—a world without this thread of consecutiveness, without this *veritas* in the sense of the old metaphysic[1].' Accordingly for Lotze the ultimate reality is a personal God, who sets before Himself the highest moral ends, and has established the 'absolutely valid system of laws which rules the world' as the best means of securing these ends. Thought is a means of attaining to complete experience ; mechanism is a means of realizing the best. 'There is no "nature of things" outside of God,' limiting the sphere of His choice. But on the other hand, His choice is not arbitrary, but is governed by His perfect idea of what is absolutely best.

In this the influence of Leibniz is so manifest that it does not surprise us to find Lotze writing to the younger Fichte : 'I went willingly through the splendid gateway which he [Herbart] is convinced that he has been able to erect as an entrance to his metaphysic ; the gateway of the Leibnitian Monad-world[2].' Thus, according to Lotze, we are constrained to conceive the real world as a world of Monads, which are ultimately one in nature. In addition to mechanism, or the system of laws governing (or expressing) the relations between things, there are the things themselves, the facts, which may be conceived as Monads. And both of these (the laws and the facts) presuppose a universal and all-pervading substance, which is merely a postulate of thought, but is a reality for feeling, and which (being intelligible only through the idea of a personal Deity) realizes the highest moral ends in the sphere of the facts by means of the laws. Things are to be thought of as Monads, because nature is to be conceived as animated throughout ; all things are endowed with 'modes of sensation and enjoyment[3].' Otherwise

---

[1] *Streitschrift*, p. 57.
[2] Ibid. p. 7.
[3] *Microcosmus*, bk. iii. ch. 4, § 3 (Eng. Tr., vol. i. p. 360). Cf. Lotze's early writing—*Pensées d'un Idiote sur Descartes, Spinoza et Leibnitz*. (*Kleine Schriften*, vol. iii. p. 564.)

we should have to regard all nature as merely machinery
for the drama of human consciousness—a view which
could never satisfy our 'longings' and 'cravings.' But
this monadology or 'hypothesis of unextended atoms' can
never, for Lotze, be more than a hypothesis. Thought
can never determine its truth, because it is a hypothesis
regarding the *nature* of things, and thought has to do
only with their *relations*. The monadology is 'a conception of whose essential truth we are convinced, yet to
which we can hardly expect any further concession than
that, among the dreams of our imagination, it may be
one of those which do not contradict actual facts[1].'

Lotze is here manifestly more in harmony with Kant
than with Leibniz[2]. And he further differs from Leibniz
in maintaining that the Monads are not completely isolated
from one another, so that each contains its own relations
within itself. If Leibniz's doctrine be true, 'while none
of the members [of the real world] condition each other,
everything goes on as if they all did so; accordingly,
while it does not really form a whole, yet to an intelligence directed to it, it will have the appearance of doing
so; and, in one word, its reality consists in a hollow and
delusive imitation of that inner consistency which was
pronounced to be, as such, the ultimate reason why its
realization was possible[3].' Accordingly for Lotze 'every
single thing and event can only be thought as an activity,
constant or transitory, of the one existence, its reality
and substance as the mode of being and substance of this
one existence, its nature and form as a consistent phase
in the unfolding of the same[4].' The pre-established
harmony of Leibniz is thus set aside by Lotze[5]. Its place

---

[1] *Microcosmus*, bk. iii. ch. 4, § 3 (Eng. Tr., i. 360; cf. i. 363).
[2] For an excellent account of the general relation of Lotze to
Kant, see Jones, *Philosophy of Lotze*, pp. 64 sqq.
[3] *Metaphysic*, bk. i. ch. 6, § 79 (Eng. Tr., vol. i. p. 184). Cf. the
whole context.
[4] *loc. cit.*
[5] 'Only if the course of all, even of the most trivial, events
were fixed by immutable predestination, could the assumption of

is taken by the conception of mechanism, through which we describe the relations in which things are for thought. Such relations as those between the phenomena of the soul and the phenomena of the body can be described on purely mechanical principles : that is to say, the conditions of their connexion can be stated as laws. And the theory of a pre-established harmony is not required (not to say that it is insufficient) to explain *how* the phenomena of the soul have any connexion with those of the body—how, for instance, physical nerve-motion passes into psychical sensation. It is impossible for our thought to explain this ; but it is just as impossible for our thought to explain how one physical phenomenon is invariably connected with another physical phenomenon—how, for instance, the burning match is connected with the exploding gunpowder[1]. In neither case can thought do more than *describe* a connexion invariable in our experience. Science must be content with a ' practical occasionalism ' as distinct from the ' theoretical ' (i. e. absolute ontological) ' occasionalism ' of the Cartesians[2].

Thus in Lotze we find the principles of the philosophy of Leibniz modified by Kantian influences. Like Leibniz, Lotze in his application of the principles of contradiction and of sufficient reason keeps them sharply apart from

---

a pre-established harmony—not, indeed, *explain* anything. but—tolerably well *describe* the facts. . . . It is only if individual things do not float independent or left to themselves in a vacuum across which no connexion can reach—only if all of them, being finite individuals, are at the same time only parts of one single infinite substance, which embraces them all and cherishes them all within itself, that their reciprocal action, or what we call such, is possible.' *Microcosmus*, bk. ix. ch. 1, § 5 (Eng. Tr., vol. ii. pp. 597, 598). Cf. *Metaphysic*, bk. i. ch. 5, §§ 63 sqq. (Eng. Tr., vol. i. p. 150).

[1] ' As in our life we see the physical motions of external nature employed as stimuli to excite that in ourselves which is far higher—conscious sensation : so, we think, throughout the universe mechanical events are but the external tissue of regularly crossing stimuli, designed to kindle at innumerable points, within innumerable beings, the true action of a more intelligent life.' *Microcosmus*, bk. iii. Conclusion. (Eng. Tr., vol. i. p. 399.)

[2] *Streitschrift*, p. 96.

one another. But, unlike Leibniz, he regards the principle of contradiction as, indeed, universally applicable but completely subordinate in importance. According to Leibniz, mechanism in the real world is subordinate to teleology, efficient to final causes. But at least the co-ordinate priority of the principle of contradiction is secured by the conception of the 'possible' things or 'essences,' the realm of ideas, in the understanding of God. Lotze, on the other hand, does away with this realm of 'possibles,' making the 'principle of the best' absolutely supreme, allowing the choice of God to be independent even of the principle of contradiction, independent of all save the ideal of absolute ethical worth. A violation of the law of contradiction is an absurdity for us ; but God might conceivably (if it had been the most perfect means to the realizing of the best) have made a world in which the law of contradiction did not hold. But as Leibniz gave no clear explanation of the relations between the two principles of contradiction and sufficient reason, so Lotze does not explain the subordination of the one to the other, but maintains that any such explanation is beyond the reach of human thought.

From early years Lotze was familiar with the works of Leibniz, and his writings continually suggest Leibnitian ways of looking at things. But, though an inheritor of Leibniz's ideas, he could not 'take over' the philosophy as a whole. 'I have, indeed, in general never had the presumption to declare myself the successor of Leibniz, in the sense of being his heir ... but I must have the presumption to admit that I could only have entered into possession of this inheritance *cum beneficio inventarii*[1].'

Other Influences of Leibniz.

It would be impossible briefly to indicate the full influence of the philosophy of Leibniz in other directions.

[1] *Kleine Schriften*, vol. iii. p. 342.

While the academic writers on philosophy missed much
of his best thought, its spirit was felt in the literature of
Germany through the works of Lessing and Herder[1].
Nor was Leibniz's thinking altogether without effect upon
English literature; for, though the doctrine is sadly
straitened into platitude, that sense of the varied wholeness and harmonious system of things which pervades the
Théodicée is cleverly expressed in the *Essay on Man* by
the phrases of which Pope was a master[2].   Again, with
regard to the influence of Leibniz upon natural science,
reference may be made to the way in which his idea that
the organism is a group of smaller organisms, has been in
various forms developed by naturalists like Buffon[3], and
has finally gained something like scientific verification in
the cell-theory of Schwann.   Johannes Müller recognized
this by giving to the cells the somewhat inappropriate
name of 'organic monads[4].'   Modern psychology also, in
the attention it directs to 'sub-conscious' processes and
in its analysis of sensations and perceptions into elements
which are individually unnoticed (e. g. the 'over-tones' of
Helmholtz and the 'local signs' of Lotze), owes much to

[1] See Merz's *Leibniz* (Blackwood's Philosophical Classics), pp. 195
sqq.   There are also traces of the influence of Leibniz in the works
of Schiller, who is said to have written his poem *Die Freundschaft*
when his mind was full of ideas suggested by the reading of
Leibniz.   This is the poem from which Hegel in his *Geschichte d.
Phil.*, vol. i. p. 91 (ed. 1840), quotes the well-known lines ' *Freundlos
war der grosse Weltenmeister*,' &c.   The poem belongs to Schiller's
'First Period.'

[2] See *Introduction* to the edition by Mark Pattison (Clarendon
Press).   Bolingbroke said of Pope that he was 'a very great wit,
but a very indifferent philosopher.'

[3] Cf. Buffon's *Histoire Naturelle*, &c. (1787), vol. iv. p. 22 : 'Living
beings contain a large number of living and active molecules.
The life of the animal or of the plant appears to be only the result
of all the activities, of all the little individual lives (if I may so
speak) of each of these active molecules, whose life is underived
[*primitive*] and appears incapable of destruction.'

[4] Weismann regards the unicellular organism as immortal.   Cf.
Essays upon Heredity, &c. (Eng. ed. by Poulton, Schönland, and
Shipley, pp. 25 and 27).   For a good account of the relation of
Leibniz's philosophy to modern scientific thought, see Watson,
Comte, Mill and Spencer, pp. 126 sqq.

Leibniz's far-reaching suggestion of the unconscious *petites perceptions*. For this suggestion also (if for little else) Hartmann's *Philosophy of the Unconscious* is indebted to Leibniz[1]. And further, in these days when we are so persistently assured that 'the real is the individual,' Monadology may be said to be in the air, and we need not be surprised to find that, in one form or another, it has its adherents in theologians like Dorner, philosophical teachers like Croom Robertson, and expositors like Dillmann.

The fruits of the philosophy of Leibniz are as widely scattered as its roots were far spread. The materials of his philosophy were derived from every sphere of thought, from every generation of thinkers, and he gave to the future as liberally as he borrowed from the past. 'Nicht Vielwisser war er, sondern, soweit der Mensch es kann, All- und Ganzwisser, und sein Erfassen, sein Erkennen, war stets zugleich schöpferischer Act[2].'

[1] See Tr. by Coupland, vol. i. pp. 16 sqq.
[2] 'He was learned not merely in many things but, so far as a man can be, in all and everything, and his very comprehending or acquiring of knowledge was also an act of creating.' E. Du Bois-Reymond, *Leibnizische Gedanken in der neueren Naturwissenschaft*, in his *Reden*, Erste Folge, p. 33.

APPENDIX A.

EXPLANATION OF THE PRE-ESTABLISHED HARMONY BY A SPECIAL INSTANCE.

In a letter to Arnauld (1687) (G. ii. 113) Leibniz gives an account of the way in which his theory may be applied to a particular case (that of the relation between a pin-prick in the body and pain in consciousness). 'We have now to inquire how the soul is conscious of the motions of its body, since we can see no way of explaining by what channels the activity of an extended mass can pass into an indivisible being. Ordinary Cartesians declare that no explanation of this union can be given. The authors of the hypothesis of occasional causes think that it is *nodus vindice dignus, cui Deus ex Machina intervenire debeat.* For my part I explain it in a natural way. From the notion of substance or concrete [*accompli*] being in general, which declares that its present state is always a natural consequence of its preceding state, it follows that the nature of each individual substance, and consequently of every soul, is to express the universe. Each has been from the first created such that, in virtue of the laws of its own nature, it must happen that it is in harmony with what takes place in bodies, and especially in its own body. We need not then be surprised to find that it has the power of representing to itself the pin-prick, when this takes place in its body. And, to complete my explanation on this point, we have :—

State of the body at moment A.	State of the soul at moment A.
State of the body at the following moment B.	State of the soul at moment B.
(Pin-prick.)	(Pain.)

'As, then, the state of the body at moment B follows from the state of the body at moment A, so the state of the soul B is a consequence of A, the preceding state of the same soul, according to the notion of substance in general. Now the

states of the soul are naturally and essentially expressions of
the corresponding states of the world, and especially of the
bodies which for the time belong to the soul. Accordingly,
since the pin-prick is a part of the state of the body at the
moment B, the representation or expression of the pin-prick
(i. e. the pain) will be a part of the soul at the moment B; for
as one motion follows from another motion, so one representation follows from another representation in a substance whose
nature is to be representative. Thus the soul must needs be
conscious of the pin-prick, when the laws of relation require
it to express more distinctly a more observable change in the
parts of its body. It is true that the soul is not always distinctly
conscious of the causes of the pin-prick and of its coming pain,
when these are still hidden in the representation of the state A,
as when we sleep or in some other way are unaware of the
approach of the pin. But that is because the motions of
the pin at that time make too little impression, and though
we are already in some way affected by all these motions and
their representations in our soul, and thus have within us the
representation or expression of the causes of the pin-prick, and
consequently the cause of the representation of the same pin-
prick, that is to say, the cause of the pain—yet we can unravel
them from the multitude of other thoughts only when they
become noticeable. Our soul reflects only upon the more
marked phenomena, which stand out from the others; not
thinking distinctly of any, when it thinks equally of all. After
this explanation, I cannot imagine where anybody can find the
least shadow of farther difficulty, unless he is prepared to
deny that God can create substances which are so made from
the beginning that each in virtue of its own nature is afterwards in harmony with the phenomena of all the others. Now
nobody seems to deny this possibility, and since we see that
mathematicians represent in a machine the motions of the
heavenly bodies (as when

> Jura poli rerumque fidem legesque deorum
> Cuncta Syracosius transtulit arte senex,

which we can do to-day much better than Archimedes could in
his day), why could not God, who excels them infinitely, from
the beginning create representative substances in such a way
that they express by their own laws, according to the natural
change of their thoughts or representations, all that is to

happen to every body?   This seems to me not only easy
to conceive, but also worthy of God and of the beauty of the
universe, and in a way necessary, since all substances must
have a mutual harmony and connexion and all must express
in themselves the same universe and the universal cause, which
is the will of their Creator, and the decrees or laws which He
has established in order to make them fit into one another as
well as possible. Thus this mutual correspondence of different
substances (which, speaking with metaphysical strictness, cannot act upon one another, and yet are in harmony as if one
did act upon another) is one of the strongest proofs of the
existence of God or of a common cause which each effect must
always express according to its point of view and its capacity
of expression. Otherwise the phenomena of different minds
would not harmonize, and there would be as many systems as
substances; or rather, it would be entirely a matter of chance
if they *were* sometimes in harmony.'

APPENDIX B.

FORMATION OF THE IDEA OF SPACE.

In § 47 of the fifth letter to Clarke, Leibniz gives an account
of the origin of the idea of space. 'I will here show how
men come to form to themselves the notion of space. They
consider that many things exist at once and they observe in
them a certain order of co-existence, according to which the
relation of one thing to another is more or less simple. This
order is their situation or distance. When it happens that
one of those co-existent things changes its relation to a multitude of others, without their changing their relations among
themselves; and that another thing, newly come, acquires
the same relation to the others as the former had; we then
say it is come into the *place* of the other; and this change we
call a *motion* in that body, wherein is the immediate cause
of the change. And though several, or even all the co-existent
things should change according to certain known rules of
direction and velocity, we can always determine the relation of

situation which each acquires with reference to every other, and we can even determine the relation which any other [co-existent] would have [to this], or which this would have to any other, if it had not changed or if it had changed otherwise. And supposing or feigning that among those co-existents there is a sufficient number of them, which have undergone no change, then we may say that those which now have to those fixed existents a relation such as that which others formerly had to them, have the same place which these latter had. And that which comprehends all these places is called space, which shows that in order to have an idea of place, and consequently of space, it is sufficient to consider these relations and the rules of their changes, without needing to fancy any absolute reality outside of the things whose situation we consider. And, to give a kind of definition : *place* is that which we say is the same for A and for B, when the relation of co-existence between B and C, E, F, G, &c., is in perfect agreement with the relation of co-existence which A formerly had with the same C, E, F, G, &c.; provided that in C, E, F, G, &c., there has been no cause of change. . . . . *Place* is that which is the same in different moments to different existent things, when the relations of co-existence between each and certain other existents, which are supposed to continue *fixed* from moment to moment, agree entirely together. And *fixed existents* are those in which there has been no cause of change in the order of their co-existence with others, or (which is the same thing) in which there has been no motion. In short, space is that which results from places taken together. And here it is right to consider the difference between place and the relation of situation which is in the body occupying the place. For the place of A and B is the same; whereas the relation of A to the fixed bodies is not exactly and individually the same as the relation which B (that comes into its place) will have to the same fixed bodies : these relations are only in agreement. For two different objects, as A and B, cannot have exactly the same individual affection ; it being impossible that the same individual accident should be in two objects or pass from one object to another. But the mind, not satisfied with mere agreement, looks for an identity, for something which should be really the same, and conceives it as outside of the objects : and this is what we here call *place* and *space*. But this can only be an ideal thing, involving a certain order, in which the mind conceives relations to be applied.' (E. 768 a; G. vii. 400.)

I have made some slight alterations in Clarke's translation for the sake of clearness. As to other details of Leibniz's doctrine of space, cf. Fraser's ed. of Locke's *Essay*, vol. i. pp. 158 and 186.

APPENDIX C.

THE MEANING OF CAUSE.

IN a draft of a letter to Arnauld (1686) (G. ii. 68) Leibniz expounds his view of cause as follows:—'The hypothesis of concomitance is a consequence of my notion of substance. For, in my view, the individual notion of a substance includes all that is ever to happen to it, and it is in this respect that concrete things [*êtres accomplis = res completae* ?] differ from those which are not so. Now, the soul being an individual substance, its notion, idea, essence or nature must include all that is ever to happen to it ; and God, who sees it perfectly, sees in it all that it will ever do or suffer and all the thoughts it will have. Accordingly, since our thoughts are nothing but the consequences of the nature of our soul and arise in it in virtue of its notion, it is useless to seek in it the influence of any other particular substance, besides that such an influence is absolutely inexplicable. It is true that certain thoughts come to us when there are certain bodily motions, and that certain bodily motions happen when we have certain thoughts ; but that is because each substance expresses the entire universe in its own way, and that expression of the universe which is a motion in the body is perhaps a pain in relation to the soul. But we attribute activity [*action*] to that substance whose expression is the more distinct, and we call it cause. Thus when a body passes through water, there is an infinity of motions of the parts of the water, such as there must be in order that the place which the body leaves may be filled up again by the shortest way. We say that this body is the cause of the motions, because by its means we can explain distinctly what happens ; but if we consider what is physical and real in the motion, we may equally well suppose that the body is at rest and that everything else moves, in accordance with the hypothesis, since the whole motion in itself is only a relative thing, viz. a change of position [*situation*] which we do not know how to explain with mathematical exactness; but we do attribute it to a body by means of which all is distinctly explained' [i. e. so far sufficiently explained, though not with mathematical exactness]. 'And in fact, taking all the phenomena little and great, there is only one hypothesis which serves to explain the whole distinctly. And we may indeed say that, although this body may not be an efficient physical cause of these effects, its idea is at least, so to speak, their final, or, if you like, archetypal [*exemplaire*] cause in the understanding of God. For, if we wish to find whether there is anything real in the motion, let us imagine that God wills directly to produce all the changes of situation in the universe exactly as if this vessel were producing them in passing through the water; is it not true that there would actually happen exactly the same thing? For it is impossible to assign any real difference. Thus, in metaphysical strictness, we have no more reason to say that the vessel compels the water to make this great number of ripples by means of which the place of the vessel is filled up, than to say that the water is compelled to make all these ripples and that it compels the vessel to move in conformity with it; but, except by saying that God has willed directly to produce so great a number of motions all tending to this one thing, we can give no reason for it, and as it is not reasonable to have recourse to God for the immediate explanation of matters of detail, we have recourse to the vessel, although actually, in an ultimate analysis, the agreement of all the phenomena of the various substances comes only from this, that they are all productions of one and the same cause, to wit, God; and consequently each individual substance expresses the resolution which God has taken with regard to the whole universe. . . . . It is quite right to say that my will is the cause of the motion of my arm and that a *solutio continui* in the matter of my body is the cause of pain, for the one expresses distinctly what the other expresses more confusedly, and activity [*action*] is to be attributed to the substance of which the expression is more distinct.' (p. 71.)

APPENDIX D.

LEIBNIZ'S LOGIC.

In the *Nouveaux Essais*, bk. iv. ch. 11, § 14 (E. 379a; G. v. 428', there is an interesting passage explaining in more detail a part of the logic of Leibniz. It contains some remarkable anticipations of more modern views. 'Propositions of fact also may become general in a way, but it is by induction or observation; so that it' [the general proposition of fact] 'is nothing but a multitude of similar facts, as when we observe that all quicksilver evaporates by the force of fire; and this is not a perfect generality, because we do not see its necessity. General propositions of reason are necessary, although reason also furnishes some which are not absolutely general and are only probable, as for instance, when we presume that an idea is possible, until a more strict investigation reveals its contrary. There are, finally, *mixed propositions*, which are drawn from premises, of which some come from facts and observations, while others are necessary propositions: and such are numerous geographical and astronomical conclusions about the globe of the earth and about the course of the stars, which conclusions are obtained by combining the observations of travellers and astronomers with the theorems of geometry and arithmetic. But as, according to the usage of logicians, *the conclusion follows the weaker of the premises*, and cannot have more certainty than they, these mixed propositions have only the certainty and generality which belong to observations. As to *eternal truths*, it is to be noted, that at bottom they are all conditional and say in effect: Granted such a thing, such another thing is. For instance, when I say, *Every figure which has three sides will also have three angles*, I say nothing but this, that supposing there is a figure with three sides, *this same figure* will have three angles. I say *this same figure*, and it is in this respect that categorical propositions, which can be stated unconditionally (although fundamentally they are conditional), differ from those that are called *hypothetical*, such as the following: *If a figure has three sides, its angles are equal to two right angles*. In this latter case we see that the *antecedent* (namely, the figure with three sides) and the *consequent* (namely, the angles of the three-sided figure are equal to two right angles) do not have the same subject, as they had in the preceding case in which the antecedent was—*This figure has three sides*, and the consequent—*The said figure has three angles*. Nevertheless the hypothetical might often be transformed into a categorical by a slight change in the terms, for instance, if in place of the preceding hypothetical I were to say: *The angles of every three-sided figure are equal to two right angles*. The Scholastics have argued much *de constantia subjecti*, as they called it, that is to say, how a proposition regarding a subject can have a real truth, if the subject has no existence. The fact is that the truth is only conditional and says that, supposing the subject ever exists, it will be found to be so-and-so. But it will still be asked: On what is this connexion founded, since there is within it reality which does not deceive? The reply will be, that it is in the connexion of ideas. But it will be asked again: Where would these ideas be, if no mind existed, and what would then become of the real foundation of this certainty of eternal truths? That leads us at last to the ultimate foundation of truths, namely, that supreme and universal spirit, which cannot but exist, whose understanding, to speak truly, is the region of eternal truths, as St. Augustine has recognized and says in a vivid way[1]. And lest it should be thought unnecessary to have recourse to this, it is to be noted that these necessary truths contain the determining reason and regulative principle of existences themselves, and, in a word, the laws of the universe. Thus these necessary truths, being anterior to the existence of contingent beings, must have their foundation in the existence of a necessary substance. It is here that I find the original of the ideas and truths which are graven in our souls, not in the form of propositions, but as sources from which application and opportunity will produce actual statements.'

[1] The reference may be to Augustine, *De Genesi ad Litteram*, bk. v. cap. 13 sqq. (Migne's ed., iii. 331 sqq.), or to *Enarratio in Psalmum* xlix. (Migne's ed., iv. 576 sqq.). Cf. *De diversis Quaestionibus*, Q. xlvi. § 2 (Migne's ed., vi. 30).

APPENDIX E.

THE Wolffians endeavoured to show that Kant's philosophy was merely a degenerate product of Leibnitian thought. In reply to Eberhard, Kant in 1790 wrote an interesting account of his own relation to Leibniz—*Über eine Entdeckung, nach der alle neue Kritik der reinen Vernunft durch eine ältere entbehrlich gemacht werden soll.* See Rosenkranz, i. pp. 478 sqq.; Hartenstein, iii. 390 sqq.

'The metaphysic of Leibniz contains three great original principles: (1) the principle of sufficient reason, especially in so far as it shows the insufficiency of the principle of contradiction for the knowledge of necessary truths; (2) the monadology; (3) the doctrine of the pre-established harmony. . . . . (1) Is it to be believed that Leibniz desired his principle of sufficient reason to be understood objectively (as a law of nature), when he attached a great importance to this principle as an addition to the principles of earlier philosophy? It is indeed so universally known and (within proper limits) so manifestly clear, that the poorest intellect could not imagine it had made a new discovery in finding it. Thus it is that critics, who have misunderstood it, have greatly ridiculed it. But for Leibniz this principle was merely a subjective one, that is to say, a principle having reference merely to a critique of reason. For what is meant by saying that, in addition to the principle of contradiction, there must be other first principles? It is as much as to say that, according to the principle of contradiction only that can be known which is already contained in the notion [*Begriff*] of the object; but if we say anything more about the object, something must be added to this notion, and thus we must find a special principle different from that of contradiction, for our assertions must have their own special reason. Now propositions of this latter kind are now-a-days called synthetic, and thus Leibniz means nothing but this: "In addition to the principle of contradiction (as the principle of analytic judgments), there must be another principle, namely that of synthetic judgments." This was a new and remarkable suggestion of investigations in metaphysics which had not yet been undertaken (and which have actually been undertaken only recently). .... (2) Is it to be believed that so great a mathematician as Leibniz held that bodies are composed of Monads (and consequently that space is made up of simple parts)? He referred not to the corporeal world, but to its substratum imperceptible [*unerkennbar*] to us, namely, the intelligible world which belongs merely to the idea of reason, and in which doubtless we must represent to ourselves as made up of simple substances everything which we think therein as compound substance. He likewise appears, like Plato, to attribute to the human mind an original, although at present only obscure, intellectual intuition [*Anschauen*] of these supersensible realities. But in this he did not refer to the things of sense, which he attributes to intuition [*Anschauung*] of a special kind, of which we are capable only in relation to things we can really know [*für uns mögliche Erkenntnisse*], and he regards the things of sense as mere phenomena (in the strict use of the term), as specific forms of intuition peculiar to us. With regard to this we must not allow ourselves to be perplexed by his explanation of sensation as a confused kind of perception, but must rather substitute for it another explanation more in harmony with his main purpose; for otherwise his system would be inconsistent with itself. To take this defect as a deliberate and careful speculation on the part of Leibniz (as copiers, in order to make their copy exactly the same as the original, reproduce its mistakes of form and language) can hardly be credited to the disciples of Leibniz as a service done to the fame of their master. Similarly, if it is taken too literally, a wrong interpretation is given to the view of Leibniz regarding the innateness of certain notions, by which he means a fundamental faculty to which the *a priori* principles of our knowledge are referable: he makes use of this idea merely as against Locke, who recognized no other than an empirical origin of these principles. (3) Is it possible to believe that, by his preestablished harmony between soul and body, Leibniz meant a mutual conformity of two beings entirely independent of one another as regards their nature and incapable of being brought into connexion through their own forces? That would have been to proclaim idealism; for why should the existence of bodies in general be admitted, if it is possible to regard everything that takes place in the soul as the effect of its own powers, which it would exercise even if it were entirely isolated? The soul and the substratum (entirely unknown to us) of the phenomena which we call bodies are indeed two quite different beings, but these phenomena themselves, as mere forms of their intuition [Anschauung] depending upon the nature of the subject (the soul), are mere perceptions [Vorstellungen]. Hence the connexion between understanding and sense in the same subject can be understood according to certain a priori laws, as well as the necessary and natural dependence of sense upon external things, without sacrificing external things to idealism. For this harmony between understanding and sense, in so far as it renders possible a priori the knowledge of universal laws of nature, criticism has given as a reason that without this harmony no experience is possible. . . . . But we can give no reason why we have just such a kind of sense and an understanding of such a nature that through their combination experience is possible; and further we can find no reason why they, as completely heterogeneous sources of knowledge, always so completely harmonize in rendering possible experiential knowledge in general and more especially (as the Critique of Judgment shows) in rendering possible an experience of nature, under its manifold special and merely empirical laws, regarding which the understanding teaches us nothing a priori. Neither we nor any one else can explain how this harmony is as complete as if nature had been arranged expressly to suit our power of comprehension. Leibniz called the principle of this union (especially with reference to the knowledge of bodies and in particular of our own body as a middle term in this relation) a pre-established harmony. Manifestly he did not in this way give an explanation of the union, nor did he profess to explain it. He merely pointed out that we must regard the order established by the supreme cause of ourselves as well as of all things outside of us as involving a certain conformity to end. This purpose is regarded as present at creation (pre-established); yet as a pre-established agreement, not between things taken as outside one another, but only between our mental powers of sense and understanding, according to the special constitution of each in relation to the other. In the same way criticism teaches that, in order to a knowledge of things *a priori*, these powers must stand in relationship to one another in the mind. That this was what Leibniz really meant, although he did not clearly develop it, appears from this, that he extends the application of the pre-established harmony beyond the relation between soul and body to the relation between the kingdom of *nature* and the kingdom of *grace* (the kingdom of ends in relation to the supreme end, i. e. man under moral laws). Here the harmony is to be thought of as a harmony between what follows from our notions of nature and what follows from our notions of freedom, and thus as a harmony between two completely different powers in us, having completely dissimilar principles, and not between two different things taken as *external to one another*. And this harmony, as the *Critique* teaches, can in no way be comprehended from the nature of created things [*Weltwesen*] but, as it is for us an essentially contingent harmony, it can only be understood by referring it to an intelligent cause of the world.'

THE MONADOLOGY

THE MONADOLOGY[1]. 1714.

----◆----

PREFATORY NOTE.

THE *Monadology* is one of the latest of the works of Leibniz, having been written at Vienna in 1714, two years before his death. On this last visit of his to Vienna he had met the soldier prince Eugene of Savoy, who (probably through Queen Sophia Charlotte of Prussia) had heard of the one great work Leibniz had hitherto published, the *Théodicée*, which appeared in 1710. Having read the *Théodicée*, Prince Eugene begged Leibniz to write for him a condensed statement of the main principles of his philosophy, and having obtained this, in the form either of what we now call the *Monadology* or of the *Principles of Nature and of Grace*, he was so delighted with it that he kept it like a jewel in a case, so that his friend, Count Bonneval, wrote to Leibniz, perhaps with a touch of humorous exaggeration :—'He keeps your writing as the priests at Naples keep the blood of St. Januarius; he lets me kiss it and immediately shuts it up again in its casket.' (Guhrauer, ii. 287.)

The *Monadology* was written in French; but it was not published in its original form until 1840, when Erdmann, who had discovered the MS. in the Royal Library at Hanover, printed it in his edition of the philosophical works of Leibniz. German and Latin translations of it appeared in 1720 and 1721, and it was for a long time combined with the *Principles of*

---

[1] Erdmann gave the name '*La Monadologie*' to this work when he published it in 1840. Köhler published a German version of it in 1720, under the title: *Lehrsätze über die Monadologie*, &c. Dutens gives a Latin translation of the German and entitles it : *Principia philosophiae seu theses in gratiam Principis Eugenii*. The original MSS. have no title.

Nature and of Grace, there being some doubt as to which of the two was the treatise written for Prince Eugene. The two writings are similar in scope and intention, and were probably written about the same time. Gerhardt holds that the work written for Prince Eugene was not the *Monadology* but the *Principles of Nature and of Grace*. (See G. vi. 483 and prefatory note to the *Principles of Nature and of Grace* in this edition.) The *Principles of Nature and of Grace* certainly appears to be the earlier of the two.

As to its contents, the *Monadology* is to be regarded, not as an introduction to the philosophy of Leibniz, but rather as a condensed statement of the principles expressed in many philosophical papers, and expounded, after a somewhat desultory fashion, in the *Théodicée*. Leibniz himself indicated this fact by putting on the margin of his manuscript of the *Monadology* a series of references to sections of the *Théodicée* in which his views are more fully expressed. Thus, as Erdmann says, the *Monadology* is (in the German sense) an 'Encyclopaedia' of the philosophy of Leibniz, and the full understanding of it presupposes some general knowledge of his thinking. It is not possible rightly to understand it at a first reading.

The *Monadology* expounds a Metaphysic of Substance, and it may for convenience be regarded as consisting of two main divisions, in the first of which an account is given of the essential nature of all the substances, created and uncreated, which constitute the reality of the universe, while the second division explains the mutual relations through which they form one world. §§ 1 to 48 make up the first of these divisions, the second consisting of §§ 49 to 90. In the first division three principal parts may be discriminated; (a) §§ 1–18, in which the nature of Created Monads is explained; (b) §§ 19–30, in which three great classes of Created Monads are discriminated; and (c) §§ 31–48, in which transition is made from the highest class of Created Monads (the self-conscious) to the Uncreated Monad (God) through the two great principles of Reason, that of Contradiction and that of Sufficient Reason. Thus a philosophic view is taken of the whole universe, considered as a hierarchy of individual beings. The second division of the *Monadology*, in which the mutual relations of substances are more fully explained, may also be subdivided into three principal parts : (a) §§ 49–60, expounding the general principles of the inter-relation of substances through the hypothesis of the Pre-established Harmony and the doctrine of 'the best of all possible worlds'; (b) §§ 61–82, explaining in more detail the relations of particular classes of substances to one another, and dealing with questions of organism and of the relations of soul and body, including birth and death, &c.; and (c) §§ 83–90, in which the whole system of relations is brought to unity in God, the distinction and harmony between efficient and final causes (which had been found to be the basis of the distinction between body and soul), being supplemented by an analogous distinction and harmony between the 'physical realm of nature and the moral realm of grace, that is to say, between God, considered as Architect of the machine of the universe and God considered as Monarch of the divine City of spirits.' This brief analysis is to be taken merely as a suggestion of the line of thought in the *Monadology*; the texture of the work is so close that it is impossible to make perfectly satisfactory divisions in it.

The translation is made from the text given by M. Boutroux, who has collated the MSS. at Hanover and corrected some errors of Erdmann. The *Monadology* is given in E. 705 sqq.; G. vi. 607 sqq.

1. The Monad, of which we shall here speak, is nothing but a *simple* substance, which enters into compounds. By 'simple' is meant 'without parts.' (*Théod.* 10.)

2. And there must be simple substances, since there are compounds; for a compound[2] is nothing but a collection or *aggregatum* of simple things[3].

---

[2] There is a slight but interesting difference between this and the corresponding passage in the *Principles of Nature and of Grace* (see p. 406). Leibniz speaks here of 'a compound' in general (*le composé*): in the other passage he uses the expression 'compound substance' (*la composée*). In both cases he must be understood to mean 'body,' which, he elsewhere tells us, is not a substance, strictly speaking (Introduction, Part iii. pp. 96 and 111). Accordingly, the expression here is more exact than that in the *Principles of Nature and of Grace*; but the difference illustrates the looseness of Leibniz's terminology in this connexion.

[3] If the 'simple things' are, like the Monads, non-quantitative, can we attach any intelligible meaning to 'compounds,' which are mere aggregates of them? Does not an aggregate always imply

3. Now where there are no parts[4], there can be neither extension nor form [*figure*] nor divisibility. These Monads are the real atoms of nature and, in a word, the elements of things[5].

4. No dissolution of these elements need be feared, and there is no conceivable way in which a simple substance can be destroyed by natural means. (*Théod.* 89.)

5. For the same reason there is no conceivable way in which a simple substance can come into being by natural means, since it cannot be formed by the combination of parts [*composition*][6].

elements which are quantities, however small? Leibniz elsewhere makes it perfectly clear that nothing quantitative can ever be absolutely simple, and thus there seems a weakness in his reasoning at this point. The difficulty is fundamental and affects the whole of Leibniz's system: it is, indeed, the crux of every Individualist or Atomist philosophy. Leibniz's hypothesis of a 'living [*formel*] atom,' a 'fertile simplicity,' a 'centre which expresses (or represents) an infinite circumference' (*Réponse aux Réflexions de Bayle*, 1702, E. 187 a; G. iv. 562), is the suggestion of a way out of Atomism; but it does not take us entirely out of the wood. We have still, in the spirit of much of Leibniz's philosophizing, to ask ourselves the question—'Are not "simple" and "compound" purely relative terms, so that to search for an absolutely simple thing is to explore blind alleys?' Kant shows us the blind alleys in his second Antinomy (*Critique of Pure Reason*, Meiklejohn's Tr., p. 271). See also the interesting analysis and criticism of Kant's arguments in Hegel's *Wissenschaft der Logik*, bk. i. div. 2, ch. i. sect. A, note. Cf. Hegel's *Geschichte der Philosophie*, vol. iii. p. 525 (Eng. Tr., p. 449).

[4] i. e. where there are no spatial distinctions.

[5] Cf. *New System*, § 3. Ordinary physical atoms have form and extension; and, though they may not be physically divisible, yet they must be ideally divisible *ad infinitum*, inasmuch as they occupy space. Thus for Leibniz all merely physical atoms are unreal. Cf. Lange's *History of Materialism*, bk. i. sect. 4, ch. iv. (Eng. Tr., vol. ii. pp. 124 sqq.).

[6] According to Leibniz a thing is produced by nature only when it comes into being gradually, bit by bit. But the Monads, having no parts, cannot come into being by the adding of part to part. Yet it may be pointed out that every Monad has an *internal* development, which is gradual. It is not born perfect, fully realized. Why, then, should it not come into being by natural means?

6. Thus it may be said that a Monad can only come into being or come to an end all at once; that is to say, it can come into being only by creation and come to an end only by annihilation, while that which is compound comes into being or comes to an end by parts[7].

7. Further, there is no way of explaining how a Monad can be altered in quality or internally changed[8] by any other created thing; since it is impossible to change the place of anything in it or to conceive in it any internal motion which could be produced, directed, increased or diminished therein, although all this is possible in the case of compounds, in which there are changes among the parts[9]. The Monads have no windows, through which anything could come in or go out. Accidents cannot separate themselves from substances nor go about outside of them, as the 'sensible species' of the Scholastics used to do[10]. Thus

[7] Consider, by way of analogy and contrast, what Spinoza says regarding the eternity of the human mind, *Ethics*, v. prop. 23. Spinoza dispenses with the idea of creation. But according to Leibniz there are created Monads, whose creation is, nevertheless, not an event in time, for time and space have to do merely with phenomena, and the Monads are not in time and space, but condition them. Cf. § 47 and Introduction, Part iii. p. 101.

[8] The meaning is that by other things the Monad can neither be altered as to its nature, i.e. changed into something else, nor even affected in those changes of state which it can undergo without a change of nature.

[9] It is implied that all changes in bodies are reducible to transposition of parts, and ultimately to changes in the amount and direction of motion. See Introduction, Part iii. pp. 89 sqq.

[10] Leibniz seems here to have in view partly the doctrines of Thomas Aquinas and partly the scholastic theories which were based on the system of Democritus. The 'species' are images or immaterial representations of material qualities. According to Thomas Aquinas, the accidents of things are known to us by means of sensible species, or particular images, while we know the essences of things by means of intelligible species or general images. The scholastic theory in general may be said to be that the sensible or intelligible 'species' in us have something in common with the accidents or essences in things, though there

neither substance nor accident can come into a Monad from outside [11].

8. Yet the Monads must have some qualities, otherwise they would not even be existing things [12]. And if simple substances did not differ in quality, there would be

is a considerable variety of more or less vague opinion as to the nature of the relation. Leibniz is evidently thinking of a theory (*not* that of Thomas Aquinas), according to which sense-perception means that particles are detached from the body perceived and pass into the percipient, in whom they are reconstructed into images or representations of qualities in the thing perceived. Images of this kind were called εἴδωλα by Democritus. Cf. Ritter and Preller, *Historia Philosophiae Graecae*, § 155. Atomists felt bound to explain the action of body upon soul by the suggestion of some kind of *influxus physicus*. Descartes has a parallel passage to this of Leibniz, in which he says that he ' desires to rid people's minds of all these little images, flying through the air, called *intentional species*, which give so much work to the imagination of philosophers.' *Dioptrique*, Discours I. Cf. other passages quoted by Veitch in his *Translation of Descartes's Method and Meditations*, note 2—'Idea.'

[11] Kant pointed out that a thing may have 'intensive' as well as 'extensive' quantity, i.e. quantity which is not divisible into spatial parts as well as quantity which is so divisible. A stone descending from a height loses a certain 'intensive quantity' without losing any of its spatial parts. And thus a simple substance may, in a certain sense, lose and receive quality. Cf. *Critique of Pure Reason* (Hartenstein, ii. 178; Rosenkranz, ii. 145; Meiklejohn's Tr., p. 125). Kant argues that the simplicity of the soul (i.e. the absence of parts in it) does not necessarily prove its indestructibility, for, though it has no parts, it may lose consciousness and the rest of its essential qualities (Hartenstein, ii. 318; Rosenkranz, ii. 792; Meiklejohn's Tr., p. 245). Compare Kant's 'intensive quantity' with Leibniz's degrees of Perception and Appetition.

[12] After this sentence Leibniz originally wrote, and then deleted, these words : 'And if simple substances were nonentities [*riens*], compounds also would be reduced to nothing.' This emphasizes the point that a being without quality is indistinguishable from nothing ; cf. Hegel's *Logic*, Wallace's Tr., pp. 158 sqq. Quantity always presupposes quality ; see Introduction, Part ii. pp. 27 sqq. Leibniz seems also to imply that each Monad must have more than one quality. On the other hand, Herbart (1776–1841), whose Monadology owes much to that of Leibniz, and who calls his Monads 'primary qualities' (*Urqualitäten*), holds that a substance cannot be perfectly simple unless it has only one ultimate quality.

absolutely no means of perceiving any change in things. For what is in the compound can come only from the simple elements it contains, and the Monads, if they had no qualities, would be indistinguishable from one another, since they do not differ in quantity [13]. Consequently, space being a *plenum*, each part of space would always receive, in any motion, exactly the equivalent of what it already had, and no one state of things would be discernible from another [14].

[13] Kant would say that they may differ in 'intensive quantity'; see note 11. Leibniz makes the distinction between quality and quantity as sharp as the Aristotelian distinction between ποῖον and πόσον. Yet in some respects his Law of Continuity suggests a different view.

[14] E. reads 'one state of things would be indistinguishable from another.' Cf. *Epistola ad Des Bosses* (1706) (G. ii. 295) : 'If we were to admit, as the Cartesians desire, the *plenum* and the uniformity of matter, adding to these motion alone, it would follow that nothing would ever take place among things but a substitution of equivalents, as if the whole universe were reduced to the motion of a perfectly uniform wheel about its axis or, again, to the revolutions of concentric circles, each made of exactly the same materials. The result of this would be that it would not be possible, even for an angel, to distinguish the state of things at one moment from their state at another. For there could be no variety in the phenomena. Accordingly, in addition to figure, size, and motion, we must allow certain Forms, whence there arises a distinction among the phenomena of matter ; and I do not see whence these Forms are to be taken, if they are to be intelligible, unless it be from Entelechies.' To avoid a possible misunderstanding, it should be noted that for Leibniz, the Monads are not in space, which is a relation between phenomena ; see Introduction, Part iii. p. 101. Cf. *Epistola ad Des Bosses* (1712) (E. 682 b ; G. ii. 450): 'Space is the order of co-existing phenomena, as time is the order of successive phenomena. There is no nearness or distance, whether spatial or absolute, among Monads, and to say that they are collected together in one point or dispersed throughout space, is to make use of certain fictions of our mind, by which we try to represent to ourselves in imagination what cannot be imagined but only understood.' Kant, misled by the position of Wolff, does not rightly interpret Leibniz's view of space, which he discusses in the *Critique of Pure Reason*, Hartenstein, ii. 256 sqq. ; Rosenkranz, ii. 216 sqq. ; Meiklejohn's Tr., pp. 191 sqq., especially p. 199. Cf. Introduction, Part iv. pp. 168 sqq.

9. Indeed, each Monad must be different from every other. For in nature there are never two beings which are perfectly alike and in which it is not possible to find an internal difference, or at least a difference founded upon an intrinsic quality [*dénomination*] [15].

10. I assume also as admitted that every created being, and consequently the created Monad, is subject to change, and further that this change is continuous in each [16].

[15] This is the principle of the 'Identity of indiscernibles'; see Introduction, Part ii. p. 36.   Cf. *Nouveaux Essais*, bk. ii. ch. xxvii. § 3 (E. 277 b ; G. v. 214).   For Kant's criticism see *Critique of Pure Reason*, Hartenstein, ii. 267 ; Rosenkranz, ii. 229 ; Meiklejohn's Tr., p. 202.   Probably the first statement of the principle is to be found in the writings of Nicholas of Cusa (1401-1464).   He says that 'there cannot be several things exactly the same [*aequalia*], for in that case there would not be several things, but the same thing itself.   Therefore all things both agree with and differ from one another.' (*De Venatione Sapientiae*, 23.)   Cf. *De docta ignorantia*, iii. 1 : 'All things must of necessity differ from one another.   Among several individuals of the same species there is necessarily a diversity of degrees of perfection.   There is nothing in the universe which does not enjoy a certain *singularity*, which is to be found in no other thing.'   His theories are full of suggestions of Leibniz.   Cf. Falckenberg, *History of Modern Philosophy*, English Tr., pp. 20 sqq. Reference may also be made to a very interesting article by Zimmermann, *Nicolaus Cusanus als Vorläufer Leibnitzens* (*Wien. Akad. Sitzungsberichte*, vol. 8, p. 306).   There is no mention of Nicholas of Cusa in any of Leibniz's philosophical writings ; but in a letter to the *Acta Eruditorum* (1697) Leibniz refers to him as a mathematician (cf. Dutens, iii. 345).—*Intrinsic* qualities are those which things have in themselves, e. g. figure, motion, &c., while *extrinsic* qualities are those which arise from their relations to other things, e. g. their being perceived, desired, &c.   Cf. *Port-Royal Logic*, part i. ch. ii. (Baynes's Tr., p. 37) : 'There are some modes which may be called *internal*, because they are conceived to be in the substance, as *round*, *square* ; and others which may be called *external*, because they are taken from something which is not in the substance, as *loved*, *seen*, *desired*, which are names taken from the actions of another—and this is what is called in the schools *external denomination*.'

[16] There is constant change in created substances, even though there may appear to be no change.   What appears to us as absence of change is really a very small degree of change.   We have here an application of the Law of Continuity.

11. It follows from what has just been said, that the natural[17] changes of the Monads come from an *internal principle*, since an external cause can have no influence upon their inner being. (*Théod.* 396, 400.)

12[18]. But, besides the principle of the change, there must be *a particular series of changes* [*un détail de ce qui change*], which constitutes, so to speak, the specific nature and variety of the simple substances.

13. This particular series of changes should involve a multiplicity in the unit [*unité*] or in that which is simple. For, as every natural change takes place gradually, something changes and something remains unchanged[19]; and consequently a simple substance must be affected and related in many ways, although it has no parts[20].

[17] i.e. other than miraculous changes or than such change as may be implied in the creation or annihilation of a Monad.

[18] At the beginning of § 12 Leibniz originally wrote : 'And generally it may be said that force is nothing but the principle of the change.' He seems afterwards to have felt that force was not a deep enough notion to be an adequate expression of the principle which, in §§ 14 and 15, he describes under the names of Perception and Appetition.

[19] The Law of Continuity. Everything is continually changing. and in every part of this change there is both a permanent and a varying element. That is to say, at any moment everything both ' is ' and ' is not,' everything is becoming something else—something which is, nevertheless, not entirely ' other.'

[20] In illustration of this and the following sections, cf. *Réponse aux Réflexions de Bayle* (1702) (E. 186 b ; G. iv. 562) : ' The state of the *soul*, as of the *atom*, is a state of change, a tendency. The atom tends to change its place, the soul to change its thought : each changes of itself in the simplest and most uniform way, that its state allows. Whence comes it, then (I shall be asked), that there is so much simplicity in the change of the *atom* ' [which is taken as being always motion in a straight line at a uniform speed] ' and so much variety in the changes of the *soul*? The reason is that the atom (as it is supposed to be, for there is no such thing in nature), although it has parts, has nothing which causes any variety in its tendency, because it is supposed that these parts do not change their relations ; while on the other hand the soul, though it is perfectly indivisible, has a composite tendency, that is to say, it contains a multitude of present thoughts, of which each tends to

14. The passing condition, which involves and represents a multiplicity in the unit [*unité*] or in the simple
substance, is nothing but what is called *Perception* [21],
which is to be distinguished from Apperception or
Consciousness, as will afterwards appear. In this matter
the Cartesian view is extremely defective, for it treats as
non-existent those perceptions of which we are not
consciously aware [22]. This has also led them to believe
that minds [*esprits*] alone are Monads, and that there are
no souls of animals nor other Entelechies. Thus, like the
crowd, they have failed to distinguish between a prolonged
unconsciousness and absolute death [23], which has made

a particular change, according to the nature of its content, and
which all are present together in the soul, in virtue of the soul's
essential relation to all the other things in the world. It is because
they do not have this relation that the atoms of Epicurus have no
existence in nature. For there is no individual thing, which is
not to be regarded as expressing all others; and consequently the
soul, in regard to the variety of its *modifications*, ought to be likened
to the *universe*, which it represents according to its point of view,
and even in a way to God, whose *infinity* it represents *finitely*, because
of its confused and imperfect perception of the infinite, rather than
to a *material atom.*' Cf. Appendix F, p. 272.

[21] Cf. *Epistola ad Des Bosses* (1706) (E. 438 a; G. ii. 311): 'Since
perception is nothing else than the expression of many things in
one, all Entelechies or Monads must necessarily be endowed with
perception.' Also *Lettre à Arnauld* (1687) (G. ii. 112): 'Because of
the continuity and divisibility of all matter, the least motion has
its effect upon neighbouring bodies, and consequently upon one
body after another *ad infinitum*, in a gradually lessening degree;
and thus our body must in some way be affected by the changes in
all other bodies. Now, to all the motions of our body there correspond certain more or less confused perceptions of our soul, and
accordingly our soul also will have some thought of all the motions
in the universe, and in my opinion every other soul or substance
will have some perception or expression of them.' See Introduction,
Part ii. p. 33.

[22] Cf. *Method*, Part 5, and *Meditations*, 2 and 6. See also *Principia
Philosophiae*, i. 48, and cf. Introduction, Part iii. p. 126. The Cartesian view is that animals and plants are purely mechanical
structures or living automata, parts of extension, entirely separate
from thought.

Sleep, which is an image of death, trances, the burying of

them fall again into the Scholastic prejudice of souls entirely separate [from bodies], and has even confirmed ill-balanced[24] minds in the opinion that souls are mortal[25].

a silkworm in its cocoon, the resuscitation of drowned flies by means of a dry powder sprinkled upon them (when they would remain quite dead, if this were not done), the resuscitation of swallows which make their winter quarters among the reeds, where they are found without any appearance of life, the cases of men frozen to death, drowned, or strangled, who have been brought to life again . . . all these things serve to confirm my opinion that these different conditions differ only in degree, and if we have not the means of bringing about resuscitation from death in other forms, it is either because we do not know what ought to be done or because, though we do know it, our hands, our instruments, and our remedies cannot accomplish it, especially when dissolution takes place too quickly and has gone too far. Accordingly we must not content ourselves with the notions which the common people may have about life and death, when we have both analogies and (what is more) solid arguments which prove the contrary. *Lettre à Arnauld* (1687) (G. ii. 123).

[24] E. reads *mal touchés* ; G. and Boutroux, *mal tournés*.

[25] Descartes regards the immortality of the soul as ultimately dependent on the will of God. See the *Abrégé* prefixed to the *Méditations* [*Synopsis* in Veitch's translation]. Cf. *Réponses aux Deuxièmes Objections*, 7. Leibniz thus criticizes the view of Descartes: 'The immortality of the soul, as it is established by Descartes, is of no use and can give us no kind of consolation. For, granting that the soul is a substance and that no substance perishes, the soul then will not be lost, as, indeed, nothing is lost in nature; but, like matter, the soul will change in appearance and, as the matter of which a man is made has at other times belonged to plants and animals, in the same way the soul may be immortal, indeed, but it will pass through innumerable changes and will have no recollection of its former states. But this immortality without recollection is ethically quite useless; for it is inconsistent with reward and punishment. What good, sir, would it do you to become king of China, on condition that you forget what you have been? Would it not be the same as if God, at the moment He destroyed you, were to create a king in China?' (G. iv. p. 300.) From his own point of view, however, Descartes can say: 'Although all the accidents of the mind be changed—although, for example, it think certain things, will others, and perceive others, the mind itself does not vary with these changes; while, on the contrary, the human body is no longer the same if a change take place in the form of any of its parts.' *Abrégé des Méditations.* It

15. The activity of the internal principle which produces change or passage from one perception to another may be called *Appetition*. It is true that desire [*l'appétit*] cannot always fully attain to the whole perception at which it aims, but it always obtains some of it and attains to new perceptions [26].

16. We have in ourselves experience of a multiplicity in simple substance, when we find that the least thought of which we are conscious involves variety in its object [27]. Thus all those who admit that the soul is a simple substance should admit this multiplicity in the Monad ; and M. Bayle [28] ought not to have found any difficulty

seems to me not improbable that in the last words of this section Leibniz may have in view, among others, the wandering Irishman, John Toland (1670-1722), author of *Christianity not Mysterious*, who was in Berlin in 1702 and had a brief correspondence with Leibniz, in which the question of the immortality of the soul is referred to. Leibniz writes to the Princess Sophia Charlotte with something like a kindly contempt of Toland's readiness to take either side of a question. See G. vi. pp. 508 sqq. Cf. *Principles of Nature and of Grace*, § 4.

[26] See *Introduction*, Part ii. p. 33. Cf. *Principles of Nature and of Grace*, § 2. In many of his writings Leibniz uses the word 'tendencies' (*tendances*) for appetitions. Force is a form of appetition or tendency, i. e. it is not merely what actually appears as motion, &c., but it includes something *potential*. And it is not *really*, but only *ideally*, an influence of one substance upon another. Cf. appetition, in respect of likeness and difference, with Spinoza's *Conatus*.

[27] Cf. *Nouveaux Essais*, bk. ii. ch. 2 (E. 227 a ; G. v. 109).

[28] Pierre Bayle, the son of a Protestant clergyman, was born at Carlat in Languedoc, in 1647. He was educated at the University of Toulouse, where, under the influence of Jesuit teachers, he became a Roman Catholic. But his Roman Catholicism was not lasting and, having returned to his original faith, he avoided the censures of the Church by going to Geneva. After some years of wandering he became a Professor of Philosophy in the University of Sedan (1675). But owing to the 'free-thinking' of Bayle and others Louis XIV summarily suppressed this Protestant University in 1681, and Bayle went, as Professor of History and Philosophy, to a newly established institution at Rotterdam. In 1684 he founded the *Nouvelles de la République des Lettres*, a monthly review of new books, &c., to which there is frequent reference in the writings of Leibniz.

in this, as he has done in his Dictionary, article ' Rorarius ' [29].

17. Moreover, it must be confessed that *perception* and that which depends upon it are *inexplicable on mechanical*

[29] In 1693, ostensibly on political as well as theological grounds, he was deprived of his professorship, and he afterwards devoted himself to his *Dictionnaire Historique et Critique* (1695-96), which was the precursor of the Encyclopaedias and the Encyclopaedist movement in the following century. Among other writings he also published a tract against religious persecution and a reply to Maimbourg's libels upon Calvinism. He died in 1706. The *Théodicée* of Leibniz is to a large extent devoted to answering the arguments of Bayle, who maintained the impossibility of reconciling faith with reason. There is much difference of opinion as to whether Bayle was sincere in his combination of philosophical scepticism with an appeal to faith in matters of religion. Probably in this regard he meant to follow the example of Descartes. Leibniz seems to have believed in the sincerity of Bayle's religious faith. He always writes of Bayle with the greatest respect, saying of him (*Théod.* § 174) : ' *Ubi bene, nemo melius,*' and again, after his death : ' We must believe that Bayle is now enlightened with that light, which is refused to earth, since, according to all appearance, he has always been a man of good will.'

[29] Like the greater part of Bayle's Dictionary, the article ' Rorarius' may be said to consist mostly of foot-notes. Jerome Rorarius (1485-1566), an Italian, was Papal Nuncio at the Court of Ferdinand of Hungary. He was so great an admirer of the Emperor Charles V that, on hearing a learned man speak of him as inferior to Otho and to Frederick Barbarossa, he was moved to write a treatise maintaining that men are less rational than the lower animals. This treatise (*Quod animalia bruta ratione utantur melius homine*) was not published until about 100 years after it was written, when Descartes's views regarding the souls of animals were under discussion. Bayle accordingly makes the name of Rorarius the occasion of a full consideration of the question, in the course of which he expounds and criticizes the opinions of Leibniz. Bayle thinks it a pity that the position of Descartes is so difficult to maintain and so unlikely to be true ; for otherwise it would be very helpful to the true faith. That is to say, the Cartesian view is regarded as confirming belief in the immortality of the soul by making a very great distinction between man and ' the brutes which perish.' But it seems to Bayle that Leibniz (whom he calls ' one of the greatest minds in Europe ') has made some suggestions (in regard to the solution of the general problem) which are worthy of being developed. These suggestions are contained in the *New*

grounds, that is to say, by means of figures and motions. And supposing there were a machine, so constructed as to think, feel, and have perception, it might be conceived as increased in size, while keeping the same proportions, so that one might go into it as into a mill. That being so, we should, on examining its interior, find only parts which work one upon another, and never anything by which to explain a perception [30]. Thus it is in a simple substance, and not in a compound or in a machine, that perception must be sought for [31]. Further, nothing but this (namely, perceptions and their changes) can be found in a simple substance. It is also in this alone that all

System, which was published in the _Journal des Savans_ of June 27, 1695 (the year before the second vol. of Bayle's _Dictionary_ appeared). Bayle's criticism is directed mainly against the pre-established harmony and the spontaneous development of all their states by simple substances. Cf. Appendix F. p. 272.

[30] That is to say, even if we had microscopes powerful enough to reveal to us, on a large scale, all the intricacies of nerve-cell and nerve-fibre in the brain, we should still never get beyond figures and motions. Cf. _Commentatio de Anima Brutorum_ (1710) (E. 463 a ; G. vii. 328): 'If in that which is organic there is nothing but mechanism, that is, bare matter, having differences of place, magnitude and figure ; nothing can be deduced and explained from it, except mechanism, that is, except such differences as I have just mentioned. For from anything taken by itself nothing can be deduced and explained, except differences of the attributes which constitute it. Hence we may readily conclude that in no mill or clock as such is there to be found any principle which perceives what takes place in it; and it matters not whether the things contained in the "machine" are solid or fluid or made up of both. Further we know that there is no essential difference between coarse and fine bodies, but only a difference of magnitude. Whence it follows that, if it is inconceivable how perception arises in any coarse "machine," whether it be made up of fluids or solids, it is equally inconceivable how perception can arise from a finer "machine"; for if our senses were finer, it would be the same as if we were perceiving a coarse "machine," as we do at present.' See also _New Essays_, Introduction, p. 400.   (G. v. 59; E. 203 a.)

[31] Mechanism always means _partes extra partes_. This is characteristic of all compounds, but not of any simple substances. Thus it can never be said that matter thinks. Matter pre-supposes a thinking or at least a 'perceiving' principle.

the *internal activities* of simple substances can consist. (*Théod. Préf.* [E. 474 ; G. vi. 37].)

18. All simple substances or created Monads might be called Entelechies [32], for they have in them a certain perfection (ἔχουσι τὸ ἐντελές); they have a certain self-sufficiency (αὐτάρκεια) which makes them the sources of their internal activities and, so to speak, incorporeal automata [33]. (*Théod.* 87.)

---

[32] ἐντελέχεια is probably derived from ἐν τέλει ἔχειν, to be complete or absolute. Leibniz's use of the term differs considerably from that of Aristotle. ἐντελέχεια in Aristotle is the *state* of perfection or realization in which ἐνέργεια, as a *process*, ends. τοὔνομα ἐνέργεια λέγεται κατὰ τὸ ἔργον, καὶ συντείνει πρὸς τὴν ἐντελέχειαν. *Metaph.* Θ, 8, 1050ª 22. But the distinction between ἐντελέχεια and ἐνέργεια in Aristotle is not by any means a sharp one. Thus he defines the soul (ψυχή) as ἐντελέχεια ἡ πρώτη σώματος φυσικοῦ δυνάμει ζωὴν ἔχοντος. *De Anima*, ii. 1. But elsewhere he calls it οὐσία καὶ ἐνέργεια σώματός τινος. *Metaph.* H, 3, 1043ª 35. *First* entelechy is related to *second* entelechy as ἐπιστήμη (implicit) is related to θεωρεῖν (explicit). Thus the soul is defined as *first* or implicit entelechy because it exists in sleep as well as awake. The entelechy of Leibniz, however, is to be understood as an individual substance or force, containing within itself the principle of its own changes. It is called entelechy, not because it is a state of perfect realization, but because it contains in germ an infinity of perfections, which it tends to develop. It is thus not so much the final developed condition of a thing, opposed to its potentiality (δύναμις or ὕλη), but it rather implies the tendency or virtuality, of which Leibniz speaks as something intermediate between the bare potency (*puissance*) and the fully developed activity (*acte*) of the Scholastics. Cf. Introduction, Part iii. pp. 91, 105. 'The Forms of the Ancients or *Entelechies* are nothing but forces.' *Lettre au Père Bouvet*, E. 146 a. Cf. Trendelenburg, *De Anima*, pp. 295, 320. In the eighth book of Aristotle's *Metaphysics* there is a remark of much interest, when considered in relation to Leibniz : ἡ οὐσία ἐν οὕτως, ἀλλ' οὐχ ὡς λέγουσί τινες οἷον μονάς τις οὖσα ἢ στιγμή, ἀλλ' ἐντελέχεια καὶ φύσις τις ἑκάστη. H, 3, 1044ª 7. μονάς is, of course, used here in its original sense of a unit.

[33] That is to say, not merely machines, such as those made by man, but entirely self-moving machines or machines which contain within themselves the ground or principle of all their states or conditions, in as complete independence of all else as if there were nothing in the universe but God and themselves. Monads alone are automata in this sense. Corporeal automata, in so far as they

19. If we are to give the name of Soul to everything which has perceptions and desires [*appétits*] in the general sense which I have explained, then all simple substances or created Monads might be called souls; but as feeling [*le sentiment*] is something more than a bare perception, I think it right that the general name of Monads or Entelechies should suffice for simple substances which have perception only, and that the name of *Souls* should be given only to those in which perception is more distinct, and is accompanied by memory [34].

20. For we experience in ourselves a condition in which we remember nothing and have no distinguishable perception; as when we fall into a swoon or when we are overcome with a profound dreamless sleep. In this state the soul does not perceptibly differ from a bare Monad; but as this state is not lasting, and the soul comes out of it, the soul *is* something more than a bare Monad. (*Théod.* 64.)

21. And it does not follow that in this state the simple substance is without any perception. That, indeed, cannot be, for the reasons already given; for it cannot perish, and it cannot continue to exist without being affected in some way, and this affection [35] is nothing but its perception. But when there is a great multitude of little perceptions, in which there is nothing distinct, one is stunned; as when one turns continuously round in the

are corporeal, cannot be said to have this αὐτάρκεια. Cf. § 64. Spinoza speaks of the soul as 'acting according to certain laws and as if it were a kind of spiritual automaton.' *De Intellectus Emendatione*, 85; Bruder's ed., ii. 34.

[34] Memory is thus the sign of consciousness as distinct from unconscious perception. This is in harmony with the view, emphasized by modern writers, that conscious sensation pre-supposes memory, because we can know one sensation only when it has been brought into comparison with others. Leibniz in one of his early writings suggestively remarks that ·body is 'momentary mind, i. e. mind without memory' (*mens momentanea, seu carens recordatione*). *Theoria Motus Abstracti* (1671) (G. iv. 230).

[35] Leibniz originally wrote 'variation.'

same way several times in succession, whence comes a giddiness which may make us swoon, and which keeps us from distinguishing anything.[36]. Death can for a time put animals into this condition[37].

22. And as every present state of a simple substance is naturally a consequence of its preceding state, in such a way that its present is big with its future[38]; (*Théod.* 350.)

23. And as, on waking from stupor, *we are conscious* of our perceptions, we must have had perceptions immediately before we awoke, although we were not at all conscious of them; for one perception can in a natural way come only from another perception, as a motion can in a natural way come only from a motion[39]. (*Théod.* 401–403.)

24. It thus appears that if we had in our perceptions nothing marked and, so to speak, striking and highly-flavoured, we should always be in a state of stupor. And this is the state in which the bare Monads are.

25. We see also that nature has given heightened perceptions to animals, from the care she has taken to provide them with organs, which collect numerous rays of light, or numerous undulations of the air, in order, by uniting them, to make them have greater effect[40]. Some-

[36] Leibniz's point is that in such states as these we are still manifestly in certain peculiar relations to the external world, although consciousness has, for the time, become so slight as to be imperceptible.

[37] Cf. *Monadology*, § 14, note 23.   [38] Cf. §§ 78 and 79.

[39] In virtue of the principle of sufficient reason, every perception must have a cause, which can be nothing but another perception (see § 17); and if the antecedent perception did not *immediately* precede the consequent, there would be a breach of continuity in the existence of the soul. Ultimately, of course, motions are themselves perceptions; but they are confused perceptions, of such a kind that their relations to one another can be stated according to mechanical laws, which, however, are abstract and pre-suppose, for their full explanation, the system of final causes or the laws of perception in general.

[40] Cf. Helmholtz, *Popular Scientific Lectures*, vol. i. p. 186. See also *Principles of Nature and of Grace*, § 4.

thing similar to this takes place in smell, in taste and in touch, and perhaps in a number of other senses, which are unknown to us [41]. And I will explain presently [42] how that which takes place in the soul represents what happens in the bodily organs.

26. Memory provides the soul with a kind of *consecu-tiveness* [43], which resembles [*imite*] reason, but which is to be distinguished from it. Thus we see that when animals have a perception of something which strikes them and of which they have formerly had a similar perception, they are led, by means of representation in their memory, to expect what was combined with the thing in this previous perception, and they come to have feelings similar to those they had on the former occasion. For instance, when a stick is shown to dogs, they remember the pain it has caused them, and howl and run away [44]. (*Théod. Discours de la Conformité*, &c., § 65.)

27. And the strength of the mental image which impresses and moves them comes either from the magnitude or the number of the preceding perceptions. For often a strong impression produces all at once the same effect as a long-formed habit, or as many and oft-repeated ordinary perceptions [45].

[41] Cf. Lubbock, *Ants, Bees and Wasps*, ch. 8, especially pp. 220 and 225.

[42] See §§ 61 and 62.

[43] *Consecutio*, concatenation or sequence of perceptions. Leibniz is referring to what would now be called association 'of ideas. Cf. *Nouveaux Essais*, bk. ii. ch. 11, § 11 (E. 237 b; G. v. 130), and bk. ii. ch. 33 (E. 296 a; G. v. 252). In the latter of these chapters ('On the Association of Ideas') he is thinking mainly of a 'non-natural connexion of ideas,' as in the case of strange prejudices or superstitions.

[44] Does Leibniz in this section, as some critics maintain, overlook his 'Pre-established Harmony' and unconsciously adopt the ordinary point of view, which implies that substances *do* really act upon one another and are not each the cause of all its own experiences?

[45] Cf. *Nouveaux Essais*, bk. ii. ch. 33 (E. 296 a; G. v. 252). 'And as the reasons' [of the connexion of things] 'are often unknown to

28. In so far as the concatenation of their perceptions is due to the principle of memory alone, men act like the lower animals, resembling the empirical physicians [46], whose methods are those of mere practice without theory. Indeed, in three-fourths of our actions we are nothing but empirics. For instance, when we expect that there will be daylight to-morrow, we do so empirically, because it has always so happened until now. It is only the astronomer who thinks it on rational grounds [47].

29. But it is the knowledge of necessary and eternal truths that distinguishes us from the mere animals and gives us *Reason* and the sciences, raising us to the knowledge of ourselves and of God [48]. And it is this in us that is called the rational soul or mind [*esprit*].

us, we must attend to particular instances in proportion to their frequency; for then the expectation or recollection of another perception, usually connected with the perception we are experiencing, is reasonable; especially in cases where we have to take precautions. But as the violence [*véhémence*] of a very powerful impression often produces all at once as much effect as the frequency and repetition of several moderate impressions could have done in the long-run, it happens that this violence engraves in the fancy an image as deep and as vivid as long experience could have done. Whence it comes that a chance but violent impression combines in our memory two ideas, which were already together there, and gives us the same inclination to connect them and to expect the one after the other, as if long custom had verified their connexion. Thus association produces the same effect, though the same reason does not exist. Authority and custom produce also the same effect as experience and reason, and it is not easy to free oneself from these inclinations.' Cf. *New Essays*, Introduction, p. 364.

[46] Until the time of Galen (*circa* 150 A.D.), there were various sects of physicians. One of these was the sect of the Empirics, who laid stress upon observation of the 'visible' antecedents of disease, &c. In later times the name of empiric fell into disrepute and was given to physicians who despised theoretical study and trusted to tradition and to their own individual experience.

[47] Cf. *New Essays*, Introduction, p. 365, note 39.

[48] The necessary and eternal truths are the first principles of all rational knowledge. They are innate in us. They are, in fact, the very principles of our nature, as of the universe, because it is of our essence to represent the whole universe. Thus conscious-

30. It is also through the knowledge of necessary truths, and through their abstract expression, that we rise to *acts of reflexion*, which make us think of what is called *I*, and observe that this or that is within us: and thus, thinking of ourselves, we think of being, of substance, of the simple and the compound, of the immaterial, and of God Himself, conceiving that what is limited in us is in Him without limits. And these acts of reflexion furnish the chief objects of our reasonings[19]. (*Théod. Préf.* [E. 469; G. vi. 27].)

ness or knowledge of these truths is knowledge of ourselves, and it is at the same time knowledge of God, who is the final reason of all things. Cf. *Nouveaux Essais*, bk. i. ch. 1, § 4 (E. 207 b; G. v. 72). 'A pretty general agreement among men is an indication and not a demonstration of an innate principle; but the exact and decisive proof of these principles consists in showing that their certainty comes only from what is in us. . . . It may be said that all Arithmetic and all Geometry are innate and are in us in a virtual manner, so that we could find them by attentively considering and arranging what is already in our mind, without making use of any truth learned by experience or by external tradition, as Plato has shown in a dialogue' [*Meno*, 82 sqq.] 'in which he introduces Socrates leading a child to abstruse truths by questions alone, without giving him any information.' Cf. *Principles of Nature and of Grace*, § 5.

[19] Thus consciousness becomes self-consciousness (reflective consciousness) when we realize the eternal truths as eternal, that is to say, as the innate principles of our being and of the whole world. Substance is always a soul of some kind, because it must be something analogous to what we find in ourselves. Cf. *Nouveaux Essais*, bk. i. ch. 1, § 21 (E. 211 b; G. v. 70). 'Very often knowledge of the nature of things is nothing but knowledge of the nature of our mind [*esprit*] and of those innate ideas, which there is no need to look for outside of it.' Cf. also § 23 (E. 212 b; G. v. 71): 'Intellectual ideas or ideas of reflexion are derived from our mind; and I should like very much to know how we could have the idea of being, were it not that we ourselves are beings and thus find being in ourselves.' We see here (in however imperfect a form) the germ of the Kantian transition from 'substance' to 'subject' as the ultimate metaphysical reality. Cf. p. 190.

Boutroux finds in this passage the indication of a succession of stages in the progress of self-conscious reflexion. The nature of God is the truth or ultimate reality of our nature. Thus in 'reflexion, that is to say, in the return of the being towards its

31. Our reasonings are grounded upon *two great princi-ples, that of contradiction,* in virtue of which we judge *false* that which involves a contradiction, and *true* that which is opposed or contradictory to the false[50]; (*Théod.* 44, 169.)

32. And *that of sufficient reason,* in virtue of which we hold that there can be no fact real or existing, no statement true, unless there be a sufficient reason, why it should be so and not otherwise, although these reasons usually cannot be known by us[51]. (*Théod.* 44, 196.)

33. There are also two kinds of *truths,* those of *reason-*

source, which is God . . . we first of all come upon the ego, or the being which is in us, in so far as it is limited and distinct from other beings, and then upon being, substance and the immaterial, coming ever nearer to the Divine Essence itself. And finally, through perception which has thus become reflective and conscious, we reach the Infinite Being, whom, from the first, created beings are seeking confusedly and unwittingly. Then the circle, so to speak, closes upon itself: the created being identifies itself with the Creator in so far as He is in it; the finite has done all that its nature allowed in the way of reproducing the infinite.' (Edition of *La Monadologie,* p. 156.)

[50] Cf. Introduction, Part ii. pp. 58 sqq. Leibniz sometimes distinguishes between the principle of contradiction and that of identity $(A = A)$. But he recognizes that they are ultimately one. Cf. *Nouveaux Essais,* bk. iv. ch. 2, § 1 (E. 339 a; G. v. 343). 'The principle of contradiction is in general : *a proposition is either true or false.* This contains two true statements ; (1) that the true and the false are not compatible in the same proposition or *that a proposition cannot be true and false at the same time* ; (2) that the opposites or negations of the true and the false are not compatible, or that there is no middle term between the true and the false, or rather *that it is impossible for a proposition to be neither true nor false.'* See Aristotle, *Metaph.* Γ, 3, 1005^b 19 and 7, 1011^b 23.

[51] In his earlier writings Leibniz calls the sufficient reason the determining reason, meaning the reason which determines the existence of this or that out of a number of possibilities, each of which involves no self-contradiction. As synonymous with the 'principle of sufficient reason,' he also sometimes uses the phrase, 'principle of fitness [*convenance*] or of harmony.' He thus suggests that the sufficient reason of a thing is always to be found in its relations to other things, its place in the general system. We give the sufficient reason of anything when we show its 'compossibility' with other

ing and those of *fact* [52]. Truths of reasoning are necessary and their opposite is impossible: truths of fact are contingent and their opposite is possible [53]. When a truth is necessary, its reason can be found by analysis, resolving it into more simple ideas and truths, until we come to those which are primary [54]. (*Théod.* 170, 174, 189, 280–282, 367. *Abrégé, Object.* 3.)

things in addition to its abstract 'possibility.' The principle of sufficient reason is the principle of final cause. Leibniz's adoption of the word 'sufficient' is supposed to have been suggested by its use in Mathematics in a sense similar to that in which we say that a certain magnitude 'satisfies' a particular equation.

[52] Cf. the Scholastic *ratio cognoscendi* and *ratio essendi*.

[53] Cf. *Théodicée*, § 174 (E. 557 b; G. vi. 217). 'It may be said of M. Bayle: *Ubi bene, nemo melius*, though it could not be said of him, as it was said of Origen: *Ubi male, nemo pejus*. . . . Yet M. Bayle adds at the end' [of a passage, quoted by Leibniz in the previous section] 'words which somewhat spoil what he has so justly remarked. "Now what contradiction would there have been if Spinoza had died at Leyden? Would nature have been less perfect, less wise, less powerful?" He here confounds what is impossible, because it involves a contradiction, with what cannot happen, because it is not well fitted to be chosen. It is true that there would have been no contradiction in the supposition that Spinoza had died at Leyden and not at the Hague: it was perfectly possible. Accordingly, as regards the power of God, the matter was indifferent. But it must not be imagined that any event, however insignificant, can be regarded as indifferent in relation to God's wisdom and goodness.'

[54] Leibniz does not give us a very clear idea of the relations of the two principles to the two kinds of truths. This is probably due to his hesitancy regarding the relations of the two principles to one another. In the Appendix to the *Théodicée* entitled *Remarques sur le livre de M. King*, Leibniz says (E. 641 b; G. vi. 414): 'Both principles must apply not only to necessary, but also to contingent truths, and, indeed, that which has no sufficient reason must necessarily be non-existent. For it may in a manner be said that these two principles are included in the definition of the true and the false. Nevertheless when, by analyzing a suggested truth, we see that it depends upon truths whose opposite involves a contradiction, we can say that it is absolutely necessary. But when, carrying our analysis as far as we like, we can never reach such elements of the given truth, it must be said to be contingent, and to have its origin in a prevailing reason, which inclines without necessitating.' But on the other hand, at a later date, Leibniz

34. It is thus that in Mathematics speculative *Theorems* and practical *Canons* are reduced by analysis to *Definitions, Axioms* and *Postulates.*

35. In short, there are *simple ideas*, of which no definition can be given [53]; there are also axioms and postulates, in a word, *primary principles*, which cannot be proved, and indeed have no need of proof; and these are *identical propositions* [56], whose opposite involves an express contradiction. (*Théod.* 36, 37, 44, 45, 49, 52, 121-122, 337, 340-344.)

36. But there must also be a *sufficient reason* for contingent *truths or truths of fact* [57], that is to say, for the sequence or connexion of the things which are dispersed throughout the universe of created beings, in which the analyzing into particular reasons might go on into endless detail, because of the immense variety of things in nature and the infinite division of bodies [58]. There is an infinity

writes to Clarke (*IIme Écrit de Leibniz*, E. 748 a; G. vii. 355): 'The principle of contradiction is by itself sufficient for the demonstration of the whole of Arithmetic and Geometry, that is to say, of all mathematical principles. But in order to pass from Mathematics to Physics, another principle also is needed, the principle of sufficient reason.' See Introduction, Part ii. pp. 66 sqq. In the *Monadology*, Leibniz's position is the same as in the earlier of the passages quoted.

[55] The definition of an idea is, for Leibniz, the statement of the elements which a complete analysis reveals in it. Cf. *Meditationes de Cognitione, Veritate et Ideis* (1684) (E. 79 b; G. iv. 423). 'When everything which is an element in a distinct idea, is in its turn distinctly known, or when analysis has been completely made, knowledge is *adequate*. I know not whether human knowledge can supply a perfect instance of this: the knowledge of numbers, however, approaches it.'

[56] Leibniz uses the word *énonciation* for *enunciatio*, which is the usual Latin translation of Aristotle's ἀπόφανσις, or λόγος ἀποφαντικός.

[57] Truths of reasoning have their sufficient reason in the self-evident, identical truths to which they may be reduced by analysis. Truths of fact can find a sufficient reason only in God.

[58] Cf. Lotze, *Microcosmus*, bk. iii. ch. 5, § 1 (Eng. Tr., i. 372). Leibniz says 'infinite *division*' instead of 'infinite *divisibility*,' because bodies are infinitely divisible only as *phenomena bene fundata* and not as *real* beings. A real thing or substance must be indi-

of present and past forms and motions which go to make
up the efficient cause of my present writing; and there is
an infinity of minute tendencies and dispositions of my
soul, which go to make its final cause [59].

37. And as all this *detail* again involves other prior or
more detailed contingent things, each of which still needs
a similar analysis to yield its reason, we are no further
forward: and the sufficient or final reason must be outside of the sequence or *series* of particular contingent
things, however infinite this series may be [60].

38. Thus the final reason of things must be in a necessary substance, in which the variety of particular changes
exists only eminently [61], as in its source; and this substance we call *God*. (*Théod.* 7.)

visible: it cannot consist of *partes extra partes*. And the 'infinite
division' of bodies is merely another way of describing the infinite number of particular substances or Monads.

[59] See Introduction, Part iii. p. 107. Cf. § 61. Here, in another
form, arises the difficulty as to the relation of Leibniz's 'principles'
to one another. Apparently the efficient and the final cause
combined make up the sufficient reason, neither by itself being
enough. Yet elsewhere Leibniz represents efficient causes as
ultimately depending on final causes. And efficient causes are by
Leibniz usually identified with mechanical causes, whose principle
is that of contradiction. See also Appendix F, p. 272.

[60] This is an argument on the same lines as that by means of
which Aristotle infers a 'prime mover.' It depends on his principle, ἀνάγκη στῆναι, i. e. we must come to a stop somewhere in the
regress of causes or conditions. Cf. *Phys.* Ξ, 6, 237[b] 3; Θ, 1, 251[a] 17;
Θ, 5, 256[a] 13. Also Kant's *Critique of Pure Reason, Transcendental
Dialectic*, bk. ii. ch. 2 and 3.

[61] *Eminently* in contrast with *formally*. The terms are Scholastic
and they were adopted by Descartes. Thomas Aquinas expresses
the difference thus: 'Whatever perfection is in the effect must
also appear in the cause, after the same manner if the agent and
the effect are of the same kind (*univocal*) (thus man begets man), or
in a more *eminent*, that is to say excellent, way, if the agent is of
another kind (*equivocal*).' Descartes says: 'By the *objective reality
of an idea*, I mean the entity or being of the thing represented by
the idea, in so far as this entity is in the idea; and in the same way
we may speak of an objective perfection or an objective design, &c.
For all that we conceive as being in the objects of ideas is objectively

39. Now as this substance is a sufficient reason of all this variety of particulars, which are also connected together throughout; *there is only one God, and this God is sufficient* [62].

40. We may also hold that this supreme substance, which is unique, universal [63] and necessary, nothing out-

or by representation in the ideas themselves. The same things are said to be *formally* in the objects of the ideas, when they exist in the objects just as we conceive them to exist ; and they are said to be *eminently* in the objects, when they do not really exist as we conceive them, but when they are so great that their excellence makes up for this defect.' *Réponses aux Deuxièmes Objections. Raisons qui prouvent l'existence de Dieu,* iii. and iv., cf. *note* on this distinction in Veitch's *Translation of Descartes.* ' *Formally*' as opposed to ' *objectively*' is almost equivalent to our ' *objectively*' (as opposed to ' *subjectively*') or ' *really*' (as opposed to ' *in idea*'). As opposed to *eminently, formally* is *secundum eandem formam et rationem,* while *eminently* is *gradu* or *modo eminentiori.*

[62] That is to say, all particular things are connected together in one system, which implies one principle, one necessary substance, one God. The argument is not merely from the existence of order in the world to the existence of an intelligence which produces this order, but from the fact that the whole forms *one* system to the existence of *one* ultimate sufficient reason of the whole. Otherwise there might be various ' orders' or 'disorders' in conflict with one another, each pre-supposing its own first principle or 'God.' This is Leibniz's form of the *Cosmological* proof of the existence of God.

[63] 'Universal' in the sense of being equally the cause or first principle of *all* things. The whole spirit of Leibniz's philosophy is opposed to the supposition of a universal substance or spirit, of which all particular substances are merely *modes.* Thus in the *Considérations sur la Doctrine d'un Esprit Universel* (1702) he endeavours to refute the view that ' there is but one spirit, which is universal and which animates the whole universe and all its parts, each according to its structure and according to the organs it possesses, as the same blast of wind produces a variety of sounds from different organ-pipes' or that ' the universal spirit is like an ocean composed of an infinite number of drops, which are separated from it when they animate some particular organic body and which are reunited with their ocean after the destruction of the organism.' This is 'the view of Spinoza and of other similar authors, who will have it that there is only one substance, viz. God, who thinks, believes and wills one thing in me, and who thinks, believes and wills quite the opposite in some one else—an opinion the absurdity

side of it being independent of it,—this substance, which is a pure sequence of possible being, must be illimitable and must contain as much reality as is possible[64].

41. Whence it follows that God is absolutely perfect; for perfection is nothing but amount of positive reality, in the strict sense, leaving out of account the limits or bounds in things which are limited. And where there are no bounds, that is to say in God, perfection is absolutely infinite. (*Théod.* 22, *Préf.* [E. 469 a; G. vi. 27].)

42. It follows also that created beings derive their perfections from the influence of God, but that their imperfections come from their own nature, which is incapable of being without limits. For it is in this that they differ from God[65]. An instance of this *original imperfection* of created beings may be seen in the *natural inertia* of bodies[66]. (*Théod.* 20, 27–30, 153, 167, 377 sqq.)

of which M. Bayle has well shown in several places in his dictionary' (E. 178 a, 181 b, 182 a; G. vi. 529, 535, 537).

[64] As God is the sufficient reason of all, nothing is independent of Him. But if His possibility were in any way limited, it must be by some possibility outside and independent of Him. Consequently His possibility cannot be limited. And unlimited possibility means unlimited reality and unlimited existence. For that which is possible must be real, unless there is something else with which it is not compossible, that is to say, unless there is some other possible thing, whose nature limits it. Cf. § 54 and Introduction, Part ii. p. 63. The argument in this and the following sections will become clear if we keep in view the idea which Leibniz seeks constantly to emphasize in every department of thought, namely that possibility or potentiality is never a mere empty capacity, a *tabula rasa*, a *potentia nuda*, but always, in however small a degree, a *tendency* to realization, which is kept back only by other similar tendencies. This is what is meant by the 'claims' and 'aspirations' of the Monads, mentioned in §§ 51 and 54.

[65] Created beings must be essentially limited; otherwise they would not be created, but would be identical with God. In the *Théodicée* Leibniz (following the Scholastic principle, *bonum habet causam efficientem, malum autem deficientem*), uses this as a hypothesis by which to remove from God the responsibility for the existence of evil. The origin of evil is the essential imperfection of created substances; and God is the cause only of the perfection or positive reality of created things.

[66] This sentence is not given by E. It seems to have been added

43. It is farther true that in God there is not only the source of existences but also that of essences, in so far as they are real, that is to say, the source of what is real in the possible[67]. For the understanding of God is the region of eternal truths or of the ideas on which they depend[68], and without Him there would be nothing real in the possibilities of things, and not only would there be nothing in existence, but nothing would even be possible. (*Théod.* 20.)

by Leibniz in revising the first copy of the *Monadology*. G. gives it in a foot-note. The natural inertia of a body is its passivity or that in it which limits its activity. So far as the passivity of the body is real (i. e. not a mere appearance to us), it consists of confused perception. But God is *actus purus*, entirely without passivity, and His perceptions are all perfectly clear and distinct.

[67] That is to say, God is not only the source of all actual existence, but also the source of all potential existence, of all that *tends* to exist. 'What is real in the possible' is its tendency to exist. In a sense, 'essences' or 'possible' things are independent of God. He does not create them as essences. They are the objects of His understanding, and 'He is not the author of His own understanding' (*Théodicée*, § 380; E. 614 b; G. vi. 341). The nature of essences or possibilities is determined solely by the principle of contradiction. And yet, in another sense, they may be said to be dependent upon God, inasmuch as they are all expressions of His nature in one or another aspect or with particular limitations. His freedom, however, extends only to a choice of those which shall actually exist, and this choice is determined by His wisdom and His goodness, having regard to the nature of the 'essences' themselves. 'Without Him there would be nothing *in existence*,' for the existence of things is the result of His will, His choice. 'Without Him nothing would be *possible*,' for all that is possible is the object of His understanding, and as His understanding is perfect (i.e. entirely free from confusion in its perceptions), its object must be the ultimate nature of things, that is, the very essence of God Himself. Thus in § 44 Leibniz practically identifies 'essences' or 'possibilities' with 'eternal truths.' Cf. Introduction, Part ii. p. 66.

[68] Leibniz connects this part of his system with Plato's world of ideas. He mentions as one of the 'many most excellent doctrines of Plato' that 'there is in the Divine mind an intelligible world, which I also am wont to call the region of ideas.' *Epistola ad Hanschium* (1707), E. 445 b.

R

44. For[69] if there is a reality in essences or possibilities, or rather in eternal truths, this reality must needs be founded in something existing and actual, and consequently in the existence of the necessary Being, in whom essence involves existence, or in whom to be possible is to be actual[70]. (*Théod.* 184–189, 335.)

45. Thus God alone (or the necessary Being) has this prerogative that He must necessarily exist, if He is possible. And as nothing can interfere with the possibility of that which involves no limits, no negation and consequently no contradiction, this [His possibility] is sufficient of itself to make known the existence of God *a priori.* We have thus proved it, through the reality of eternal truths. But a little while ago[71] we proved it also *a posteriori*, since there exist contingent beings, which can have their final or sufficient reason only in the necessary Being, which has the reason of its existence in itself.

46. We must not, however, imagine, as some do, that eternal truths, being dependent on God, are arbitrary and depend on His will, as Descartes[72], and afterwards

---

[69] G. reads *car*, E. *cependant.*

[70] See Appendix G. p. 274.   [71] §§ 36–39.

[72] Cf. Descartes, *Lettre au Père Mersenne* (Cousin's ed., vol. vi. p. 109). 'The metaphysical truths which you call eternal have been established by God and are entirely dependent upon Him, like all other created things. Indeed, to say that these truths are independent of God is to speak of God as a Jupiter or a Saturn and to subject Him to Styx and the Fates. . . . God has established these laws in nature, just as a king establishes laws in his kingdom.' Cf. *loc. cit.*, p. 103. 'We cannot without blasphemy say that the truth of anything precedes the knowledge which God has of it, for in God willing and knowing are one.' Elsewhere he says that God was perfectly free to make it untrue that the three angles of a triangle should be equal to two right-angles. As early as 1671. in a letter to Honoratus Fabri, Leibniz writes: 'If truths and the natures of things are dependent on the choice of God, I do not see how knowledge [*scientia*] or even will can be attributed to Him. For will certainly presupposes some understanding, since no one can will except in view of some good [*sub ratione boni*]. But understanding presupposes something that can be understood, that is to say, some nature. But if all natures are the result of will,

M. Poiret[73], appear to have held. That is true only of contingent truths, of which the principle is *fitness* [*convenance*][74] or choice of the *best*, whereas necessary truths depend solely on His understanding and are its inner object. (*Théod.* 180–184, 185, 335, 351, 380.)

47. Thus God alone is the primary unity or original simple substance, of which all created or derivative Monads are products and have their birth, so to speak, through continual fulgurations[75] of the Divinity from

understanding also will be the result of will. How, then, does will presuppose understanding?' (G. iv. 259). The point was much discussed by the Scholastics, with special reference to the question whether or not the moral law is independent of the will of God. Descartes's view is in harmony with that of Duns Scotus, while Leibniz follows Thomas Aquinas. For Descartes, the Divine and the human understanding differ in kind: for Leibniz they differ merely in degree.

[73] Pierre Poiret (1646-1719), a Calvinist minister, who held a charge in the Duchy of Zweibrücken, in the Rhine Palatinate. He was at first a Cartesian and published a book, *Cogitationes rationales de Deo, Anima et Malo*, which Bayle attacked. Afterwards he came under the influence of Antoinette Bourignon, the Dutch religious enthusiast, whose life he wrote and whose views he expounded at very great length. This influence led him to attack Cartesianism with much fervour, and he is now remembered as a mystic rather than as a philosopher.

[74] By *convenance* is meant mutual conformity, of such a kind that things 'fit into' one another in the most perfect way. Thus the principle of *convenance* or of the *best* is what we should now call the idea of system. With Leibniz it is the same as the principle of sufficient reason, which is the principle of *conditioned*, as distinct from *unconditional* reality or truth. Cf. note 85.

[75] That is to say, 'flashings' or 'sudden emanations.' 'God is the primary centre from which all else emanates' (G. iv. 553). Cf. the Stoic τόνος which Cleanthes calls a 'stroke of fire' (πληγὴ πυρός), Frag. 76. The relation of God to the other Monads is the crux of Leibniz's philosophy. He wishes to maintain both the individuality of the Monads and their essential unity with God. Thus he seems to take fulguration as a middle term between creation and emanation. 'Creation' would mean too complete a severance between God and the other Monads; 'emanation' would mean too complete an identity between them. 'Fulguration' means that the Monad is not absolutely created out of nothing nor, on the other hand, merely a mode or an absolutely necessary product of the Divine

moment to moment, limited by the receptivity of the
created being, of whose essence it is to have limits. (*Théod.*
382–391, 398, 395.)

48. In God there is *Power*, which is the source of all,
also *Knowledge*, whose content is the variety of the ideas,
and finally *Will*, which makes changes or products
according to the principle of the best [76]. (*Théod.* 7, 149,

nature, but that it is a possibility tending to realize itself, yet
requiring the assistance, choice or will of God to set it free from
the counteracting influence of opposite possibilities. As a possibility
it has essential limits (i. e. it is not entirely perfect, *actus purus*) ;
but it is ready to spring or 'flash' into being, at the will of God,
If there were no choice of God, possibilities would simply counteract
one another. But His choice means no more than the removal of
hindrances to development, in the case of certain 'elect' possibilities. Creation adds no new being to the universe, and yet it
is not emanation, in the sense of a mere modification of the one
Eternal Being. Thus the 'continual fulgurations' of Leibniz
are to be distinguished from the 'continual creation' of Descartes.
According to Leibniz, conservation is not, as with Descartes,
a miraculous renewal of the existence of things from moment
to moment, an absolute re-creation constantly repeated ; but it is
the continuance of the activity, choice or will of God, by which
certain possible things were set free to exist and through which
alone they can persist. The successive states of any being are
neither completely independent of one another, so that at each
moment there is a new creation (Descartes), nor are they so
absolutely dependent on one another that each proceeds from its
predecessor by a logical or mathematical necessity (Spinoza), but
they are connected together in a sequence which has its ground
in the nature of the being, so that each is automatically unfolded
from its predecessor according to a regular law, provided that God
chooses to allow this unfolding. The 'continual fulgurations' are
the continual exercise of God's will in allowing the Monads of the
actual world to unfold or develop their nature. Cf. *On the ultimate
Origination of Things*, p. 344.

[76] In the *Théodicée* (§ 150; E. 549 a; G. vi. 199) Leibniz hints at
a connexion between this characterization of God's nature and the
doctrine of the Trinity. 'Some have even thought that there is in
these three perfections of God a hidden reference to the Holy
Trinity : that power has reference to the Father, that is to say, to
the Godhead [*Divinité*] ; wisdom to the eternal Word, which is
called λόγος by the most sublime of the evangelists ; and will or
love to the Holy Spirit.'   •

150.) These characteristics correspond to what in the created Monads forms the ground or basis [77], to the faculty of Perception and to the faculty of Appetition. But in God these attributes are absolutely infinite or perfect ; and in the created Monads or the Entelechies (or *perfectihabiae.* as Hermolaus Barbarus translated the word [78]) there are only imitations of these attributes, according to the degree of perfection of the Monad. (*Théod.* 87.)

49. A created thing is said to *act* outwardly [79] in so far as it has perfection, and to *suffer* [or be *passive, pâtir*] in relation to another, in so far as it is imperfect. Thus *activity* [*action*] is attributed to a Monad, in so far as it has distinct perceptions, and *passivity* [*passion*] in so far as its perceptions are confused. (*Théod.* 32, 66, 386.)

50. And one created thing is more perfect than another, in this, that there is found in the more perfect that which serves to explain *a priori* what takes place in the less perfect, and it is on this account that the former is said to act upon the latter [80].

[77] Leibniz does not elsewhere discriminate three elements in the created Monad, and we must not suppose that the 'ground or basis' is anything in itself, apart from the two 'faculties.' Leibniz wishes to emphasize the view that the Monad, whether created or uncreated, is essentially force or activity, manifesting itself in perception and appetition.

[78] *Perfectihabia* (from *perfecte* and *habeo*) was formed to correspond to ἐντελέχεια (from ἐντελῶς and ἔχειν). Cf. note 32. Hermolaus Barbarus or Ermolao Barbaro (1454-1493) was an Italian scholar who endeavoured, by means of translations of Aristotle and of the Aristotelian commentaries of Themistius, to make known the true Aristotelian doctrine as against the degenerate forms which Scholasticism had given it. He came of a Venetian family and was Professor of Philosophy at Padua, where he lectured on Aristotle's *Ethics.*

[79] Of course, no Monad really does act outside itself. This is merely Leibniz's explanation of what we mean when we speak of outward action, just as the Copernican system explains what we mean when we speak of 'sunrise' and 'sunset,' though the sun neither 'rises' nor 'sets.'

[80] Thus the explanation or reason of an event is its actual cause. This connects itself with Leibniz's view that the existence of

51. But in simple substances the influence of one Monad upon another is only ideal, and it can have its effect only through the mediation of God, in so far as in the ideas of God any Monad rightly claims that God, in regulating the others from the beginning of things, should have regard to it. For since one created Monad cannot have any physical influence upon the inner being of another, it is only by this means that the one can be dependent upon the other [81]. (*Théod.* 9, 54, 65, 66, 201. *Abrégé, Object.* 3.)

52. Accordingly, among created things, activities and passivities are mutual. For God, comparing two simple substances, finds in each reasons which oblige Him to adapt the other to it [82], and consequently what is active in certain respects is passive from another point of view [83];

a thing arises solely from the liberating of its essential activities, and that the Monads claim existence in proportion to their perfection, that is to say, to the distinctness of their perceptions. Cause and effect are relative : every created Monad is both at once. God alone is pure cause or reason (*actus purus*). Cause = relative activity = relative distinctness of perception. This may instructively be compared and contrasted with the views of Berkeley and Hume regarding cause and ‘necessary connexion.’ See Introduction. Part iii. p. 105. Cf. also Spinoza, *Ethics*, Part iii. Def. 1 and 2, and Prop. 1, 2 and 3.

[81] We have here the principle of the Pre-established Harmony (further referred to in §§ 80 and 81). It is a harmony or mutual compatibility in the very nature of things, anterior to their creation. Its perfection in the actual world is the ground of God's choice of that world ; and thus it is not in any sense a created harmony. In this respect it differs from every form of Occasionalism. See Introduction, Part ii. pp. 39 sqq.

[82] No two simple substances are exactly the same, yet all represent the same universe. Therefore a perception which is comparatively distinct in one must be comparatively confused in another or others, and whatever changes take place in one must be accompanied by corresponding changes in the others. Thus each fits into the others.

[83] Leibniz's expression here is *point de considération*. But he generally uses the phrase *point de vue*, which he introduced as a regular term in philosophical literature. It need hardly be remarked that the term has a peculiar importance in Leibniz's philosophy.

active in so far as what we distinctly know in it serves to explain [*rendre raison de*] what takes place in another, and *passive* in so far as the explanation [*raison*] of what takes place in it is to be found in that which is distinctly known in another. (*Théod.* 66.)

53. Now, as in the Ideas of God there is an infinite number of possible universes, and as only one of them can be actual, there must be a sufficient reason for the choice of God, which leads Him to decide upon one rather than another[81]. (*Théod.* 8, 10, 44, 173, 196 sqq., 225, 414–416.)

54. And this reason can be found only in the *fitness* [*convenance*], or in the degrees of perfection, that these worlds possess[85], since each possible thing has the right to aspire to existence in proportion to the amount of perfection it contains in germ[86]. (*Théod.* 74, 167, 350, 201, 130, 352, 345 sqq., 354.)

[81] See Introduction, Part ii. p. 65.

[85] See *Monadology*, note 74. God is not compelled by an absolute, *metaphysical* necessity, but 'inclined' by a *moral* necessity to create the world which, as one harmonious system, is the best. The distinction between moral necessity and absolute compulsion is of Scholastic origin. 'Possible things are those which do not involve a contradiction. Actual things are nothing but the possible things which, all things considered, are the best. Therefore things which are less perfect are not on that account impossible; for we must distinguish between the things which God can do and those He wills to do. He can do everything, He wills to do the best.' *Epistola ad Bernoullium* (1699), (G. Math. iii. 574).

[86] This aspiration to existence is the tendency to pass into existence and to proceed from confused to distinct perceptions, which makes the 'possible' things of Leibniz real essences as distinct from purely indeterminate capacities. Possibilities, according to Leibniz, are never quite empty: they are always realities in germ. Cf. notes 64 and 67. 'From the very fact that there exists something rather than nothing, we must recognize that in possible things, or in possibility or essence itself, there is a certain need of existence [*exigentiam existentiae*] or (so to speak) a certain aspiration to exist, and, in a word, that essence by itself tends to existence. Whence it further follows that all possible things, i. e. things expressing essence or possible reality, tend with equal right to existence in proportion to the quantity of essence or reality they

55. Thus the actual existence of the best that wisdom makes known to God is due to this, that His goodness makes Him choose it, and His power makes Him produce it [87]. (*Théod.* 8, 78, 80, 84, 119, 204, 206, 208. *Abrégé, Object.* 1 and 8.)

56. Now this connexion or adaptation of all created things to each and of each to all, means that each simple substance has relations which express all the others, and, consequently, that it is a perpetual living mirror of the universe [88]. (*Théod.* 130, 360.)

57. And as the same town, looked at from various sides, appears quite different and becomes as it were numerous in aspects [*perspectivement*]; even so, as a result of the infinite number of simple substances, it is as if there were so many different universes, which, nevertheless are nothing but aspects [*perspectives*] of a single universe, according to the special point of view of each Monad [89]. (*Théod.* 147.)

contain or to their degree of perfection ; for perfection is nothing but quantity of essence.' *Ultimate Origination of Things*, p. 340.

[87] This section states briefly the principles of Leibniz's *Optimism*, which are fully expounded and defended in the *Théodicée*. A world entirely free from evil would be indistinguishable from God Himself. The evil of the world arises entirely from the essential limitations of created things—their limitations as essences or possibilities. Consequently evil is not created by God ; but He creates the universe in which there is the least amount of evil that is possible in any system of things.

[88] Cf. Nicholas of Cusa, *Dialogi de ludo globi* (1454-59), i. 157 a : 'The whole is reflected in all the parts; all things keep their own relation [*habitudo*] and proportion to the universe.' Also *De docta ignorantia* (1440), i. 11 : 'Visible things are images of the invisible, and the Creator can be seen and known by the creatures as in a mirror darkly [*quasi in speculo et aenigmate*].'

[89] The 'point of view' of each Monad is its body. But we must not give a spatial meaning to the expression, as if the Monad's point of view depended on its having this or that position in space. For the Monad is absolutely non-spatial, and the nature of its body depends on the degree of confusedness (or distinctness) of its perceptions. Thus to say that the body is the point of view of the soul means simply that the particular way in which the soul represents or perceives the universe is determined by the degree

58. And by this means there is obtained as great
variety as possible, along with the greatest possible order;
that is to say, it is the way to get as much perfection as
possible [90]. (*Théod.* 120, 124, 241 sqq., 214, 243, 275.)

59. Besides, no hypothesis but this (which I venture to
call proved) fittingly exalts the greatness of God; and
this Monsieur Bayle recognized when, in his *Dictionary*
(article *Rorarius* [91]), he raised objections to it, in which

of distinctness of its perceptions. Cf. *Théodicée*, § 357 (E. 607 b;
G. vi. 327). ' The projections of perspective, which, in the case of
the circle, are the same as the Conic Sections, show that one and
the same circle can be represented by an ellipse, by a parabola
and by a hyperbola, and even by another circle, by a straight line
and by a point. Nothing seems more different, nothing more
unlike, than these figures; and yet there is an exact relation
between them, point for point. Thus it must be recognized that
each soul represents to itself the universe, according to its point of
view and by a relation peculiar to itself; but in this there always
continues to be a perfect harmony.'

[90] For Leibniz the highest perfection is the most complete unity
or order in the greatest variety. The Monads have the most
complete unity, because the essence of each consists in representing
the same universe, while they have the greatest variety, because
the points of view from which they represent it are infinitely
various. 'For a world to be possible, it is enough that it should
have intelligibility; but in order to exist it must have a pre-
eminence [*prévalence*] in intelligibility or order; for there is *order* in
proportion as there is much to distinguish in a manifold [*multitude*].'
Lettre à Bourguet (1712 ?) (E. 718 b; G. iii. 558).

[91] See note 29. Bayle compares Leibniz's theory to the supposition that a ship might be constructed of such a kind that
entirely by itself, without captain or crew, it could sail from place
to place for years on end, accommodating itself to varying winds,
avoiding shoals, casting and weighing anchor, seeking a haven
when necessary and doing all that a normal ship can. He admits
that the omnipotence of God could give such a power to a ship, but
he maintains that the nature of the ship would make it impossible
for it to receive such a power. And 'however infinite be the
knowledge and power of God, He cannot, by means of a machine
which lacks a certain part, do that which requires the help of that
part.' Thus Bayle argues against the possibility of complete
spontaneity in the Monads, and consequently maintains that the
Deus ex machina is involved in Leibniz's Pre-established Harmony
quite as much as in Occasionalism.

indeed he was inclined to think that I was attributing too much to God—more than it is possible to attribute. But he was unable to give any reason which could show the impossibility of this universal harmony, according to which every substance exactly expresses all others through the relations it has with them.

60. Further, in what I have just said there may be seen the reasons *a priori* why things could not be otherwise than they are. For God in regulating the whole has had regard [92] to each part, and in particular to each Monad, whose nature being to represent, nothing can confine it to the representing of only one part of things ; though it is true that this representation is merely confused as regards the variety of particular things [*le détail*] in the whole universe, and can be distinct only as regards a small part of things, namely, those which are either nearest or greatest [93] in relation to each of the Monads ; otherwise each Monad would be a deity. It is not as regards their object, but as regards the different ways in which they have knowledge of their object, that the Monads are limited [94]. In a confused way they all strive after [*vont à*] the infinite, the whole [95] ; but they are limited and differentiated through the degrees of their distinct perceptions.

61. And compounds are in this respect analogous with

[92] So G. E. reads 'has a regard' [*a un égard*].

[93] If the Monads are non-spatial, how can we speak of anything being nearest or greatest in relation to a Monad ? Every Monad has a body of some kind and this body is confusedly perceived as spatial in itself and in relation to other bodies, though *really* it is nothing but an aggregate of non-spatial Monads. When therefore it is said that certain things are near or great in relation to a Monad, what is meant is that they are near or great in relation to the body of the Monad.

[94] That is to say, thought in the widest sense, conscious or unconscious, is limited only by itself: there can be nothing that is not an object of thought, more or less adequate. Contrast with this the position of Kant. See Introduction, Part iv, pp. 178 sqq.

[95] Cf. Nicholas of Cusa, *Dialogus de Genesi* (1447) 72 b : 'All things seek the same, which is something absolute.'

[*symbolisent avec* [96]] simple substances. For all is a *plenum* (and thus all matter is connected together) and in the *plenum* every motion has an effect upon distant bodies in proportion to their distance, so that each body not only is affected by those which are in contact with it and in some way feels the effect of everything that happens to them, but also is mediately affected by bodies adjoining those with which it itself is in immediate contact. Wherefore it follows that this inter-communication of things extends to any distance, however great. And consequently every body feels the effect of all that takes place in the universe, so that he who sees all might read in each what is happening everywhere, and even what has happened or shall happen, observing in the present that which is far off as well in time as in place : σύμπνοια πάντα, as Hippocrates said [97]. But a soul can read in itself only

[96] The expression 'symbolize' suggests the 'calculus' idea which is so continually in Leibniz's mind. As numbers are symbols of the things numbered, and we make accurate calculations without referring at every step to the particular things for which our symbols stand, so in general unanalyzed thoughts may be symbols of their simple elements. In the same way compound things are symbols of the simple substances which compose them. What is perceived confusedly in compounds is not a mere illusion but an imperfect representation or symbol of the real characteristics of simple substances. Thus, in this section, Leibniz would say that the spatial or material *plenum* (which is a confused perception of ours) is a symbol of the infinite (or perfectly complete) series of Monads, which has no gaps, since the Monads differ from one another by infinitely small degrees. Similarly, the material action and re-action throughout the universe, such that a change at any one point affects every other, is a symbol of the Pre-established Harmony among the Monads. And, again, the fact that everything that happens, has happened or shall happen in the universe might be read in any one body is a symbol of the representative character of each Monad as ideally containing the whole within itself. It is because they are thus symbolic that the phenomena of the material world are *phenomena bene fundata*.

[97] Σύμπνοια (the noun) is probably a corruption from σύμπνοα (the adjective), ' in agreement,' lit. ' breathing together,' *conspirantia*. Leibniz makes the same quotation in the *New Essays*, Introduction, p. 373. He there translates the phrase by the words '*tout est*

that which is there represented distinctly; it cannot all at once unroll everything that is enfolded in it [98], for its complexity is infinite [99].

---

conspirant.' The mistake may be due to an imperfect recollection of the phrase in Hippocrates: ξύρροια μία, ξύμπνοια μία, ξυμπαθέα πάντα. (*De Alimento,* 4, Littré, *Œuvres d'Hippocrate,* vol. ix. p. 106). Cf. Plutarch, *De fato,* 574 E: τὸ φύσει διοικεῖσθαι τόνδε τὸν κόσμον σύμπνουν, καὶ συμπαθῆ, αὐτὸν αὑτῷ ὄντα. For a later statement of the same position, see Fichte, *Werke,* ii. 178 sqq. 'In every moment of her duration, nature is one connected whole : in every moment each part must be what it is, because all the others are what they are. . . . You cannot conceive even the position of a grain of sand other than it is in the present without being compelled to conceive the whole indefinite past as having been other than it has been, and the whole indefinite future other than it will be . . . I am what I am because in this conjuncture of the great whole of nature only such, and no other, was possible ; and a spirit who could look through the secrets of nature would, from knowing one single man, be able distinctly to declare what men had formerly existed and what men would exist at any future moment; in *one* individual he would cognize *all* real individuals. My connexion, then, with the whole of nature is that which determines what I have been, am, and shall be, and the same spirit would be able, from any possible moment of my existence, to discover infallibly what I had been and what I was to become.' [Trans. by Prof. Adamson, *Philosophy of Kant,* p. 221.]

[98] E. reads *ses règles*: G. reads *ses replis.* The latter phrase is used in the *Principles of Nature and of Grace,* § 13.

[99] Cf. *Leibnitiana,* Dutens, vol. vi. Part i. p. 332. 'I admit that after death we do not at first remember what we were, for this is neither naturally right nor in accordance with the fitness of things [*ni propre ni bienséant dans la nature*]. Nevertheless I believe that whatever has once happened to the soul is eternally imprinted upon it, although it does not at all times come back to us in memory ; just as we know a number of things which we do not always recollect, unless something suggests them and makes us think about them. For who can remember all things? But since in nature nothing is futile and nothing is lost, but everything tends to perfection and maturity, each image our soul receives will ultimately become one [*un tout*] with the things which are to come, so that we shall be able to see all as in a mirror and thence to derive that which we shall find to be more fitted to satisfy us. Whence it follows that the more virtuous we have been and the more good deeds we have done, the more shall we have of joy and satisfaction.'

62. Thus, although each created Monad represents the whole universe, it represents more distinctly the body which specially pertains to it, and of which it is the entelechy [100]; and as this body expresses the whole universe through the connexion of all matter in the *plenum*, the soul also represents the whole universe in representing this body, which belongs to it in a special way. (*Théod.* 400.)

63. The body belonging to a Monad (which is its entelechy or its soul) constitutes along with the entelechy what may be called a *living being*, and along with the soul what is called an *animal* [101]. Now this body of a living being or of an animal is always organic; for, as every Monad is, in its own way, a mirror of the universe, and as the universe is ruled according to a perfect order, there must also be order in that which represents it, i. e. in the perceptions of the soul, and consequently there must be order in the body, through which the universe is represented in the soul [102]. (*Théod.* 403.)

[100] See note 32. The entelechy or soul is at once the final cause of the body and the power which controls it or the force which acts through it. As dominant Monad, the soul has more clearly the perceptions which are relatively confused in the Monads implied by the body. The soul is thus relatively the perfection of the body. And similarly, in the soul is to be read the reason (i. e. the distinct perception) of what takes place in the body, and it is therefore the *activity* or force of the body. Cf. Introduction, Part iii. p. 110.

[101] See § 19. Leibniz uses the term *living being* not as including all beings which have life, but specifically with reference only to those whose dominant Monad is unconscious, while in the *animal* (as distinct from the *living being*) the dominant Monad has consciousness and memory.

[102] Thus order and organism are conceived by Leibniz under the idea of an infinite series of elements, each differing from its neighbour to an infinitely small extent. The Monad-series of the universe, extending from God to the lowest of Monads, is reflected in the structure of the individual organism, extending from the dominant Monad downwards, and that again is reflected in the series of perceptions within each Monad itself, extending from the most distinct perceptions to which it has attained down to the most obscure.

64. Thus the organic body of each living being is a kind of divine machine or natural automaton, which infinitely surpasses all artificial automata. For a machine made by the skill of man is not a machine [103] in each of its parts. For instance, the tooth of a brass wheel has parts or fragments which for us are not artificial products, and which do not have the special characteristics of the machine, for they give no indication of the use for which the wheel was intended. But the machines of nature, namely, living bodies, are still machines in their smallest parts *ad infinitum* [104]. It is this that constitutes the dif-

[103] i. e. not a machine *made by man*. From another point of view, as a product of *nature*, it is (as this section says) a machine in its smallest parts, for in reality all bodies are living bodies. Thus the words 'for us' in the next sentence of this section were added by Leibniz in a revision of his original manuscript, evidently in order to suggest that while the fragments of the wheel are not products of ' human art,' they are yet products of 'divine art.'

[104] Cf. *Lettre à M. l'Évêque de Meaux* (Bossuet) (1692), (Foucher de Careil, i. 277; Dutens, i. 531). 'The machines of nature are machines throughout, however small a part of them we take; or rather the least part is itself an infinite world, which even expresses in its own way all that there is in the rest of the universe. That passes our imagination, yet we know that it must be so; and all that infinitely infinite variety is animated in all its parts by a constructive [*architectonique*] wisdom that is more than infinite. It may be said that there is Harmony, Geometry, Meta-physics, and, so to speak, Ethics [*morale*] everywhere, and (what is surprising) in one sense each substance acts spontaneously as independent of all other created things, while in another sense, all others compel it to adapt itself to them; so that it may be said that all nature is full of miracles, but miracles of reason, miracles which become miracles in virtue of their being rational, in a way which amazes us. For the reasons of things follow one another in an infinite succession [*s'y pousse à un progrès infini*], so that our mind while it sees that things must be so, cannot follow so as to comprehend. Formerly people admired nature without in any way understanding it, and that was supposed to be the right thing to do. Latterly they have begun to think nature so easy to understand that they have developed a contempt for it, and some of the new philosophers even encourage themselves in idleness by imagining that they know enough about nature already.' See also Introduction, Part iii. p. 108.

ference between nature and art, that is to say, between the divine art and ours[105]. (*Théod.* 134, 146, 194, 403.)

65. And the Author of nature has been able to employ this divine and infinitely wonderful power of art, because each portion of matter is not only infinitely divisible, as the ancients observed[106], but is also actually subdivided without end[107], each part into further parts, of which

[105] Cf. Nicholas of Cusa, *Idiotae Libri quatuor*, iii. 2, 82 a. '*Humanae artes imagines Divinae artis.*'

[106] See Aristotle, *Phys.*, Z, 9, 239^b 5. Οὐ γὰρ σύγκειται ὁ χρόνος ἐκ τῶν νῦν ἀδιαιρέτων, ὥσπερ οὐδ' ἄλλο μέγεθος οὐδέν. Cf. *Phys.*, Z, 1, 231^b 18; Z, 4 (τὸ δὲ μεταβάλλον ἅπαν ἀνάγκη διαιρετὸν εἶναι); *De Caelo*, Γ, 1, 298^b 33. See also Bayle's *Dictionary*, article 'Zeno,' notes F and G.

[107] Cf. *Réponse à la lettre de M. Foucher* (1693), (E. 118 b.; G. i. 416). 'There is no part of matter which is not, I do not say divisible, but actually divided; and consequently the smallest particle must be considered as a world filled with an infinity of different creatures.' The paradox in such statements as these arises from the way in which Leibniz speaks of matter as composed of non-spatial elements. Leibniz regards matter as a mere aggregate and as therefore not *itself* a real substance. But he never explains what he means by an aggregate of Monads, each of which is non-quantitative. Again it may be asked whether a real whole can consist of an infinite number of real parts? Does not infinite divisibility mean that it is impossible to bring to an end the enumeration of parts, because the relation of whole to parts is so indefinite that we have no means of determining what exactly is a part? Thus the term 'infinite' here means that the process of division is one which can never be completed. Consequently it seems self-contradictory to speak of things as 'actually sub-divided without end' or infinitely. (Cf. Kant's *Critique of Pure Reason*, First and Second Antinomies. See also Bosanquet's *Logic*, vol. i. pp. 172 sqq.) It was Euler, the mathematician, who first brought this criticism against Leibniz, saying that the existence of units in the shape of Monads implies the finite divisibility of matter, while Leibniz at the same time maintains its infinite divisibility. (*Lettres à une Princesse d'Allemagne* (1761), Brewster's Trans, vol. ii. pp. 30 sqq.) Euler's argument is directed mainly against the Wolffian adaptation of Leibniz's position. Leibniz might reply that matter as infinitely divisible, is a mere pheno-menon, resulting from an actual infinity of real Monads. But even in this explanation the idea of 'infinite' seems to be used in two opposite senses (1) as equivalent to 'incapable of completion,' (2) as equivalent to 'absolutely complete.'

each has some motion of its own ; otherwise it would be impossible for each portion of matter to express the whole universe [108]. (*Théod. Prélim., Disc. de la Conform.* 70, and 195.)

66. Whence it appears that in the smallest particle of matter there is a world of creatures, living beings, animals, entelechies, souls.

67. Each portion of matter may be conceived as like a garden full of plants and like a pond full of fishes. But each branch of every plant, each member of every animal, each drop of its liquid parts is also some such garden or pond.

68. And though the earth and the air which are between the plants of the garden, or the water which is between the fish of the pond, be neither plant nor fish ; yet they also contain plants and fishes, but mostly so minute as to be imperceptible to us [109].

[108] The 'portions of matter,' of which Leibniz here speaks, are ultimately Monads, each of which must ideally contain the whole universe. The Monads are infinite in number, and each, as it ideally contains all, must therefore contain an infinity of 'parts.' Or the argument which Leibniz implies may be otherwise put thus : If the 'portions of matter' are not actually subdivided without end, there must be ultimate undivided atoms. But such atoms necessarily imply a void ; they are inconsistent with a *plenum*. And unless there is a *plenum* it is impossible for each portion of matter to 'express' or be affected by all the rest.

[109] Leibniz had a deep interest in the remarkable development of microscopic investigation, which took place during his lifetime. He frequently refers to the work of Leuwenhoek, the discoverer of spermatozoa, Swammerdam, the entomologist, and Malpighi, who, among many other works, made a microscopic study of the physiology of animals and plants. In a *Méditation sur la notion commune de la Justice* (Mollat, p. 66), Leibniz says : 'It is very necessary to advance our microscopical knowledge. Scarce ten men in the world are earnestly devoted to it ; and though there were a hundred thousand, they would not be too many for the discovery of the important wonders of this new world which is the inside of the world we know and which is capable of making our knowledge a hundred thousand times as extensive as it is. For this reason I have often wished that great princes might be led to make arrangements for this and to support people who would devote

69. Thus there is nothing fallow, nothing sterile, nothing dead in the universe, no chaos, no confusion save in appearance [110], somewhat as it might appear to be in a pond at a distance, in which one would see a confused movement and, as it were, a swarming of fish in the pond, without separately distinguishing the fish themselves. (*Théod. Préf.* [E. 475 b ; 477 b ; G. vi. 40, 44].)

70. Hence it appears that each living body has a dominant entelechy, which in an animal is the soul ; but the members of this living body are full of other living beings, plants, animals, each of which has also its dominant entelechy or soul [111].

themselves to it.' The view of Leibniz also suggests the cell-theory of modern physiology ; but the analogy must not be pushed too far. However numerous, for instance, may be the cells in any portion of an organism, they are not, like Leibniz's 'portions of matter,' infinitely subdivided in their turn. In fact, the cell-theory has in many ways a closer relation to the mechanical view of things than to the position of Leibniz. See Sandeman, *Problems of Biology*, pp. 53 sqq.

[110] Cf. *Epistola ad Bernoullium* (1699) (G. Math. iii. 565) : 'God, out of the infinite number of possible things, chooses by His wisdom that which is most fitting. But it is evident that if there were a vacuum (and similarly if there were atoms) there would remain sterile and fallow places, in which, nevertheless, without prejudice to any other things, something might have been produced. But it is not consistent with wisdom that such places should remain. And I think that there is nothing sterile and fallow in nature, although many things appear to us to be so.'

[111] See Introduction, Part iii. p. 111. May not the whole world, then, be conceived as one body, whose dominant soul is God, the Monad of Monads?

'All are but parts of one stupendous whole,
Whose body nature is and God the soul.'

Pope, *Essay on Man*, Epistle i. 267.

Yet Leibniz maintains that God has no body. Cf. *Monadology*, § 72. The difficulty is a fundamental one. Leibniz repeatedly disclaims the doctrine of a 'world-soul,' if it is understood as in any way destroying the independence of individual souls. 'Although a soul may have a body composed of parts, each of which has a soul of its own, the soul or form of the whole is not composed of the souls or forms of the parts.' *Lettre à Arnauld* (1687) (G. ii. 100).

71. But it must not be imagined, as has been done by some who have misunderstood my thought, that each soul has a quantity or portion of matter belonging exclusively to itself or attached to it for ever[112], and that it consequently owns other inferior living beings, which are devoted for ever to its service. For all bodies are in a perpetual flux like rivers[113], and parts are entering into them and passing out of them continually.

72. Thus the soul changes its body only by degrees, little by little, so that it is never all at once deprived of all its organs; and there is often metamorphosis in animals, but never metempsychosis or transmigration of souls[114]; nor are there souls entirely separate [from

---

[112] The misunderstanding probably arose from a confusion of *materia prima*, the passive element in the individual created Monad, which is inseparable from the active or soul element, with *materia secunda*, the changing body of a compound substance, which is phenomenal and not perfectly real, although it is founded upon reality. Cf. Introduction, Part. iii. pp. 95 sqq.

[113] The phrase is as old as Heraclitus, who, according to Plato, 'likened things to the flowing of a river,' *Cratylus*, 402 A. Cf. Aristotle, *Metaph.*, A, 6, 987ª 32. See also Burnet, *Early Greek Philosophy*, p. 149.

[114] While soul and body are quite distinct from one another, their union is of the closest possible kind. Changes in the one correspond to changes in the other. But as the perceptions of the soul are clearer and more distinct than those of the body, the changes in the soul cause or explain the changes in the body. Transmigration of souls is inconsistent with this, because it means that the body remains the same, though the soul is changed. Accordingly, in Leibniz's view, the identity of any individual substance means 'the preservation of the same soul.' *Nouveaux Essais*, bk. ii. ch. 27, § 6. (E. 278 b; G. v. 216.) He argues against Locke that identity is not fixed by time and place, and that the identity of plant, animal, and man does not consist in the possession of the same organic body. Thus, according to Leibniz, every soul or entelechy, whether conscious or not, has what he calls 'real and physical identity' (i. e. not a derived identity, but an identity belonging to its own nature, φύσις), and is, in virtue of this, imperishable (*incessable*), while the self-conscious soul has in addition a 'personal' or 'moral' identity, in virtue of which it is immortal. Neither continued consciousness nor memory is essential to the maintenance of this 'moral' identity. 'If I were to forget all the

bodies] nor unembodied spirits [*génies sans corps*]. God alone is completely without body [115]. (*Théod.* 90, 124.)

73. It also follows from this that there never is absolute birth [*génération*] nor complete death, in the strict sense, consisting in the separation of the soul from the body. What we call *births* [*générations*] are developments and growths, while what we call *deaths* are envelopments and diminutions.

74. Philosophers have been much perplexed about the origin of forms [116], entelechies, or souls; but nowadays

past, if I had even to be taught anew my own name and how to read and write, I could always learn from other people my life in former times, just as I should still retain my rights, so that it would not be necessary to divide me into two people and to make me my own heir. No more is required to maintain the *moral identity*, which constitutes the same person' (*loc. cit.*, § 9; E. 280 b; G. v. 219). 'An immaterial being or a mind [*esprit*] *cannot be deprived* of all perception of its past existence. It retains impressions of all that has formerly happened to it; but these feelings are usually too small to be capable of being distinguished and of being consciously perceived, although they may perhaps be developed some day. This continuing and connexion of *perceptions* makes the being really the same individual, but *apperceptions*—that is to say, when one is conscious [*s'aperçoit*] of past feelings—prove also a moral identity and make the real identity apparent' (*loc. cit.*, § 14; E. 281 b; G. v. 222). Cf. *New Essays*, Introduction, p. 373.

[115] A soul without body (in the sense of *materia secunda*) would be a soul without any relation to other Monads. For a compound substance (i. e. soul and body) consists ultimately in the relation of a dominant Monad to subordinate Monads. 'Creatures free or freed from matter would at the same time be separated from the universal connexion of things, and, as it were, deserters from the general order.' *Considérations sur les Principes de Vie* (1705) (E. 432 b; G. vi. 546). Again, a soul without body (in the sense of *materia prima*) would be a Monad without passivity or confused perception, i. e. it would be *actus purus* or God. Kirchmann (*Erläuterungen zu Leibniz' Schriften*) dismisses Leibniz's statement as 'a mere assertion, which indeed does not necessarily follow from Leibniz's own principles.' The difficulty is the same as that mentioned in note 111.

[116] The form is the life or vital principle in any organic being. Cf. *Lettre à Arnauld* (1687) (G. ii. 116): 'I proceed to the question of forms or souls, which I hold to be indivisible and indestructible. Parmenides (of whom Plato speaks with veneration), as well as Melissus, maintained that there is no generation nor corruption

it has become known, through careful studies of plants, insects, and animals, that the organic bodies of nature are never products of chaos or putrefaction, but always come from seeds, in which there was undoubtedly some *pre-formation* [117]; and it is held that not only the organic

except in appearance: Aristotle mentions this (*De Caelo*, bk. iii. ch. 2). And the author of the *De Diaeta*, bk. i. (which is attributed to Hippocrates), expressly says that an animal cannot be engendered absolutely [*tout de nouveau*] nor completely [*tout à fait*] destroyed. Albertus Magnus and John Bacon seem to have thought that substantial forms were already hidden in matter from the beginning of time. Fernel makes them descend from heaven, to say nothing of those who regard them as taken off from the soul of the world. They have all seen a part of the truth; but they have not developed it. Several have believed in transmigration, others in the traduction of souls' [i.e. in the soul of the offspring being as it were begotten of the soul of the parent] 'instead of transmigration and the transformation of an animal already formed. Others, not being able to explain otherwise the origin of forms, have admitted that they begin in a real creation, but while I allow that this creation takes place in time only in respect of the rational soul, and hold that all forms which do not think were created along with the world, they believe that this creation takes place every day when the smallest worm is begotten.' Cf. *New System*, notes 43 and 44.

[117] 'The living [*animée*] and organic seed is as old as the world.' *Lettre à la Reine Sophie Charlotte* (G. vi. 517). Immediately before the time of Leibniz, the origin of life in the individual plant, animal, or man was explained either by a theory of traduction or by a theory of eduction. According to the theory of traduction, the 'form' of the offspring comes from the parental 'form' or 'forms' in the same way as the body of the offspring comes from the parental body or bodies. According to the theory of eduction, on the other hand, life comes from inorganic matter, from 'chaos or putrefaction.' Eduction thus corresponds to what we now call 'spontaneous generation.' According to the theory of preformation, adopted by Leibniz, the germ contains in miniature the whole plant or animal, point for point, and accordingly the 'form' of the plant or animal exists in the spermatozoon in a contracted or 'enveloped' state, and it has existed since the beginning of time. For, as we have seen (§ 65), there is no limit to the smallness of things, and even a spermatozoon may contain an indefinite number of other living beings. This theory of preformation, which was based on the microscopic investigations of Malpighi and Leuwenhoek, has now been entirely abandoned, as the result of more thorough observations. Cf. Sande-

body was already there before conception, but also a soul in this body, and, in short, the animal itself; and that by means of conception this animal has merely been prepared for the great transformation involved in its becoming an animal of another kind. Something like this is indeed seen apart from birth [*génération*], as when worms become flies and caterpillars become butterflies. (*Théod.* 86, 89. *Préf.* [E. 475 b; G. vi. 40 sqq.]; 90, 187, 188, 403, 86, 397.)

75. The *animals*, of which some are raised by means of conception to the rank of larger animals, may be called *spermatic*, but those among them which are not so raised but remain in their own kind (that is, the majority) are born, multiply, and are destroyed [118] like the large animals, and it is only a few chosen ones [*élus*] that pass to a greater theatre.

76. But this is only half of the truth [119], and accordingly

man, *Problems of Biology*, p. 92. While rejecting traduction in its ordinary form, Leibniz recognizes its affinity to his own view, which he describes as 'a kind of traduction, more satisfactory [*traitable*] than that which is commonly taught.' *Théodicée*, § 397 (E. 618 b; G. vi. 352).

[118] According to Leibniz, they are not entirely, but only apparently destroyed. The statement is made in the form in which scientific observers of Leibniz's time would have put it, and it is subject to the qualification made in § 76. Leibniz's point is that, just as there is a visible world of larger organisms, so there is a microscopic world of spermatozoa, undergoing in miniature all the changes which take place in the larger visible world. The larger organisms of the visible world are certain elect members of the spermatic world which, 'by means of conception,' have been enabled to grow from microscopic minuteness to visibility.

[119] The scientific observers have only stated half of the truth; but Leibniz thinks that they would have no objection to the other half. 'I think that if this opinion had occurred to them, they would not have found it absurd, and there is nothing more natural than to believe that what does not begin does not perish.' *Lettre à Arnauld* (1687) (G. ii. 123). Cf. Plato, *Phaedrus*, 245 D : Ἐπειδὴ δὲ ἀγένητόν ἐστι, καὶ ἀδιάφθορον αὐτὸ ἀνάγκη εἶναι. Leibniz elsewhere speaks of the view of Plato 'that the object of wisdom is τὰ ὄντως ὄντα, that is, simple substances, which are called by me' [Leibniz] 'Monads, and which once existing always continue to exist, πρῶτα δεκτικὰ τῆς ζωῆς, that is, God and souls, and of these the chief are

I hold that if an animal never comes into being by natural means [*naturellement*], no more does it come to an end by natural means ; and that not only will there be no birth [*génération*], but also no complete destruction or death in the strict sense [120]. And these reasonings, made *a posteriori* and drawn from experience are in perfect agreement with my principles deduced *a priori*, as above [121]. (*Théod.* 90.)

77. Thus it may be said that not only the soul (mirror of an indestructible universe) is indestructible, but also the animal itself [122], though its mechanism [*machine*] may often perish in part and take off or put on an organic slough [*des dépouilles organiques* [123]].

78. These principles have given me a way of explaining naturally [124] the union or rather the mutual agreement [*conformité*] of the soul and the organic body. The soul follows its own laws, and the body likewise follows its own laws ; and they agree with each other in virtue of

minds, images of the Deity, produced by God.' *Epistola ad Hanschium* (1707) (E. 445 b). This last passage involves a misunderstanding of Plato's ἰδέαι, which are universals, not Monads. Democritus calls his atoms τὸ ὄν.

[120] 'There is always going on in the animal what goes on in it at the present moment ; that is, its body is in a continual change, like a river ; and what we call generation or death is only a greater and more rapid change than usual, such as would be the leap or cataract of a river. But these leaps are not absolute and such as I have refused to admit, as would be that of a body which should go from one place to another without going through intervening places [*sans passer par le milieu*].' *Lettre à Remond* (1715) (E. 724 a ; G. iii. 635).

[121] *Monadology*, §§ 3, 4, and 5. This endeavour to show the agreement of *a priori* with *a posteriori* conclusions is specially characteristic of Leibniz. It illustrates his belief in the harmony of the physical with the metaphysical, the mechanical with the dynamical or final.

[122] Because the soul must always have a body of some kind, which itself ultimately consists of imperishable Monads. Animals, however, are not *immortal*. Immortality belongs only to rational souls or self-conscious Monads.

[123] 'As a snake casts its old skin.' *Lettre à la Princesse Sophie* (1696) (G. vii. 544).

[124] That is, in contrast to the Occasionalist theory, which according to Leibniz implies an endless series of miracles.

the pre-established harmony between all substances, since they are all representations of one and the same universe [125]. (*Préf.* [E. 475 a ; G. vi. 39] ; *Théod.* 340, 352, 353, 358.)

79. Souls act according to the laws of final causes through appetitions, ends, and means. Bodies act according to the laws of efficient causes or motions. And the two realms, that of efficient causes and that of final causes, are in harmony with one another [126].

80. Descartes recognized that souls cannot impart any force to bodies, because there is always the same quantity

---

[125] That is to say, the problem of the connexion between soul and body is a special case of the wider problem as to the relation of any one simple substance or Monad to another.

[126] They are in harmony, because ultimately the one is reducible to the other. When it is said that 'souls act,' what is meant is that they pass from one perception to another, i. e. that they have appetition. When it is said that 'bodies act,' what is meant is that they change their state or their relation to other bodies, i. e. that they have motion. What we call the 'state' of a body and its 'relations to other bodies' ought in strictness to be called the (unconscious) perceptions of the Monads which constitute the body. And similarly, the 'motion' of the body is really the (unconscious) appetition of its constituent Monads. Thus the difference between efficient and final causes, like that between the unconscious and the conscious, is merely a difference of degree. Cf. *Principles of Nature and of Grace,* § 11. From a psychological point of view, Leibniz describes the parallelism of soul and body thus : 'I have carefully examined this matter and I have shown that there are really in the soul some materials of thought or objects of the understanding, which the external senses do not supply, namely, the soul itself and its functions (*nihil est in intellectu quod non fuerit in sensu, nisi ipse intellectus*) ... but I find nevertheless, that there is never an abstract thought which is not accompanied by some material images or marks [*traces*], and I have made out a perfect parallelism between what passes in the soul and what takes place in matter, having shown that the soul, with its functions, is something distinct from matter but yet is always accompanied by material organs, and also that the functions of the soul are always accompanied by functions of its organs, which must correspond to them, and that this is and always will be reciprocal.' *Considérations sur la Doctrine d'un Esprit Universel unique* (1702) (E. 180 a ; G. vi. 532).

of force in matter. Nevertheless he was of opinion that
the soul could change the direction of bodies. But that
is because in his time it was not known that there is
a law of nature which affirms also the conservation of the
same total direction in matter [127]. Had Descartes noticed
this he would have come upon my system of pre-established harmony [128]. (*Préf.* [E. 477 a; G. vi. 44]; *Théod.*
22, 59, 60, 61, 63, 66, 345, 346 sqq., 354, 355.)

81. According to this system bodies act as if (to
suppose the impossible) there were no souls, and souls
act as if there were no bodies, and both act as if each
influenced the other [129].

---

[127] See Introduction, Part iii. p. 89. Descartes 'believed he had
found a law of nature, to the effect that the same quantity of
motion is conserved in bodies. He did not think it possible for
the influence of the soul to break this law of bodies ; but he thought
that the soul might nevertheless have the power of changing the
direction of the motions which take place in the body; somewhat
as a horseman, although he does not give any force to the horse he
rides, nevertheless guides it by directing its force in the way that
he thinks right. As this is done by means of bridle, bit, spurs,
and other material aids, we see how it can take place; but there
are no instruments which the soul could employ for this purpose
—nothing in soul or in body, that is to say, in thought or in mass,
which could serve to explain this change of one by the other.'
Théodicée, § 60 (E. 519 b ; G. vi. 135).

[128] That is to say, Descartes would have seen that neither soul
nor body has any influence whatever upon the other, and that they
must therefore be regarded as acting merely in harmony.

[129] 'All that ambition or any other passion brings to pass in the
soul of Caesar is also represented in his body, and all the motions
of these passions come from the impressions of objects combined
with internal motions. And the body is so constituted that the
soul never makes any resolution without the motions of the body
agreeing with it. This applies even to the most abstract reasonings,
because of the characters which represent them to the imagination.
In a word, everything takes place in bodies, as regards the particular series [*détail*] of their phenomena, as if the evil doctrine of
those who, like Epicurus and Hobbes, believe that the soul is
material, were true; or as if man himself were only a body or an
automaton.... Those who show the Cartesians that their way of
proving that the lower animals are only automata amounts to
justifying him who should say that all men, except himself, are

82. As regards *minds* [*esprits*] or rational souls, though I find that what I have just been saying is true of all living beings and animals (namely that animals and souls come into being when the world begins and no more come to an end than the world does), yet there is this peculiarity in rational animals, that their spermatic animalcules, so long as they are only spermatic, have merely ordinary or sensuous [*sensitive*] souls; but when those which are chosen [*élus*], so to speak, attain to human nature through an actual conception, their sensuous souls are raised to the rank of reason and to the prerogative of minds [*esprits* [130]]. (*Théod.* 91, 397.)

also mere automata, have said exactly what I need for that half of my hypothesis which concerns body. But, apart from the principles which make it certain that there are Monads, of which compound substances are only the results, the Epicurean doctrine is refuted by inner experience, by our consciousness of the Ego which consciously perceives the things which take place in the body; and as perception cannot be explained by figures and motions, the other half of my hypothesis is established, and we are obliged to recognize that there is in us an *indivisible substance*, which must be itself the source of its phenomena. Consequently, according to this second half of my hypothesis, everything takes place in the soul as if there were no body; just as, according to the first half, everything takes place in the body as if there were no soul. . . . Whatever of good there is in the hypotheses of Epicurus and of Plato, of the greatest Materialists and the greatest Idealists, is combined here.' *Réponse aux Réflexions de Bayle* (1702) (E. 185; G. iv. 559).

[130] This elevation of the merely sensuous soul to the rank of reason might, says Leibniz, 'be attributed to the extraordinary operation of God.' But he 'prefers to dispense with miracle in the generation of man as in that of the other animals,' and says that 'among the great number of souls and animals (or at least living organic bodies) which are in the seed, only those souls which are destined some day to attain to human nature contain in germ [*enveloppent*] the reason which will some day appear in them, and that only the organic bodies of these souls are preformed and predisposed to take the human form some day, the other animalcules or seminal living beings, in which nothing of this kind is pre-established, being essentially different from them and containing only what is lower.' *Théodicée*, § 397 (E. 618 a; G. vi. 352). This question of the relation of rational to sub-rational souls is treated by Leibniz in a very unsatisfactory way. If we follow out Leibniz's

83. Among other differences which exist between ordinary souls and minds [*esprits*], some of which differences I have already noted [131], there is also this : that souls in general are living mirrors or images of the universe of created things, but that minds are also images of the Deity or Author of nature Himself, capable of knowing the system of the universe [132], and to some extent of imitating it through architectonic ensamples [*échantillons* [133]], each mind being like a small divinity in its own sphere. (*Théod.* 147.)

84. It is this that enables spirits [or minds—*esprits*] to enter into a kind of fellowship with God, and brings it about that in relation to them He is not only what an inventor is to his machine (which is the relation of God to other created things), but also what a prince is to his subjects, and, indeed, what a father is to his children [134].

main principles, it ought to be impossible to draw a sharp line between these two classes of souls. Yet, while not regarding as absolute the distinction between the rational and the merely sensuous, Leibniz is afraid of minimizing this distinction and of thus putting in jeopardy the pre-eminence of man and the immortality of the soul. In the draft of a letter to Arnauld (1686) he speaks of this question as 'a special point [*une particularité*] about which I have not light enough' (G. ii. 73). Cf. Introduction, Part iii. p. 116.

[131] §§ 19-30.

[132] 'The difference between intelligent substances and those which are not so, is as great as the difference there is between a mirror and him who looks therein.' Paper without a title (1686) (G. iv. 460).

[133] That is, subsidiary creations or imitative constructions. Man can not merely express in himself the 'machine' of the universe, but he can also make for himself small 'machines,' constructed on similar principles. Cf. § 64 ; also *Principles of Nature and of Grace*, § 14. An ἀρχιτέκτων is literally a 'master of works.'

[134] 'Concerning the human soul I dare not assert anything as to its origin nor as to its state after death, because rational or intelligent souls, such as ours is, having been so fashioned that they have a peculiar relation to the image of God, are governed by very different laws from those to which souls without understanding are subject.' *Epistola ad Bernoullium* (1699) (G. Math. iii. 565). 'Spirits [*esprits*] alone are made in His image, and are, as it were, of His

85. Whence it is easy to conclude that the totality [*assemblage*] of all spirits [*esprits*] must compose the City of God [135], that is to say, the most perfect State that is possible, under the most perfect of Monarchs. (*Théod.* 146 ; *Abrégé, Object.* 2.)

86. This City of God, this truly universal monarchy, is a moral world in the natural world, and is the most exalted and most divine among the works of God [116]; and it is in it that the glory of God really consists, for He would have no glory were not His greatness and His goodness known and admired by spirits [*esprits* [157]]. It is

race or like children of the house, since they alone can serve Him freely and act with knowledge, in imitation of the Divine nature : one single spirit [*esprit*] is worth a whole world, since it not only expresses the world but also knows it and governs itself in the world [*s'y gouverne*] after the manner of God.' Paper without title (1686) (G. iv. 461).

[135] The reference is to the *civitas Dei* of St. Augustine; but the difference of meaning is very great. St. Augustine's *civitas Dei* is the Christian Church as opposed to the *civitas terrena* or earthly state. Leibniz's City of God, on the other hand, is not set in opposition to an earthly state, but is the moral order of the universe, as distinct from its natural order. The City of God, according to Leibniz, includes not Christians alone, but all men.

[136] Cf. Fichte, *Darstellung der Wissenschaftslehre* (*Werke*, ii. 35): 'The ground of the universe is . . . spirit itself . . . a kingdom of spirits and absolutely nothing else.' Also *Werke*, v. 188 : 'It is in no way doubtful, or rather it is the most certain of all things, and indeed the foundation of all certitude, the sole absolutely indisputable objective reality, that there is a moral order in the universe ; that each rational individual has his definite place in this universal order, a place indicated by his special work ; that each of the accidents of his existence, in so far as it does not result from his personal conduct, is a consequence of this general plan ; that, except in conformity with this plan, not a hair can fall from his head, any more than a sparrow from its roof ; that every truly good action succeeds, every bad action fails ; and that all things necessarily work for the greatest good of those who only rightly love the good.' See Introduction, Part iv. p. 180 note.

[137] Cf. Nicholas of Cusa, *Cribratio Alchoran*, 16 : 'God created all things for the manifestation of His glory ; an unknown king is wanting in honour and in beneficence.' Cf. also *Excitationes ex*

also in relation to this divine City that God specially has goodness [138], while His wisdom and His power are manifested everywhere. (*Théod.* 146 ; *Abrégé, Object.* 2.)

87. As we have shown above that there is a perfect harmony between the two realms in nature, one of efficient, and the other of final causes, we should here notice also another harmony between the physical realm of nature and the moral realm of grace [139], that is to say, between God, considered as Architect of the mechanism [*machine*] of the universe and God considered as Monarch of the divine City of spirits [*esprits*]. (*Théod.* 62, 74, 118, 248, 112, 130, 247.)

Sermonibus, vi. 112 a : 'God desired to manifest the riches of His glory, and on this account He created the rational or intellectual creature, that He might manifest to him the riches of His glory ; for this creature alone can perceive the glory of God with intellectual appreciation [*intellectuali gustu*] ; but these riches [of the glory of God] are eternal life.' 'God wishes to be known, and hence on this account all things are' (*loc. cit.*, 104 a). Cf. also Schiller's 'Freundlos war der grosse Weltenmeister,' &c. (*Die Freundschaft*).

[138] Because moral distinctions and moral qualities belong specially to the moral order, i. e. to the society of rational souls.

[139] The question of the relation between the realm of nature and that of grace is, in one form or another, perennial. Leibniz seeks to apply the principles of his philosophy in a reconciling spirit to the seventeenth-century discussion of the question in its theological form. The harmony, of which Leibniz speaks, must not be taken as meaning (like the harmony between the Monads) that the two realms of nature and of grace are entirely exclusive of one another. The realm of final causes, for instance, does not belong entirely to nature : the realm of grace is the realm of final causes in its highest form. The relation between nature and grace is analogous to that between body and soul. Just as body, considered as an aggregate, is merely phenomenal and therefore quite distinct from soul or real substance, while yet it is a *phenomenon bene fundatum* and its *reality* is that of its component Monads or souls ; so nature, considered as subject to the law of efficient causes, is quite distinct from grace, while yet, since efficient causes, even in nature itself, derive their meaning and force from final causes, nature finds its perfection in grace, which is the highest expression of final cause. §§ 88 and 89 illustrate this. Cf. *Principles of Nature and of Grace*, § 15.

88. A result of this harmony is that things lead to grace by the very ways of nature, and that this globe, for instance, must be destroyed and renewed by natural means at the very time when the government of spirits requires it, for the punishment of some and the reward of others. (*Théod.* 18 sqq., 110, 244, 245, 340.)

89. It may also be said that God as Architect satisfies in all respects God as Lawgiver [140], and thus that sins must bear their penalty with them, through the order of nature, and even in virtue of the mechanical structure of things; and similarly that noble actions will attain their rewards by ways which, on the bodily side, are mechanical, although this cannot and ought not always to happen immediately [141].

90. Finally, under this perfect government no good action would be unrewarded and no bad one unpunished, and all should issue in the well-being of the good, that is to say, of those who are not malcontents in this great state, but who trust in Providence, after having done their duty, and who love and imitate, as is meet, the Author of all good, finding pleasure in the contemplation of His perfections, as is the way of genuine 'pure love [142],'

[140] That is to say, the world is built on a plan which perfectly harmonizes with the moral government of its inhabitants.

[141] Leibniz regards sin as seeking one's own good in an imperfect, unenlightened way, without regard to the moral law or order, which is the only way of securing the highest possible good of all and of each. Thus sin brings punishment as inevitably as neglect or defiance of natural laws brings disease and pain. But owing to the harmony (above explained) between spirit and body, the moral and the natural worlds, the punishment of sin is not merely spiritual: the bodily or natural has a share in it. Similarly virtue has its reward, both spiritual and natural, because it is enlightened action in accordance with the ultimate law of the whole universe, the principle of the highest good.

[142] That is to say, disinterested love, as distinct from interested or selfish love. One of the great subjects of theological discussion in the seventeenth century was the question whether there is such a thing as purely disinterested love. About this a long pamphlet controversy (lasting from 1694 to 1699) took place between Bossuet

which takes pleasure in the happiness of the beloved. This it is which leads wise and virtuous people to devote their energies to everything which appears in harmony with the presumptive or antecedent will of God, and yet makes them content with what God actually brings to pass by His secret, consequent and positive [*décisive*] will [143], recognizing that if we could sufficiently under-

and Fénelon. Fénelon (partly in defence of Mme. Guyon) maintained the possibility of a disinterested love of God, that is, a love which has no regard to rewards and punishments. Ultimately, however, Pope Innocent XII condemned the views of Fénelon, at the same time censuring the controversial methods of Bossuet. The view of Leibniz is more fully given in his Preface, *On the Notions of Right and Justice* (1693), p. 285; cf. Butler, Sermons xi, xiii, and xiv.

[143] The distinction between the antecedent and the consequent will of God is due to Thomas Aquinas. He says : 'This distinction is not founded upon the Divine will itself, for in it there is neither before nor after; but it is founded upon the objects of His will. . . . A thing may be considered either in itself, absolutely, or with some particular circumstance, which forms a subsequent consideration. For instance it is good in itself that man should live and bad that he should be killed, considering the matter absolutely; but if we add, with regard to some particular man, that he is a murderer or that his living is a source of danger to a large number of people, in this case it will be good that the man should be killed, and bad that he should live. Accordingly it may be said that a judge wills with an antecedent will that every man should continue to live, but wills with a consequent will that a murderer should be hanged.' *Summa Theol.* i. Qu. 19, Art. 6 *ad primum.* Cf. *De Veritate*, Qu. 23, Art. 2. Leibniz brings this into relation with his own hypothesis regarding the region of possible things and the actual, existing world. 'In a general sense it may be said that will consists in the inclination to do something in proportion to the good it contains. This will is called *antecedent*, when it is separate [*détachée*] and has regard to each good by itself, in so far as it is good. In this sense it may be said that God tends to all good in so far as it is good, *ad perfectionem simpliciter simplicem*, in Scholastic language, and that by an antecedent will. He has an earnest inclination to sanctify and save all men, to do away with sin and to prevent damnation. It may even be said that this will is efficacious *in itself* (*per se*), that is to say, so that the effect would follow, were there not some stronger reason which prevents it; for this will does not go to the extreme of effort (*ad summum*

stand the order of the universe, we should find that it exceeds all the desires of the wisest men, and that it is impossible to make it better than it is, not only as a whole and in general but also for ourselves in particular, if we are attached, as we ought to be, to the Author of all, not only as to the architect and efficient cause of our being, but as to our master and to the final cause, which ought to be the whole aim of our will, and which can alone make our happiness. (*Théod.* 134, 278. *Préf.* [E. 469; G. vi. 27, 28].)

conatum), otherwise it would never fail to produce its full effect, since God is master of all things. Complete and infallible success belongs only to *consequent will*, as it is called. It is complete, and this rule applies to it, namely, that we never fail to do what we will, when we can. Now this consequent, final and decisive will results from the conflict of all the antecedent volitions ['wills'], both those which tend towards good and those which oppose evil, and it is from the concurrence of all these particular volitions that the total volition comes: as in mechanics the composite motion is the result of all the tendencies which concur in one and the same movable body, and equally satisfies each of them so far as it is possible to do so at once. ... In this sense it may be said that antecedent will [volition] is in a way efficacious and even effective and successful. From this it follows that God wills *antecedently* the good, and *consequently* the best.' *Théodicée*, §§ 22 and 23 (E. 510 b; G. vi. 115, 116). God *antecedently* wills the absolute good of all beings; but He *consequently* wills the greatest good of each that is *possible*, considering the essential limitations of their natures and their relations to one another in the system of things. This greatest *possible* good is thus compatible with a certain amount of evil.

[14] This is not to be taken as meaning that it is impossible to make the world better than it is *at this or any particular moment of time*. Leibniz is speaking of the world as a system including all time, and accordingly he does not exclude progress in time.

APPENDIX F.

THE DISCUSSION BETWEEN LEIBNIZ AND BAYLE REGARDING THE MULTIPLICITY IN THE MONAD.

THE 'difficulty' regarding the possibility of a multiplicity in the Monad, to which Leibniz refers in § 16 of the *Monadology*, is variously expressed by Bayle in his *Dictionary* (article 'Rorarius'). He says : 'As Leibniz with much reason supposes that all souls are simple and indivisible, it is impossible to understand how they can be likened to a clock' [see *Third explanation of the New System*, and Introduction, Part ii. p. 45], ' that is to say, how by their original constitution they can diversify their operations, by means of the spontaneous activity they receive from their Creator. We conceive clearly that a simple being will always act uniformly, if no extraneous cause interferes with it. If it were composed of several pieces, like a machine, it would act in divers ways, because the special activity of each piece might change at any moment the course of the activity of the others; but in an independent simple substance [*substance unique*], where will you find the cause of any variety in its operation ?' Leibniz's answer to this appears in the *Réponse aux Réflexions de Bayle* ; see *Monadology*, note 20 ; cf. *Lettre à Basnage* (1698) (E. 153 a; G. iv. 522): ' I compared the soul to a clock, only as regards the regulated precision of its changes. This is but imperfect in the best of clocks, but it is perfect in the works of God. And the soul may be said to be an immaterial automaton of the very best kind. When it is said that a simple being will always act uniformly, a distinction must be made : if *acting uniformly* means constantly following the same law of order or varying succession [*continuation*], as in a certain order or series of numbers, I admit that of itself every simple being, and even every compound being, acts uniformly ; but if *uniformly* means exactly in the same way [*semblablement*], I do not admit it. . . . The soul, though it is perfectly simple, has always a feeling [*sentiment*] composed of several perceptions at once ; and this is as much to our purpose as if it were composed of pieces, like a machine. For each preceding perception influences those which follow, according to a law which there is in perceptions as in motions.' Bayle allows that Leibniz's view contains the promise of a theory which will solve all difficulties; but he still feels dissatisfied as to the power of a simple substance, like the soul of man, to develop spontaneously all the variety of thought, &c. It has not 'the necessary instruments' for doing this. 'Let us freely imagine an animal created by God and intended to sing incessantly. It will always sing, that is indubitable; but if God assigns to it a certain piece of music to sing [*une certaine tablature*], He must necessarily either place this before its eyes, or imprint it on its memory, or give it an arrangement of muscles which, in accordance with the laws of mechanics, shall make one note follow another exactly according to their order in the musical score [*tablature*]. Otherwise it is inconceivable that the animal should ever be able to conform to the whole succession of notes indicated by God. Let us apply this to the soul of man. M. Leibniz thinks that it has received not only the faculty of continually supplying itself with thoughts, but also the faculty of always following a certain order in its thoughts, corresponding to the continual changes of the bodily mechanism. This order of thoughts is like the musical score assigned to the animal musician of which we have been speaking. In order that the soul may from moment to moment change its perceptions or its modifications in accordance with the "score" of thoughts, must not the soul know the succession of the notes and actually think of it? Now experience shows us that it does nothing of the kind. And, failing this knowledge, must there not at least be in the soul a succession of special instruments which might each be a necessary cause of this or that particular thought? Must not these instruments be so situated that one acts upon another, in exact accord with the *pre-established* correspondence between the changes of the bodily mechanism and the thoughts of the soul? Now it is quite certain that no immaterial, simple and indivisible substance can be composed of this countless multitude of special instruments placed one before another in the order required by the "score" in question. Accordingly it is impossible for the human soul to carry out this law.' (This illustration of Bayle's may be compared with Leibniz's simile of the choirs, see Introduction, Part ii. p. 47. The letter containing Leibniz's simile was written in 1687.) In a paper written in 1702 (G. iv. 549 sqq.) Leibniz makes the following reply to Bayle (referring in the first place to Bayle's supposition of an animal created by God to sing incessantly): 'It is enough if we suppose a singer paid to sing at certain hours in church or at the opera, and

T

that he finds there a music-book, in which there are the pieces of music or the " score " he is to sing on the particular days and hours. The singer sings with open book [à *livre ouvert*], his eyes are directed by the book, and his tongue and throat are directed by his eyes, but his soul sings, so to speak, by memory or by something equivalent to memory; for since the music-book, the eyes and the ears cannot act upon the soul, it must by itself, and indeed without trouble or application and without seeking it, find what his brain and organs find with the help of the book. The reason is that the whole " score " of the book or books that shall, one after another, be followed in singing is potentially [*virtuellement*] graven in his soul from the beginning of its existence ; as this "score" was in some way graven in its material causes before the pieces of music were composed and the book made out of them. But the soul cannot be conscious of it [*s'en apercevoir*], for it is enveloped in the confused perceptions of the soul, which express all the detail of the universe. And the soul is distinctly conscious of it only at the time when its organs are markedly affected by the notes of the " score." . . . I have already shown more than once that the soul does many things without knowing how it does them, when it does so by means of confused perceptions and unconscious [*insensibles*] inclinations or appetitions, of which there is always a very great number, and which it is impossible for the soul to be conscious of, or to unravel distinctly. . . . The soul has all the instruments which M. Bayle thinks necessary, arranged [*placé*] as they ought to be. But they are not material instruments. They are the preceding perceptions themselves, from which the succeeding perceptions arise by the laws of appetitions [*appétits*].'

APPENDIX G.

PROOF OF THE EXISTENCE OF GOD.

THE view of Leibniz, expressed in the *Monadology* (§§ 44 and 45), must be carefully distinguished from the Cartesian argument (derived from Anselm) that the idea of God involves His existence, because if He does not exist, a more perfect Being may be conceived, namely one who does exist. It is also to be distinguished from the view of Spinoza, which amounts to saying that the essence of God involves His existence, because

all essence exists, all that is possible is actual. As against
Descartes's proof Leibniz argues that it is incomplete, for the
idea of a most perfect being might perhaps be self-contradictory, like the idea of the swiftest possible motion or the
greatest possible number. Thus, after stating the Cartesian
argument, Leibniz says: 'But it is to be noted that the only
logical conclusion is: "If God is possible, it follows that He
exists." For we cannot safely use definitions in order to reach
a conclusion, until we know that these definitions are real or
that they involve no contradiction. The reason of this is that
from notions which involve a contradiction opposite conclusions
may be drawn at the same time, which is absurd. To illustrate
this I usually take the instance of the swiftest possible motion,
which involves an absurdity. For, suppose a wheel to revolve
with the swiftest possible motion, is it not evident, that if any
spoke of the wheel be made longer' [*produced*, in the mathematical sense] 'its extremity will move more swiftly than
a nail on the circumference of the wheel; wherefore the
motion of the circumference is not the swiftest possible, as was
supposed by the hypothesis. Yet at first sight it may appear
that we have an idea of the swiftest possible motion; for we
seem to understand what we are saying, and nevertheless we
have no idea of impossible things.' *Meditationes de Cognitione,
Veritate et Ideis* (1684), (E. 80 a; G. iv. 424.) 'Therefore there is
assuredly reason to doubt whether the idea of the greatest of all
beings is not uncertain, and whether it does not involve some
contradiction. For I quite understand, for instance, the nature
of motion and velocity, and what "the greatest" is. But I do
not understand whether these are compatible, and whether
it is possible to combine them into the one idea of the greatest
velocity of which motion is capable. In the same way, although
I know what "being" is, and what the "greatest" and the
"most perfect" are, nevertheless I do not therefore know that
there is not a hidden contradiction involved in combining these
together, as there actually is in the instances I have just given
. . . Yet I admit that God has here a great advantage over
all other things. For, in order to prove that He exists, it is
sufficient to prove that He is possible, which is not the case
with regard to anything else that I know of. . . . Simple
forms [i. e. living principles] are the source of things. Now
I maintain that all simple forms are compatible with one
another. . . . If this be granted, it follows that the nature of

God, which contains all simple forms taken absolutely, is possible. Now we have proved above that God is, provided He is possible. Therefore He exists.' (G. iv. 294 and 296.) Thus Leibniz, as he himself says (G. iv. 405), holds a middle position between those who regard the Cartesian proof as a sophism and those who say that it is a complete demonstration. God's existence, for Leibniz, follows immediately from His possibility, for all real possibility includes a tendency to existence, and there can be nothing to hinder this tendency in a being supposed to be perfect. In the *Réponses aux Deuxièmes Objections*, Descartes maintains the possibility of the idea of a most perfect being. But he does not make this a prominent or essential part of his proof, as Leibniz does. Cf. Descartes, *Méditation* 5; *Principia Philosophiae*, Part i. §§ 14 sqq.

In the *Animadversiones in partem generalem Principiorum Cartesianorum* (1692) (G. iv. 359) Leibniz suggests that the argument might be simplified by omitting the reference to 'perfection,' and merely saying 'a necessary Being exists—or a Being whose essence is existence, or Being in itself [*ens a se*] exists—as is evident from the terms. Now God is such a being (from the definition of God), therefore God exists. This argument holds if it be granted that a necessary being is possible and does not involve a contradiction, or, what is the same thing, that the essence from which existence follows is possible.' Elsewhere (E. 177 b; G. iv. 406) Leibniz points out that 'those who hold that from notions, ideas, definitions or possible essences alone we can never infer actual existence . . . deny the possibility of being in itself' [*ens a se*]. But 'if *being in itself* is impossible, all beings through another' [*entia ab alio*] 'are also impossible, since indeed they are only through *being in itself*: thus nothing can exist.'

As against Spinoza, Leibniz's argument would be that not all that is possible is actual, but only the compossible or compatible. There are unrealized 'possibles,' essences which do not involve existence, and consequently the necessary being, whose essence involves existence, is not the all, but is something distinct from the world of created things. The essence of a created being does not involve its existence, because it is limited, and thus its existence depends upon its 'fitting into' other essences so as to constitute, along with them, the best possible world. But the essence of a necessary being involves its existence because it is unlimited. There is nothing to

hinder or condition its existence, and accordingly, if it be possible, it must exist. The value of Leibniz's argument depends
on the worth of the distinction he makes between 'possible'
and 'compossible,' that is to say between a metaphysical or
absolute necessity and a moral or inclining necessity. How
are these two kinds of necessity related to one another ? It is
hardly a satisfactory solution of the opposition between them
to refer the one to the understanding and the other to the
will of God. We have here again the fundamental weakness
of Leibniz's philosophy, the uncertainty of the relation between
the principle of contradiction and that of sufficient reason.

Kant rejects the whole argument as a paralogism, on the
ground that 'existence' can never be a predicate, that is to
say, that we are never justified logically in passing from a
mere idea to the existence of its content. (See *Critique of
Pure Reason*, Rosenkranz, ii. 462 ; Hartenstein, ii. 456 ; Meiklejohn's Tr., 364.) It is true that we can never pass from a mere
idea to the existence of its content; but to adduce this as an
argument here is to beg the question. For a mere idea is an
idea of that which may be non-existent ; while the idea of
a necessary being is the idea of that which cannot be non-
existent. Gaunilo in his *Liber pro insipiente*, anticipates the
objection of Kant, and to this Anselm replied in his *Liber
apologeticus contra respondentem pro insipiente*, saying, among
other things : 'Let us assume that the *Summum cogitabile*
need not exist merely because it is thought. Mark the consequence. That which can be thought without really existing
would not, if it did exist, be the *summum cogitabile* ; so that,
by the hypothesis, the *summum cogitabile* is and is not the
summum cogitabile, which is in the last degree absurd' (Rigg's
St. Anselm of Canterbury, p. 71. See the whole of his chap. v).
Cf. Introduction, Part iv. p. 173.

OTHER PHILOSOPHICAL WRITINGS

OF LEIBNIZ

ON THE NOTIONS OF RIGHT AND JUSTICE. 1693.

PREFATORY NOTE.

LEIBNIZ was deeply interested in the maintenance of the rights of the Empire as against the pretensions of Louis XIV. He observed that the French took every opportunity of obtaining and preserving documents on which they might found claims. And accordingly, on behalf of the Empire, he set himself to make a collection of Treaties and State papers (international and national) affecting the European nations. His plan was to publish them in three volumes under the title *Codex Juris Gentium Diplomaticus*. In 1693 the first volume appeared, containing papers of date from 1100 to 1500 A.D. The work was never finished; but an Appendix (*mantissa*) to the first volume was published in 1700. Writing to the Count de Kinsky in 1697, Leibniz remarks that his book 'is a little less in season than it was at first, for we are assured that a general peace is on the point of being concluded' (Klopp, vi. 454).

To this work Leibniz says he 'contributed only the title, the preface, and the trouble of reading it over' (Klopp, vi. 441). The preface, however, contains the most convenient summary of its author's views in an important department of ethics. The whole preface is given by Dutens (iv. 287) and by Klopp (vi. 457); but Erdmann (118) gives only the paragraphs dealing with 'the eternal rights [or laws] of a rational nature,' and Gerhardt includes no part of it in his edition. I have translated the portion given by Erdmann, adding a few sentences from the succeeding paragraphs which deal with 'voluntary' and 'divine' right. In the foot-notes will be found translations of a number of illustrative passages from the very interesting collection of papers from the Hanover

MSS. published by Dr. Georg Mollat under the title, *Rechts-philosophisches aus Leibnizens ungedruckten Schriften* (Leipzig, Robolsky, 1885).

The following statement of Leibniz may be used as a summary of this part of the Preface to the *Codex Diplomaticus*: 'In stating the elements of natural right there must be expounded, *first*, the common principles of justice, the charity of the wise man; *secondly*, private right or the precepts of commutative justice, concerning what is observed among men in so far as they are regarded as equal; *thirdly*, public right, concerning the dispensing of common goods and evils among unequal people for the greatest common good in this life; *fourthly*, inward right, concerning universal virtue and natural obligation towards God, that we may have regard to perpetual happiness. To these must be added the elements of legitimate human and divine right: human right both in our own commonwealth and between nations, divine right in the universal Church.' (*De tribus juris naturae et gentium gradibus*, Mollat, p. 21.)

The ideas expressed in this *Preface* are to a large extent derived from Grotius.

The doctrine of right, confined by nature within narrow limits, has been immensely extended by the human intellect [1]. I am not sure that, even after so many distinguished writers have discussed them, the notions of *Right* and *Justice* may be considered sufficiently clear. *Right* is a certain moral power, and *obligation* a moral necessity [2]. Now by *moral* I mean that which is equivalent to 'natural' in a good man: for as a Roman lawyer admirably says, it is not to be believed that we are capable of doing things

[1] 'Medical science is the science of the pleasant, political science is the science of the useful, ethical science is the science of the just.' *Juris et aequi elementa* (Mollat, p. 23).

[2] 'Nothing impossible is a duty or, as it is commonly put, of impossible things there is no obligation. . . . Everything necessary is permissible or, as it is commonly put, necessity has no law.' *De debitis et illicitis* (Mollat, p. 92). 'Necessity is the avoiding of misery,' which is defined as 'lasting sadness' or 'that state in which the aggregate of evils preponderates over the aggregate of goods.' *Juris et aequi elementa* (Mollat, pp. 32, 33).

which are contrary to good morals [*contra bonos mores*][3]. Further, *a good man* is one who loves all men, so far as reason allows[4]. *Justice*[5], therefore, which is the virtue[6] governing that disposition of mind [*affectus*] which the Greeks call φιλανθρωπία, will, if I mistake not, be most fittingly defined as the *charity of the wise man* [*caritas sapientis*[7]], that is to say, charity in obedience to the

[3] 'When the nature of justice and (as is necessarily involved in this) the nature of wisdom and charity is understood, it is manifest that that which to a good man is possible, impossible, necessary (if he wishes to retain the name), is just or permissible, unjust, and finally, *obligatory* [*debitum*]. For it is not to be believed that we are capable of doing things which are contrary to good morals, and in this sense it may be said that the *right* we have of acting or not acting is a certain power or moral liberty, while *obligation* is a necessity.' *De tribus juris naturae et gentium gradibus* (Mollat, p. 13).

[4] 'He who loves God, that is he who is wise, will love all men, but each in proportion as the traces of divine virtue in him shine out, and in proportion as he hopes to find in him a companion ready and able to promote the common good, or (what comes to the same thing) the glory of God, the Giver of good things,' *loc. cit.*

[5] The doctrine of Right must, according to Leibniz, be deduced from definitions, for the idea of justice is *a priori*. 'Since justice consists in a certain congruity and proportion, the just may have a meaning, although there may neither be any one who practises justice nor any one towards whom it is practised, just as the ratios of numbers are true, although there may neither be any one who numbers nor anything which is numbered, and it may be predicted of a house that it will be beautiful, of a machine that it will be effective, of a commonwealth that it will be happy, if it comes into existence, although it may never come into existence.' *Juris et aequi elementa* (Mollat, p. 24). I have in most places translated the word '*jus*' by '*Right*.' Regarding the ambiguities of these words see E. C. Clark's *Practical Jurisprudence*, ch. 2 and 6.

[6] 'All virtue is the bridling of the desires [*affectus*] so that nothing can oppose the commands of right reason.' *Juris et aequi elementa* (Mollat, p. 26). Cf. G. vii. 92 sqq.

[7] Leibniz gives various longer definitions of justice. In a letter to Kesner (1709) (Dutens, iv. 261) he says: 'Justice is perfection in accordance with wisdom, so far as concerns a person's conduct in relation to the goods and ills of other persons.' Again, 'Justice is nothing but that which is in conformity with wisdom and goodness combined; the end of goodness is the greatest good, but

dictates of wisdom [8]. Therefore the saying attributed to Carneades [9] that justice is supreme folly, because it bids us attend to the interests of others, neglecting our own, proceeds from ignorance of the definition of justice [10]. *Charity* is universal benevolence, and *benevolence* is the habit of loving or esteeming [*amandi sive diligendi*] [11]. But to *love*

in order to recognize it we require wisdom, which is nothing but the knowledge of the good. . . . Wisdom is in the understanding and goodness in the will. And justice consequently is in both.' *Méditation sur la notion commune de la justice* (Mollat, p. 62). ' The true and perfect definition of justice is the habit of loving others or of taking pleasure in the thought of other people's good, as often as it comes into consideration.' ' Justice is prudence in bringing about the good of others or not bringing evil upon them for the sake of bringing about one's own good (by thus manifesting one's mind), or not bringing evil upon oneself (that is, for the sake of gaining reward or avoiding punishment).' *Juris et aequi elementa* (Mollat, pp. 32 and 35). Regarding the last statement, it should be remarked that Leibniz says : ' God Himself is the reward,' *loc. cit.*

[8] ' . . . even in those who have not attained to this wisdom. For, setting God apart, the majority of those who would act in accordance with justice in all things, even against their own interests, would in fact do what is required by the wise man who finds his pleasure in the general good, but in certain cases they would not themselves act as wise men, not being sensitive to the pleasure of virtue.' *Méditation sur la notion commune de la justice* (Mollat, p. 75).

[9] The saying comes from the *Epitome* of the *Divinae Institutiones* of Lactantius, ch. i. Cf. *Instit.* v. 14 and Cicero, *De Rep.* iii. 23 (Ritter and Preller, *Hist. Phil. Graec.* §§ 436 and 438). Carneades (about 213–129 B.C.), a native of Cyrene, was founder of the New Academy. In 156 B.C. he visited Rome as an ambassador from Athens and caused much astonishment by his skill in arguing successively for and against justice. Cf. Grotius, *De jure belli et pacis, Prolegomena,* § 5.

[10] ' There cannot be justice without prudence, nor can prudence be separated from one's own good.' *Juris et aequi elementa* (Mollat, p. 26).

[11] ' There are two ways of desiring the good of others, the one when we desire it on account of our own good, the other when we desire it as if it were our own good. The first is the way of him who esteems, the second of him who loves ; the first is the feeling of a master to his servant, the second that of a father to his son ; the first is the feeling of a man towards the tool he

or *esteem* is to take pleasure in the happiness of another, or what comes to the same thing, to adopt another's happiness as our own.   In this way there is solved the difficult problem, which is also of great importance in theology, how there can be a disinterested love [*amor non mercenarius*] [12], a love apart from hope and fear and every consideration of advantage; the solution being that the happiness of those in whose happiness we take pleasure becomes a part of our own happiness [13], for things which give us pleasure are desired for their own sakes [14].   And as the very con-

requires, the second that of friend to friend; in the first case the good of others is sought for the sake of something else, in the second for its own sake.' *Juris et aequi elementa* (Mollat, p. 30). In this note the word translated 'esteem' is *aestimare*, while in the text it is *diligere*.   Benevolence is a ἕξις in the Aristotelian sense, 'not an act, but a *habit* or strong inclination of the mind, which we have acquired either by the fortune of birth, or by a special gift of God, or by repeated practice.' *De justitia* (Mollat, p. 37).

[12] Cf. *Monadology*, § 90, note 142.   In the Preface to the second part of the *Codex Juris Gentium Diplomaticus*, § 10 (Dutens, iv. 313), Leibniz replies to those who objected to his solution on the ground that 'it is more perfect to cast oneself entirely upon God, so as to be moved by His will alone and not by one's own pleasure.' This, says Leibniz, 'is contrary to the nature of things: for the endeavour to act springs from a tendency to perfection, the feeling of which is pleasure; and there is no action or volition otherwise.' Cf. a paper on the views of Fénelon (1697) (E. 790 a ; G. ii. 578): 'We do everything for our own good, and it is impossible for us to have other opinions, although we can speak about others.   But nevertheless, we do not yet love quite purely, when we do not seek the good of the loved object for its own sake and because it pleases us in itself, but because of some advantage which comes to us from it.   But . . . we seek at once our own good for our own sakes and the good of the loved object for its own sake, when the good of this object is immediately, finally (*ultimato*) and by itself our aim, our pleasure and our good, as happens with regard to all the things which we desire because they please us in themselves and are consequently good in themselves without regard to consequences : they are ends, not means.'

[13] 'The prerogative of true happiness is that it is increased by the multitude of those who share it.' *De justitia* (Mollat, p. 41).

[14] This is a convertible statement.   'Everything pleasant is

templation of beautiful things is pleasant [15], and a picture
by Raphael moves him who understands it, although it
brings him no gain, so that it becomes dear and delightful
to him, inspiring in him something like love [16]; so when
the beautiful thing is also capable of happiness, his feeling
for it passes into real love. But *Divine love* [17] excels
other loves, for God can be loved with the happiest result,
since nothing is happier than God and nothing more
beautiful or more worthy of happiness can be conceived [18].
And since He possesses supreme power and wisdom, His
happiness not only becomes a part of ours (if we are wise,
that is, if we love Him) but even constitutes it [19]. But
since wisdom ought to direct charity, wisdom also requires

sought for its own sake, and whatever is sought for its own sake
is pleasant. Other things are sought on account of what is
pleasant, that they may produce it, contribute to it, or remove
what is opposed to it. All men feel this whatever they may say,
or at any rate they do it, whatever they may feel.' *Juris et aequi
elementa* (Mollat, p. 30).

[15] 'We seek beautiful things because they are pleasant. I define
a beautiful thing as that the contemplation of which is pleasant.'
loc. cit. (Mollat, p. 31).

[16] 'He who finds pleasure in the contemplation of a beautiful
picture and would suffer pain if he saw it spoiled, even though it
belong to another man, loves it so to speak with a disinterested
love; but this is not the case with him who thinks merely of
making money by selling or getting applause by showing it,
without caring whether it is spoiled or not, when it no longer
belongs to him.' *Lettre à Nicaise* (1698) (E. 791 b; G. ii. 581). Cf. Kant,
Critique of Judgment, Part i. div. i. bk. i. §§ 1-5.

[17] i.e. love for God.

[18] 'He Himself is always happy and will never be a cause of
grief to us through His misfortune, nor will He be in need of our
help. And again, since He always does everything in the most
reasonable way, we can act in relation to Him otherwise than
in relation to those who, being carried away by their emotions,
follow no fixed rule of conduct and may even be offended by those
who are most anxious to honour them. But He is always content
with a good will and richly rewards all things well done or
intended, that is, all things which are in harmony with His
presumptive will.' *De justitia,* 5 (Mollat, p. 38).

[19] 'The happiness of God constitutes . . . the whole of ours.'
(E. 790 a; G. ii. 578.)

to be defined.   And I think that the notion men have of
it will best be satisfied, if we say that *wisdom* is nothing
but the very science of happiness [20].   So we are brought
back again to the notion of *happiness*, which this is not
the place to explain [21].

Now from this source flows *natural Right* [*jus naturae*]
of which there are *three degrees: Right in the narrow sense*
[*jus strictum*] in commutative justice, *equity* (or charity
in the narrower sense of the word) in distributive justice [22],
and lastly, *piety* (or uprightness) in universal justice [23].

[20] 'Wisdom is the science of the best, as prudence is the science
of the good.' *Specimen demonstrationum politicarum* (1669), prop. 38
(Dutens, iv. 559).

[21] 'Happiness is a lasting state of joy.' *Initium institutionum juris
perpetui* (Mollat, p. 4).   'Nothing contributes more to happiness
than the enlightenment of the understanding and the inclination
of the will always to act according to reason, and such an enlightenment is especially to be sought in the knowledge of those things
which can lead our understanding ever onward to a higher light ;
because from this there arises a continual progress in wisdom and
virtue, and consequently in perfection and joy, the fruit of which
remains with the soul even after this life.' *Von der Glückseligkeit*
(E. 672 b ; G. vii. 88).   Cf. E. 792 a ; G. ii. 581.

[22] These correspond respectively to Aristotle's τὸ ἐν τοῖς συναλλάγ-
μασι δίκαιον or δίκαιον διορθωτικόν and his διανεμητικὸν δίκαιον or δίκαιον
ἐν ταῖς διανόμαις.   *Ethics*, v. 2, 1130ᵇ 30 ; v. 4, 1131ᵇ 27 and 33.   Cf.
Pol. iii. 9.   'Commutative justice has to do with private right,
distributive with public right.'   *De tribus juris naturae et gentium
gradibus* (Mollat, p. 14).   Cf. *loc. cit.*, p. 17, where they are called
' right of property, and right of society.'   But Aristotle recognizes
a ' catallactic' or ' commutative' justice (τὸ ἀντιπεπονθός) distinct
(at least according to what seems the best interpretation of *Eth*. v.
5) both from ' corrective' justice (τὸ διορθωτικόν) and 'distributive'
justice (τὸ διανεμητικόν); ' corrective' and 'distributive' justice
pre-supposing the existence of a state (πόλις), while ' catallactic'
justice is pre-supposed by the state. See Prof. Ritchie 'On Aristotle's
subdivisions of Particular Justice,' *Classical Review*, viii. p. 185.

[23] 'While justice is only a particular virtue, when we make
abstraction from God or from a government which imitates that
of God ; and while this virtue, thus limited, includes only what is
called commutative and distributive justice, we may say that as
soon as it is founded upon God or upon the imitation of God, it becomes *universal justice* and contains all the virtues.' *Méditation sur la
notion commune de la justice* (Mollat, p. 75).   Cf. *infra*, note 42.

Hence come the precepts that we should do injury to no
one, that we should give each his own, that we should
live virtuously (or rather piously), the universal and
commonly accepted precepts of Right [*jus*] [24] ; as I
suggested, when a youth, in my little book *De Methodo
Juris* [25]. The precept of bare Right or *Right in the narrow
sense* [*jus strictum*] [26] is that *no one is to be injured*, lest if
it be within the state, the person should have ground for
an action at law, or if it be without the state, he should
have the right to make war [27]. From this there comes
the justice which the philosophers call *commutative* and
the right which Grotius calls *right proper* [*facultas*] [28].

[24] The precepts are given by Ulpian. See *Justiniani Institutiones*,
Lib. i. Tit. i. 3 (Moyle's ed., vol. i. p. 100). In his *De tribus juris
naturae et gentium gradibus* (Mollat, p. 14), Leibniz says that the three
precepts flow from 'the supreme rule of Right,' which is ' to direct
all things to the greater general good.'

[25] *Methodus nova discendae docendaeque Jurisprudentiae* (1667), §§ 74–76
(Dutens, iv. 213). This was the work through which Leibniz
obtained an introduction to the Elector of Mainz. See Introduction,
Part i. p. 4.

[26] Grotius distinguishes between *jus strictum* and *jus laxius*, the
latter being *moral* right. *De jure belli et pacis*, bk. i. ch. 1, § 9, 1 and 2.
Cf. *Prolegomena*, § 10. Leibniz holds, as against Hobbes, that 'there
is a right and even a *jus strictum* before the foundation of the State.
He who produces a new thing or puts himself in possession of an
already existing thing, which no one has already taken possession
of, and who cultivates it and fits it for his use, cannot as a rule be
deprived of it without injustice.' *Méditation sur la notion commune de
la justice* (Mollat, p. 78).

[27] 'Against him who knowingly injures without necessity, there
is a right of war.' *Juris et aequi elementa* (Mollat, p. 33). The object
of this first degree of Right is the preservation of peace, which does
not necessarily secure happiness but is an essential condition of
happiness. 'It is an evil to a man that there is another man who
wishes him ill, and it is a good to a man that there is another man
who wishes him well.' *Axiomes ou principes de droit* (Mollat, p. 54).

[28] *De jure belli et pacis*, bk. i. ch. 1, §§ 5 sqq. *Facultas* is *jus proprie
aut stricte dictum*. It includes power (*potestas*) whether over one's
self (which is liberty), or over another (which is authority), also
ownership (*dominium*), whether full (as of property), or less full
(as of compact, pledge, credit, to which corresponds debt on the
other side). Whewell translates *facultas* 'jural claim' in contrast

The higher degree I call *equity*[29], or if you prefer it, charity (that is, in the narrower sense), which I extend beyond the rigour of bare Right to those obligations also on account of which those to whom we are obliged have no ground of action to compel us to perform them, such as gratitude, pity, and the things which are said by Grotius to have *imperfect right* [or *fitness, aptitudo*] not *right proper* [*facultas*]. And as the precept of the lowest degree was to do injury to no one, so that of the middle degree is to do good to everybody[30]; but that so far as befits each person or so far as each deserves, since we cannot equally befriend all men[31]. Therefore to this place belong *distributive* justice[32] and that precept of Right [*jus*] which bids us *give to each his own*. And to this political laws in the state are related, laws which have to do with the happiness of subjects and which usually bring it about that those who had only moral claim [*aptitudo*] acquire a jural claim [*facultas*][33], that is to say, that they are

with 'moral claim' (*aptitudo*). 'Commutative justice' (*justitia expletrix*) concerns *facultas*, while 'distributive justice' (*justitia attributrix*) concerns *aptitudo*.

[29] This degree of Right presupposes some sort of 'society' or social arrangement among men. There may be such a 'society' in which the first degree of Right is alone recognized, but it cannot be a happy state, for there must be 'perpetual quarrels' in it, and thus the higher degree of Right comes to be recognized. *De tribus juris naturae et gentium gradibus* (Mollat, pp. 17 sqq.).

[30] 'Do not do to others what you do not wish to be done to yourself, and do not deny to others what you wish to be done to yourself. It is the rule of reason, and it is our Lord's rule. Put yourself in the place of others and you will be at the true point of view for judging what is just or not.' *Méditation sur la notion commune de la justice* (Mollat, p. 70).

[31] See note 4.

[32] 'In which I include *contributive* justice,' that is, not merely the giving to each his due, but the promoting of the common good and the averting of the common evil. *De tribus juris naturae et gentium gradibus* (Mollat, p. 16).

[33] The different degrees of Right are merely *degrees*, not absolute divisions, and thus one passes into another. Thus to refuse to give a man his due is to injure him, for 'the absence of good is an evil

U

enabled to demand what it is fair that others should give.
But while in the lowest degree of Right no regard was
paid to the differences among men (except to those which
arise from the particular matter in hand), and all men
were regarded as equal, now in this higher degree merits
are weighed, and hence privileges, rewards and punishments appear [34].   Xenophon has cleverly represented this
difference in the degrees of Right by the case of the young
boy Cyrus [35], who was chosen to decide between two boys
the stronger of whom had forcibly exchanged clothes with
the other, because he had found that the other boy's gown
fitted him better, while his own fitted the other boy
better.   Cyrus decided in favour of the robber; but his
tutor pointed out to him that the question here was not
whom the gown fitted but whose it was, and that some
day he would more rightly make use of this way of judging when he himself had gowns to distribute.   For equity

and the absence of evil is a good.' (Mollat, p. 70.) Thus 'the gover-
nors of societies and certain magistrates are obliged not only to
prevent evil but also to promote good.' (Mollat, p. 68.) 'The science
of the just and that of the useful, that is, the science of public and
that of private good are mutually involved, and it is not easy for
any one to be happy in the midst of the miserable.' *Juris et aequi
elementa* (Mollat, p. 23).

[34] Regarding the lowest degree of right, Leibniz says : 'This is
that equality which is commonly called *arithmetical*, that all are so
far regarded as having the same merit, and, no account of persons
being taken, each receives just as much as he gave up.' *De tribus
juris naturae et gentium graditus* (Mollat, p. 15). 'The distribution of
goods and evils is often made in proportion to people's virtues and
merits, or vices and faults, and this is called *geometrical* equality,
because in this very inequality an equality of ratios is observed, so
that unequal things are given to unequal persons, the same proportion being kept between the things given as there is between
the persons,' *loc. cit.*, p. 16. The distinction and the names are due
to Aristotle, although Leibniz's application of them is somewhat
different. Cf. *Ethics*, v. 3, 1131^b 12 sqq. and v. 4, 1131^b 25 sqq. See
also Plato, *Laws*, bk. vi. 757 A sqq., and Grotius, *De jure belli et pacis*,
bk. i. ch. 1, § 8, 2.

[35] *Cyropaedia*, bk. i. ch. 3, 17. The story is quoted by Grotius.
bk. i. ch. 1, § 8.

itself leads us in business to act upon Right in the narrow
sense [*jus strictum*], that is, the equality of men, unless
when a weighty reason of greater good requires us to
depart from it [36]. Moreover, what is called respect of
persons has place, not in the exchanging of goods with
others, but in the distributing of our own goods or those
of the public.

I have called the highest degree of Right by the name
of uprightness or rather *piety* [37]. For what has been said
so far may be understood in such a way as to be limited
to the relations of a mortal life. And indeed bare Right
or Right in the narrow sense [*jus strictum*] has its source
in the need of keeping the peace; equity or charity

[36] ' It is not allowable to take from the rich their goods in order
to supply the poor with them. . . . Because the disorder which
would arise from this would cause more evil and inconvenience in
general than the special inconvenience of the present state of
things. . . . Thus the state should maintain individuals in their
possessions. Yet it may make a tolerable breach in them for the
common security, and even for a great common good.' *Méditation
sur la notion commune de la justice* (Mollat, p. 81).

[37] ' The third principle of Right is the will of a superior. . . . But
the superior is either superior by nature, as God is: and His will
again is either natural, hence *piety*, or law, hence positive Divine
Right; or the superior is superior by agreement [*pactum*], as a man
is; hence civil Right. Piety therefore is the third degree of natural
Right, and it gives perfection and effect to the others. For God,
since He is omniscient and wise, confirms bare right and equity;
and, since He is omnipotent, He carries them out. Hence the
advantage of the human race, and indeed the beauty and harmony
of the world, coincide with the Divine will.' *Methodus Nova,* &c.
(1667), § 76 (Dutens, iv. 214). Elsewhere Leibniz argues that
there must be a higher degree of right than mere equity, for
' God is supremely just and supremely good,' and the justice of
God differs not in kind but in degree from the justice of man.
' But it is not for his ease nor in order to keep the peace with us,
that God shows us so much goodness; for we could not make war
upon Him. What, then, will be the principle of His justice and
what will be its rule? It will not be that equity or that equality,
which has place among men. . . . We cannot regard God as having
any other motive than perfection.' *Méditation sur la notion commune
de la justice* (Mollat, p. 72).

strives after something more, to wit that while each to other does as much good as possible, each may increase his own happiness through that of others ; and, to put it in a word, Right in the narrow sense [*jus strictum*] avoids misery, Right in the higher sense [*jus superius*] tends to happiness, but of such a kind as falls to our mortal lot. But that we ought to subordinate life itself and whatever makes life desirable to the great good of others so that it behoves us to bear patiently the greatest pains for the sake of others [38], this is beautifully inculcated by philosophers rather than thoroughly proved by them.   For the moral dignity and glory and our soul's feeling of joy on account of virtue, to which philosophers [39] appeal under the name of rectitude, are certainly good things of thought or of the mind, and are indeed great goods, but not such as to prevail with all men nor to overcome all the sharpness of evils, since all men are not equally moved by imagination ; especially those who have not become accustomed to the thought of honour or to the appreciation of the good things of the soul, either through a liberal education, or a noble way of living, or the discipline of life or of method. But in order that it may be concluded by a universal demonstration that everything honourable is beneficial [*omne honestum utile*] and that everything base is hurtful [*omne turpe damnosum*] [40], we must assume the immor-

[38] 'The principles of charity are abnegation of self, esteem of others.' *Tabulae duae disciplinae juris*, &c. (Mollat, p. 9). 'Love feels not the wounds which it suffers, but those which it makes,' *loc. cit.* p. 12. 'Among true friends all things are common, even to misery.' *Juris et aequi elementa* (Mollat, p. 33).

[39] ' If you had listened very attentively to Cicero declaiming on behalf of rectitude as against pleasure, you would have heard him magnificently perorate about the beauty of virtue, the deformity of base things, about a conscience at peace with itself in the depth of a rejoicing soul, about the good of an untarnished reputation, about an immortal name and the exultation of glory.' *Juris et aequi elementa* (Mollat, p. 30).

[40] In his *Initium institutionum juris perpetui* (Mollat, p. 4) Leibnïz, using a similar expression, adds: ' And moral qualities are turned into natural.' Cf. *Monadology*, §§ 88–90.

tality of the soul [41] and the Ruler of the universe, GOD [42]. Thus it is that we think of all men as living in the most perfect City [*civitas*] [43], under a Monarch who on account of His wisdom cannot be deceived [*falli*] and on account of His power cannot be avoided [44] ; and a Monarch who is also so loveable that it is happiness to serve such a master. Therefore he who spends his soul for Him gains it, as Christ teaches [45]. By His power and providence it comes to pass that every *right* passes into fact [*omne jus in factum transeat*] [46], that no one is injured except by him-

[41] If the soul were not immortal, Leibniz thinks it would be impossible for even a wise man to have a sufficient regard for his own perfection. (Mollat, p. 21.) To a similar effect he writes against the view of Puffendorf, of whom he had a very poor opinion. ('He is not much of a lawyer and very little of a philosopher,' Dutens, iv. 261.) Puffendorf limited natural right to external laws and regarded all virtues or moral qualities as based on principles not of reason but of revelation. See *Monita quaedam ad Samuelis Puffendorfii principia* (Dutens, iv. 275 sqq., and 262).

[42] Grotius held that 'there would be a certain natural obligation, even if it were granted (which it cannot be) that there is no God.' *De jure belli et pacis, Prolegomena*, § 11. 'It is true that Aristotle recognized this universal justice, although he did not refer it to God, and I think it admirable in him to have had, nevertheless, so high an idea of it. But this is due to the fact that for him a well-constituted government or state takes the place of God as regards earthly things, and such a government will do what it can to compel men to be virtuous.' *Méditation sur la notion commune de la justice* (Mollat, p. 76).

[43] 'Finding, as I do, the principle of justice in the good, Aristotle takes as the rule of expediency [*convenance*] the best, that is to say, what would be expedient for the best government (*quod optimae reipublicae conveniret*), so that, according to this author, natural right is that which is most expedient for order.' *loc. cit.* (Mollat, p. 80). Cf. *Monadology*, § 85.

[44] 'So that the honourable and the advantageous are the same, and no sin is without punishment, no noble deed is in vain or goes without reward.' (Mollat, p. 96.) Cf. *Monadology*, § 90.

[45] St. Luke, ix. 24 ; xvii. 33 ; St. John, xii. 25.

[46] When power is combined with wisdom and goodness 'it makes right become fact, so that what ought to be really exists, in so far as the nature of things allows. And this is what God does

self[47], that nothing done rightly is without a reward and no sin without a punishment. For, as Christ divinely taught, all our hairs are numbered, and not even a draught of water is given in vain to one who thirsts, and thus nothing is disregarded in the commonwealth of the universe[48]. It is on this account that *justice* is called *universal* and comprehends all other virtues[49], for things which otherwise do not seem to concern any one else, as for instance whether we abuse our own body or our own property, and which are beyond the range of human laws, are nevertheless forbidden by the law of nature [*jus naturale*][50], that is, by the eternal laws of the Divine Monarchy, since we owe ourselves and all that is ours to God[51]. For as it is of importance to a commonwealth[52], so much more is it to the universe, that no one should make a bad use of that which is his own[53]. Accordingly from this is derived

in the world.' *Méditation sur la notion commune de la justice* (Mollat, p. 62). Cf. *Monadology*, § 55.

[47] 'The immortal soul, exposed to no injuries except from itself, is always in the hand and keeping of God, and Christ has divinely bidden us not to fear those who can kill the body but cannot harm the soul.' *De justitia* (Mollat, p. 40).

[48] 'If a draught of cold water has its reward, what will those receive, who have done something great in human affairs for the glory of God and the common good, seeing that those who bring many to righteousness [*justitia*] shall shine as the stars.' *De tribus juris naturae et gentium gradibus* (Mollat, p. 20). Cf. G. iv. 462, 463.

[49] Cf. Aristotle, *Ethics*, v. 1, 1130ᵃ 8.

[50] 'Right [*jus*] cannot be unjust: that would be a contradiction. But law [*lex*] may be. For it is power that ordains and upholds law; and if this power is lacking in wisdom or goodwill, it may ordain and uphold very wicked laws. But happily for the universe, the laws of God are always just, and He is in a position to uphold them, as He undoubtedly does, although He does not always visibly and immediately do so, for which He has doubtless excellent reasons.' *Méditation sur la notion commune de la justice* (Mollat, p. 61).

[51] 'We were not born merely for ourselves, but others claim for themselves a part of us, and God the whole.' *Monita ad Puffendorfii principia*, § 5 (Dutens, iv. 281). '*Quicquid sumus Dei sumus*' (Mollat, p. 3).

[52] '*Salus publica suprema lex est*' (Mollat, p. 3).

[53] 'For when we are vicious, we not only injure ourselves, but

the force of that highest precept of Right, which bids us *live virtuously* (that is, piously). And in this sense learned men have rightly put it down among things to be desired, that natural law and the law of nations [*jus naturae et gentium*] should be formulated in accordance with the doctrines of Christianity, that is (according to the teaching of Christ) τὰ ἀνώτερα [54], the sublime things, the divine things of the wise. Thus I think I have very fitly explained the three precepts of Right or three degrees of justice, and have pointed out the sources of natural law.

Besides the eternal rights of a rational nature which flow from the Divine Source, there is also observed a *voluntary Right*, derived from customs or made by a superior. And indeed in the commonwealth civil Right receives its force from him who has the supreme power [55];

we also diminish, in so far as it depends upon us, the perfection of the great commonwealth, of which God is the Monarch.' *Méditation sur la notion commune de la justice* (Mollat, p. 76).

[54] Possibly Leibniz is thinking of ἡ ἄνωθεν σοφία (St. James, iii. 15, 17). Leibniz seems himself to have intended to supply the want to which he here refers, for he sketched the outline of a book on the subject, which is printed by Mollat (pp. 8 sqq.), under the title *Tabulae duae disciplinae juris naturae et gentium secundum disciplinam Christianorum*. In this he refers to St. James as 'calling charity νόμος βασιλικός, the royal law (ch. ii. 8), inasmuch as it comes from the supreme King (St. Paul, *Romans*, i. 32, δικαίωμα τοῦ θεοῦ).' (Mollat, p. 11.)

[55] While admitting a right of this kind as distinct from natural right, Leibniz maintains that the two ought always to be in harmony. He thus condemns the view of Hobbes, that the basis of right is power, which he identifies with the view of Thrasymachus in Plato's *Republic*, bk. i. (see Mollat, p. 57 sqq.). Cf. *Le Portrait du Prince* (Klopp, iv. 461): 'As the order of States is established on the authority of those who govern them and on the dependence of their peoples, nature which destines men for civil life endows them at birth with different qualities, some for commanding, others for obeying, in order that the power of the sovereign in a monarchy and the inequality between those who command and those who obey in a republic, be no less founded on nature than on law, on virtue than on fortune. So princes ought to be above their subjects by their virtue and their natural qualities, as they are above them by the authority which the laws give them, in

outside of the commonwealth or among those who are sharers in supreme power (of whom there are sometimes several even in the same commonwealth) there is the sphere of the *voluntary law of nations*, accepted by the tacit consent of the peoples. . . .

But Christians have also another common bond, namely the *positive Divine law* [*jus*] which is contained in the sacred books. To which are to be added the sacred canons received by the whole Church and afterwards in the West the Papal law [*jures*] to which kings and peoples submit themselves. And in general (and certainly not against reason) it seems for a long time to have been accepted, before the schism of last century, that there should be understood to be a certain general commonwealth of the Christian nations, the heads of which were in sacred things the Pope [*Pontifex Maximus*] and in temporal things the Emperor of the Romans, who also seemed to retain so much of the law of the old Roman monarchy as was needed for the common good of Christendom, without prejudice to the Right of kings and the liberty of princes.

order to reign both by natural right and by civil right, like the first kings in the world, who having been raised to the government of their peoples by their virtue and their intellectual gifts, commanded as much by nature as by law, by merit as by fortune.'

NEW SYSTEM OF THE NATURE OF SUB-STANCES AND OF THE COMMUNICATION [1] BETWEEN THEM, AS WELL AS OF THE UNION THERE IS BETWEEN SOUL AND BODY [2]. 1695.

PREFATORY NOTE.

IN this paper, which appeared anonymously in the *Journal des Savants* of June, 1695, we have Leibniz's first public statement of his *New System* (see Introduction, Part i. p. 12). In character it is much more tentative than his later writings, and it is only towards the end of the paper (§ 17) that he ventures to speak of his view as 'more than a hypothesis.' This is very characteristic of Leibniz : he likes to advance by suggestion and hypothesis. But he regards hypothesis as merely a stepping-stone : he will not rest there if it is possible to go farther. 'In matters where certainty can be obtained, I will not use hypotheses,' he says to Bernouilli (G. Math. iii. 575). And nearly twenty years after he published the *New System*, Leibniz writes of 'this hypothesis, which I venture to call proved' (*Monadology*, § 59). Thus the peculiar interest of the *New System* is that it lets us see something of Leibniz's philosophy in the making. For in this work he writes historically, indicating to us the course which his thought took.

The *New System* may be divided into two main parts, in the first of which (§§ 1-11 inclusive) Leibniz shows us how he was

---

[1] i. e. inter-relation or interaction.
[2] The title in the First Draft is *New system for explaining the nature of substances and their communication with one another, as well as the union of soul with body.*

led to re-introduce into philosophy the 'substantial forms' of the Scholastics, and in what sense these forms, souls, simple substances or real units are to be understood; while in the second (§§ 12-18) he applies his theory of substance to the question of the relation between soul and body, mind and matter, and finds that the problem can be satisfactorily solved only through the hypothesis of a pre-established harmony between all simple substances. Analyzing the title of the paper, we may say that the first part deals with the *nature* of substances and the second with their *communication*.

Erdmann (E. 124 sqq.) gives the *New System* as it was originally published. Gerhardt (G. iv. 477 sqq.) gives it as it was afterwards revised and altered by Leibniz, and he also prints an interesting First Draft of it. I have translated from Gerhardt's text, indicating its differences from Erdmann's; and in the notes will be found some passages from the First Draft. The paragraphs are numbered in E.; but not in G.

1. Several years ago I conceived this system and had communications about it with learned men, especially with one of the greatest theologians and philosophers of our time [3], who, having been informed of some of my opinions by a person of the highest rank [4], had found them very paradoxical [5]. But having received explanations from me, he withdrew what he had said in the

---

[3] 'Mons. Arnauld.' Note by Leibniz, who tells us also that with regard to his *New System* he 'followed the rule of Horace: *nonumque prematur in annum*' (G. iv. 490). There is an interesting account of Arnauld and his friends in Stephen's *Essays in Ecclesiastical Biography*, vol. i, Essay vi, *The Port-Royalists*.

[4] Landgraf Ernest of Hesse-Rheinfels (1623-1693), who in 1652, shortly after the close of the Thirty Years' War, became a Roman Catholic and published a justification of the course he had taken. A copy of this work he sent to the Duke of Brunswick, and he thus came into communication with Leibniz. They kept up a correspondence on theological and ecclesiastical subjects until the death of the Landgraf in 1693.

[5] Arnauld writes to the Landgraf:—'I find in these thoughts so many things which alarm me and at which almost all men, if I am not mistaken, will be so shocked, that I do not see what use there could be in a writing which apparently will be rejected by everybody' (G. ii. 15). Leibniz felt this very keenly; but Arnauld made ample explanations and apologies in a letter to Leibniz himself. (G. ii. 25.)

most generous and exemplary way; and having approved
a number of my propositions, he praetermitted his cen-
sure as regards the others, to which he was still unable
to agree. Since that time I have continued my meditations, as I had opportunity, in order that I might give
to the public only well-tested opinions, and I have also
endeavoured to meet the objections raised against my
essays on Dynamics, which have some connexion with
this[6]. And in short, as some people of consideration
have desired to see my opinions[7] more elucidated, I have
ventured upon these meditations, although they are by no
means popular nor such as to be relished by every kind
of mind. I have been led to this mainly in order that
I may profit by the judgment of those who are enlightened in these matters; since it would be too troublesome a task to seek out and call to my aid individually
those who might be disposed to give me suggestions,
which I shall always be glad to receive, provided they
are marked by a love of truth rather than by a passion for
preconceived opinions[8].

2. Although I am one of those who have worked much
at mathematics, I have none the less meditated upon
philosophy from my youth up; for it always seemed to
me that there was a possibility [*moyen*] of establishing
something solid in philosophy by clear demonstrations.
I had penetrated far into the country of the Scholastics,
when mathematics and modern authors brought me out
again, while I was still quite young. The beauty of
their mechanical explanations of nature charmed me,

[6] Leibniz's principal essay on Dynamics is the *Specimen Dynamicum*, published in the *Acta Eruditorum* for April, 1695. (G. Math.
vi. 234.)

[7] The First Draft has in addition the words: 'Which they
think may be useful in harmonizing faith with reason as regards
matters of importance.'

[8] 'I desire objections to be made against me, which oblige me
to go beyond what I have already said. Objections of this kind
are instructive and I like them because I may profit by them
and make others profit by them; but it is not easy to make them.'
Lettre à Masson (1716) (G. vi. 629).

and I rightly contemned the method of those who make use only of forms and faculties, from which we learn nothing[9]. But afterwards, having tried to go deeply into mechanical principles themselves, in order to find a reason for the laws of nature which experience makes known, I perceived that the mere consideration of an *extended mass* is not sufficient and that use must also be made of the notion of *force*, which is very intelligible, though it belongs to the sphere of metaphysics[10]. It appeared to me also that the view of those who transform or degrade the lower animals into mere machines, although it seems possible, is improbable and indeed is contrary to the order of things.

3. At first, when I had freed myself from the yoke of Aristotle, I took to the void and the atoms, for that is the view which best satisfies the imagination. But having got over this, I perceived, after much meditation, that it is impossible to find *the principles of a real unity* in matter alone, or in that which is only passive, since it is nothing but a collection or aggregation of parts *ad infinitum*[11]. Now a multiplicity [*multitude*] can derive its reality only *from genuine units* [*unités*] which come from elsewhere and are quite other than the mathematical points which are only extremities of the extended and

[9] See Introduction, Part i. p. 3, and Part iv. p. 156.

[10] The meaning is that, although force is not anything that can be pictured or represented in imagination, it can nevertheless be quite well understood. The notion of force is 'metaphysical,' because force is not merely a physical thing that can be perceived in the same way as other physical things. For instance, we can understand, but we cannot perceive, the potential energy of a mass. In the First Draft, Leibniz says: 'By force or power [*puissance*] I do not mean the power [*pouvoir*] or mere faculty, which is nothing but a near possibility of acting and which, being as it were dead, never produces an action without being stimulated from without, but I mean something between power to act [*pouvoir*] and action, something which includes an effort, an actual working [*acte*], an entelechy, for force passes of itself into action, in so far as nothing hinders it. Wherefore I regard force as constitutive of substance, since it is the source [*principe*] of action, which is the characteristic of substance' (G. iv. 472).

[11] Cf. Introduction, Part ii. p. 23.

modifications [12], of which it is certain that the *continuous* [*continuum*] cannot be composed [13]. Accordingly, in order to find these *real units* [*unités*] I was constrained to have recourse to a *real and animated point*, so to speak, or to an atom of substance which must contain some kind of form or active principle, so as to make a complete being [14]. It was, then, necessary to recall and, as it were, to rehabilitate the *substantial forms* [15], which are so much decried now-a-days, but in a way which renders them intelligible and separates the use to which they should be put from the abuse which they have suffered. I found, then, that the nature of the substantial forms consists in force, and that from this follows something analogous to feeling [*sentiment*] and desire [*appétit*]; and that thus they must be conceived after the manner of the notion we have of *souls* [16]. But as the soul ought not to be used to explain in detail the structure of the animal's body, I held that similarly these forms must not be used to solve the particular problems of nature, although they are necessary for establishing true general principles [17]. Aristotle calls them *first entelechies*. I call them (in a way that may

[12] That is, not independent beings, but properties or relations, like the two ends of a stick.

[13] E. reads: 'quite other than the points of which it is certain,' &c. See Prefatory Note.

[14] E. reads: 'I was constrained to have recourse to a formal atom, since a material being cannot be at once material and perfectly indivisible or possessed of a genuine unity.'

[15] *Substantial* forms as distinct from *accidental* forms, the former being used to explain substances, the latter to explain their accidents.

[16] The transition from point to point is here rather rapid. The analogy between desire and force is manifest, but that between feeling and force is more obscure. The essence of feeling, according to Leibniz, is not consciousness but the representation or concentration of many in one; and similarly the manifold actions of any substance are 'enveloped' or potentially contained in its force or vital principle. Cf. *Monadology*, §§ 13 sqq.

[17] In the First Draft, Leibniz says: 'In my opinion everything in nature takes place mechanically, and to give an exact and complete explanation of any particular phenomenon (such, for instance, as weight or elasticity), nothing but figure and motion need be used' (G. iv. 472.)

perhaps be more easily understood) *primary forces*[18], which contain not only *actuality* [*l'acte*] or the complement of possibility, but also an original *activity*.

4. I saw that those forms and those souls, as well as our mind [*esprit*], ought to be indivisible, and in fact I remembered that this was the opinion of St. Thomas with regard to the souls of the lower animals[19]. But this truth[20] renewed the great difficulty about the origin and the duration of souls and forms. For, as every *simple*[21] *substance* which has a genuine unity can have a beginning and an end only by miracle, it follows that they can come into being only by creation and come to an end only by annihilation[22]. Thus I was obliged to recognize that (with the exception of the souls which God still intends specially to create) the constitutive forms of substances must have been created with the world and must always continue to exist[23]. So some of the Scholastics, like Albertus Magnus and John Bacon, had an inkling of part of the truth regarding the origin of these forms[24]. And all this ought not to appear ex-

[18] 'To distinguish it from the secondary, which is called moving force, and which is an accidental limitation or variation of primary force.' First Draft (G. iv. 473).

[19] Possibly Leibniz refers to the passage in which Aquinas says: 'The substantial form, which requires diversity in the parts, for instance the soul and especially the soul of complete animals, does not stand in exactly the same relation to the whole and to the parts. And hence it is not divided *per accidens*, that is to say, by a quantitative division.' *Summa Theol.* i. qu. 76, art. 8. Elsewhere, however, Aquinas says: 'The sensitive soul in the lower animals is corruptible; but in man, since it is the same in substance as the rational soul, it is incorruptible.' *De Anima*, art. 14 *ad primum*.

[20] Janet reads *cette nouveauté*, 'this new view,' instead of *cette vérité*.

[21] E. omits 'simple.'

[22] The First Draft has in addition the words: 'brought about expressly by the supreme power of God' (G. iv. 474).

[23] Cf. *Principles of Nature and of Grace*, § 6; *Monadology*, §§ 4, 5, 6, and 76. The First Draft has: 'genuine unity is absolutely indissoluble' (G. iv. 474).

[24] Cf. *Monadology*, note 116. The statement of Leibniz is so vague that one can hardly fix the passage in Albertus Magnus of which he is thinking. In his *Summa de Creaturis* (part ii. qu. 16, art. 3), Albertus Magnus says: 'We hold that the souls of the

traordinary, for we are only attributing to forms the duration which the Gassendists [25] accord to their atoms.

5. Nevertheless I held that we must not include among these, without distinction (or confound with other forms or souls [26]), minds [*esprits*] or rational souls, which are of a higher rank and have incomparably more perfection than those forms which are sunk in matter, which in my opinion are to be found everywhere [27], and

lower animals and plants are educed from the matter of the seed through generation. But if it be asked whether they are in the seed or not, we say that they are there in one way, and in another way they are not. . . . They are not there actually [*actu*], but they are there in the potency [*potentia*] of the efficient cause and the matter [*efficientis et materiae*]. And if it be asked: What is this efficient cause? Is it the soul or not? We say . . . that it is not the soul. . . .' Cf. *De Animalibus* (xvi. 11): 'The principle of life is in the seed in the way in which the act is in the instruments of the act. . . . And in this way also the soul is in the seed like an act and not like the entelechy of an organic body. . . . That which is in the seed is something of the soul [*aliquid animae*] and not the soul.' See also *De Anima*, bk. i. Tract. 2, cap. 13: 'The soul is indivisible, and nothing can be cut off from it.' John Bacon or Bacho, is better known as John Baconthorp, from the place in Norfolk where he was born towards the close of the thirteenth century. He was a Carmelite monk and a schoolman, and in 1329 he became Provincial of the English Carmelites. He lived much in Oxford and Paris, where he obtained a great reputation for learning. He was called the Resolute Doctor. He died in 1346. Besides a book on the rule of his order, his chief work is the *Commentaria seu quaestiones in quatuor libros Sententiarum*. Leibniz probably refers to a passage in this book, *In Secundum*, Dist. xii. Qu. 1, Art. 3, § 3.

[25] Pierre Gassendi (1592-1655), a French priest and a disciple of Bacon, expounded the doctrines of Epicurus and endeavoured to adapt them to the conditions of modern thought. His attitude was both anti-Scholastic and anti-Cartesian. He severely criticized Descartes's *Méditations* and thus began a long controversy with Descartes regarding the origin of knowledge, Gassendi taking a purely experiential standpoint as against Descartes's belief in innate ideas. See Descartes, *Méditations, Cinquièmes Objections* (by Gassendi). Gassendi himself does not attribute eternity to his atoms, which he regards as created by God. The spirit of his thinking is well expressed in his own words: 'The shadow of truth which I everywhere pursue suffices to fill me with joy. I say "the shadow," for, as to truth itself, God alone can know it.' *Lettre à Golius*.

[26] This clause within brackets is given by G., but not by E.

[27] 'Which in my opinion are to be found everywhere' is given by G., but not by E. Cf. *Monadology*, §§ 65 sqq.

in comparison with which minds or rational souls are like little gods, made in the image of God and having within them some ray of the Divine enlightenment [*lumières*]. For this reason God governs minds [*esprits*] as a prince governs his subjects, and indeed as a father looks after his children; while, on the other hand, He deals with other substances as an engineer works with his machines. Thus minds [*esprits*] have special laws which put them above the revolutions of matter through the very order which God has put in them [28]; and it may be said that everything else is made only for them, these revolutions themselves being arranged for the felicity of the good and the punishment of the wicked [29].

6. However, to return to ordinary forms or *material souls* [30], the duration which must be attributed to them (in place of that which used to be attributed to atoms) might lead to a doubt whether they do not go from body to body; which would be *metempsychosis*, something almost analogous to the transmission of motion and the transmission of species [31] which certain philosophers have maintained. But this fancy is very far from the nature of things. There is no such passing [32]. And here the *transformations* noted by MM. Swammerdam, Malpighi, and Leuwenhoek [33], who are among the most excellent

[28] 'Through the very order which God has put in them' is given by G., but not by E.

[29] Cf. *Monadology*, §§ 83, 84, 89.

[30] E. has *âmes matérielles* while G. has *âmes brutes*. Leibniz probably wrote *brutes* in order to avoid the ambiguity of the other expression, which seems to suggest that some souls are 'material,' while Leibniz, of course, holds that all are 'immaterial.' By 'material or brute souls' he means the souls which are 'sunk in matter' (§ 5), i.e. unconscious souls, in which matter as a *phenomenon* is *bene fundatum*.

[31] i.e. transference of quality from one body to another, as when the quality of the leaven is imparted to the whole lump or the red colour of a drop of wine is diffused throughout water. Cf. *Monadology*, note 10.

[32] The First Draft says: 'This transmigration of souls is an absurdity. The principles of substance do not flutter outside of substances' (G. iv. 474).

[33] The reference is to such changes as that from caterpillar to

observers of our time, have come to my aid and have led me the more readily to admit that no animal nor any other organic substance comes into existence at the time at which we think it does, and that its apparent generation is only a development and a kind of growth [*augmentation*]. I have noticed also that the author of the *Recherche de la Vérité* [34], M. Régis [35], M. Hartsoeker [36],

butterfly. 'God has *preformed* things, so that new organisms are nothing but a mechanical consequence of a preceding organic constitution; as when butterflies come from silkworms, which M. Swammerdam has shown to be merely a process of development.' *Théodicée, Preface* (E. 476 a; G. vi. 41); cf. *Monadology*, § 74. John Swammerdam (1637-1680), of Amsterdam, is famous as an observer of insect life. Marcello Malpighi (1628-1694), of Bologna, the famous anatomist, is probably mentioned by Leibniz because of his work on the process of incubation. Anton van Leeuwenhoek (1632-1723), of Delft, did much to support Harvey's theory of the circulation of the blood. Leibniz refers to him on account of his investigations regarding spermatozoa, in connexion with which he may be regarded as one of the founders of the science of embryology.

[34] Nicolas Malebranche (1638-1715) published his *De la Recherche de la Vérité* in 1674. Descartes had already given a similar title to one of his writings. While differing greatly from Malebranche's general theory, Leibniz endeavours to harmonize Malebranche's view with his own on many particular points. See Foucher de Careil, *Lettres et opuscules inédits de Leibniz*, Introduction. Leibniz corresponded intermittently with Malebranche upon philosophical and other questions between 1674 and 1711. In his *Recherche de la Vérité*, bk. ii. ch. 7, § 3 (*Œuvres*, Jules Simon's ed., vol. iii. pp. 199 sqq.), Malebranche uses expressions which indicate a belief in the theory of preformation.

[35] Pierre Sylvain Régis or Leroy (Petrus Silvanus Regius) (1632-1707) was an exponent of the philosophy of Descartes, which, in opposition to the idealism of Malebranche, he developed in an empirical direction. Descartes, however, disowned the views of Régis. See *Œuvres de Descartes* (ed. Cousin), vol. x. p. 70. Cf. Veitch, *Method &c.* of Descartes, note vi. on *Innate Ideas*. Cf. Kuno Fischer, *Descartes and his School*, bk. iii. ch. 2. Régis, whose philosophical school at Paris was in 1675 closed by Archbishop Harlay on account of its Cartesian teaching, wrote a violent attack upon Leibniz, charging him with injustice towards Descartes. This attack, anonymously published, will be found, along with Leibniz's reply, in E. 140; G. iv. 333.

[36] Nicolas Hartsoeker (1656-1725) was a Dutch physicist, whose earlier work had mainly to do with the making of microscopes and telescopes. Leibniz, writing to Des Bosses in 1709, calls him *vir clarissimus in Dioptricis* (E. 461 a; G. ii. 377). In 1694 Hartsoeker published an atomist philosophy of nature, based on the sup-

and other able men have not been very far from this opinion.

7. But there still remained the greater question, what becomes of these souls or forms at the death of the animal or on the destruction of the individual, of the organic substance? This is a most perplexing question, inasmuch as there seems little reason in thinking that souls remain uselessly in a chaos of confused matter [37]. Accordingly I came to the conclusion that there is only one view that can reasonably be taken, namely, that which affirms the conservation not only of the soul but also of the animal itself and its organic mechanism; although the destruction of its grosser parts has reduced it to a minuteness which makes it as little perceptible to our senses as it was before its birth [38]. Thus no one can exactly note the real time of death, which for a time may be taken for a mere suspension of perceptible activities and which at bottom is never anything else than this in the case of mere animals: witness the *resuscitation* of flies which have been drowned and then buried in powdered chalk, and several similar instances which are sufficient to inform us that there might be other resuscitations, even when the destruction of the organic substance had gone much farther, if men were in a position to reconstruct the [animal] mechanism [39]. And apparently it was about something like this that the great Democritus spoke (thorough atomist as he was), though Pliny laughs at what he said [40]. Accord-

position of perfectly hard atoms in a perfect fluid. In 1704 he became Professor of Mathematics and Physics at Düsseldorf, and from 1706 to 1712 he discussed his philosophy of nature with Leibniz in a correspondence to which Leibniz frequently refers in his letters to Des Bosses. The correspondence is given by Gerhardt, iii. 483. Cf. *Third Explanation of the New System*, p. 334.

[37] That is, matter which is (comparatively) inorganic.

[38] Cf. *Monadology*, §§ 73 and 77.

[39] Cf. *Monadology*, § 14, note 23 and § 21; *Principles of Nature and of Grace*, §§ 6 and 12.

[40] Cf. *Lettre à des Maizeaux* (1711) (E. 676 b; G. vii. 535): 'Plato believed that material things are in a perpetual flux, but that

ingly it is natural that an animal, having always been living and organic (as some people of great penetration are beginning to recognize), should likewise always remain so. And thus, since an animal has no first birth or entirely new begetting [*génération*], it follows that it will have no final extinction or complete death, in the strict metaphysical sense, and that consequently, in place of the *transmigration* of souls, there is nothing but a *transformation* of one and the same animal, according as its organs are differently enfolded [*pliés*] and more or less developed [41].

8. Nevertheless rational souls follow much higher laws and are exempt from everything which could make them lose the rank [*la qualité*] of citizens of the society of spirits [*esprits*]; God having provided for this so carefully that all the changes of matter cannot make them lose the moral qualities of their personality. And it may be said that everything tends to the perfection, not only of the universe in general, but also of these created

genuine substances continue to exist. By "genuine substances" he appears to have meant only souls. But perhaps Democritus, thorough atomist as he was, believed in the conservation of the animal also. For he taught that there is resuscitation [*réviviscence*], as Pliny says of him: *reviviscendi promissa Democrito vanitas, qui ipse non revixit'* [the false opinion of a coming to life again, put forth by Democritus, who himself did not come to life again]. 'We hardly know anything about this great man, except what has been borrowed from him by Epicurus, who was not capable of always taking his best things.' The words quoted from Pliny occur in his *Historia Naturalis*, bk. vii. cap. 55. (Sillig's ed., vol. ii. p. 60.)

[41] *Monadology*, §§ 72 and 73. In the First Draft (G. iv. 474) Leibniz writes: 'As the minuteness of organic bodies may be infinite (which may be seen from the fact that their seeds, enclosed in one another, contain enfolded a continual succession of organized and animate bodies), it is easily seen that even fire, which is the most penetrating and violent agent, will not destroy an animal, since it will at most reduce it to such a smallness that fire can no longer act upon it.' In the correspondence with Arnauld, to which Leibniz refers in § 1 of the *New System*, Arnauld had asked (as an objection to Leibniz's theory of the indestructibility of animals) what became of the ram which Abraham sacrificed in place of Isaac. The foregoing passage contains in brief Leibniz's answer.

beings in particular, which are destined to such a degree
of happiness that the universe is concerned in it, in
virtue of the Divine goodness which is imparted to each,
so far as supreme wisdom can allow.

9. As to the ordinary body [42] of animals and other
corporeal substances, which have hitherto been supposed
to suffer total extinction and whose changes are dependent rather upon mechanical rules than upon moral
laws, I observed with pleasure that the author of the
book *De Diaeta* (which is attributed to Hippocrates [43])
had some inkling of the truth, when he expressly said
that animals are not born and do not die and that
the things which we suppose to come into being and
perish merely appear and disappear. This was also the
opinion of Parmenides and of Melissus according to
Aristotle [44]; for these men of old had more worth than
we suppose.

10. I am as ready as man can be to do justice to the
moderns, yet I think they have carried reform too far;
among other things, in confounding natural with arti-

---

[42] G. has *corps ordinaire*. E. reads *cours ordinaire* ('usual history').

[43] Hippocrates, 'the father of medicine,' is no longer regarded
as the author of the *De Diaeta* (περὶ διαίτης). The passage to which
Leibniz refers is most probably the following: ἀπόλλυται μὲν νυν
οὐδὲν ἁπάντων χρημάτων, οὐδὲ γίνεται ὅ τι μὴ καὶ πρόσθεν ἦν ... καὶ
οὔτε, εἰ ζῷον, ἀποθανεῖν οἷόν τε, εἰ μὴ μετὰ πάντων· ποῦ γὰρ ἀποθανεῖται;
οὔτε τὸ μὴ ὂν γενέσθαι· πόθεν γὰρ ἔσται; ἀλλ' αὔξεται πάντα μειοῦται
καὶ ἐς τὸ μήκιστον καὶ [ἐς τὸ] ἐλάχιστον, τῶν γε δυνατῶν, i. 4. 'Now
none among all things is destroyed, and there does not come into
being that which was not in existence before. . . . And neither is it
possible for an animal to die, except along with all things (for
how shall it die?); nor can that which is not come into being
(for whence shall it be?); but all things grow and diminish to
the greatest and to the least that is possible.' See Bywater,
Heracliti Ephesii Reliquiae, Appendix ii.

[44] *De Cae'o*, Γ I, 298[b] 14: οἱ μὲν γὰρ αὐτῶν ὅλως ἀνεῖλον γένεσιν καὶ
φθοράν· οὐθὲν γὰρ οὔτε γίγνεσθαί φασιν οὔτε φθείρεσθαι τῶν ὄντων, ἀλλὰ
μόνον δοκεῖν ἡμῖν οἷον οἱ περὶ Μέλισσόν τε καὶ Παρμενίδην, οὕς, εἰ καὶ
τἄλλα λέγουσι καλῶς, ἀλλ' οὐ φυσικῶς γε δεῖ νομίσαι λέγειν. Cf.
Monadology, § 74, note 116. But the views of Parmenides and
Melissus, who deny the reality of change or of becoming, are very
far removed from the position of Leibniz. They deny change or
becoming of τὸ ἕν, not of each of a plurality of substances.

ficial things, through not having great enough ideas of the majesty of nature. They think that the difference between nature's machines and ours is only a difference of size. This has lately led a very able man [45] (the author of the *Entretiens sur la pluralité des Mondes* [46]) to say that, when we look closely at nature, we find it less wonderful [*admirable*] than we had thought, it being merely a kind of workshop. It seems to me that this is to give an idea of nature which is not quite just nor worthy of it [47], and that it is only our system which shows how real and immense after all is the distance between the least productions and mechanisms that are made by the Divine wisdom and the greatest artistic masterpieces of a limited mind [*esprit*]—the difference being not merely one of degree, but even one of kind. Accordingly it is to be observed that the machines of nature have a really infinite number of organs [48] and are so well equipped and so proof against all accidents that it is not possible to destroy them. A natural machine still remains a machine in its smallest parts, and moreover

[45] Bernard le Bovier de Fontenelle (1657–1757), a nephew of Pierre Corneille, was secretary of the *Académie des Sciences* at Paris from 1699 to 1741. One of his duties as secretary was to prepare every year *Éloges* or tributes to the memory of those members of the academy who had died during the year, and among the ablest of these papers is his *Éloge de Leibniz*, published in the *Histoire de l'Académie Royale des Sciences de Paris, année* 1716. He wrote a great deal of indifferent verse; but his main work consisted in the popularizing of scientific ideas. There is a saying of his (which sounds like a parody of Leibniz) that 'everything is possible, and everybody is right.'

[46] 'Conversations on the Plurality of Worlds.' This book (published 1686) was intended to popularize the astronomical theories of Copernicus. It has been several times translated into English.

[47] É. has merely 'which is not worthy of it.'

[48] A machine made by man has a finite number of 'organs' or parts having each a definite function in relation to the whole. The tooth of a wheel is an 'organ' of the wheel and of the whole machine. But the material particles which make up this tooth are not 'organs' of the wheel or the machine. Nature, on the other hand, is organic throughout : no part of it is not an 'organ' of the whole. Thus a natural machine has 'a really infinite number of organs.' Cf. *Monadology*, § 64.

it always remains the same machine it originally was, being merely transformed through different foldings [*plis*] it receives, and sometimes expanded, sometimes contracted and, as it were, concentrated, when we think that it is lost.

11. Further, by means of the soul or form, there is a real unity which corresponds to what in us is called the Ego; but this cannot be the case in regard to the machines of art or to mere material mass, however well organized it may be, which can be considered only as an army or a flock, or as a pond full of fish[49], or as a watch composed of springs and wheels. Nevertheless if there were no real *substantial units* [*unités*] there would be nothing substantial or real in the collection. It was this that compelled M. Cordemoi[50] to give up Descartes and to adopt Democritus's doctrine of atoms in order to find a real unit [*unité*]. But *atoms of matter* are contrary to reason, besides being still composed of parts, since the invincible attachment of one part to another (even if it could rationally be conceived or supposed) would not

---

[49] 'When I say "I," I speak of one substance only; but an army, a flock, a pond full of fish, even though it were frozen and had become solid with all the fish in it, will always be a collection of several substances.' First Draft (G. iv. 473). Cf. Introduction, Part iii. pp. 96–98.

[50] Géraud de Cordemoi (born early in the seventeenth century, died 1684), a French Cartesian, arrived independently at an Occasionalist position, about the same time as Geulincx developed his more famous system. See Kuno Fischer, *Descartes and his School*, bk. iii. ch. 2. His most important philosophical work is *Le discernement du corps et de l'âme* (1666), and it was in this book that he so far gave up Descartes as to adopt a theory of atoms. Cf. Leibniz's *Lettre à la Princesse Sophie* (1705) (G. vii. 561): 'M. Cordemoi, seeing that compound things must be the result of simple things, was forced, Cartesian though he was, to have recourse to atoms, abandoning his master. . . .' Also *Lettre à Arnauld* (1686) (G. ii. 78): 'M. Cordemoi . . . in order to account for the substantial unity in bodies, felt obliged to admit atoms or indivisible extended bodies in order to find something fixed to constitute a simple being. . . . He appears to have recognized something of the truth, but he had not yet seen in what the real notion of a substance consists.' Cordemoi, however, was more devoted to history than to philosophy.

make one part any the less different from another[51]. Only *atoms of substance*, that is to say real units [*unités*] absolutely devoid of parts, are the sources of actions, and the absolute first principles of the composition of things and, as it were, the ultimate elements in the analysis of substantial things[52]. They might be called *metaphysical points*; they have *something of the nature of life* and they have a kind of *perception*, and *mathematical points* are their *points of view*[53] for expressing the universe. But when a corporeal substance is contracted, all its organs together make but one *physical point* for us[54]. Thus physical points are only apparently indivisible. Mathematical points are indivisible [*exacts*], but they are only modalities. None but metaphysical or substantial points (consisting of forms or souls) are indivisible [*exact*] and real; and without them nothing would be real, since without genuine units [*unités*] there would be no multiplicity[55].

12. Having settled these things, I thought I had gained my haven, but when I set myself to meditate upon the union of soul and body I was as it were driven back into the deep sea. For I found no way of explaining how the body transmits anything to the soul or *vice versa*, nor how one substance cau communicate with another created substance. So far as can be gathered from his writings, M. Descartes gave this up[56]; but his disciples,

[51] See Introduction, Part ii. p. 30.

[52] E. reads 'substances.' In the First Draft, Leibniz says: 'What constitutes corporeal substance must be something which corresponds to what is called *ego* in us, which is indivisible and nevertheless active [*agissant*], for being indivisible and without parts, it will no longer be a being by aggregation, but being active [*agissant*] it will be something substantial' (G. iv. 473).

[53] E. reads 'point of view.' Mathematical points are merely positions in space, and when we speak of positions in space, wo are describing in a confused way the essential differences between Monads. Cf. *Monadology*, §§ 60-62.

[54] Cf. *Monadology*, §§ 68 und 69.

[55] Cf. Introduction, Part ii. pp. 28 sqq.

[56] 'The human mind is not capable of distinctly conceiving the difference of essence between soul and body and, at the same time,

seeing that the common opinion is inconceivable, held
that we are aware of the qualities of bodies, because God
makes thoughts arise in the soul on occasion of the
motions of matter ; and, on the other hand, when our
soul wishes to move the body, they hold that it is God
who moves the body for it.   And as communication of
motions also appeared to them inconceivable, they were
of opinion that God gives motion to a body on occasion
of the motion of another body.   This is what is called
the *system of occasional causes*, which has been brought
into wide repute by the excellent reflexions of the author
of the *Recherche de la Vérité* [57].

13. It must be admitted that they have gone far into
the difficulty in telling us what cannot take place ; but
they do not appear to have removed it by their explanation of what actually does happen.   It is quite true that
one created substance has, in the strict metaphysical
sense, no real influence upon another, and that all things
and all their reality are continually produced by the
power [*vertu*] of God.   But to solve problems it is not
enough to make use of a general cause and to introduce
what is called *Deus ex machina*.   For to do this, without
offering any other explanation which can be derived from
the order of secondary causes, is just to have recourse to
miracle.   In philosophy we must endeavour to give a
reason for things by showing how they are carried out
by the Divine wisdom in conformity with the notion of
the matter we are dealing with [58].

14. Accordingly, being obliged to admit that it is im-

their union, for it would then be necessary to conceive both as
a single being and at the same time as two different things, which
is a contradiction.' *Œuvres* (ed. Cousin), vol. ix. p. 132.

[57] Arnold Geulincx (1625-1669) was the real founder of Occasionalism. The first part of his *Ethica* appeared in 1665, while
Malebranche's great work was published in 1674. See Introduction,
Part ii. pp. 42 sqq. Cf. Kuno Fischer, *Descartes and his School*, bk. iii.
ch. 3.

[58] We must not make a vague reference to the Divine wisdom,
but must show how it is present in particular departments of
experience.

possible the soul or any other real substance should receive
anything from outside, unless through the Divine omnipotence, I was insensibly led to an opinion which
surprised me, but which seems inevitable and which, in
fact, has very great advantages and very considerable
beauties. It is this, that God at first so created the soul,
or any other real unity, that everything must arise [59] in
it from its own inner nature [*fonds*] with a perfect
spontaneity as regards itself and yet with a perfect *conformity* to things outside of it. And thus our inner
feelings [*sentiments*] (that is to say, those which are in
the soul itself and not in the brain or in the finer parts
of the body), being only connected phenomena of external
things or rather genuine appearances and, as it were,
well-ordered dreams [60], these internal perceptions in the
soul itself must come to it from its original constitution,
that is to say from the representative nature (capable of
expressing beings outside of it in relation to its organs [61])
which was given to it at creation and which constitutes
its individual character. And accordingly, since each of
these substances accurately represents the whole universe
in its own way and from a certain point of view, and
the perceptions or expressions of external things come
into the soul at their appropriate time, in virtue of its
own laws, as in a world [62] by itself and as if there existed
nothing but God and the soul (to adopt the phrase of
a certain person of high intellectual power, renowned
for his piety [63]), there will be a perfect agreement between
all these substances, which will have the same result as
would be observed if they had communication with one

[59] E. has 'arises.' As to the 'spontaneity' of the soul and its
'creation,' see *Monadology*, § 47, note 75.

[60] 'And so genuine that they can be successfully foreseen.' First
Draft (G. iv. 477). See Introduction, Part iii. p. 98 sqq.

[61] That is, according to the nature and disposition of its organs.

[62] E. has 'the world.'

[63] Kirchmann suggests that this may perhaps refer to Foucher.
But Leibniz uses the phrase, without any special reference or
acknowledgment, in a letter to Foucher, written in 1686. (G. i. 382.)

another by a transmission of species or of qualities, such as the mass of ordinary philosophers suppose [64]. Further, as the organized mass, in which is the point of view of the soul, is more nearly expressed by the soul [65] and, conversely, is ready of itself to act, according to the laws of the corporeal mechanism, at the moment the soul desires it, without either of them interfering with the laws of the other—the animal spirits [*les esprits*] [66] and the blood having exactly at that moment the right motions to correspond to the passions and perceptions of the soul—this mutual relationship, prearranged in each substance in the universe, produces what we call their *communication* and alone constitutes *the union of soul and body*. And in this way we can understand how the soul has its seat in the body through an immediate presence, which is as near as possible, since the soul is in the body as the unit [*unité*] is in the multiplicity which is the resultant of units [*unités*] [67].

[64] See *Monadology*, § 7, note 10.

[65] E. omits 'by the soul' (*par elle*).

[66] 'Animal spirits' was the name given by Descartes to certain 'very fine particles of the blood,' by means of which he explained muscular movement. The name was derived from the Stoic πνεῦμα, through the early medical philosophers, such as Galen, who speaks of 'natural spirits' and 'vital spirits'; but Descartes's use of the term is original. 'What I here call "spirits" are only bodies, and they have no other property except that they are very small bodies which move very quickly, like the particles of flame which come from a lighted torch; so that they do not stay in any place, and as soon as some of them enter the cavities of the brain, others go out again through the pores in its substance, which pores lead them to the nerves and thence to the muscles, by means of which they move the body in all the different ways it can be moved.' *Les Passions de l'Âme*, part i. art. 10. See also articles 11-13, and *Method*, part v, where he says that the 'animal spirits' are 'like a very subtle wind, or rather a very pure and vivid flame.' The name survives in common language, and the hypothesis was only set aside by the results of microscopic study in anatomy. Cf. Kuno Fischer, *Descartes and his School*, bk. ii. ch. 9, § 2.

[67] Descartes also held that the soul must be present to the whole organism. But he maintained that 'nevertheless there is in the body a part in which the soul exercises its functions more specially than in any other part,' this special 'seat of the soul' being the pineal gland in the brain. (*Les Passions*, part i. articles 30-33.)

15. This hypothesis is very possible. For why might not God in the beginning give to substance an inner nature or force which could regularly produce in it —as in an *automaton* that is *spiritual or endowed with a living principle*[68], *but free* in the case of a substance which partakes of reason[69]—everything that will happen to it, that is to say, all the appearances or expressions it will have, and that without the help of any created thing? This is the more likely since the nature of substance necessarily requires and essentially involves a progress or change, without which it would have no force to act[70]. And as the nature of the soul is to represent the universe in a very exact way (though with greater or less distinctness), the succession of representations which the soul produces for itself will correspond naturally to the succession of changes in the universe itself; while, on the other hand, the body has also been adapted to the soul to fit the circumstances in which the soul is conceived as acting outwardly. This adaptation of the body to the soul is the more reasonable inasmuch as bodies are made only for spirits [*esprits*][71], which alone are capable of entering into fellowship with God and celebrating His glory. Thus as soon as we see that this *hypothesis of agreements* [*accords*][72] is possible, we see

Leibniz seeks to show that, on *his* hypothesis, the connexion between soul and body is much closer. The soul is 'immediately' present to the body and thus has no special seat but is in every part (independently of the part's position) as the unit is in every part of the whole.

[68] The French is: *un automate spirituel ou formel. Formel* conveys the idea of the form or individual unity of the thing, as in the phrase 'substantial form.'

[69] Every substance has *spontaneity*, inasmuch as it produces from within itself the series of its states or phenomena; but rational souls alone have *liberty*, for liberty is action under the guidance of right reason.

[70] No substance can act upon anything outside of it. Thus its action must appear in some internal change.

[71] That is to say, bodies are entirely subordinate to spirits, as the realm of efficient causes is to that of final causes. See *Monadology*, concluding §§.

[72] In the First Draft, Leibniz says: 'I call this the system of

also that it is the most reasonable hypothesis and that it gives a wonderful idea of the harmony of the universe and the perfection of the works of God.

16. There is also this great advantage in our hypothesis, that instead of saying that we are free only apparently and enough for practical purposes, as several clever people have held, we must rather say that we are only apparently constrained, and that, to use strict metaphysical language, we possess a perfect independence as regards the influence of all other created things [73]. This also throws a wonderful light upon the immortality of our soul and the ever unbroken preservation of our individuality, which is perfectly well-ordered by its own nature and independent of all external contingencies, whatever appearance there may be to the contrary. Never has any system more completely shown our high calling. Every spirit [*esprit*] being like a world apart, sufficient to itself, independent of every other created thing, involving the infinite, expressing the universe, is as lasting, as continuous in its existence and as absolute as the very universe of created things. Thus we should hold that each spirit should always play its part [*faire figure*] in the universe in the way that is most fitted to contribute to the perfection of the society of all spirits, which constitutes their moral union in the City of God. There is also here a new and surprisingly clear proof of the existence of God. For this perfect agreement of so many substances which have no communication with one another can come only from their common cause [74].

17. In addition to all these advantages which this

---

correspondence' (G. iv. 476). He is still feeling for the name 'Pre-established Harmony,' which he uses for the first time in the *First Explanation of the New System* (1696).

[73] See Introduction, Part iii. pp. 141 sqq.

[74] In the First Draft, Leibniz says : 'It is true that this is only by a participation, though limited, in the Divine perfections; for the agreement among the effects arises from their expressing the common cause' (G. iv. 475). Cf. *Principles of Nature and of Grace*, § 11, note 49.

hypothesis has in its favour, it may be said that it is
something more than a hypothesis, since it hardly
appears possible to explain things in any other intelligible way, and since several great difficulties, which
have hitherto perplexed men's minds [*les esprits*], seem
to disappear of themselves when we rightly comprehend
this hypothesis. The expressions of ordinary language
may also be quite well adapted to it. For we may say
that the substance whose condition [*disposition*] explains
a change in an intelligible way (so that we may hold
that it is this substance to which the others have on this
point been adapted from the beginning, according to the
order of the decrees of God) is the substance which, in
respect of this change, we should consequently conceive
as *acting* upon the others[75]. Thus the action of one
substance upon another is not an emission nor a trans-
plantation of an entity as is commonly supposed, and it
can be rationally understood only in the way I have
just mentioned. It is true that we quite well conceive
in matter both the emission and the receiving of parts
through which we are entitled to explain mechanically
all the phenomena of physics; but as material mass is
not a substance[76], it is evident that action as regards
substance itself can only be what I have just said that
it is.

18. These considerations, however metaphysical they
may appear, are also of remarkable service in physics
for establishing the laws of motion, as our *Dynamics* will
be able to show. For it may be said that in the impact
of bodies each suffers only through its own elasticity,
caused by[77] the motion which is already in it[78]. And

[75] See Introduction, Part iii. pp. 105 sqq.
[76] See Introduction, Part iii. p. 110.
[77] E. has *cause du*, 'a (or the) cause of the.' G. has *causé du*,
'caused by the.' The First Draft has: 'which comes from a motion
already existing in it' (G. iv. 476).
[78] Leibniz opposes the idea that there is a fixed quantity of
motion dispersed throughout the universe and passing indifferently

as to absolute motion, nothing can determine it mathematically, since all ends [se termine] in relations, with
the result that there is always a perfect equivalence of
hypotheses as in astronomy [79]; so that, whatever number
of bodies we take, we may arbitrarily assign rest or such
and such a degree of velocity to whichever we like, without it being possible for us to be refuted by the phenomena of motion, whether it be in a straight line, in
a circle, or composite.   Yet it is reasonable to attribute
to bodies real motions, according to the supposition
which explains the phenomena in the most intelligible
way, for this is in harmony with the notion of activity
[action] which we have here maintained [80].

from one body to another.   Each body, he would say, has a force,
which is the cause of its actual motions, and when two bodies
collide, there is not a transference of motion from one to the other,
but a certain release of the pent-up force in each, and this release
shows itself in the elasticity of their rebound.   See Introduction,
Part iii. pp. 89 sqq.

[79] 'Absolute motion' would be motion that is not in any degree
rest.   But motion must always be determined through relation.
One body has motion only in reference to another, and, accordingly,
if we wish to determine which of the two *really* (i. e. absolutely)
moves, we must refer them both to some third body and so *ad
infinitum*.   The 'equivalence of hypotheses in astronomy' probably
refers to the fact that the hypothesis of Copernicus (1473-1543),
according to which all the planets move round the sun, and the
hypothesis of Tycho Brahe (1546-1601), according to which the sun
moves round the earth and the other planets move round the sun,
equally well explained the phenomena as observed at that time.
Cf. G. iv. 369, and Descartes, *Principia*, Part iii. §§ 15-18.

[80] See Appendix C, p. 204.

EXPLANATION OF THE NEW SYSTEM OF THE COMMUNICATION BETWEEN SUBSTANCES, BY WAY OF REPLY TO WHAT IS SAID ABOUT IT IN THE *JOURNAL* OF SEPTEMBER 12, 1695[1]. 1696.

PREFATORY NOTE.

IN the *Journal des Savants* for September, 1695, there appeared a letter to Leibniz from Foucher in which various objections to the *New System* were stated. Simon Foucher (1644-1696) was a Canon of Dijon, who professed philosophical scepticism and endeavoured to restore the teaching of the later Academics, somewhat as Gassendi sought to interpret anew the doctrines of Epicurus. Between 1676 and 1695 Leibniz corresponded with Foucher, discussing in the earlier letters questions regarding the theory of knowledge and in the later letters questions of Physics. Foucher's comparatively early death was to some extent due to overwork. In 1697 Leibniz writes to Nicaise (G. ii. 566) : 'I am grieved at the death of M. Foucher. His curiosity was limited, and was directed only to certain somewhat dry matters, and even these he did not treat with the accuracy they required. Perhaps his aim was merely to be the resuscitator of the Academics, as M. Gassendi has resuscitated the Sect of Epicurus. But he ought not to have confined himself to generalities. Plato, Cicero, Sextus Empiricus and others might have enabled him to make a real advance. And under pretext of doubting, he might have established good and useful truths. I took the liberty of giving

---

[1] The reference is of course to the letter of Foucher in the *Journal des Savants*.

him my opinion as to this ; but he had perhaps other views of which I did not know enough. Yet he had much cleverness and subtlety and he was a most virtuous man, and hence I lament him.' (Cf. G. i. 365.) Leibniz replied to the objections of Foucher in an *Explanation of the New System*, which appeared in the *Journal des Sarants* for April, 1696. A further *Explanation* (called by Erdmann the *Troisième Éclaircissement*) was published in the *Journal* for November, 1696. I have translated these two *Explanations*, omitting that which Dutens and Erdmann call *Second Éclaircissement* (E. 133, J. S. Feb. 1696, cf. G. iv. 498), as the *Troisième Éclaircissement* contains practically the whole of it.

In Foucher's letter of objections there appears the simile of the clocks, which Leibniz passes over in his immediate reply but takes up and develops in the *Second* and *Third Explanations*. Foucher writes : ' It will be granted you that God, the great Artificer of the universe, can so perfectly adjust all the organic parts of a man's body, that they may be capable of producing all the motions which the soul combined with this body will desire to produce in the course of his life, without the soul having the power to change these motions or to modify them in any way, and that on the other hand God can make a construction in the soul (be it a mechanism of a new kind or not), by means of which all the thoughts and modifications which correspond to these motions might successively arise at the same moment in which the body performs its corresponding functions, and it will also be granted you that this is no more impossible than to make two clocks keep time [*s'accorder*] so well and go so uniformly that at the moment clock A strikes twelve, clock B will strike twelve also, so that we imagine the two clocks to be kept going by the same weight or the same spring' (E. 129 b ; G. iv. 488). The simile was originally applied in this way by Geulincx. See Introduction, Part ii. p. 43 note ; cf. *Third Explanation of the New System*, p. 331 note.

In the translation of the *Explanations* I follow G.'s revised text (G. iv. 493, 500 sqq.). E. gives them as they were originally published (E. 131, 134 sqq.).

I recollect, Sir, that in compliance with what I understood to be your desire, I communicated to you my hypothesis in philosophy several years ago, although at

the same time I indicated to you that I had not yet
resolved to make it known. I asked your opinion of it
in exchange; but I do not recollect having received
objections from you: otherwise, teachable [*docile*] as
I am, I should not have caused you to offer the same
objections twice over. Nevertheless they still come in
time, although they come after I have published. For
I am not of those with whom the committing of themselves to an opinion takes the place of reason, as you will
find when you are able to say that you have brought
forward[2] any precise and urgent reason against my
opinions; which apparently has not been your purpose[3].
Your intention was to speak as an able Academic[4], and
thus to give an opportunity for a thorough investigation
of things.

1[5]. I intended to explain here, not the principles of
extension [*l'étendue*], but the principles of that which
is actually extended [*l'étendu effectif*] or of bodily mass;
and these principles, in my opinion, are real unities, that
is to say, substances possessing a genuine unity[6].

2. The unity of a clock, which you mention, is in my
view quite other than that of an animal; for an animal
may be a substance possessing a genuine unity, like what
is called ego [*moi*] in us; while a clock is nothing but an
aggregate [*assemblage*].

3. I do not find the principle of the animal's consciousness [*le principe sensitif*] in the arrangement [*disposition*]
of its organs; and I agree that this arrangement concerns
only the bodily mass[7].

[2] E. has 'when you are able to bring forward.'
[3] E. adds 'on this occasion.'
[4] In reference to Foucher's philosophical position. See Prefatory
Note.
[5] In G.'s text the paragraphs are numbered. In E.'s text they
are not numbered, and the paragraphs are differently divided.
[6] Foucher had maintained that 'the essential principles of extension cannot really exist,' i.e. that extension has no ultimate
real elements. (E. 129 a; G. iv. 487.) Cf. Appendix H, p. 329.
[7] Foucher had said: 'Whatever arrangement [*disposition*] the
organs of an animal might have, that is not enough to make it

4. I notice these things in order to prevent misunder-standings, and to show that what you say on this point is by no means contrary to what I have brought forward [8]. Thus it appears that you do not make me out to be wrong in requiring genuine unities, and in consequently rehabilitating the substantial forms. But when you appear to say that the soul of the lower animals must have reason, if we attribute feeling [*sentiment*] to it [9], that is an inference [10] of which I do not see the proof [11].

5. With laudable candour you recognize that my hypothesis of harmony or concomitance is possible. But you still have a certain repugnance to it; doubtless because you think that it is purely arbitrary, through not being aware that it follows from my view regarding unities; for everything in my theory is connected to-gether.

6. Accordingly you ask, Sir, of what use is all this elaborate contrivance which I attribute to the Author of nature [12]? As if one could attribute too much contrivance to Him, and as if this exact mutual correspondence of

conscious [*sensible*]; for in short this has to do with nothing but the organic and mechanical structure, and I do not see that you are right in attributing to the lower animals a principle of conscious-ness, substantially different from that of men' (E. 129 b; G. iv. 488).

[8] E. does not have this sentence.

[9] Foucher wrote: 'After all, it is not without ground that the Cartesians acknowledge that if we allow to the animals a principle of consciousness, capable of distinguishing good from evil, we must also, as a consequence, allow to them reason, discrimination and judgment' (E. 129 b; G. iv. 488). In the *Remarques sur les Objections de M. Foucher* Leibniz replies: 'I do this' [attribute to the animals a principle of consciousness, substantially different from that of men] 'because we do not find that the animals make the reflexions which constitute reason and which, producing the knowledge of necessary truths or science, make the soul capable of personality. The lower animals, having perception, distinguish good and evil; but they are not capable of moral good and evil, which presuppose reason and conscience' (G. iv. 492). Cf. *Monadology*, §§ 25-30.

[10] E. reads 'you make use of an inference.'

[11] E. reads 'force.'

[12] Foucher's question is: 'Of what use is all this great elaborate contrivance among substances, unless to make us believe that they act upon one another, although this is not the case?' (E. 130 a; G. iv. 489).

substances, through the special laws which each has at the beginning received, were not a thing most admirable in itself and worthy of its Author! You ask also what advantage I find in it.

7. I might refer to what I have already said; but I reply, first, that when a thing cannot but be[13], there is no need to ask of what use it is, before we admit it. Of what use is the incommensurability of the side with the diagonal?

8. I reply in the second place, that this correspondence is of use in explaining the communication of substances and the union of the soul with the body, through the laws of nature which have been established from the first [*par avance*], without having recourse either to a transmission of species[14] [qualities], which is inconceivable, or to a new intervention of God, which seems out of accord with the fitness of things. For it is to be observed that as there are laws of nature in matter, so there are also laws of nature in souls or forms; and the meaning of these laws is that which I have just indicated.

9. Again, I am asked[15] whence it comes that God does not think it enough to produce all the thoughts and *modifications* of the soul, without these *useless* bodies, which the soul, it is said, can neither *move nor know*. The answer is easy. It was God's will that there should

---

[13] Has Leibniz shown that his pre-established harmony 'cannot but be'? In the *Remarques* already quoted, he says: 'This elaborate contrivance, which makes each substance correspond to all others, is necessary because all substances are the effect of a supreme wisdom; and it was not otherwise possible (at any rate in the order of nature and without miracles) to bring about their interdependence and the changing of one by another or in consequence of another. It nevertheless remains true that they act upon one another, provided we give a right sense to these words. . . . God is not obliged to make a system, about which we are not liable to make mistakes; as He was not obliged to avoid the system of the earth's motion, in order to save us from the error into which almost all astronomers fell until Copernicus' (G. iv. 492).

[14] See *Monadology.* § 7, note 10.

[15] E. has 'I shall be asked.' The question was put by Foucher in his letter of objections.

be more substances rather than fewer, and He thought it right that these *modifications* of the soul should correspond to something outside [16].

10. No substance is *useless*; they are all made to co-operate [17] towards fulfilling the plan of God.

11. I am also far from admitting that the soul *does not know* bodies, although this knowledge arises without any influence of the one upon the other.

12. I will not even shrink from saying [18] that the soul *moves* the body; and as a Copernican speaks truly of the rising of the sun, a Platonist of the reality of matter, and a Cartesian of the reality of sensible qualities [19], provided we rightly understand them, in the same way I hold that it is most true to say that substances act upon one another, provided we understand that one is the cause of changes in the other in consequence of the laws of the harmony.

13. The objection which is based on the supposed *lethargy* of bodies, which would be without activity [*action*] while the soul believes them to be in motion, cannot hold because of this very unfailing correspondence, which the Divine wisdom has established [20].

[16] In the *Remarques* Leibniz says: 'Bodies were necessary so that there might be produced not only our unities and souls but also those of the other corporeal substances, animals and plants, which are in our bodies and in those which surround us' (G. iv. 493). This last sentence indicates Leibniz's real answer to the difficulty (the answer he would have given in later years', viz. that ultimately all bodies are souls or Monads, so that to ask why there are bodies is to ask why there are other souls. Is the answer sufficient?

[17] E. has 'they all co-operate.'

[18] E. has 'I will even raise no objection against saying.'

[19] i. e. the qualities of bodies, as they are perceived by our senses. As sensations, facts of consciousness, these are real, according to Descartes; but as qualities of bodies they are confused and therefore unreal. See *Principia*, Part i. §§ 66-70.

[20] Foucher says that, on Leibniz's hypothesis, 'even although no motion took place in bodies' [in harmony with the action of the soul], 'the soul would nevertheless always think that such a motion does take place ; in the same way as sleeping people think they are moving their limbs and walking, while nevertheless their limbs

14. I have no knowledge of these *idle, useless, and inactive masses*, to which reference is made. There is activity [*action*] everywhere, and I maintain it even more fully than does the received philosophy; because I hold that there is no body without motion, no substance without force [*effort*][21].

15. I do not understand the nature of the objection that is contained in the words :—*In truth, Sir, is it not evident that these opinions were formed with a special purpose in view, and that these systems, appearing by way of afterthought [venant après coup], were constructed merely to safeguard certain principles?* All hypotheses are made *with a special purpose in view*, and all systems appear *by way of afterthought [viennent après coup]*, in order to safeguard phenomena or appearances; but I do not see what are the principles in favour of which I am said to be prejudiced and which I wish to safeguard.

16. If it is meant that I am led to my hypothesis also by reasons *a priori* or by fixed principles, as is actually the case; this is rather a commendation of the hypothesis than an objection to it. It is usually enough that a hypothesis be proved *a posteriori*, by being adequate to the phenomena; but when there are in addition other reasons for it, and these *a priori*, it is so much the better.

17. But perhaps what is meant is that, having invented a new opinion, I have delighted to make use of it, rather to give myself airs because of its novelty than because I have found any usefulness in it. I am not sure, Sir, that you have so bad an opinion of me as to attribute to me these thoughts. For you know that I love truth, and that, if I were so fond of novelties, I should have more

are at rest and do not move at all. So, when wide awake, souls would always continue to be persuaded that their bodies move in obedience to their volitions, though nevertheless these idle and useless masses would be inactive and would remain in a continual lethargy' (E. 130 a ; G. iv. 489).

[21] That is, force which is not necessarily observed, but includes tendency or the active potentiality of observed force.

eagerness to produce them—especially those whose sound-
ness is recognized.   But, lest those who know me less
should give to your words a meaning which we should
not like [22], it will be enough to say, that in my opinion
it is impossible otherwise to explain *transeunt activity*
[*l'action émanente*] [23] in conformity with the laws of nature,
and that I thought that the use of my hypothesis would
be evident, owing to the difficulty which the most able
philosophers of our time have found as to the inter-
relation [*communication*] of minds [*esprits*] and bodies,
and even of bodily substances with one another: and
I do not know but that you yourself have found some
difficulty in this.

18. It is true that, in my view, there are forces [*efforts*]
in all substances; but these forces [*efforts*] are, rightly
speaking, only in the substance itself, and what follows
from them in other substances takes place only in virtue
of a *harmony pre-established* [24] (if I may use the word), and
in no wise by a real influence or by the transmission of
some *species* or quality [25].   As I have explained what
activity [*action*] and passivity [*passion*] are, the nature
of force [*effort*] and of resistance may be inferred.

19. You say, Sir, that *you know there are still many
questions to be put, before those which we have been discussing
can be decided.*   But perhaps you will find that I have
already put these questions; and I am not sure that your
Academics have applied what is good in their method
more rigorously and effectively than I [26].   I strongly

---

[22] E. reads 'contrary to my intentions.'

[23] That is, activity which apparently passes beyond the substance
itself and has effects in other substances.   It is the same thing as
the 'influence' of one substance upon another.   See *De ipsa Natura*
(1698), § 10 (E. 157 b; G. iv. 510), where Leibniz uses the expression
transeuntes creaturarum actiones.

[24] This is the first use of the term by Leibniz.

[25] See *Monadology,* § 7, note 10.

[26] Foucher wrote: 'We ought to observe the laws of the
Academics, the second of which forbids us to put in question
matters which we clearly see cannot be settled, as are almost all
those of which we have been speaking; not that these questions

approve of seeking to demonstrate truths from first
principles: it is more useful than people think, and
I have often[27] put this precept in practice. Thus I commend what you say on this point, and I would that your
example may lead our philosophers to think of it as they
ought.

20. I will add a further reflexion, which seems to me
helpful in making the reality and use of my system better
understood. You know that M. Descartes believed in
the conservation of the same quantity of motion in bodies.
It has been shown that he was wrong in this; but I have
shown that it is still true that there is conservation of
the same moving force, instead of which he put quantity
of motion. Nevertheless, he was perplexed by the
changes which take place in the body in consequence
of modifications of the soul, because they seemed to
break this law. But he thought he had found a way
out of it (which is certainly ingenious) in saying that
we must distinguish between motion and direction; and
that the soul cannot increase nor diminish the moving
force, but that it changes the direction or determination
of the course of the animal spirits, and that it is in this
way that voluntary motions take place[28]. It is true that
he made no attempt to explain how the soul acts so as to
change the course of bodies, for there seems as much
difficulty in this as there is in saying that the soul gives
motion to bodies, unless with me you have recourse to
the pre-established harmony; but it is to be observed
that *there is another law of nature,* which I have discovered
and proved, and which M. Descartes was unaware of,
namely, that *there is conservation* not only of the same
quantity of moving force, but also *of the same quantity*

are absolutely insoluble, but because they are soluble only in
a certain order, which requires that philosophers should begin by
coming to an agreement as to the infallible mark of truth, and
should confine themselves to demonstrations from first principles'
(E. 130 b; G. iv. 490).

[27] E. omits 'often.' Cf. Introduction, Part ii. p. 59.

[28] See *Monadology*, § 80, note 127, and Introduction, Part iii. p. 89.

of direction in whatever line [*de quelque côté*] [29] *we take it in the world.*   That is to say, drawing any straight line you please, and taking also such bodies and so many of them as you please, you will find that, considering all these bodies together, without omitting any of those which act upon any one of those which you have taken, there will always be the same amount [*quantité*] of progression in the same direction [*du même côté*] in all lines parallel to the straight line you have taken—observing that the total amount of progression is to be calculated by subtracting from the amount of progression of the bodies which go in the given direction, the amount of progression of those which go in the opposite direction [30].   This law, being as good and as general as the other, deserved as

[29] E. reads *vers quelque côté.*

[30] See *Principles of Nature and of Grace,* § 11, note 48. Cf. *Epistola ad Bernoullium* (1696) (G. Math. iii. 243 ; E. 108 note): 'In the next place it is to be observed that I make a distinction between absolute force and directing force, although I can deduce and demonstrate directing force from the sole consideration of absolute power. And indeed I prove that there is conservation not only of the same absolute force or quantity of action in the world, but also of the same directing force and the same quantity of direction in the same lines [*ad easdem paries*], i. e. the same quantity of progression, its direction being taken into account and the quantity of progression being counted equal to the mass multiplied by the velocity, and not by the square of the velocity' [mv, not mv^2]. 'Nevertheless this quantity of progression differs from quantity of motion in this way, that when two bodies are moving in opposite directions their total quantity of motion (in the Cartesian sense) is to be got by adding together the quantity of motion of each (calculated as the mass into the velocity); but the quantity of progression is to be got by subtracting the one from the other; for in such a case the difference between the quantities of motion will be the quantity of progression.   Therefore when Descartes thought that he could safeguard the soul's power of acting on the body in this way, that while the soul cannot increase or diminish the quantity of motion in the world, it can nevertheless increase or diminish the quantity of direction of the [animal] spirits, he erred through not knowing this new law of ours regarding the conservation of the quantity of direction, which is no less beautiful and inviolable than the law of the conservation of absolute force [*virtus*] or power of action.'   The 'quantity of progression' would now be called a projection of the quantity of motion.   A full explanation, with diagrams, will be found in the appendix to Boutroux's edition of the *Monadologie.*

little to be broken, and this is so, according to my system [31], in which there is conservation of force and direction, and none of the natural laws of bodies are broken, notwithstanding the changes which take place in body in consequence of changes in the soul.

APPENDIX H.

ON THE ELEMENTS OF EXTENSION.

ONE of Foucher's objections to the *New System* was based on the contention that extension has no ultimate real elements (E. 129a; G. iv. 487). In some *Remarques sur les Objections de M. Foucher* (G. iv. 490) Leibniz replies: 'The author of the objection does not seem to have rightly understood my view. Extension or space, and the surfaces, lines and points that can be conceived in it, are nothing but relations of order or orders of co-existence, both as regards that which actually exists and as regards the possible thing that might be put in place of that which exists. Thus they have no ultimate component elements [*principes*], any more than number has. And as a broken number, for instance $\frac{1}{2}$, can be further broken into two-fourths or four-eighths and so on *ad infinitum*, without our being able to reach the absolutely smallest fractions or to conceive the number as a whole formed by the combination of ultimate elements, so it is with a line which can be divided, just like this number. Again, strictly speaking, the number $\frac{1}{2}$ in the abstract is a perfectly simple ratio [*rapport*], not at all formed by the compounding of other fractions, although in numbered things there is equality between two-fourths and one-half. And we may say as much regarding an *abstract* line, since compounding takes place only in *concrete* things, or the masses of which these abstract lines indicate the relations. And it is also in this way that mathematical points are to be regarded : they are merely modalities, that is to say extremities. And as in the abstract line all is indefinite, it has reference to everything which is possible, as in the case of

[31] E. reads 'and this' [i. e. the breach of the law] 'is avoided by my system.'

fractions of a number, without our troubling about divisions actually made, which indicate points in the line in various ways. But in actual substantial things the whole is a sum or aggregate of simple substances or rather of a multitude of real units [*unités*]. And it is the confounding of the ideal and the actual that has brought the whole matter into confusion and has produced the labyrinth *de compositione continui*. Those who have supposed the line to be made up of points have sought for the primary elements in ideal things or relations, which was quite a mistake; and those who have found that relations like number or space (which includes the order or relation of possible co-existent things) cannot be formed by the aggregation of points, have usually made the mistake of denying the primary elements of substantial realities, as if they had no primary unities, or as if there were no simple substances. Nevertheless number and the line are not *chimerical* things, although they are not thus compounded, for they are relations which involve eternal truths, in accordance with which the phenomena of nature are ordered. Hence it may be said that, considered in the abstract, $\frac{1}{2}$ and $\frac{1}{4}$ are independent of one another, or rather the total ratio [*rapport*] $\frac{1}{2}$ is anterior—in the order of reason [*dans le signe de la raison*], as the Scholastics say—to the partial ratio $\frac{1}{4}$, since it is by the subdivision of the half that we come to the fourth, following the order of what is ideal; and the same is the case with the line, in which the whole is anterior to the part because the part is only possible and ideal. But in realities, in which there are only divisions actually made, the whole is merely a sum or aggregate, as in the case of a flock of sheep. It is true that the number of simple substances which enter into a mass, however small it be, is infinite, since in addition to the soul which constitutes the real unity of the animal, the body of the sheep (for instance) is actually subdivided, that is to say it is also an aggregate of invisible animals or plants (which are likewise compound) besides that which constitutes also their real unity; and although this proceeds *ad infinitum*, it is manifest that ultimately all is reducible to these unities, the remainder or the aggregates being merely well-founded phenomena.'

THIRD EXPLANATION [1]—EXTRACT FROM A LETTER OF M. D. L. REGARDING HIS PHILOSOPHICAL HYPOTHESIS AND THE CURIOUS PROBLEM, PROPOUNDED TO THE MATHEMATICIANS BY ONE OF HIS FRIENDS, WITH AN EXPLANATION REGARDING SOME DISPUTED POINTS IN PRECEDING *JOURNALS* BETWEEN THE AUTHOR OF THE *PRINCIPLES OF PHYSICS* [2] AND THE AUTHOR OF THE *OBJECTIONS.* 1696.

SOME learned and acute friends of mine having considered my new hypothesis on the great question of *the union of soul and body*, and having found it of value, have asked me to give some explanations regarding the objections which have been brought against it and which arose from its not having been rightly understood. I think the matter may be made intelligible to minds of every kind by the following illustration.

Suppose two clocks [3] or two watches which perfectly

---

[1] E. has 'Third Explanation,' which is omitted by G.

[2] Nicholas Hartsoeker. 'M.D.L.' is a pseudonym of Leibniz.

[3] See Prefatory Note. Geulincx's use of the simile is as follows: 'My will certainly does not move the moving power that it may move my limbs; but He who imparted motion to matter and laid down laws for it, Himself also formed my will. Therefore He bound together these most diverse things (the motion of matter and the choice of my will), so that when my will wills, such a motion as it wills occurs, and on the other hand when

keep time together [*s'accordent*].   Now that may happen
in three ways.   The first way consists in the mutual influence of each clock upon the other ; the second, in the
care of a man who looks after them ; the third, in their
own accuracy.   *The first way*, that of influence, was
ascertained on trial by the late M. Huygens[4], to his great
astonishment.   He attached two large pendulums to the
same piece of wood.   The continual swinging of these
pendulums imparted similar vibrations to the particles of
the wood ; but as these different vibrations could not

the motion occurs, the will wills it, without any causality or
influence [*influxus*] of the one upon the other ; as in the case of
two clocks which are carefully adjusted together to the daily
course of the sun, as often as the one strikes and tells us the
hours, the other strikes in the same way and indicates the hours,
and *that* apart from any causality, by which the one might produce
this effect in the other, but solely on account of the connexion
which comes from the fact that both were made by the same
art and with similar workmanship.   Thus, for example, the
motion of the tongue accompanies our volition to speak, and this
volition accompanies that motion : and the motion does not depend
upon the volition, nor the volition upon the motion, but both
depend upon the same Supreme Artificer, who has so wonderfully
connected and bound them together.'   *Ethica, Tract.* I. cap. 2, § 2,
note 19 ; Land's ed., vol. iii. p. 211.   Cf. ibid. note 48 ; Land, iii. 220.
Cf. also Introduction, Part ii. p. 43.

    [4] Christian Huygens (1629-1695) was a mathematician, phy-
sicist and astronomer, who lived for the most part in Holland,
where he was born, and in France, where Leibniz, coming to
Paris in 1672, met him.   Anticipating the revocation of the Edict
of Nantes, the Protestant Huygens left Paris in 1681 and returned
to Holland, but he continued to correspond with Leibniz on
mathematical subjects.   In 1673 Huygens published his great
work *Horologium Oscillatorium, sive de motu pendulorum ad horologia
adaptato*, in which he gave a full account of a discovery he had
made in 1656, that of the pendulum clock.   Among the other
great works of Huygens were discoveries in connexion with the
astronomy of the planets, the undulatory theory of light, and
the use of spiral springs for regulating the balances of watches.
Leibniz frequently acknowledges his great indebtedness to
Huygens in regard to mathematics, and in July, 1695, he writes
to Nicaise : 'Nothing can equal the loss of the incomparable
M. Huygens.   Most certainly he ought to be named immediately
after Galileo and Descartes.   He might still have given us great
light upon nature' (G. ii. 552).   But elsewhere he says that
'M. Huygens had no taste for metaphysics.'   *Lettre à Remond* (1714)
(E. 702 b ; G. iii. 607).

continue in their proper order, without interfering with one another, unless the pendulums kept time together, it happened, by a kind of wonder, that even when their swinging was deliberately disturbed they soon came to swing together again, somewhat like two stretched strings that are in unison.

The second way of making two clocks (even though they be bad ones) constantly keep time together would be to put them in charge of a skilled workman who should keep them together from moment to moment. I call this the way of assistance.

Finally, *the third way* will be to make the two clocks [*pendules*] at first with such skill and accuracy that we can be sure that they will always afterwards keep time together. This is the way of pre-established agreement [*consentement*].

Now put the soul and the body in place of the two clocks. Their agreement [*accord*] or sympathy will also arise in one of these three ways. *The way of influence* is that of the common philosophy; but as we cannot conceive material particles or immaterial species or qualities which can pass from one of these substances into the other, we are obliged to give up this opinion. *The way of assistance* is that of the system of occasional causes; but I hold that this is to introduce *Deus ex machina* in a natural and ordinary matter, in which it is reasonable that God should intervene only in the way in which He supports [*concourt à*] all the other things of nature. Thus there remains only my hypothesis, that is to say, *the way of the harmony pre-established* by a contrivance of the Divine foresight, which has from the beginning formed each of these substances in so perfect, so regular and accurate a manner that by merely following its own laws which were given to it when it came into being, each substance is yet in harmony with the other, just as if there were a mutual influence between them, or as if God were continually putting His hand

upon them, in addition to His general support [con-
currence].

I do not think that I need offer any further proof[5]
unless I should be required to prove that God is in
a position[6] to make use of this contrivance of foresight,
of which we have instances even among men, in proportion to the skill they have. And supposing that
God is able to make use of this means, it is very evident
that this is the best way and the most worthy of Him.
It is true that I have also other proofs of it[7], but they
are deeper and it is unnecessary to adduce them here[8].

. . . .

Let me say a word about the dispute between two very
clever people, the author of the recently-published *Principles of Physics*[9] and the author of the *Objections*[10] (which
appeared in the *Journal* of August 13 and elsewhere),
because my hypothesis serves to bring these controversies
to an end. I do not understand how matter can be

[5] It should be observed that Leibniz's argument from analogy
proceeds upon the assumption that body and soul, or soul and
soul, are in reality quite independent and separate from one
another. If this be not admitted his 'proof' breaks down: the
'three ways' do not exhaust the possible hypotheses. Leibniz
seems rather to have prided himself on emphasizing, by his
hypothesis, the difference between body and soul. In the post-
script to a letter to Basnage de Beauval (1696), part of which is
printed as the *Second Éclaircissement* (E. 134 b; G. iv. 499), Leibniz
says: 'You had a suspicion that my explanation would be irre-
concilable with the great difference which, in our opinion, there
is between mind [*esprit*] and body. But now you see clearly, Sir,
that no one has established their independence more completely
than I. For since hitherto we have been obliged to explain their
inter-relation [*communication*] by a kind of miracle, we have constantly given occasion to many people to fear that the distinction
between mind and body is not so real as people think, since our
reasons for maintaining it are so far-fetched. Now all these scruples
cease.'

[6] The *Second Éclaircissement* reads 'is skilful enough.'

[7] The reference is probably to such arguments as those which
he afterwards gave in the *Monadology*.

[8] I have omitted two paragraphs dealing with a purely mathematical problem.

[9] Hartsoeker. See *New System*, § 6, note 36.

[10] Foucher.

conceived as extended and yet without either actual or ideal [11] parts; and if it is so, I do not know what is meant by being extended [12]. I even hold that matter is essentially an aggregate, and consequently that there are always actual parts. Thus it is by reason, and not merely by the senses, that we judge that it is divided, or rather that it is ultimately nothing but a collection [*multitude*]. I hold it as true that matter (and even each part of matter) is divided into a greater number of parts than it is possible to imagine. And accordingly I often say that each body, however small it may be, is a world of creatures infinite in number. Thus I do not believe that there are atoms, that is to say, parts of matter which are perfectly hard or of invincible solidity; while, on the other hand, I as little believe that there is a perfectly fluid matter [13], and my opinion is that each body is fluid in comparison with more solid bodies and solid in comparison with the more fluid. I am surprised that it is still said that an equal quantity of motion, in the Cartesian sense, is always conserved; for I have proved the opposite, and already excellent mathematicians have admitted it. Nevertheless I do not regard the solidity or consistence of bodies as a primary quality, but as a consequence of motion, and I hope that my Dynamics will show in what this consists, as the understanding of my hypothesis will also serve to remove several difficulties which still engage the attention of philosophers. In fact, I believe I can intelligibly answer all the doubts to which *the late M. Bernier* [14] has specially devoted a

[11] *mentales*, i. e. thinkable.

[12] The reference is probably to the views of Foucher, who denied that the essence of matter is extension, holding that all our ideas (including those of external objects) are merely modifications of ourselves and that, in order to represent an object, an idea must be like it. See Foucher de Careil, *Lettres et Opuscules inédits de Leibniz*, Introduction.

[13] Hartsoeker's theory was that the ultimate elements of things are perfectly hard atoms in a perfect fluid, the atoms combined forming tangible bodies, while the fluid transmits light, &c.

[14] François Bernier (d. 1688) was more famous as a traveller

book; and those who will think out what I have
formerly published will perhaps find that they already
have the means of making this answer.

than as a philosopher. After travelling in Syria and Egypt, he
went to India (where he was physician to Aurungzebe), and
afterwards to Cashmir. In Paris he was nicknamed 'the Mogul.'
He assisted Boileau in preparing the *Mock Decree, given in the hall
of Parnassus, in favour of the Masters of Arts, Physicians, and Professors of
the University of Stagira, in the land of chimeras, for the support of the
doctrine of Aristotle,* which by its ridicule killed the serious proposal
that the French Parliament should officially condemn the philosophy of Descartes. Bernier's principal philosophical works were
Abrégé de la philosophie de Gassendi (8 vols., 1678) and, by way of
supplement to this, *Doutes de M. Bernier sur quelques-uns des principaux
chapitres de son abrégé de la philosophie de Gassendi* (7 vols., 1684). The
latter is probably the work to which Leibniz refers. There is
an English translation of Bernier's *Travels in the Mogul Empire* (new
ed., Constable, 1897).

ON THE ULTIMATE ORIGINATION
OF THINGS.   1697.

PREFATORY NOTE.

THIS paper, written in Latin, is dated by Leibniz, November 23, 1697.   It may have been intended for the *Acta Eruditorum*; but it remained unpublished until 1840, when Erdmann included it in his edition.   Leibniz here explains the function of the principle of sufficient reason in his philosophy, expanding what he had already said in a paper written about 1685, to which Erdmann gives the title, *De Scientia Universali seu Calculo philosophico* (see E. 83 b; G. vii. 200).   §§ 36–48 of the *Monadology* may be regarded as a condensation of the main argument of this Essay *On the Ultimate Origination of Things*. In the latter part of the Essay we have a vindication of the optimism of Leibniz (that this is the best of all possible worlds), and some of the chief doctrines of the *Théodicée* are given in outline.

The *Ultimate Origination of Things* is given by E. 147 sqq.; G. vii. 302 sqq.

BESIDES the world or the aggregate of finite things there is a certain unity [*unum*] which is dominant, not only as the soul is dominant in me or rather as the ego itself is dominant in my body, but also in a much higher sense[1].   For the dominant unity of the universe not only rules the world but constructs or[2] fashions it.   It is higher than the world and, so to speak, extramundane, and is thus the ultimate reason of things.   For the

[1] Cf. *Monadology*, §§ 70 and 72, notes 111 and 115.
[2] E. reads 'and.'

z

sufficient reason of existence cannot be found either in any particular thing or in the whole aggregate and series of things. Let us suppose that a book of the elements of geometry existed from all eternity and that in succession one copy of it was made from another, it is evident that although we can account for the present book by the book from which it was copied, nevertheless, going back through as many books as we like, we could never reach a complete reason for it, because we can always ask why such books have at all times existed, that is to say, why books at all, and why written in this way. What is true of books is also true of the different states of the world ; for, in spite of certain laws of change, the succeeding state is, in some sort, a copy of that which precedes it. Therefore, to whatever earlier state you go back, you never find in it the complete reason of things, that is to say, the reason why there exists any world and why this world rather than some other.

You may indeed suppose the world eternal ; but as you suppose only a succession of states, in none of which do you find the sufficient reason, and as even any number of worlds does not in the least help you to account for them, it is evident that the reason must be sought elsewhere. For in eternal things, even though there be no cause, there must be a reason[3] which, for permanent things, is necessity itself or essence[4]; but for the series of changing things, if it be supposed that they succeed one another from all eternity, this reason is, as we shall presently see, the prevailing of inclinations[5] which con-

---

[3] If a thing is eternal, it cannot have a cause in time ; but there must still be some reason (other than a cause in time) for its existence. Cf. Aristotle's αἴτιον (which is wider than our 'cause') and the German *Grund*.

[4] By 'permanent things' is meant things that are not contingent, and these, in Leibniz's language, are 'possible' things = 'necessary' things = essences. Cf. *Monadology*, §§ 40 and 43, notes 64 and 67.

[5] The sufficient reason of changing or contingent things is not an absolute principle, whose opposite would be self-contradictory,

sist not in necessitating reasons, that is to say, reasons of an absolute and metaphysical necessity, the opposite of which involves a contradiction [6], but in inclining reasons. From this it is manifest that even by supposing the eternity of the world, we cannot escape the ultimate extramundane reason of things, that is to say, God [7].

Accordingly the reasons of the world lie hid in something extramundane, different from the concatenation of states or the series of things, the aggregate of which constitutes the world. And thus we must go beyond the physical or hypothetical necessity, according to which the later things of the world are determined by the earlier, to something which is of absolute or metaphysical necessity [8], of which a reason cannot be given. For the present world is necessary physically or hypothetically, but not absolutely or metaphysically. That is to say, the nature of the world being such as it is, it follows that things must happen in it just as they do. Therefore, since the ultimate root of all must be in something which has metaphysical necessity, and since the reason of any existing thing is to be found only in an existing thing, it follows that there must exist one Being which has metaphysical necessity, one Being of whose essence

but a superiority of the good or desirable over the bad or undesirable in the things which come to pass. The balance or preponderance of goodness inclines the will of God (without absolutely necessitating it) to create these contingent things.

[6] The word *contradictionem* seems to have been omitted *per incuriam*. Neither E. nor G. gives it.

[7] Even though the world be taken as eternal, its necessity is not on that account absolute or compelling but merely 'inclining,' and it therefore presupposes some one whose will is 'inclined,' i. e. God.

[8] E. reads 'something which is absolute or metaphysical necessity.' Absolute or metaphysical necessity is a necessity that is independent of actual things, in contrast with hypothetical (conditional, relative) or physical necessity, which is the necessity arising out of the natures of actual things, the necessity which a system of 'compossible' things imposes on its members. Cf. Introduction, Part ii. p. 67.

it is to exist[9]; and thus there must exist something different from that plurality of beings, the world, which as we admitted and showed, has no metaphysical necessity[10].

But to explain more distinctly how from eternal or essential or metaphysical truths there arise temporal, contingent or physical truths, we must first observe that, from the very fact that there exists something rather than nothing, it follows that in possible things, or in possibility or essence itself, there is a certain need of existence or, so to speak, a claim to exist, in a word, that essence of itself tends to existence[11]. From this it further follows that all possible things, that is, things expressing essence or possible reality, with equal right tend to existence[12] in proportion to the quantity of essence or reality, or in proportion to the degree of perfection which belongs to them. For perfection is nothing but quantity of essence[13].

Hence it is most evident that out of the infinite possible combinations and series of possible things there exists that one through which the greatest amount of essence or possibility is brought into existence. Indeed, there is always in things a principle of determination according to maximum and minimum, so that, for instance, the maximum effect is produced with the minimum outlay[14]. And the time, the place, or, in a word, the

[9] Cf. Spinoza's distinction between Substance as *id quod in se est* and Mode as *id quod in alio est*. *Ethics*, Part i. deff. 3 and 5. See *Monadology*, §§ 36 sqq.

[10] For Kant's criticism of the cosmological proof of the existence of God, see *Critique of Pure Reason, Transcendental Dialectic*, bk. ii. ch. 2, § 2, *Fourth Antinomy*.

[11] Cf. *Monadology*, § 40, note 64.

[12] Both E. and G. read *essentiam*, which is manifestly a slip for *existentiam*. E. corrects the error in his *Errata*.

[13] Cf. *Monadology*, §§ 41 and 54.

[14] Outlay or cost is in itself loss or limitation. But if there is to be a world at all, there must be loss or limitation, for if the elements of the world were not in different degrees limited, there would be no variety. All would be one 'splendidly null' perfection. Yet the world is the best possible world in the sense that it

receptivity or capacity of the world [16] may here be considered as the outlay or ground on which the world is
to be built as fittingly [*quam commodissime*] as possible,
while the variety of forms corresponds to the fitness
[*commoditas*] of the building and to the number and
elegance of its rooms. The whole matter may be likened
to certain games in which all the spaces on a board are
to be filled up according to definite rules, so that, unless
you make use of some ingenious contrivance, you find
yourself in the end kept out of some refractory spaces
and compelled to leave empty more spaces than you
intended and some which you might otherwise have
filled. Yet there is a definite method by which the
most complete filling up of the spaces may most easily
be accomplished. So if we have to draw a triangle, no
other determining condition being given, it will be an
equilateral triangle; and if a line is to be drawn from
one point to another, no further condition being assigned,
the easiest or shortest way will be chosen. So if once
it is given that being is superior to not-being (that is to
say, that there is a reason why something should exist
rather than nothing [16]), or that possibility must pass into
actuality, it follows that, though nothing further is
determined, there must exist as much as is possible considering the capacity of time and space (that is, of the
possible order of existing [17]), just as tiles are put together

contains the greatest balance of perfection over limitation or of
good over evil, i. e. the maximum of advantage at the minimum
of cost. In this sense the 'principle of the best,' to which Leibniz
constantly refers, is a 'principle of determination according to
maximum and minimum.' That the cost should be minimum
might be taken as a way of stating the 'law of parsimony.'

[15] That is, the natural or essential limits within which the
actual world may express an ideal possibility, which has no limits.
This limiting 'receptivity or capacity' (which is to the world what
the body is to the individual Monad) might be regarded as the
passivity or matter of the world, in contrast with its activity or
form.

[16] Cf. *Principles of Nature and of Grace*, § 7.

[17] i. e. not merely the order which we discover among actual
things, but the order which is a condition of possible things

in such a way that as many as possible may be contained in a given area.

Thus it is wonderfully made known to us how in the very origination of things a certain Divine mathematics [18] or metaphysical mechanics is employed and the greatest quantity is brought into existence [*lit.* the determination of the greatest quantity takes place]. So among all angles the determined [fixed] angle in geometry is the right angle [19], and so also liquids put into heterogeneous media take the form of greatest capacity, that of a sphere. But best of all is the illustration we get in ordinary mechanics, where, when several heavy bodies act against one another, the resultant motion is that which produces the greatest fall on the whole [20]. For as all possible things by an equal right tend to exist in proportion to their reality, so all weights by an equal right tend to fall in proportion to their gravity; and as in the case of the latter there is produced a motion which involves the greatest possible fall of the heavy bodies, so in the case of the former there is produced a world in which the greatest number of possible things comes into existence.

And thus we have physical necessity coming from metaphysical necessity; for although the world is not metaphysically necessary, so that its opposite involves a contradiction or logical absurdity, it is nevertheless physically necessary or so determined that its opposite involves imperfection or moral absurdity. And as possibility is the principle of essence, so perfection or degree

coming into existence. Only compossible essences can give rise to co-existing phenomena, and time and space are the order of co-existence of these phenomena. See Introduction, Part iii. p. 102.

[18] 'When God calculates and employs thought, the world is made.' *De connexione inter res et verba* (1677) (E. 77 a; G. vii. 191). The phrase was written by Leibniz on the margin of the MS. and may accordingly be of later date.

[19] The right angle is always 90°; but an acute or an obtuse angle is variable in size. The right angle is thus 'fixed' or 'determined,' and the right angle is the greatest angle at which one line can meet another.

[20] The suggestion is of some such arrangement as we have in a system of pulleys.

of essence (through which more things are compossible the greater it is) is the principle of existence. Whence at the same time it is manifest how the Author of the world is free, although He does all things determinately, for He acts from a principle of wisdom or perfection. Indifference springs from ignorance, and the wiser a man is the more is he determined towards that which is most perfect [21].

But, you will say, however beautiful may seem this comparison of a certain metaphysical determining mechanism with the physical mechanism of heavy bodies, it nevertheless fails in this respect that heavy bodies really exist and act, but possibilities or essences anterior to existence or apart from it are imaginary or fictitious and therefore no reason [22] of existence is to be sought in them. I reply that neither these essences nor what are called eternal truths regarding these essences are fictitious, but that they exist in a certain region (if I may so call it) of ideas, that is to say, in God Himself, the source of all essence and of the existence of other things. That this is not a mere gratuitous assertion of mine is shown by the existence of the actual series of things. For since the reason of the series is not to be found in itself, as has been shown above, but is to be sought in metaphysical necessities or eternal truths, and since existing things can come only from existing things, as we have already remarked, eternal truths must have existence in some absolutely or [23] metaphysically necessary subject, that is, in God, through whom these things which would otherwise be imaginary are (to use a barbarous but expressive word) realized [24].

And indeed we actually find that all things in the

---

[21] Cf. Introduction, Part iii. p. 145.

[22] Or 'ground.' [23] E. reads 'and.'

[24] That is to say, God gives them a certain reality or existence *in His understanding*, as distinct from existence *in the actual world*, which belongs to contingent things. Cf. *Monadology*, §§ 43, 44, 46 and 47, note 75.

world take place in accordance with the laws, not only
geometrical but also metaphysical, of eternal truths, that
is, not only in accordance with material necessities but
also in accordance with formal reasons[25].   And this is
not only true in general as regards the reason (which we
have just explained) why a world exists rather than not,
and why it exists thus rather than otherwise (a reason
which is to be found only in the tendency of possible
things to exist); but also when we come down to particular things we see that metaphysical laws of cause,
power, activity, are present in a wonderful way throughout the whole of nature, and that they are even superior
to the purely geometrical laws of matter, as to my great
astonishment I found when I was explaining the laws
of motion, so that, as I have elsewhere more fully explained[26], I was ultimately compelled to give up the law
of the geometrical composition of forces [conatus] which
I had maintained in my youth when I had more belief
in the material view.

Accordingly we have the ultimate reason of the reality
both of essences and of existences in one Being who is
necessarily greater, higher, and older [anterius] than the
world itself, since through Him not only the existing
things which the world contains but also possible things
have reality.   But this ultimate reason can be found
only in one source on account of the inter-connexion of
all these things[27].   But it is manifest that from this
source existing things continually come forth [promanare],
that they are being and have been produced by it, since
it does not appear why one state of the world rather
than another, the state of yesterday rather than that of
to-day, should flow from it[28].   It is also manifest how

[25] E. reads 'necessities' instead of 'reasons.'
[26] See Appendix I, p. 351.
[27] That is to say, the actual system of things is one and therefore
its source is one.   Cf. *Monadology*, § 39.
[28] The reference is not quite clear.   Janet translates 'from the
world itself.'   Kirchmann translates 'from this source.'   On Janet's

God acts not only physically but also freely, how not only the efficient but also the final cause of things is in Him, and how He manifests not only His greatness and power in the mechanism of the world as already constructed, but also His wisdom and goodness in the constructing of it [29].

And lest any one should think that we are here confounding moral perfection or goodness with metaphysical perfection or greatness and, allowing the latter, should deny the former, it is to be observed that it follows from what has been said not only that the world is most perfect physically, or, if you prefer it, metaphysically, that is to say, that that series of things has come into existence in which the greatest amount of reality is actually manifested, but also that the world is most perfect morally because genuine moral perfection is physical [30] perfection in minds [*mentes*] themselves. Wherefore the world is not only the most admirable mechanism, but it is also, in so far as it is made up of minds [*mentes*], the best commonwealth, through which there is bestowed upon minds the greatest possible happiness or joy, in which their physical perfection consists [31].

interpretation, the passage would mean that all the states of the world must come from God, in whose nature is to be found the sufficient reason of all and of each, and not from the world itself, which cannot supply the sufficient reason of any. On Kirchmann's interpretation, the meaning would be that each state of the world comes from God by a ' *continual* creation,' because there is no reason why God should create one state rather than another. Both interpretations are possible ; but Janet's seems the more natural.

[29] Cf. *Monadology*, §§ 47, 48, 55.

[30] 'Physical' here means 'natural' or 'according to the specific nature (φύσις) of the thing' in contrast with 'metaphysical' in the sense of 'absolute, independent of the specific nature of the thing.' Thus (cf. *supra*) 'the world is most perfect physically' means that its individual members or elements are as perfect as the nature of each allows, while 'the world is most perfect metaphysically' means that the world as a whole is the most perfect possible. So also 'genuine moral perfection is physical perfection in minds themselves' means that the specific natural perfection of mind is moral perfection.

[31] Cf. *Monadology*, §§ 86 sqq. 'Felicity is to persons what perfection is to beings.' Paper without a title (1686) (G. iv. 462).

But, you will say, we find that the opposite of this takes place in the world, for very often the best people suffer the worst things, and those who are innocent, both animals and men, are afflicted and put to death even with torture; and indeed the world, especially if we consider the government of the human race, seems rather a confused chaos than anything directed by a supreme wisdom. So, I confess, it seems at a first glance, but when we look at it more closely the opposite conclusion manifestly follows *a priori* from those very considerations which have been adduced, the conclusion, namely, that the highest possible perfection of all things, and therefore of all minds, is brought about.

And indeed, as the lawyers say, it is not proper to judge unless we have examined the whole law. We know a very small part of eternity which is immeasureable in its extent; for what a little thing is the record of a few thousand years, which history transmits to us! Nevertheless, from so slight an experience we rashly judge regarding the immeasureable and eternal, like men who, having been born and brought up in prison or, perhaps, in the subterranean salt-mines of the Sarmatians[32], should think that there is no other light in the

---

[32] The reference is probably to some of the salt-mines in or near the Carpathians, which are the richest in Europe. The most famous salt-mines in the world are at Wielicza, near Cracow in Galicia (which in Leibniz's time was still part of the kingdom of Poland). They have been worked for about 600 years, and many of the workers live permanently underground, there being streets and houses and, in short, something like a village in the lower levels. In Jeremy Collier's *Dictionary*, published towards the end of the seventeenth century, the famous salt-mines are said to be those of Eperies, in northern Hungary, on the other side of the Carpathians from Cracow. Sarmatia is a very vague word. According to Ptolemy it included all the eastern European plain from the Vistula and the Dniester to the Volga. In any case it included the district of the salt-mines referred to. Leibniz elsewhere seems to identify Sarmatian with Slavonic speech. (*Nouveaux Essais*, iii. 2, § 1; E. 299 b; G. v. 259, 260.) In English verse, Sarmatia is often used as synonymous with Poland, e.g. 'Sarmatia fell, unwept, without a crime' (Campbell, *Pleasures of Hope*, Part i. line 376; see also l. 407).

world than that of the feeble lamp which hardly suffices
to direct their steps. If you look at a very beautiful
picture, having covered up the whole of it except a very
small part, what will it present to your sight, however
thoroughly you examine it (nay, so much the more, the
more closely you inspect it), but a confused mass of
colours laid on without selection and without art? Yet
if you remove the covering and look at the whole picture
from the right point of view, you will see that what
appeared to have been carelessly daubed on the canvas
was really done by the painter with very great art[33].
The experience of the eyes in painting corresponds to
that of the ears in music. Eminent composers very
often mingle discords with harmonies so as to stimulate
and, as it were, to prick the hearer, who becomes anxious
as to what is going to happen, and is so much the more
pleased when presently all is restored to order ; just as
we take pleasure in small dangers or risks of mishap,
merely from the consciousness of our power or our luck
or from a desire to make a display of them ; or, again, as
we delight in the show of danger that is connected with
performances on the tight-rope or sword-dancing (*sauts
périlleux*)[34], and we ourselves in jest half let go a little
boy, as if about to throw him from us, like the ape which
carried Christiern, King of Denmark[35], while still an
infant in swaddling-clothes, to the top of the roof, and
then, as in jest, relieved the anxiety of every one by
bringing him safely back to his cradle. On the same
principle sweet things become insipid if we eat nothing
else ; sharp, tart, and even bitter things must be combined with them, so as to stimulate the taste. He

---

[33] A most interesting variant of this illustration occurs in
Bosanquet's *Essentials of Logic*, pp. 55 sqq.

[34] Leibniz gives the French phrase to explain his Latin.

[35] Probably Christiern or Christian V (1646-1699), the first
hereditary (not elected) King of Denmark, who was reigning at
the time when Leibniz wrote. In the text he is called Christiernus,
Christiern or Kristiern being the Danish form of the name.

who has not tasted bitter things does not deserve sweet
things and, indeed, will not appreciate them.   This
is the very law of enjoyment, that pleasure does not
have an even tenor, for this begets loathing and makes
us dull, not happy [36].

But as to our saying that a part may be disturbed
without destroying harmony in the whole, this must not
be understood as meaning that no account is taken of the
parts or that it is enough for the world as a whole to be
perfect, although it may be that the human race is
wretched, and that there is in the universe no regard
for justice and no care for us, as is the opinion of some
whose judgment regarding the totality of things is
not quite just.   For it is to be observed that, as in
a thoroughly well-constituted commonwealth care is
taken, as far as may be, for the good of individuals,
so the universe will not be sufficiently perfect unless
the interests of individuals are attended to, while the
universal harmony is preserved [37].   And for this   no

----

[36] 'To have a thousand well-bound Virgils in your library, always
to sing airs from the opera of Cadmus and Hermione, to break all
your porcelain that you might have nothing but cups of gold, to
have diamonds alone for buttons, to eat nothing but partridges,
to drink only Hungarian or Shiras wine—would you call that
reason?'   *Théodicée*, § 124 (E. 539 b; G. vi. 179).   Cf. *Principles of
Nature and of Grace*, § 18; also Bacon, *De Augmentis*, iii. 1.

[37] Cf. *Théodicée*, § 118 (E. 535 a; G. vi. 169): 'No substance is
absolutely contemptible or precious in the sight of God. . . . It
is certain that God gives more importance to a man than to
a lion; yet I do not know if we can be certain that God prefers
one man to the whole species of lions in all respects.   But even if
it were so, it would not follow that the interest of a certain number
of men should prevail in face of a general disorder, extending to an
infinite number of created things.   This opinion would be a relic
of the old maxim, now quite out of repute, that everything happens
solely on man's account.'   Cf. *Méditation sur la notion commune de la
justice* (Mollat, p. 63): 'There are people who think that we are of
too little consequence, in the sight of an infinite God, for Him to
have any care for us: we are supposed to be in relation to God
what the worms, which we crush without thinking about it, are in
relation to us.   But this is to suppose that God is like a man and
cannot think of everything.   Just because God is infinite, He does
things without labour by a kind of consequence of His will, as it is
a consequence of my will and that of my friend that we are in

better standard could be set up than the very law of justice which declares that each should participate in the perfection of the universe and in a happiness of his own in proportion to his own virtue and to the degree in which his will has regard to the common good ; and by this is fulfilled that which we call charity and the love of God, in which alone, in the opinion of wise theologians, consists the force and power even of the Christian religion [38]. Nor ought it to appear wonderful that so great a place should be given to minds in the universe, since they most closely resemble the image of the Supreme Author ; they are related to Him, not (like other things) as machines to their constructor, but as citizens to their prince ; they are to last as long as the universe itself, and in a manner they express and concentrate the whole in themselves, so that it may be said that minds are whole parts [*partes totales*] [39].

But as to the special question of the afflictions of good men, it is to be held as certain that these afflictions have as their result the greater good of those who are afflicted, and this is true not only theologically but also naturally [*physice*], as the grain cast into the earth suffers before it bears fruit. And in general it may be said that afflictions are for the time evil but in the end good, since they are short ways to greater perfection. So in physics, liquids which ferment slowly take also a longer time to purify,

agreement, no new action being required to produce our agreement, beyond the resolve which each of us has made. Now if the human race and even the smallest thing were not well governed, the universe itself would not be well governed, for the whole consists in its parts.'

[38] Cf. Pope, *Essay on Man*, Fourth Epistle, lines 327 sqq. Nature, says Pope, connects
    'Man's greatest virtue with his greatest bliss.
    .   .   .   .
    Self-love thus push'd to social, to divine,
    Gives thee to make thy neighbour's blessing thine.
    .   .   .   .
    Happier as kinder, in whate'er degree
    And height of bliss but height of charity.'
[39] See Introduction, Part ii. p. 31.

while those which undergo a greater agitation throw off certain of their ingredients with greater force, and are thus more quickly rectified. And this is what you might call going back in order that you may put more force into your leap forward (*qu'on recède pour mieux sauter*[40]). Wherefore these things are to be regarded not only as agreeable and comforting, but also as most true. And in general I think there is nothing more true than happiness, and nothing more happy and pleasant than truth.

Further, to realize in its completeness the universal beauty and perfection of the works of God, we must recognize a certain perpetual and very free progress of the whole universe, such that it is always going forward to greater improvement [*cultus*]. So even now a great part of our earth has received cultivation [*cultura*] and will receive it more and more. And although it is true that sometimes certain parts of it grow wild again, or again suffer destruction or degeneration, yet this is to be understood in the way in which affliction was explained above, that is to say, that this very destruction and degeneration leads to some greater end, so that somehow we profit by the loss itself[41].

And to the possible objection that, if this were so, the world ought long ago to have become a paradise, there is a ready answer. Although many substances have

---

[40] Cf. *Principles of Nature and of Grace*, § 12, note 51.

[41] Cf. *Lettre à la Princesse Sophie* (1706) (G. vii. 568) : 'And as there is reason to think that the universe itself develops from more to more and that all tends to some end, since all comes from an Author whose wisdom is perfect, we may similarly believe that souls, which last as long as the universe, go also from better to better, at least naturally [*physiquement*] and that their perfections go on increasing, although most often this takes place imperceptibly and sometimes after great circuits backward.' See also *Lettre à Bourguet* (1716) (G. iii. 589) : 'Although the universe has always been equally perfect' [i. e. each momentary state of the universe equally perfect with every other] 'it will never be supremely perfect ; for it always changes and gains new perfections, though it loses old ones.'

already attained a great perfection, yet on account of the infinite divisibility of the continuous, there always remain in the abyss of things slumbering parts which have yet to be awakened, to grow in size and worth, and, in a word, to advance to a more perfect state [*ad meliorem cultum*]. And hence no end of progress is ever reached.

APPENDIX I.

THE GROWTH OF LEIBNIZ'S THEORIES REGARDING FORCE AND MOTION.

IN the second of two dialogues, entitled *Phoranomus seu de Potentia et Legibus Naturae* (1689), Leibniz gives an account of the progress of his views regarding dynamics and physics. What follows is a portion of this account, combined with part of a similar statement in the *Specimen Dynamicum*. 'When first I escaped from the prickly thorn-brakes of the schools into the more pleasant fields of later philosophy, I was greatly taken with that fascinating ease of understanding, in which I saw a lucid imagination comprehending all the things which formerly were wrapped in dark notions. And after long and careful deliberation I at length rejected the "forms" and "qualities" of material things, and reduced all things to purely mathematical principles; but since I was not yet versed in geometry, I was convinced that a *continuum* consists of points and that a very slow motion is broken by little bits of rest, and I was inclined to other doctrines of this kind, which commend themselves to those who seek to comprehend all things with the imagination and who do not notice the infinite which is everywhere latent in things. But although, when I became a geometrician, I put off these opinions, there yet remained for a while atoms and the void, as relics of a state of mind that was in revolt against the idea of the infinite; for although I granted that every *continuum* can in thought be divided *ad infinitum*, yet I did not really accept the view that in things there are innumerable parts which follow from motion in the *plenum*. At last, not only was I freed from this scruple, but also I began to recognize something deeper in bodies, which could not be comprehended by the imagination. . . . This ought not to seem wonderful, for it is the nature of foundations to be humble, but if they are securely laid, great masses arise upon them. Accordingly, when I as yet acknowledged the jurisdiction of imagination alone in regard to material things, I was of opinion that any natural inertia in bodies was unintelligible, and that a body at rest *in vacuo* or in a free space must receive the velocity of another, however small that other might be; and that this does not actually happen in our experience I attributed to the system established by the wisdom of the Supreme Author of things, in which all things are ruled by the most just laws. Nor indeed did I doubt that the origin of the system might be rationally thought out on mechanical principles from those very laws of natural bodies, which explain occurrences by the composition of motions, such as I expounded regarding several cases in a treatise which I published when a young man.' *Phoranomus,* see *Arch. f. Gesch. d. Phil.* i. 577. 'When I was a young man and, at that time, following Democritus and his adherents in this matter, Gassendi and Descartes, I regarded the nature of body as consisting in mere inert mass, I issued a treatise with the title *Hypothesis Physica,* in which I expounded a theory of motion both abstract (independent of the system of things) and concrete (as it appears in the system of things), which I see has pleased many distinguished men better than its moderate worth deserved. In this treatise I maintained that, supposing my view of the nature of body to be right, every impinging body gives its impulse [*conatus*] to the body on which it impinges or which is directly in its way, as such. For when the impact takes place, the body impinged upon endeavours to move forward and thus to go away, and (since, as I then thought, body is indifferent to motion or rest) this endeavour [effort, *conatus*] must have its full effect in the body impinged upon, unless it is hindered by an opposite effort, and even if it is so hindered, since these different efforts must be compounded together. Accordingly it was manifest that no cause can be given why the impinging body should not achieve the effect towards which it tends or why the body impinged upon should not receive the whole impulse [*conatus*] of the impinging body, and therefore the motion of the body impinged upon is compounded of its own original impulse and the new or foreign impulse it has received. Whence I further showed that if in body there were recognized only mathematical notions, magnitude, figure, place, and their changes or their tendency [*conatus*] to change at the very moment of impact, and no account were taken of metaphysical notions, namely, of moving power [*potentia*] in the form, and of inertia (or resistance to motion) in the matter [of the body], and if it were thus necessary that the result of the impact should be determined by a purely geometrical composition of forces [*conatus*], as we have explained: then it ought to follow that the impulse of the impinging body, however small that body may be, is communicated to the whole of the body impinged upon, however large it may be, and thus the very largest body at rest is moved away by an impinging body, however small, without any retarding of the latter, since matter, thus understood, is not repugnant but rather indifferent to motion. Hence it would not be more difficult to move a large body at rest than a small one, and therefore there would be action without reaction, and no estimate of power could be made, since anything might be accomplished by anything. . . . But afterwards, having considered the whole matter more profoundly, I saw in what the systematic explanation of things' [i. e. the explanation of things as they actually are] 'should consist, and I observed that my former hypothesis regarding the nature of body was not complete, and that this as well as other arguments proved that body must be regarded as having, in addition to magnitude and impenetrability, something from which arises the consideration of forces [*vires*], the metaphysical laws of which, when combined with the laws of extension, give rise to those very laws of motion which I had called systematic. . . .' *Specimen Dynamicum*, &c. (1695) (G. Math. vi. 240). 'I am of opinion that the mechanical principles and reasons of the laws of motion do themselves arise not from the necessity of matter, but from some higher principle than imagination, and one independent of mathematics. . . . Besides I began to have considerable doubts as to the nature of motion. For when formerly I regarded space as an immovable real place, possessing extension alone, I had been able to define absolute motion as change of this real space. But gradually I began to doubt whether there is in nature such an entity as is called space; whence it followed that a doubt might arise about absolute motion. Certainly Aristotle had said that place is nothing but the surface of what surrounds us [*superficies ambientis*][1], and Descartes, following him, had defined motion (that is, change of place) as change of neighbourhood [*mutatio viciniae*]. Whence it seemed to follow that that which is real and absolute in motion consists not in what is purely mathematical, such as change of neighbourhood or situation, but in motive force [*potentia motrix*] itself; and if there is none of this, then there is no absolute and real motion. . . . Accordingly I found no other Ariadne thread to lead me out of this labyrinth than the calculation of forces [*potentiae*], assuming this metaphysical principle, "That the total effect is always equal to its complete cause" [*Quod effectus integer sit semper aequalis causae suae plenae*]. When I discovered that this agrees perfectly with experience and satisfies all doubts, I was more confirmed in my opinion that the causes of things are not, so to speak, senseless [*surdus*] and purely mathematical, like the concourse of atoms or the blind force of nature, but proceed from an intelligence which employs metaphysical reasons.' *Phoranomus*, see *Arch. f. Gesch. d. Phil.* i. 577. In the first of these dialogues (*Phoranomus*, &c.) Leibniz says: 'As in geometry and numbers, through the principle of the equality of the whole to all its parts, geometry is brought within the scope of an analytical calculus, so in mechanics, through the principle of the equality of the effect to all its causes or of the cause to all its effects, we obtain certain equations, as it were, and a kind of algebraic mechanics.' *loc. cit.* p. 576. Cf. Introduction to this book, Part iii. p. 107 note.

---

[1] *Phys.* Δ. 4. 212ᵃ 20.

NEW ESSAYS ON THE HUMAN[1] UNDER-STANDING. 1704.

By the Author of the System of Pre-established Harmony.

PREFATORY NOTE.

THE *New Essays* contain the fullest statement of Leibniz's appreciation and criticism of Locke. Leibniz became acquainted with the main outline of Locke's *Essay*, before it was actually published in English, by means of an abstract of the book, prepared by Locke, translated into French and published in Le Clerc's *Bibliothèque Universelle* (1688), vol. 8, pp. 49 sqq. When in 1690 the *Essay* itself was published Leibniz read it, making notes as he went, and his criticisms were expressed in various short papers, some of which were transmitted to Locke through Thomas Burnet of Kemnay. Locke, however, seems rather to have disparaged Leibniz's criticisms and he did not count them worthy of a reply. Meanwhile Locke's *Essay* passed through several editions, and in 1700 Coste's French translation of it was published. This enabled Leibniz, whose knowledge of English was somewhat imperfect, to make a thorough study of the *Essay*, and after writing some papers on special parts of it, he set himself to the task of preparing the elaborate exposition and criticism of the *Essay* which was afterwards published as the *New Essays*. The book was written somewhat hurriedly and discontinuously, during scraps of

---

[1] G., with over-accuracy, omits 'human,' which Leibniz cannot deliberately have intended to omit, for he includes it in the titles of the first three books of the *New Essays*.

leisure time. Accordingly Leibniz, in view of publication, submitted his work to Hugony and Barbeyrac (the great jurist), who revised a considerable portion of it, including the Introduction, and made numerous changes in its expression. Meanwhile a new edition of Coste's translation, revised and corrected by Locke himself, was promised, and Leibniz was strongly advised by Coste to delay publication until after he had seen this new edition. Locke died in the end of 1704, and Leibniz, understanding that he had made considerable changes in his opinions, felt that it was now of little use to publish his own criticism.

Accordingly the *New Essays* remained in manuscript until 1765, when they were published by Raspe. He printed the text in the form which it had finally assumed after the correction and revision of Hugony, Barbeyrac and Leibniz himself. Erdmann (E. 194 sqq.) follows this text. Gerhardt (G. v. 39 sqq.), however, has thought it better to reconstruct the original text, by going behind the corrections, on the ground that, while these corrections often improve the French style of the original, they do not always so well express Leibniz's thought. Boutroux, approving the course taken by Gerhardt, has in various points corrected the text made by that editor. My translation is made from Boutroux's text. Such variations as involve a change in translation are mentioned in foot-notes.

In the Introduction to the *New Essays* (which was written later than the rest of the book), Leibniz summarizes the main points regarding which he differs from Locke, while he characteristically suggests that, after all, the differences between his view and that of Locke are not altogether insurmountable. After some prefatory sentences, the Introduction deals in the first place (*a*) with the question whether (as Locke held) the mind is *tabula rasa* or whether (as Leibniz thought) there are innate ideas, necessary truths, including the question whether or not all our knowledge comes from the senses (pp. 357-367). (*b*) This leads naturally to the question whether (as Locke seems to say) there is nothing in our mind of which we are not actually conscious or whether (as Leibniz maintains) we have unconscious perceptions (pp. 367-385). Leibniz here connects his psychology with his metaphysics by showing how the *petites perceptions* throw light upon the pre-established harmony, the law of continuity, the identity of indiscernibles and the indestructibility of souls, as well as their inseparability from bodies. (c) The next question considered is that of atoms and the void (in which Locke believes) as against a *plenum* (Leibniz's view) (pp. 385 sqq.). (d) References to the criticism of Locke by Stillingfleet lead to a consideration of the question whether matter can think, Locke maintaining the possibility of this, while Stillingfleet and Leibniz deny it (pp. 390 sqq.). This gives occasion to Leibniz to draw a distinction between the physical or real genus of a thing and its logical or ideal genus (p. 394), and in the remainder of the Introduction he applies this distinction, maintaining that as matter and soul are heterogeneous (i.e. not of the same physical or real genus), thinking, which is a mode of soul, cannot be a mode of matter, except by miracle, and that accordingly, if Locke's contention were true, we should have to adopt a philosophy of unintelligible qualities or faculties, which would be even worse than the Scholastic theories of 'occult' qualities or faculties, so justly derided by later thinkers.

INTRODUCTION.

As the *Essay on the Understanding*[2], by an illustrious Englishman, is one of the best and most highly esteemed works of the present time, I have resolved to make some remarks upon it, because, having for a long time given considerable attention to the same subject and to most of the matters with which the essay deals, I have thought that this would be a good occasion for publishing some of my opinions under the title of *New Essays on the Understanding*, in the hope that my thoughts will obtain a favourable[3] reception through appearing in such good company. I have hoped also to be able to profit by the work of another, not only in the way of lessening my own work (as in fact it is less trouble to follow the thread of a good author than to work on entirely untrodden ground)[4], but also in the way of adding some-

---

[2] E. reads 'human understanding.'
[3] E. reads 'more favourable.'
[4] E. omits the clause in brackets.

thing to what he has given us, which is always easier than making an independent beginning [5]. For I think I have removed some difficulties which he left entirely alone. Thus his reputation is helpful to me ; and besides, being disposed to do justice and very far from wishing to lessen the esteem in which his work is held, I would increase his reputation, if my approval have any weight [6]. It is true that I often differ from him in opinion ; but, far from [7] denying the worth of famous writers, we bear witness to it by making known in what respect and for what reasons we differ from their opinion, when we think it necessary to prevent their authority from prevailing against reason on some important points [8] ; and besides, in replying to such excellent men, we make it easier for the truth to be accepted, and it is to be supposed that it is principally for truth that they are working.

In fact, although the author of the *Essay* says a thousand fine things of which I cordially approve, our systems greatly differ. His has more relation to Aristotle and mine to Plato [9], although in many things both of us have

---

[5] E. omits 'always' and adds (after 'beginning'), 'and working on entirely untrodden ground.'

[6] E. omits from 'For I think' to 'any weight.'

[7] E. reads 'denying on that account the worth of this famous writer, I do him justice,' &c.

[8] E. omits the remainder of the sentence, from this point.

[9] The main principles of Leibniz's philosophy are really much more akin to the philosophy of Aristotle than to the doctrines which are peculiar to Plato. But, as regards Aristotle, Leibniz is here thinking of that side of his philosophy which led the Scholastics to attribute to him the saying, *Nihil est in intellectu quod non prius fuerit in sensu.* (Cf. Duns Scotus, *Super Universalibus Porphyrii*, Question 3 : *Illa propositio Aristotelis, nihil est in intellectu quin prius fuerit in sensu. . . .*) This phrase does not occur in any of Aristotle's writings ; but it serves as a fair enough analysis of several passages in the *Posterior Analytics*, in which ἐπιστήμη is traced to αἴσθησις, though other passages supplement this by bringing in the work of νοῦς. (See especially *Anal. Post.* ii. 19, and *Eth.* vi. 3, § 3.) The view that the soul is a *tabula rasa* is suggested by the passage :

departed from the doctrine of these two ancient writers. He is more popular, and I for my part am sometimes compelled to be a little more *acroamatic*[10] and abstract, which is not of advantage to me, especially when a living language is used. But I think that by introducing two speakers, one of whom expounds opinions taken from this author's *Essay*, while the other adds my observations, I show the relation between us in a way that will be more satisfactory to the reader than if I had put down mere remarks, the reading of which would have been constantly interrupted by the necessity of turning to his book in order to understand mine. Nevertheless it will be well also to compare our writings sometimes, and not to judge of his opinions except from his own work, although I have usually retained his expressions. It is true that owing to the limitations involved in following the thread of another person's argument and making remarks upon it, I have been unable even to think of achieving the graceful turns of which dialogue is susceptible; but I hope that the matter will make up for the defects of the style.

δυνάμει πώς ἐστι τὰ νοητὰ ὁ νοῦς, ἀλλ' ἐντελεχείᾳ οὐδέν, πρὶν ἂν νοῇ. δεῖ δ' οὕτως ὥσπερ ἐν γραμματείῳ ᾧ μηθὲν ὑπάρχει ἐντελεχείᾳ γεγραμμένον (*De Anima*, iii. 4. 429^b 30). Cf. note 12, *infra*. In regard to Plato, on the other hand, Leibniz is probably thinking mainly of the Platonic theory of reminiscence, according to which our knowledge of realities, in so far as we can attain to it, is a recollection or restoration of knowledge possessed by the soul in a previous state, so that necessary and eternal truths are, in a sense, innate in us. On the whole matter cf. Nolen, *Quid Leibnizius Aristoteli debuerit*, and Trendelenburg, *Hist. Beiträge*, vol. ii.

[10] i. e. esoteric. See Aulus Gellius, *Noctes Atticae*, xx. 5 (quoted by Ritter and Preller, *Hist. Phil. Graec.* § 298), where a distinction is drawn between the exoteric and the 'acroatic' writings of Aristotle. Leibniz himself defines the word : 'The acroamatic way of philosophizing is that in which all things are demonstrated, the exoteric is that in which certain things are said without demonstration, and yet are confirmed by the consistency they have with various other things and by probable [*topicae*] reasons (or even reasons that might demonstrate, but are put forward only as

The differences between us have regard to subjects [11] of some importance.　There is the question whether the soul, in itself, is entirely empty, like a writing-tablet on which nothing has yet been written (*tabula rasa*), (which is the opinion of Aristotle [12] and of the author of the *Essay*), and whether everything that is inscribed upon it comes solely from the senses and experience; or whether the soul originally contains the principles [13] of several notions and doctrines, which are merely roused on certain occasions by external objects, as I hold along with Plato and even with the Schoolmen, and with all those who interpret in this sense the passage of St. Paul (Romans, ii. 15), in which he shows that the law of God is written in men's hearts.　The Stoics called these principles [14] προλήψεις [15], that is, fundamental assumptions or what

---

probable), and are illustrated by instances and similar cases.'　*De stilo philosophico Nizolii* (1670) (E. 63 a ; G. iv. 146).

[11] E. reads 'objects.'

[12] Cf. note 9. Aristotle's meaning, however, is very different from that of Locke.　ὁ νοῦς is not the 'soul,' but reason as opposed to sense.　And there is a νοῦς ἀπαθής.　The context of the passage in which νοῦς is compared to the writing-tablet shows that Aristotle merely meant to protest against the view that reason has certain complete 'ready-made' ideas, apart from all sense-experience.　But this is quite consistent with holding that there are in reason potential or virtual forms or ideas.　Even the clean writing-tablet is at least a writing-tablet and not a sheet of water on which nothing can be written.　Cf. *De Anima*, iii. 4. 429ᵃ 27 : καὶ εὖ δὴ οἱ λέγοντες τὴν ψυχὴν εἶναι τόπον εἰδῶν, πλὴν ὅτι οὔτε ὅλη ἀλλ' ἡ νοητική, οὔτε ἐντελεχείᾳ ἀλλὰ δυνάμει τὰ εἴδη.　Cf. *Analytica Post.* ii. 19, 99ᵇ 20 sqq.

[13] ἀρχαί, grounds or sources.

[14] E. reads 'common notions' after 'principles.'

[15] The original has *prolepses*.　The Stoic πρόληψις, however, was not an anticipation prior to, or presupposed by, all experience, but the common image resulting from a series of sense-impressions, which leads us to expect other similar impressions.　The distinguishing characteristic of the προλήψεις is that they arise φυσικῶς (naturally), and are not deliberately constructed by us.　Thus Diogenes Laertius, vii. 54 : ἔστι δ' ἡ πρόληψις ἔννοια φυσικὴ τῶν καθόλου.　Cf. *Placita*, iv. 11, quoted by Ritter and Preller, *Hist. Phil. Graec.* § 393, in which the Stoics are represented as holding a view

we take for granted beforehand. Mathematicians call them *common notions* (κοιναὶ ἔννοιαι) [16]. Modern philosophers give them other excellent names; and, in particular, Julius Scaliger [17] named them *semina aeternitatis item zopyra* [18], as much as to say, living fires, flashes of light [*traits lumineux*] [19], hidden within us but appearing at the instance of the senses, like the sparks which come from the steel when it strikes the flint. And not without reason it is thought that these flashes [*éclats*] indicate something divine and eternal, which appears above all in necessary truths. Hence there arises another question, whether all truths are dependent on experience, that is, on induction and instances; or whether there are some which have yet another foundation. For if some events can be foreseen before we have made any trial of them, it is manifest that we contribute

much more akin to that of Locke than to that of Leibniz : οἱ Στωϊκοί φασιν· ὅταν γεννηθῇ ὁ ἄνθρωπος, ἔχει τὸ ἡγεμονικὸν μέρος τῆς ψυχῆς ὥσπερ χάρτην εὔεργον εἰς ἀπογραφήν· εἰς τοῦτο μίαν ἑκάστην τῶν ἐννοιῶν ἐναπογράφεται. But the peculiarity of the Stoic Monism makes it possible to regard this as less inconsistent with Leibniz's view than at first sight it appears to be. Cf. Rendall's *Marcus Aurelius Antoninus*, Introduction, pp. lxxvi-lxxviii ; and Bonhöffer, *Epictet und die Stoa*, pp. 187 sqq.

[16] Euclid calls axioms κοιναὶ ἔννοιαι.

[17] Julius Caesar Scaliger (1484-1558), one of the great scholars of the Renaissance. Among his chief works (besides many translations from Greek into Latin) were a treatise on Latin grammar, *De causis linguae Latinae*, and a book in opposition to the views of Cardan, *Exotericae Exercitationes de Subtilitate ad Hieronymum Cardanum*.

[18] 'Seeds of the eternal and kindling sparks.' The reference is to *Poetice*, Lib. iii. cap. 11. (5th ed., 1617, p. 211) : 'Sunt in nobis insita zopyra quaedam, id est, semina aeternitatis.' For similar expressions cf. *Poetice*, Lib. iii. cap. 1 and 20 ; *Poemata, Pars Altera* (1574), pp. 79 and 160; and *Ad Arnoldum Ferronum Atticum Oratio* (*Epistolae et Orationes*, p. 427). Zopyra is the Greek ζώπυρα, 'lights used for kindling fires.' In the *Laws*, bk. iii. 677 B, Plato speaks of the survivors of the Flood as ἐν κορυφαῖς που σμικρὰ ζώπυρα τοῦ τῶν ἀνθρώπων διασεσωσμένα γένους.

[19] *Trait de lumière* is used in French for an illuminating *thought*, and probably Leibniz's phrase is intended to suggest this.

to them something of our own [20]. The senses, although they are necessary for all our actual acquiring of knowledge, are by no means sufficient to give us the whole of our knowledge, since the senses never give anything but instances [21], that is to say particular or individual truths [22]. Now all the instances which confirm a general truth, however numerous they may be, are not sufficient to establish the universal necessity of this same truth ; for it does not at all follow that what has happened will [23] happen in the same way. For example, the Greeks, the Romans, and all the other peoples of the earth, as it was known to the ancients [24], always observed that before twenty-four hours have passed, day changes into night

[20] E. reads 'on our part.'

[21] i. e. special cases.

[22] In a *Lettre touchant ce qui est indépendant des Sens et de la Matière* written to Queen Sophia Charlotte in 1702 (during the time when he was working at the *New Essays*), Leibniz says : ' We use our external senses as a blind man uses his stick (after the simile of an ancient writer), and they make known to us their particular objects, which are colours, sounds, odours, tastes, and touch-qualities. But they do not make known to us what these sense-qualities are, nor in what they consist. . . . It may be said that *sense-qualities* are in fact *occult qualities*, and that there must be other *more manifest* qualities, which can make them explicable. And far from its being true that we understand things of sense alone, these are the very things we understand least. And although they are familiar to us, we do not on that account comprehend them better, as a pilot does not understand better than other people the nature of the magnetic needle which turns to the north, although he has it always before his eyes in the compass, and on that account has almost ceased to wonder at it. . . . Nevertheless I admit that, in our present state, the external senses are necessary for our thinking, and that, if we had none of them, we should not think. But what is necessary for anything is not on that account the essence of the thing. Air is necessary to us for life ; but our life is something else than air. The senses furnish us with matter for reasoning, and we never have thoughts so abstract that something of sense is not mingled with them ; but reasoning requires in addition something other than that which is of sense.' (G. vi. 499, 500, 506.)

[23] E. adds ' always.'

[24] E. has merely 'and all other peoples.'

and night into day. But they would have been wrong
if they had thought that the same rule is observed
everywhere else[25], for since that time, the opposite has
been experienced[26] by people on a visit to Nova Zembla.
And he would still be wrong who should think that, in
our regions at least, it is a necessary and eternal truth
that shall endure for ever[27], since we must hold that the
earth and the sun itself do not exist necessarily, and that
perhaps there will come a time when this beautiful star
with its whole system will no longer exist, at least in its
present form[28]. Whence it seems that necessary truths,
such as we find in pure mathematics and especially in
arithmetic and geometry, must have principles whose
proof does not depend upon instances nor, consequently,
upon the witness of the senses, although without the
senses it would never have come into our heads to think
of them. This is a point which should be carefully noted,
and it is one which Euclid so well understood that he
often proves by reason that which is evident enough
through experience and through sense-images[29]. Logic
also, along with metaphysics and ethics [la morale], of
which the one forms natural theology[30] and the other
natural jurisprudence, are full of such truths ; and consequently their demonstration[31] can come only from the

[25] E. omits ' else.' [26] E. reads ' seen.'

[27] E. omits ' that shall endure for ever.'

[28] Cf. *Monadology*, § 28.

[29] Cf. the letter to Queen Sophia Charlotte, quoted above: 'The
senses can indeed in a way make known to us that which is, but
they cannot make known that which ought to be or which cannot
be otherwise. . . . The senses and inductions never yield us truth
perfectly universal nor that which is absolutely necessary, but only
that which is and that which occurs in particular instances.'
(G. vi. 504, 505.)

[30] 'True metaphysics is hardly different from true logic, that is
to say, from the art of discovery in general ; for in fact metaphysics
is natural theology, and the same God, who is the source of all good
things, is also the principle of all parts of knowledge.' *Lettre à la
Princesse Sophie* (undated) (G. iv. 292).

[31] i.e. the certainty of logic, metaphysics and ethics as sciences.

inner principles which are called innate.   It is true we
must not imagine that we can read these eternal laws of
reason in the soul as in an open book[32], as the edict
of the praetor may be read on his *album*[33] without trouble
or investigation ; but it is enough that we can discover
these laws in ourselves by means of attention, for which
opportunities are furnished by the senses ; and the
success of experiments serves also as a confirmation of
reason, somewhat as in arithmetic ' proofs' are useful in
helping us to avoid errors of calculation when the process
is a long one.   In this also lies the difference between
human knowledge and that of the lower animals.   The
lower animals are purely empirical and direct themselves by particular instances alone ; for, so far as we can
judge, they never succeed in forming necessary propositions ; while men, on the other hand, have the capacity
for demonstrative science.   It is also on this account that
the power of making *concatenations* [of ideas] which the
lower animals possess is something inferior to the reason
which is in men[34].   The concatenations [of ideas] made by
the lower animals are simply like those of mere empirics,
who maintain that what has sometimes happened will
happen again in a case which resembles the former in
characteristics which strike them, although[35] they are
incapable of judging whether or not the same reasons
hold good in both cases.   That is why it is so simple
a matter for men to entrap animals, and so easy for
mere empirics to make mistakes.   From this making of
mistakes even persons who have become skilful through
age and experience are not exempt, when they trust too
much to their past experience, as some have done in civil
and military affairs ; because enough consideration is
not given to the fact that the world changes and that

[32] *à livre ouvert*, lit. = *ad aperturam libri.*

[33] i. e. the tablets with 'notices,' posted up in a public place, so
that he who runs may read.

[34] Cf. *Monadology*, §§ 26-29.   [35] E. adds ' for all that.'

men become more skilful by finding countless new con-
trivances, while on the other hand the stags or the hares
of our time do not become[36] more full of shifts than
those of former times. The concatenations [of ideas] in
the lower animals are only a shadow of reasoning, that is
to say they are only connexions[37] of imagination and
passings[37] from one image to another, because in new
circumstances which seem to resemble others which have
occurred before we[38] expect anew what we[38] at other
times found along with them, as if things were actually
connected together because their images are connected in
memory. It is true that reason also leads us to expect,
as a rule, that there will occur in the future what is in
harmony with a long experience of the past, but this is,
nevertheless, not a necessary and infallible truth; and
our forecast may fail when we least expect it, because
the reasons which have hitherto justified it no longer
operate[39]. And on this account the wisest people do not
trust altogether to experience, but try, so far as possible,
to get some hold of the reason of what happens, in order
to decide when exceptions must be made. For reason
is alone capable of laying down trustworthy rules and

[36] E. reads ‘are not.’
[37] E. reads ‘a connexion’ and ‘a passing.’
[38] E. reads ‘they.’
[39] Cf. *Lettre à la Reine Sophie Charlotte* (1702) : ‘For instance, though
we may have observed a thousand times that iron, when it is put
by itself on the surface of water, goes to the bottom, we have no
assurance that it must always be so. And without referring to the
miracle of the prophet Elisha who made iron to swim, we know
that we can make an iron pot so hollow that it floats, and that it
can even carry a considerable load, as do boats made of copper and
tin. And even abstract sciences, like geometry, afford instances in
which that which usually happens no longer happens. For
instance, we usually find that two lines which continually approach
one another ultimately meet, and many people will be ready to
take oath that this can never fail to happen. Nevertheless geometry makes known to us unusual lines (called, on that account,
Asymptotes) which, if prolonged to infinity, continually approach one
another and yet never meet.’ (G. vi. 505.)

of supplying what is lacking in those which were not trustworthy, by stating the exceptions to them, and in short of finding sure connexions in the force of necessary consequences; and this often enables us to foresee the event without having to experience the sense-connexions of images, to which the animals are confined, so that that which shows that the sources [*principes*] of necessary truths are within us also distinguishes man from the lower animals.

Perhaps our able author may not entirely differ from me in opinion. For after having devoted the whole of his first book to the rejection of innate knowledge [*lumières*], understood in a certain sense, he nevertheless admits, at the beginning of the second book and in those which follow, that the ideas which do not originate in sensation come from reflexion. Now reflexion is nothing but an attention to that which is in us, and the senses do not give us what we already bring with us. That being so, can it be denied that there is much that is innate in our mind [*esprit*], since we are, so to speak, innate to ourselves, and since in ourselves there are being, unity, substance, duration, change, activity [*action*], perception, pleasure and a thousand other objects of our intellectual ideas [40]? And as these objects are immediate objects of our understanding and are always present [41] (although they cannot always be consciously perceived [*aperçus*] because of our distractions and wants), why should it be surprising that we say that these ideas, along with all that depends on them, are innate in us? Accordingly I have taken as illustration a block of veined

[40] As distinguished from ideas or images of sense. Cf. *Monadology*, § 30, and *Principles of Nature and of Grace*, § 5; also *Petit discours de Métaphysique* (1686) (G. iv. 452): 'Those expressions which are in our soul, whether they are conceived or not, may be called *ideas*, but those which are conceived or formed may be said to be *notions*, *conceptus*.'

[41] E. reads 'these objects are immediate and always present to our understanding.'

marble, rather than a block of perfectly uniform marble or than empty tablets, that is to say, what is called by philosophers *tabula rasa*. For if the soul were like these empty tablets, truths would be in us as the figure of Hercules is in a block of marble, when the block of marble is indifferently capable of receiving this figure or any other. But if there were in the stone veins, which should mark out the figure of Hercules rather than other figures, the stone would be more determined towards this figure, and Hercules would somehow be, as it were, innate in it, although labour would be needed to uncover the veins and to clear them by polishing and thus removing what prevents them from being fully seen. It is thus that ideas and truths are innate in us, as natural inclinations, dispositions, habits or powers [*virtualités*] [42], and not as activities [*actions*], although these powers [*virtualités*] are always accompanied by some activities [*actions*], often imperceptible, which correspond to them.

Our able author seems to maintain that there is in us nothing *virtual*, and even nothing of which we are not always actually conscious [43]. But this cannot be understood in a strict sense ; otherwise his opinion would be too paradoxical, since, for instance [44], we are not always conscious

[42] Cf. *Monadology*, §§ 40, 43 and 54, with the notes. By a *virtualité* Leibniz means something between a mere potency or capacity and a fully-developed activity or actual idea. Thus necessary and eternal truths are not innate in the soul in a fully-developed form, nor, on the other hand, does the soul merely have a capacity for receiving or acquiring them, but they are innate in germ, as imperfectly perceived ideas with a tendency to become perfectly perceived. See Introduction, Part iii. pp. 125 sqq. and 130.

[43] Cf. Locke's *Essay*, bk. i. ch. 1, § 5. This position is an immediate result of Cartesian principles. See Introduction, Part iii. p. 126. Cf. Geulincx, *Metaphysica Vera*, Part i. (*Opera*, Land's ed., vol. ii. p. 150) : 'It is impossible that he who does not know how a thing is done should do it. If you do not know how a thing is done you do not do it.'

[44] E. reads 'since, although we are not, &c. . . . we often bring, &c.'

of acquired habits and of the things stored in our memory, and, indeed, they do not always come to our aid when we require them, although we often bring them back easily into our mind on some slight occasion which recalls them to us, as we need only the beginning of a song in order to remember it [45]. Our author also limits his thesis in other places, saying that there is in us nothing of which we have not at least been conscious [aperçus] formerly. But in addition to the fact that nobody can, through reason alone, be quite certain how far our past *apperceptions* have extended, for we may have forgotten them, especially in light of the Platonic doctrine of reminiscence, which, though a myth [46], contains, in part at least [47], nothing incompatible with bare reason—in addition, I say, to this fact, why must everything be acquired by us through apperception of external things, and why should it be impossible to unearth anything in

[45] E reads 'to make us remember the rest of it.'

[46] Leibniz's objection to the Platonic doctrine is that it implies a complete (or clear and distinct) knowledge of the 'ideas' in a previous state. He accepts the Platonic doctrine in so far as it implies that knowledge of the eternally true comes to the soul not through external sense, but by development from its own inner being. Cf. *Nouveaux Essais*, bk. i. ch. 1, § 5 (E. 209 a ; G. v. 75) : ' It was the opinion of the Platonists that all our ideas [*connaissances*] were reminiscences, and that thus the truths which the soul brings with it at a man's birth, and which are called innate, must be remains of a former definite knowledge. But this opinion has no foundation. And we may readily believe that the soul must have already had innate ideas [*connaissances*] in its preceding state (if it did pre-exist), however far back that state might be, just as it has them now ; accordingly they must in turn have come from another preceding state, in which they would ultimately be innate, or at least created along with it ; or else we should have to go *ad infinitum* and regard souls as eternal, in which case these ideas [*connaissances*] would in fact be innate, because they would never have had a beginning in the soul ; and if any one maintains that each prior state has received from another, prior to itself, something which it has not transmitted to those which follow, the answer is that it is manifest that certain evident truths must have belonged to all these states.'

[47] E. omits ' in part at least.'

ourselves? Is our soul, then, so empty that, beyond [48] images borrowed from outside, it is nothing? That, I am sure, is not a view which our judicious author can approve. And where shall we find tablets which have not some variety in themselves? For there is never [49] such a thing as a perfectly unbroken [*uni*] and uniform surface. Why, then, should not we also be able to provide ourselves with some sort [50] of thought out of our own inner being, when we deliberately try to penetrate its depths [51]? Thus I am led to believe that his opinion on this point is not fundamentally different from mine, or rather from the common opinion, inasmuch as he recognizes two sources of our knowledge, the senses and reflexion [52].

I do not know that it will be so easy to reconcile him with us and with the Cartesians, when he maintains that the mind does not always think, and especially that it is without perception when we sleep without dreaming; and he holds that, since bodies can exist without motion, souls might also quite well exist without thinking [53]. But here I reply in a way somewhat different from that which is usual; for I maintain that, naturally [54], a sub-

[48] E. reads 'without.'

[49] In E. the sentence is interrogative : ' Is there ever,' &c.

[50] E. reads 'object.'

[51] Leibniz is here applying his principle of the 'identity of indiscernibles,' viz. that no two things are absolutely identical, which implies that no real thing is an absolute unity, exclusive of all difference or variety, but that everything has some essential characteristic or internal quality. See *Monadology*, § 9.

[52] If the mind is really *tabula rasa*, what are those 'internal operations' or 'actings of our own minds,' which Locke regards as the objects of reflexion? Leibniz suggests that Locke may not really mean all that he seems to mean by the *tabula rasa*, and that, accordingly, Locke is fundamentally at one with him in admitting at least innate 'dispositions.'

[53] *Essay*, bk. ii. ch. 1, § 9 (Fraser's ed., vol. i. p. 127). See Introduction, Part iii. p. 129.

[54] i. e. 'in the ordinary course of things,' 'otherwise than by miracle.'

stance cannot exist without activity [*action*], and indeed
that there never is a body without motion. Experience
is already in my favour as regards this, and to be persuaded of it one has only to refer to the book of the
illustrious Mr. Boyle [55] against an absolute rest. But
I think that reason also supports it, and this is one of the
proofs which I use to overthrow the theory of atoms [56].

Besides there are countless indications which lead us
to think that there is at every moment an infinity of
perceptions within us, but without apperception and
without reflexion; that is to say, changes in the soul
itself of which we are not conscious [*s'apercevoir*], because
the impressions are either too small and too numerous
or too closely combined [*trop unies*], so that each is not
distinctive enough by itself, but nevertheless in combination with others each has its effect and makes itself
felt, at least confusedly, in the whole. Thus it is that,
through being accustomed to it, we take no notice of the
motion of a mill or a waterfall when we have for some
time lived quite near them. Not that this motion does
not continually affect our organs, nor that something
does not pass into the soul, which responds to it because
of the harmony of the soul and the body, but these
impressions which are in the soul and in the body,

[55] Robert Boyle (b. Lismore, 1627, d. London, 1691), the famous
chemist and physicist, who (almost contemporaneously with
Mariotte) discovered the law of the pressure of gases, which is
called the Boyle-Mariotte law. He maintained that there is no
such thing as absolute rest, in the book here referred to, under the
title *Of Absolute Rest in Bodies.* [Boyle's *Works* (London, 1744), vol. i.
p. 281.] It was also published in Latin in his *Opera Varia* (Geneva,
1680). Leibniz had some intercourse with Boyle during his stay
in London in 1673. See Introduction, Part i. p. 7.

[56] As rest is infinitely small motion, everything moves. Consequently the essence of body cannot be absolutely unmoved
extension, but must be force, which is the source of motion. But
a force is a real unity, absolutely indivisible, while the atom is only
physically indivisible, it being ideally divisible. Hence physical
atoms are not the elements of things. Cf. *New System*, § 11.

having lost the attractions of novelty, are not strong enough to attract our attention and our memory, busied [57] with more engrossing objects. For [58] all attention requires memory, and often [59] when we are not, so to speak, admonished [59] and warned to take notice of some of our present perceptions, we let them pass without reflexion and even without observing them; but if some one directs our attention to them immediately afterwards [60], and for instance bids us notice some sound that has just been heard, we remember it, and we are conscious that we had some feeling of it at the time. Thus there were perceptions of which we were not immediately conscious [*s'apercevoir*], apperception arising in this case only from our attention being directed to them after [61] some interval, however small. And for an even better understanding of the *petites perceptions* which we cannot individually distinguish in the crowd, I am wont to employ the illustration of the moaning or sound of the sea, which we notice when we are on the shore. In order to hear this sound as we do, we must hear the parts of which the whole sound is made up, that is to say the sounds [62] which come from each wave, although each of these little sounds makes itself known only in the confused combination of all the sounds taken together, that is to say, in the moaning of the sea [63], and no one of the sounds would be observed if the wave which makes it were alone. For we must be affected a little by the motion of this wave, and we must have some perception of each of these sounds, however little they may be; otherwise we should not have the perception of a hundred thousand waves, for a hundred thousand

[57] E. reads 'which are busied only.'   [58] E. omits 'for.'

[59] E. omits 'often' and 'admonished and.'

[60] E. omits 'afterwards.'

[61] E. reads 'in this case of our attention being directed to them only after,' &c.

[62] E. reads 'sound.'

[63] E. omits 'that is to say, in the moaning of the sea.'

nothings cannot make something. We never sleep so
profoundly as not to have some feeble and confused
feeling, and we should never be wakened by the greatest
noise in the world if we had not some perception of its
beginning which is small, just as we should never break
a cord by the greatest effort [64] in the world, if it were
not strained and stretched a little by less efforts, though
the small extension they produce is not apparent [65].

These *petites perceptions* have thus through their consequences [66] an influence greater than people think. It is
they that form this something I know not what, these
tastes, these images of sense-qualities, clear in combination
but confused in the parts [67], these impressions which

[64] G. reads 'effect.'

[65] Cf. Montaigne, *Essais*, bk. ii. ch. 14 : 'If we suppose a piece
of twine equally strong throughout, it is utterly impossible that it
should ever break. For in what part of it is the breaking to begin,
the flaw to appear? And for it to break in every part at once is
against all nature.' See Introduction, Part iii. p. 144 note.

[66] E. omits 'through their consequences.'

[67] Sense-qualities, according to Leibniz, are each *clear* as a whole,
that is to say, each can be perfectly distinguished from others.
But they are not also *distinct* ; that is to say, we cannot perfectly
analyze their elements. Such an analysis is possible ; but *we* cannot
perform it, for it would involve an infinite process. Each sense-
quality 'contains infinity,' for it has connexions with everything
else in the universe. Cf. *Lettre à la Reine Sophie Charlotte* (1702) :
'We know by what kind of refraction blue and yellow are made,
and that these two colours when mixed make green. But we
cannot yet understand, for all that, how our perception of green
results from our perceptions of the two colours which compose it,
nor how our perceptions of these colours arise from their causes. We
have not even nominal definitions of such qualities so as to explain
the terms for them. . . . If I were to say to some one : You know that
green means a colour consisting of blue and yellow mixed, he would
not make use of this definition as a means of recognizing green
when he came upon it. But this is the function of nominal
definitions. For the blue and the yellow which are in the green
are not distinguishable or recognizable, and it is only by chance, so
to speak, that we have found this by observing that this mixture
always makes green. Thus the only way to enable a man to
recognize green in future is to show it to him at present ; but this

surrounding bodies make upon us, who contain infinity[68], this connexion which each being has with all the rest of the universe. It may even be said that in consequence of these *petites perceptions* the present is big with[69] the future and laden with the past, that there is a conspiration of all things (σύμπνοια πάντα, as Hippocrates said[70]), and that in the least of substances eyes as penetrating as those of God might read the whole succession of the things of the universe,

Quae sint, quae fuerint, quae mox futura trahantur[71].

These unconscious [*insensible*] perceptions also indicate and constitute the identity of the individual, who is characterized by the traces or expressions[72] of his previous states which these unconscious perceptions preserve, as they connect his previous states with his present state; and these unconscious perceptions[73] may be known by

is not necessary in the case of more distinct notions, which can be made known to people by description, although we do not have them at hand.... For this reason we are wont to say that the *notions* of sense-qualities are *clear*, for they enable us to recognize the qualities; but that these notions are not *distinct*, because we cannot discriminate nor unfold what they contain within them. What they contain is an *I know not what*, of which we are conscious but of which we can give no account.' (Passages combined from G. vi. 492, 493, 500.)

[68] E. reads 'and which contain infinity.'

[69] E. reads 'full of.'

[70] See *Monadology*, note 97.

[71] 'What things are, what things have been, and what future things may soon be brought forth.' Virgil, *Georgics*, iv. 393. Virgil ascribes this knowledge to Proteus. Leibniz misquotes *futura* for *ventura*: *futura* would not scan.

[72] E. omits 'or expressions.'

[73] Leibniz merely says 'and they,' so that the reference is doubtful. He may mean 'the traces of previous states.' What is meant is simply that as the unconscious perceptions are the development of previous states of perception and at the same time contain, in a germinal or confused way, all future states of perception, they give continuity to the individual possessing them, i. e. they constitute his identity. Contrast Locke's view, *Essay*, bk. ii. ch. 27. Cf. *Monadology*, note 114.

a higher mind [*esprit*], although the individual himself
may not be conscious of them, that is to say, though he
may no longer have a definite recollection of them.   But
they [these perceptions] furnish also the means of re-
covering this recollection, when it is needed, through
periodic developments which may some day occur[74].   That
is why death, owing to these perceptions[75], can only be
a sleep, and cannot even last as a sleep, for in animals
perceptions merely cease to be distinct [*distingué*] enough[76],
and are reduced to a state of confusion, in which consciousness [*aperception*] is suspended, but which cannot
last for ever[77], not to speak here of man who must have
great privileges in this regard in order to keep his
personality[78].

Further, the unconscious [*insensible*] perceptions explain[79] that wonderful pre-established harmony of body
and soul, and indeed of all Monads or simple substances,
which takes the place of the untenable theory of the
influence of one upon another, and which, in the opinion

---

[74] What is meant is that, as perceptions are not isolated but
linked together, they do not each independently rise and fall in
distinctness by a kind of chance, but as one group or system of
perceptions falls out of consciousness another rises into consciousness, so that there is a kind of periodicity in our perceptions, with
troughs and crests as in wave-motion. Thus the recollection of any
former perception means that the system or group of which it is
a member has passed from the crest of consciousness to the trough
of sub-consciousness and so back to the crest again. Cf. *Considérations
sur la Doctrine d'un Esprit Universel Unique* (1702) (E. 181 a ; G. vi.
535): 'The organs' [of the animal] 'are merely "enveloped" and
reduced to a small size, but the order of nature requires that some
day all shall re-develop and return to an observable condition, and
that in these vicissitudes there be a certain well-ordered progress,
which serves to mature things and to bring them to perfection.'
For a development of this idea cf. James's *Psychology*, vol. i. ch. 9.

[75] E. omits 'owing to these perceptions.'

[76] i. e. distinct enough to produce consciousness.

[77] The remainder of this sentence is omitted by E.

[78] Cf. *Principles of Nature and of Grace*, § 12, note 51 ; *Monadology*, § 82,
note 130.   See also Introduction, Part iii. p. 116.

[79] E. reads ' by the unconscious perceptions I explain.'

of the author of the most excellent of Dictionaries [80], exalts the greatness of the Divine perfections beyond what has ever been conceived. After this I should add little, if I were to say that [81] it is these *petites perceptions* which *determine* us on many occasions without our thinking it, and which deceive people by the appearance of an *indifference of equilibrium*, as if, for instance, we were completely [82] indifferent whether to turn to the right or to the left [83]. It is also unnecessary for me to point out here, as I have done in the book itself, that they cause that *uneasiness* which I show to consist in something which differs from pain only as the small from the great, and which nevertheless often constitutes our desire and even our pleasure, giving to it a kind of stimulating relish [84]. It is also due to these unconscious [*insensible*] parts of our conscious [*sensible*] perceptions that there is a relation between these perceptions of colour, heat, and other sensible qualities, and the motions in bodies which correspond to them; while the Cartesians, along with our author, in spite of all his penetration, regard the perceptions we have of these qualities as arbitrary, that is to say, as if God had given them to the soul according to His good pleasure, without regard to any essential relation between the perceptions and their objects; an opinion which surprises me, and which seems to me not very worthy of the wisdom of the Author of things, who does nothing without harmony and without reason [85].

[80] Pierre Bayle. See *Monadology*, § 16, notes 28 and 29. The reference is to the article *Rorarius* in Bayle's *Dictionary*, where he says (note L, 1): 'It' [the system of pre-established harmony] 'exalts above all that can be conceived the power and intelligence of Divine art.' Bayle, however, makes this remark by way of objection to the system.

[81] E. reads 'after this I ought also to add that.'

[82] E. omits 'completely.'

[83] Cf. Introduction, Part iii. p. 141.

[84] Cf. Introduction, Part iii. p. 140.

[85] See Descartes, *Principia*, Part iv. §§ 196–198 and 204. Descartes

In a word, *unconscious* [*insensible*] *perceptions* are of as great use in pneumatics [86] as imperceptible [*insensible*] [87] corpuscles are in physics; and it is as unreasonable to reject the one as the other on the ground that they are beyond the reach of our senses [88]. Nothing takes place all at once, and it is one of my great maxims, one among the most completely verified of maxims, that *nature never makes leaps;* which I called the *law of continuity* [89] when I spoke of it in the first [90] *Nouvelles de la République des Lettres* [91]; and the use of this law in physics is very considerable: it is to the effect that we always pass from

held that 'colour, heat,' &c., as we perceive them, are not to be attributed to external bodies, the qualities of which are all forms of motion. There is on his view no absolute reason why one kind of motion should produce in us the sensation of colour and another the sensation of heat. Leibniz, on the other hand, regards motions as themselves perceptions of a very low degree of distinctness, and the unconscious perceptions which in combination give rise to our conscious sensation form a connecting link between the motions of bodies and our corresponding sense-perception of their qualities.

[86] A name for the philosophy of mind or spirit, derived from the New Testament use of πνεῦμα. In Scholastic times it included natural theology and the doctrines regarding angels and demons, as well as 'psychology.' In the seventeenth century it was used in the more limited sense by Alsted in his *Encyklopädie* (1630), a work which, according to Diderot, Leibniz thought of re-modelling, with the assistance of other scholars (*Œuvres de Diderot*, ed. Assézat, vol. xv. p. 440). Cf. G. vii. 67. The terms *Pneumaticks* and *Pneumatology* (in the sense of philosophy of the mind) were used in the Scottish Universities in the end of the seventeenth and beginning of the eighteenth centuries. The word *Pneumatics* has now ceased to have any connexion with the philosophy of mind and is used to describe the branch of hydrodynamics which is concerned with gases.

[87] E. omits 'imperceptible [*insensible*].'

[88] The reference is probably to the views of Descartes. See *Principia*, Part iv. § 201.

[89] Cf. Introduction, Part ii. p. 37; Part iii. p. 83.

[90] E. reads 'when I spoke of it elsewhere in the *Nouvelles*,' &c.

[91] This was Bayle's magazine, and Leibniz formulated his law for the first time in the letter to Bayle (1687) to which reference is here made. (See G. iii. 51; E. 104.) For a translation of this see Introduction, Part iii. p. 83 note.

small to great, and *vice versa*, through that which is intermediate in degrees as in parts [92] ; and that a motion never immediately arises from rest nor is immediately reduced to rest, but comes or goes through a smaller motion, just as we never completely traverse any line or length without having traversed a smaller line, although hitherto those who have laid down the laws of motion have not observed this law, and have thought that a body can in a moment receive a motion contrary to that which it had immediately before [93]. And all this leads us to think that *noticeable perceptions* also [94] come by degrees from those which are too small to be noticed. To think otherwise is to know little of the illimitable fineness [*subtilité*] of things, which always and everywhere contains [*enveloppe*] an actual infinity [95].

I have also noticed that, in virtue of imperceptible [*insensible*] variations, two individual things cannot be perfectly alike, and that they must always differ more than *numero* [96]. This makes an end of 'the empty tablets of the soul,' 'a soul without thought,' 'a substance without activity' [*action*], 'the void in space,' 'atoms,' and

[92] i. e. in degree as in quantity.

[93] Cf. Introduction, Part iii. pp. 87 sqq.

[94] E. omits 'also.'

[95] See *Monadology*, § 65, note 107.

[96] Cf. Introduction, Part ii. pp. 36 sqq. Also *Monadology*, § 9, note 15, and *Nouveaux Essais*, bk. ii. ch. 27, § 1 (E. 277 b ; G. v. 213): ' Besides the difference of time and place, there must always be an internal *principle* of *distinction*, and although there are several things of the same kind, it is nevertheless true that none of them are ever perfectly alike. Thus although time and place (that is to say, external relation) enable us to distinguish things, which we do not readily distinguish by themselves, the things are none the less distinguishable in themselves. The exact determination of *identity* and *diversity* is not a matter of time and place, although it is true that the diversity of things is accompanied by that of time and place ; because they' [i. e. time and place] 'bring with them different impressions about the thing. Not to mention the fact that it is rather by means of the things that we must distinguish one place or time from another, for in themselves they are perfectly alike, but of course they are not substances or complete realities.'

even particles not actually divided in matter, 'absolute rest,' 'complete uniformity in one part of time, place or matter,' 'perfect globes of the second element, arising from original perfect cubes [97],' and a thousand other fictions of philosophers, which come from their incomplete notions and which the nature of things does not admit of, and which are made passable by our ignorance and the slight attention we give to the imperceptible [*insensible*], but which cannot be made tolerable unless in the limited sense of abstractions of the mind, which protests that it does not deny what it sets aside and thinks ought not to come into any present consideration. Otherwise, if we seriously meant this, namely that the things of which we are not conscious [*s'apercevoir*] are neither in the soul nor in the body, we should err in philosophy as is done in statecraft [*politique*], when no account is taken of τὸ μικρόν [98], imperceptible [*insensible*]

[97] The reference is to the vortex hypothesis of Descartes. According to Descartes, as body is ultimately extension in three dimensions, the original division of it (as the result of motion imparted by God) would result in perfectly cubical parts. This original motion Descartes supposes to have been such as to make the parts revolve on their own axes and also in groups round different centres. As a result of this (matter being a *plenum*) the angles of the cubes are rubbed down, and the detrition proceeds at an ever-increasing rate, because the smaller the body, the larger (in proportion to its bulk) is the surface it exposes to the rubbing of other bodies. Accordingly there are three primary elements of the visible world, (1) the detritus, which includes the sun and the fixed stars, (2) the remains of the original cubes in the form of exceedingly minute globules, of which element the sky consists, and (3) some parts of matter which have been less easy to move than the globules of the second element and consequently have not been rubbed down so quickly; such as the earth, the planets and comets. In short, the first element consists of luminous bodies, the second of transparent bodies and the third of opaque bodies. See Descartes, *Principia*, Part iii. §§ 46 sqq. In a letter to Nicaise (1692) Leibniz speaks about the 'useless chatter regarding little bodies and the first, second or third element, which are of as little value as the occult qualities' (G. ii. 534).

[98] Δεῖ . . . τὸ μικρὸν φυλάττειν (Aristotle, *Politics*, v. 8, § 2, 1307[b] 32).

progressions; but on the other hand an abstraction is not an error, provided we know that what we ignore is actually there. So mathematicians make use of abstractions when they speak of the perfect lines which they ask us to consider, the uniform motions and other regular effects, although *matter* (that is to say, the intermingling of the effects of the surrounding infinite[99]) always makes some exception. We proceed thus in order to discriminate conditions [*considérations*] from one another and in order to reduce effects to their grounds [*raisons*], as far as possible, and to foresee some of their consequences: for the more we are careful to neglect none of the conditions which we can control, the more does practice correspond to theory[100]. But it belongs only to the supreme reason, which nothing escapes, to comprehend distinctly all the infinite and to see[101] all grounds [*raisons*] and all consequences. All that we can do as regards infinities is to recognize them confusedly, and to know at least distinctly that they are there; otherwise[102] we have a very poor idea of the beauty and greatness of the universe, and also we cannot have a sound physics, which explains the nature of bodies[103] in general, and still less a sound pneumatics[104], which includes the knowledge of God, of souls, and of simple substances in general.

This knowledge of unconscious [*insensible*] perceptions serves also to explain why and how no two souls, human

The chapter deals with maxims for avoiding revolutions. § 3 refers to the fallacy of the spendthrift: 'Each expense is little, therefore the whole is little.' Cf. *Politics*, v. 4, § 1, 1303[b] 18 : γίνονται μὲν οὖν αἱ στάσεις οὐ περὶ μικρῶν ἀλλ' ἐκ μικρῶν.

[99] E. reads 'the infinite which surrounds us.'

[100] That is to say, the more do actual occurrences correspond to our explanation of them.

[101] E. omits ' and to see.'

[102] 'Otherwise' = 'but if we entirely ignore the infinities in things.'

[103] E. reads 'things.'

[104] See note 86.

or other, of one and the same kind [103], ever come perfectly
alike from the hands of the Creator, and each has always
from the first a reference to the point of view it will have
in the universe [106]. But this indeed follows already from
what I observed regarding two individuals, namely, that
their *difference* is always *more than a numerical one.* There
is also another important point, as to which I must differ,
not only from the opinions of our author, but also from
those of the majority of modern writers. I believe, with
the majority of the ancients, that all superhuman spirits
[*génies*], all souls, all created simple substances are always
combined [107] with a body, and that there never are souls
entirely separated [from body] [108]. I have *a priori* reasons
for this, but it will also be found that the doctrine is of
advantage in this respect, that it solves all the philosophical difficulties about the state of souls [109], about their
perpetual preservation, about their immortality and about
their working ; for the difference between one state of
the soul and another never is and never has been anything but a difference between the more and the less
conscious [*sensible*], the more and the less perfect, or vice
versa, and thus the past or the future state of the soul
is as explicable as its present state [110]. The slightest
reflexion makes it sufficiently evident that this is in
accordance with reason, and that a leap from one state to
another infinitely different state could not be natural.
I am surprised that the philosophic schools have without
reason given up natural explanation [111], and have deliberately plunged themselves into very great difficulties and

[103] E. reads 'no two human souls or two things of one and the
same kind.'

[106] Cf. *Monadology*, §§ 51 sqq.

[107] E. omits 'combined,' reading '*sont toujours à un corps.*'

[108] God alone is *actus purus*, without body. Cf. Introduction,
Part iii. pp. 108 sqq., and *Monadology*, § 72, note 115.

[109] This probably means questions as to what has been the state
of souls in the past and what will be their state in the future.

[110] See Introduction, Part iii. pp. 113 sqq.

[111] E. reads 'nature.'

given occasion for the apparent triumphs of freethinkers
[*esprits forts*][112], all of whose arguments fall at once
through this explanation of things, according to which
there is no more difficulty in conceiving the preservation
of souls (or rather, as I think, of the animal), than there
is in the change of the caterpillar into the butterfly, and
in the preservation of thought during sleep, to which
Jesus Christ has divinely likened death[113]. But then
I have already said that no sleep can last for ever; and
it will last for the shortest time or almost not at all in
the case of rational souls, which are destined always to
preserve the personal character [*personnage*] which has
been given them in the City of God, and consequently
to retain memory; and this is so, in order that they may
be more susceptible of punishments and rewards. And
I add further that no derangement of its visible organs
is capable of reducing things to complete confusion in
an animal, or of destroying all its organs and depriving

---

[112] Cf. *Monadology*, § 14, note 25. See also *Considérations sur la
Doctrine d'un Esprit Universel Unique* (1702) (G. vi. 532; E. 179 b):
'What has also, in my opinion, contributed greatly towards
making men of intellect believe in the doctrine of a single universal spirit is this, that ordinary philosophers have set forth
a doctrine about souls separate [from bodies] and about the
, functions of the soul being independent of the body and its organs,
which doctrine they could not sufficiently justify. They were
perfectly right in wishing to maintain the immortality of the soul
as in conformity with the Divine perfections and with a genuine
morality, but seeing that by death those organs in animals which
we observe are deranged and ultimately corrupted, they thought
it necessary to have recourse to separated souls, that is to say, to
the opinion that the soul continues to exist without any body and
none the less retains its thoughts and functions. And in order to
give a better proof of this they tried to show that the soul has
already in this life thoughts which are abstract and independent
of ideas of matter. Now those who rejected this separated condition and independence [of the soul] as contrary to experience
and to reason were so much the more led to believe in the
extinction of the individual soul and the preservation of the
universal spirit alone.'
[113] St. John xi. ver. 11.

the soul of the whole of its organic body and of the ineffaceable remains of all its former impressions [114]. But the ease with which people have given up the ancient doctrine that the angels have ethereal [subtils] bodies connected with them (which has been confounded with the corporeality of the angels themselves), the introduction of supposed unembodied [séparés] intelligences among created things (to which Aristotle's theory of intelligences that make the skies revolve has greatly contributed) [115], and finally the ill-considered opinion people

[114] Cf. *Monadology*, §§ 72-77; *New System*, §§ 7 and 8.

[115] According to Aristotle the heavens are moved by the πρῶτον κινοῦν or prime mover, i. e. by God, who (as Leibniz also admits) is *actus purus*. But this is an eternal (ἀίδιον) motion, and Aristotle describes the heavens as σῶμά τι θεῖον (*De Caelo*, ii. 3, 286ᵃ 11). Accordingly the heavens are not moved by '*intelligences*.' On the other hand, Aristotle represents the planets as having motions of their own, different from that of the fixed stars or the sphere of the heavens in general. These planetary motions are attributed to an activity (πρᾶξις) similar to that which exists in animals and plants (*De Caelo*, ii. 12, 292ᵇ 1). But even so, Aristotle cannot be regarded as meaning that the planets are moved by 'separate' intelligences. It seems likely that Leibniz was thinking of the views of Thomas Aquinas, who says: 'A heavenly body is moved by some intellectual substance' (*Contra Gentes*, iii. 23, 1); and also : 'Heavenly bodies are moved by the substances which move them through apprehension : not however a sense-apprehension .... and therefore an intellectual one.' At the end of the chapter quoted, he says: 'For our present purpose it does not matter whether a heavenly body is moved by an intellectual substance conjoined with it as its soul, or by a separate substance : or whether each of the heavenly bodies is moved by God or none of them is immediately so moved, but all through the mediation of created intellectual substances : or whether the first heavenly body alone is immediately moved by God and the others by the mediation of created substances—provided we hold that the motion of the heavens is due to an intellectual substance.' There is here a suggestion of the Neo-Platonic influences to which Thomas Aquinas was necessarily subject. The theory mentioned by Leibniz is stated also by Albertus Magnus, *Metaphysica*, Lib. xi. Tract. 2, cap. 10 (*Opera*, ed. Jammy, 1651, vol. iii. p. 374 b), and by J. C. Scaliger, *Comm. in Hippocratis lib. de Somniis* (1539), p. 12. Cf. Leibniz's *Considérations sur la Doctrine d'un Esprit Universel Unique* (E. 178 b ; G.

have held that we cannot believe in the preservation
of the souls of the lower animals without falling into
metempsychosis and making them go [*promcner*] from
body to body, and the perplexity in which people have
been through not knowing what to do with them[116],
have, in my opinion, led to the neglect of the natural
way of explaining the preservation of the soul. This
has done great injury to natural religion and has led
a good many to believe that our immortality is only
a miraculous grace of God; and our celebrated author
also speaks of it with some doubt, as I shall mention
presently[117]. But it were well if all those who are of
this opinion had spoken about it as wisely and as
sincerely as he; for it is to be feared that a good many
people who speak of immortality through grace, do so
only to save appearances, and are at bottom nearly of
the same opinion as those Averroists[118] and some erring

vi. 530): 'It is true, the Peripatetic philosophers did not regard this
spirit as absolutely universal; for besides the intelligences which,
according to them, animate the stars, they had an intelligence for
this lower world, and this intelligence performed the function
of active understanding in the souls of men.' See also Bayle's
Dictionary, vol. iv, article *Ricius*, note C.

[116] E. omits from 'and making' to 'with them.'

[117] Infra, pp. 389 sqq. See Locke, *Essay*, bk. iv. ch. 3, § 6 (Fraser's
ed., vol. ii. p. 195, with note), and bk. iv. ch. 4, § 15 (Fraser, vol. ii.
p. 240 note). Cf. also Locke's *Reasonableness of Christianity* (opening
paragraphs), where Locke seems to make the immortality of the
soul conditional on religious faith.

[118] Averroes (or Ibn Roschd) was born at Cordova in 1126 and
died in 1198. Much of his philosophizing was concerned with the
relation between the νοῦς ποιητικὸς (a phrase never actually used by
Aristotle) and the νοῦς παθητικὸς of Aristotle. (See *De Anima*, iii.
5, 430ᵃ 10 sqq.) Developing a suggestion of Aristotle, Averroes
regards the νοῦς ποιητικὸς as one principle appearing in all men,
while the νοῦς παθητικὸς is peculiar to the individual. The νοῦς
ποιητικὸς is ultimately identical with the Divine Spirit and is thus
immortal; but there is no individual immortality, for the νοῦς
παθητικὸς is mortal. Cf. Leibniz's *Considérations sur la Doctrine d'un
Esprit Universel Unique* (1702) (E. 178 a; G. vi. 529): 'Several people of
intellect have thought and do still think that there is only one spirit,

Quietists [119], who imagine an absorption of the soul and its reunion with the ocean of divinity, a notion

which is universal and which animates the whole universe and all its parts, according to the structure of each and the organs it finds in each, as the same blast of wind produces the various sounds from different organ-pipes. And thus when the organs of an animal are rightly arranged, this spirit appears in it as an individual soul, but when the organs are broken up, this individual soul comes to nothing again or returns, so to speak, into the ocean of the universal spirit. To many people Aristotle appears to have had an opinion of this kind, which has been revived by Averroes, a famous Arabian philosopher. He held that there is in us an *intellectus agens*, or active understanding, and also an *intellectus patiens*, or passive understanding; and that the former of these, coming from outside of us, is eternal and universal for all, while the passive understanding, which is peculiar to each, passes away at the man's death. This doctrine was held by some of the Peripatetics, two or three centuries ago, such as Pomponatius, Contarenus and others.'

[119] See *Considérations sur la Doctrine d'un Esprit Universel Unique* (E. 178 b; G. vi. 530): 'Apparently Molinos, and some other new Quietists, among others a certain author called Joannes Angelus Silesius, who wrote before Molinos, and some of whose works have lately been reprinted, and even Weigelius before them, favoured this opinion of the Sabbath or rest of souls in God. And for this reason they held that the cessation of individual functions is the highest state of perfection.' Miguel de Molinos was born at Saragossa in 1627 and died (in the prison of the Inquisition) in 1697. His chief book was his *Spiritual Guide*, published in Spanish and afterwards translated into many languages. Madame Guyon and Fénelon were much influenced by his work. Valentine Weigel was born at Hayn in Thuringia in 1533 and died in 1588. He was a Protestant minister in a village near Dresden, and although only one book of his was published in his lifetime, he left a large number of works in manuscript, many of which are still unpublished. He was a believer in the direct revelation of truth by the 'inward light,' in answer to prayer. Leibniz elsewhere mentions him as 'a clever man, who was indeed too clever,' and he says that Angelus was 'the author of certain rather pretty little bits of devotional verse, in the form of epigrams.' *Discours de la Conformité de la Foi avec la Raison*, § 9 (E. 482 b; G. vi. 55). There has been much dispute as to the identity of Angelus and little is known about him. His best known poem is the *Cherubinischer Wandersmann*. See Vaughan, *Hours with the Mystics*, bk. vii. ch. 1; and Schrader, *Angelus Silesius u. seine Mystik*. Leibniz distinguishes between the Quietist 'Sabbath' and the 'beatific vision,' saying that the 'beatific vision of completely

which perhaps my system alone clearly shows to be impossible [120].

We seem also to differ as regards matter in this, that the author thinks there must be a void in it [matter] [121] for the sake of motion, because he believes that the particles of matter are indivisible [*roide*]. And I admit that if matter were composed of such parts, motion in the *plenum* would be impossible, as if a room were filled with a great many little pebbles, so that not even the smallest place in it was empty. But this supposition is not by any means granted, and indeed there does not seem to be any reason for it; although this able author goes so far as to think that the rigidity or cohesion of its particles constitutes the essence of the body. Space must rather be conceived as full of an ultimately fluid matter,

happy souls is compatible with the functions of their glorified bodies, which will still remain organic in their own way.' *Esprit Universel Unique* (E. 182 a ; G. vi. 536).

[120] For, according to Leibniz, no substance can be without an activity of its own, and thus none can be lost in the ocean of the one spirit. Against this idea that 'the universal spirit is like an ocean composed of an infinity of drops, which are separated from it when they animate some particular organic body, but are reunited to their ocean after the destruction of the body's organs,' Leibniz argues that 'as the ocean is a quantity of drops, God would thus be an assemblage of all souls, somewhat in the same way as a swarm of bees is an assemblage of these insects, but as the swarm is not itself a genuine substance, it is clear that in this way the universal spirit itself would not be a genuine being, and in place of saying that it is the only spirit, we should have to say that in itself it is nothing at all, and that in nature there is nothing but individual souls of which it is the aggregate. . . . If we hold that the souls, when reunited to God, are without any functions of their own, we fall into an opinion contrary to reason and to all good philosophy, as if any being with a continued existence could ever reach a state in which it is without function or impression. For when one thing is combined with another it retains nevertheless its peculiar functions, which, when combined with the functions of the others, produce the functions of the whole, otherwise the whole would have no functions, if the parts had none.' *Esprit Universel Unique* (E. 181 b ; G. vi. 535).

[121] E. omits 'in it' [*y*].

susceptible of all divisions and even subjected actually to divisions and subdivisions *ad infinitum* [122]; but nevertheless with this difference that it is divisible and divided unequally in different places, because of the motions, more or less tending to division, which are already in the particular place. Consequently matter has every-where some degree of rigidity as well as of fluidity, and there is no body which is hard or fluid in the highest degree, that is to say, there is no atom of invincible hardness, and no quantity of matter [*masse*] completely indifferent to division [123]. Thus the order of nature and especially the law of continuity make both [124] equally inadmissible.

I have also shown that *cohesion*, if not itself the effect of impulse or motion, would cause a *traction*, strictly speaking [125]. For if there were a fundamentally hard

[122] Cf. *Monadology*, § 65.

[123] Two extremes are both impossible : (1) the absolutely hard or solid, (2) the absolutely soft or fluid. An absolutely hard piece of matter would be one in which the force holding it together should be so strong that no combination of other forces could overcome it. An absolutely soft portion of matter would be one in which there is no force of cohesion whatever, nothing to resist division, so that it would be 'completely indifferent to division.' Hardness or solidity is, according to the law of continuity, simply a low degree of softness or fluidity.

[124] i. e. both a perfect atom and a perfect fluid. Cf. *Third Explanation of the New System*, p. 335 with note. Also *Nouveaux Essais*, bk. ii. ch. 4. § 4 : 'I am also of opinion that all bodies have some degree of cohesion, as in the same way I hold that there are none which have not some *fluidity* and of which the cohesion cannot be overcome : and consequently in my opinion the atoms of Epicurus, the hardness of which is supposed to be invincible, cannot exist any more than the perfectly fluid minute [*subtile*] matter of the Cartesians.' (E. 229 b ; G. v. 114.)

[125] But, according to Leibniz, *traction* or *attraction* is unintelligible, unless in the sense of a force or impulse which can be overcome by counteracting forces. A 'traction, strictly speaking.' would imply that one part of matter is for ever bound ('thirled') to another and must therefore always be dragged along with it. Leibniz, however, does admit that there is an *apparent traction*, even though there be no visible contact between the parts which draw one another, as

body, for instance, one of the atoms of Epicurus, which should have a part projecting in the form of a hook (as we can imagine atoms of all kinds of shapes) [126], the hook when impelled would draw with it the rest of the atom, that is to say, the part which is not impelled and which does not lie in the line of impulsion. Yet our able author is himself opposed to these philosophical tractions, such as were formerly attributed to nature's abhorrence of a vacuum ; and he reduces them to *impulses*, maintaining, with the moderns, that one part of matter acts immediately upon another only by impelling it through contact [127]. In this I think they are right, because otherwise there would be nothing intelligible in the operation.

Nevertheless I must not conceal the fact that I have observed a kind of retraction regarding this matter on the part of our excellent author, whose unpretending straightforwardness in this respect I cannot but praise, as much as I have admired his penetrating genius on other occasions. I refer to his reply to the second letter of the late Bishop of Worcester [128], printed in 1699,

in the case of the magnet and some electrical phenomena. But in any such case, there is contact and 'impulse' between the bodies concerned, although it may not appear so to our senses. Cf. *Nouveaux Essais*, bk. ii. ch. 4, § 4 ; ch. 8, § 11 (E. 229 a, 231 b ; G. v. 113, 118).

[126] According to Democritus, atoms differ in 'shape, arrangement and position.' (Aristotle, *Metaph.* A. 4, 985^b 13.)

[127] See Locke's *Essay*, bk. ii. ch. 8, § 11 (cf. Fraser's note, vol. i. p. 171), and bk. ii. ch. 23, § 17 sqq.

[128] Edward Stillingfleet, born at Cranbourne, Dorsetshire, 1635, died at Westminster, 1699, having for ten years been Bishop of Worcester. His chief work was the *Origines Sacrae* (1662). His controversy with Locke originated in the anti-religious use to which Toland (in his *Christianity not Mysterious*) turned some of Locke's views. In 1696 Stillingfleet published *A Discourse in Vindication of the Doctrine of the Trinity with an answer to the late Socinian objections*, in which there appeared a criticism of Locke's 'way of ideas.' To this Locke replied at great length and the controversy continued until Stillingfleet's death. Cf. Fraser's ed. of Locke's

p. 408, in which, by way of justifying the opinion he had maintained against the learned prelate, namely that matter might think, he says among other things: 'It is true, I say, "that bodies operate by impulse and nothing else" (*Essay*, bk. ii. ch. 8, § 11). And so I thought when I writ it, and can yet conceive no other way of their operation. But I am since convinced by the judicious Mr. Newton's incomparable book, that it is too bold a presumption to limit God's power, in this point, by my narrow conceptions. The gravitation of matter towards matter, by ways inconceivable to me, is not only a demonstration that God can, if He pleases, put into bodies powers and ways of operation above what can be devised from our idea of body, or can be explained by what we know of matter, but also an unquestionable and everywhere visible instance, that He has done so. And therefore in the next edition of my book I shall take care to have that passage rectified[129].' I find that in the French translation of this book, doubtless made from the latest editions[130], this section 11 reads thus: 'It is evident, *at least so far as we can conceive it*, that bodies act upon one another by impulse and not otherwise; for it is impossible for us to understand that a body can act upon that which it does not touch, which is as much as to imagine that it can act where it is not[131].'

Essay, vol. i. *Prolegomena*, p. xli; Stillingfleet's *Works* (1710), vol. iii. pp. 413 sqq.; Locke's *Works* (1823), vol. iv.

[129] See Fraser's ed. of Locke's *Essay*, vol. i. p. 171 note. Also Locke's *Works* (10 vol. ed., 1823), vol. iv. p. 467.

[130] See Prefatory Note. The italics are by Leibniz. The English edition has merely: 'The next thing to be considered is, how bodies produce ideas in us; and that is manifestly by impulse, the only way which we can conceive bodies to operate in.'

[131] Of course the Newtonian theory does not necessarily imply that a body can act where it is not. ' *The whole is greater than the part:* how exceedingly true! *Nature abhors a vacuum:* how exceedingly false and calumnious! Again, *Nothing can act but where it is:* with all my heart; only, WHERE is it?' Carlyle, *Sartor Resartus*, bk. i. ch. 8 (Library ed., vol. i. p. 52). Cf. Newton, *Principia*, def. 8, and *Scholium Generale*; also Stallo, *Concepts of Modern Physics*, ch. 5.

I cannot but praise the modest piety of our celebrated author, who recognizes that God can do beyond what we can understand, and that thus there may be inconceivable mysteries in the articles of faith ; but I would rather that we were not compelled to have recourse to miracle in the ordinary course of nature and to admit absolutely inexplicable powers and operations. Otherwise too great a licence will be given to bad philosophers on the strength of what God can do ; and if we admit those *centripetal powers* [*vertus*] [132] or those *immediate attractions* from a distance, without its being possible to make them intelligible,

---

[132] In *Nouveaux Essais*, bk. ii. ch. 8, § 11, he calls them *vires centripetae* (E. 231 b; G. v. 118). Cf. *Antibarbarus Physicus pro Philosophia reali contra renovationes qualitatum scholasticarum et intelligentiarum chimaericarum* (G. vii. 342) : 'And all who are not content to recognize with us qualities which are so far occult, that is, which are unknown, have supposed qualities which are perpetually occult, ἄρρητοι, inexplicable, which not even the highest spirit [*genius*] could thoroughly know and make intelligible. Such are they who, led on by the success of the observation that the large bodies of the world exert among themselves and upon their own perceptible parts the attraction of this system, suppose that every body is attracted by every other through the very force of matter ; whether, as it were, like feels like and delights in it even from afar, or whether God by a perpetual miracle secures that they shall strive towards one another, as if they had feeling. However that may be, these people neither can reduce attraction to impulse or to explicable reasons (as Plato did in the *Timaeus*) nor do they wish they could. . . . It is surprising that even now, in the great light of this age, there are some who hope to persuade the world of a doctrine so opposed to reason. John Locke, in the first edition of his *Essay on the Understanding*, declared rightly, and in accordance with the mechanical physics established by his illustrious countrymen, Hobbes, Boyle, and their numerous followers, that no body is moved except by the impulse of a body coming into contact with it. But afterwards (obeying, I think, the authority of his friends rather than his own judgment) he withdrew this opinion, and held that there may lie hid in the essence of matter I know not what extraordinary things [*mirabilia*] ; which is just as if one were to think that there are occult qualities in number, time, space and motion, taken by themselves, that is to say, as if one were to seek a knot in a bulrush' [a difficulty where there is none], 'or to try deliberately to make clear things obscure.'

I see nothing to hinder our Scholastics from saying that everything happens merely through their 'faculties,' and from maintaining their 'intentional species,' which go from objects to us and find it possible to enter even into our souls [133]. If that is so,

Omnia jam fient, fieri quae posse negabam [134],

so that it seems to me that our author, judicious as he is, goes here a little too much from one extreme to the other. He raises difficulties about the operations of *souls* when the question is merely whether that which is not *perceptible* [*sensible*] is to be admitted; and here we have him giving to *bodies* that which is not even *intelligible*, attributing to them powers and activities which surpass all that a created spirit can, in my opinion, do or understand, for he attributes to them attraction, and that at great distances without any limit to the sphere of its activity; and he does this in order to support an opinion which seems to me [135] no less inexplicable, namely, the possibility that within the order of nature matter may think.

The question which he discusses with the distinguished prelate who had attacked him is *whether matter can think*; and, as it is an important point, even for the present work, I cannot avoid entering into it a little and examining their controversy [136]. I will state the substance of

---

[133] See *Monadology*, § 7. note 10.

[134] 'All the things will presently happen, which I said could not happen.' Ovid, *Tristia*, bk. i. el. 8, ver. 7. The whole passage is:—

Omnia naturae praepostera legibus ibunt,
Parsque suum mundi nulla tenebit iter :
Omnia jam fient, fieri quae posse negabam,
Et nihil est, de quo non sit habenda fides.

[All things by the laws of nature will go topsy-turvy, and no part of the world will hold on its own way; all the things will presently happen which I said could not happen, and there is nothing we may not believe.]

[135] E. reads 'which is' instead of 'which seems to me.'

[136] That Leibniz was deeply interested in the controversy appears from his letters to Thomas Burnet of Kemnay (G. iii. 151 sqq.), in

the controversy on this subject, and will take the liberty of saying what I think about it. The late Bishop of Worcester, fearing (in my opinion without much ground) that our author's doctrine of ideas was liable to some abuses prejudicial to the Christian faith, set himself to examine certain parts of it in his *Vindication of the Doctrine of the Trinity;* and having done justice to this excellent author, in recognizing that he thinks the existence of the mind [*esprit*] as certain as that of the body, although the one of these substances is as little known as the other, he asks (pp. 241 sqq.)[137] how reflexion can assure us of the existence of the mind [*esprit*] if God can give to matter the faculty of thinking, according to the opinion of our author (bk. iv. ch. 3), since thus the way of ideas, which should enable us to discriminate[138] what may be proper to the soul and what to the body, would become useless, while yet it was said in the second book of the *Essay on the Understanding* (ch. 23, §§ 15, 27, 28), that the operations of the soul furnish us with the idea of the mind [*esprit*], and that the understanding along with the will makes this idea as intelligible to us as the nature of body is made intelligible to us by solidity and impulse. This is how our author replies in his first letter (p. 65)[139]: 'I think I have proved that there is a spiritual substance in us,

which he frequently refers to it and likens it to his own controversy with Arnauld. He has 'no doubt that Locke will come well out of it. He [Locke] has too much judgment to give an advantage to *messieurs les ecclesiastiques*, who are the natural directors of the peoples and whose formularies must be followed as much as possible.' (G. iii. 216.) Leibniz also wrote two accounts of the controversy, with comments of his own. (G. iii. 223 sqq.) See also Foucher de Careil, *Lettres et Opuscules inédits de Leibniz,* Introduction, pp. lxii-lxxxiii.

[137] Stillingfleet's *Works* (1710), vol. iii. p. 505.

[138] E. reads 'investigate' [*discuter*] instead of *discerner*.

[139] Locke's *Works* (ed. 1823), vol. iv. pp. 32 sqq.; Bohn's ed., vol. ii. p. 387; Fraser's ed. of the *Essay*, vol. ii. p. 193 note. Here, and in other passages quoted, I give the words of the author—not re-translating from Leibniz.

for we experiment in ourselves thinking. The idea of
this action or mode of thinking is inconsistent with the
idea of self-subsistence, and therefore has a necessary connexion with a support or subject of inhesion: the idea
of that support is what we call substance. . . . For *the
general idea of substance being the same everywhere*[140], the
modification of thinking, or the power of thinking joined
to it, makes it a spirit, without considering what other
modification it has, as whether it has the modification of
solidity or no. As on the other side, substance that has
the modification of solidity is matter, whether it has
the modification of thinking or no. And therefore if
your lordship means by a spiritual an immaterial substance, I grant I have not proved, nor upon my principles can it be proved (your lordship meaning, as I think
you do, demonstratively proved) that there is an immaterial substance in us that thinks. Though I presume,
from what I have said about the supposition of a system
of matter thinking (bk. iv. ch. 10, § 16) (which there de-
monstrates that God is immaterial), it will prove in the
highest degree probable that the thinking substance in
us is immaterial. . . . Yet I have shown' (adds the author,
p. 68)[141] 'that all the great ends of religion and morality
are secured barely by the immortality of the soul, without
a necessary supposition that the soul is immaterial.'

The learned Bishop in his reply to this letter, in order
to show that our author was of another opinion when
he wrote the second book of the *Essay*, quotes from it
(p. 51)[142] the passage (taken from the same book, ch. 23,
§ 15), in which it is said that 'by the simple ideas we
have taken from our own minds[143] we are able to frame

---

[140] Leibniz's italics.   [141] Ed. 1823, vol. iv. p. 34.
[142] Stillingfleet's *Works*, vol. iii. p. 534.
[143] Leibniz's translation has 'from the operations of our mind.'
I give the words as they are in Stillingfleet, who condenses Locke's
sentence, which is as follows: ' By the simple ideas we have taken
from those operations of our own minds, which we experiment
daily in ourselves, as thinking, understanding, willing, knowing,

the complex idea of a spirit. And thus by putting together the ideas of thinking, perceiving, liberty and power of moving themselves [144], we have as clear a perception and notion of immaterial substances as well as material [145].' He also quotes other passages to show that our author opposed spirit [*esprit*] to body, and says (p. 54) [146] that the ends of religion and morality are best secured by proving that the soul is immortal by its nature, that is to say that it is immaterial. He also quotes (p. 70) [147] this passage that 'all the ideas we have of particular distinct sorts of substances are nothing but several combinations of simple ideas,' and that thus our author thought that the idea of thinking and of willing presupposes another substance, different from that which is presupposed by solidity and impulse, and that thus (§ 17) [148] he indicates that these ideas constitute body as opposed to spirit [*esprit*].

The Bishop of Worcester might have added that from the fact that the *general idea* of substance is in body and in spirit, it does not follow that their *differences* are

and power of beginning motion, &c., co-existing in some substance, we are able to frame the complex idea of an immaterial spirit.'

[144] Leibniz reads 'our body' instead of 'themselves.'

[145] Leibniz reads 'as of material.' Stillingfleet here again shortens Locke's statement, though he gives a more exact quotation of it on p. 540. Locke wrote: 'And thus by putting together the ideas of thinking, perceiving, liberty, and power of moving themselves and other things, we have as clear a perception and notion of immaterial substances as we have of material. For putting together the ideas of thinking and willing, or the power of moving or quieting corporeal motion, joined to substance, of which we have no distinct idea, we have the idea of an immaterial spirit ; and by putting together the ideas of coherent solid parts, and a power of being moved, joined with substance, of which likewise we have no positive idea, we have the idea of matter.'

[146] Stillingfleet's *Works*, vol. iii. p. 535: 'I am of opinion that the great ends of religion and morality are best secured by the proofs of the immortality of the soul from its nature and properties, and which I think prove it immaterial.'

[147] Stillingfleet, iii. 539 ; Locke's *Essay*, ii. 23, § 6.

[148] *Essay*, ii. 23, § 17 ; Stillingfleet, iii. 540.

modifications of one and the same thing, as our author
said in the passage I have quoted from his first letter[149].
We must certainly distinguish between modifications
and attributes. The faculty of having perception and
that of acting, extension, and solidity are attributes or
perpetual and principal predicates ; but thinking, impetus
[*impétuosité*], figures and motions are modifications of
these attributes[150]. Further, we ought to distinguish between *physical* (or rather real) *genus* and *logical* or ideal
genus. Things which are of the same physical genus,
or which are *homogeneous*, are of the same *matter*, so to
speak, and can often be changed one into another by
changing their modification, like circles and squares.
But two *heterogeneous* things may have a common logical
genus, and then their *differences* are not mere accidental
modifications of one and the same subject [*sujet*][151], or
one and the same matter, metaphysical or physical. Thus
time and space are very heterogeneous things, and it would.
be a mistake to suppose I know not what real common
ground [*sujet*], having nothing but continuous quantity
in general, from the modifications of which time and
space arise. Nevertheless their common logical genus is
continuous quantity[152]. Some one will perhaps ridicule
this distinction[153] of the philosophers between two genera,
the one merely logical, the other real[154], and between
two matters, the one physical (that of bodies), the other
merely metaphysical or general, as if one were to say
that two parts of space have the same matter, or that
two hours also have each the same matter as the other.
Yet these distinctions are distinctions not only of terms
but of things themselves, and they appear to be most

---

[149] *Supra*, p. 392.
[150] Cf. Introduction, Part ii. p. 34 ; Part iii. p. 127 ; *Monadology*,
§§ 14 sqq.
[151] Or ' ground.'   [152] E. gives this sentence ; G. omits it.
[153] E. reads ' these distinctions.'
[154] E. reads ' also real.'

pertinent here, where confusion between them has produced a false conclusion[155]. These two genera have a
common notion, and the notion of the real genus is
common to the two matters, so that their filiation will
be as follows[156] :—

GENUS
- Merely *logical*, its variations consisting of mere *differences*.
- *real*, the differences of which are *modifications*, that is to say, *matter*[157]
  - *metaphysical* merely, in which there is homogeneity,
  - *physical*, in which there is a solid homogeneous mass.

I have not seen the second letter of our author to the
Bishop; and the answer which the prelate makes to it
hardly touches the point about the thinking of matter.
But *our author's reply* to this second answer returns to
that point. 'God' (he says, nearly in these words,
p. 397)[158], 'superadds to the essence of matter what
qualities and perfections He pleases: to some parts mere
motion, but to plants vegetation, and to animals feeling
[*sentiment*]. Those who agree with me so far exclaim

[155] The point simply is that no real thing can have two or more
conflicting *attributes*, though it may at different times have *modifications* which in themselves are conflicting. Nevertheless attributes
which, in a real thing, would be impossible because conflicting,
may abstractly or 'ideally' be comprehended under the same
concept or in the same class, on the ground that there is an
essential (not merely accidental) community between them. They
are thus species of a logical genus. Modifications, on the other
hand, are more or less accidental variations of some real thing,
which is the bond of union between them. They are thus species
of a real genus. Ultimately, perhaps, the modifications may turn
out to be species of a logical genus (it is probable that they are so in
the mind of God) ; but, for us, an infinite analysis would be needed
to show this.

[156] This 'filiation' as a whole is, of course, an arrangement of
logical genera and species.

[157] 'Matter' here is equivalent to 'real genus.'

[158] *Works* (ed. 1823), vol. iv. p. 460 ; Bohn's ed., vol. ii. p. 390.
In translating this passage I have used Locke's words as much as
possible.

against me when I go a step further and say, God may
give to matter thought, reason and volition, as if that
were to destroy the essence of matter. But to make
good this assertion they say that thought and reason are
not included in the essence of matter; which proves
nothing, for motion and life are just as little included in
it. They also urge that we cannot conceive how matter
can think; but our conception is not the measure of God's
omnipotency [159].' He afterwards takes as an instance
the attraction of matter, on p. 99 [160], but especially on
p. 408 [161], where he speaks of the gravitation of matter
towards matter, attributed to Mr. Newton (in words
which I have quoted above), declaring that we can never
conceive the 'how' of it. This is practically to go back
to occult qualities [162], nay more, to inexplicable qualities.
He adds (p. 401) [163] that nothing is more calculated to
favour scepticism than to deny what one does not understand, and (p. 402) [163] that we do not conceive how even
the soul thinks. He thinks (p. 403) [163] that as the two
substances, material and immaterial, can be conceived
in their bare essence without any activity, it is in the
power of God to give to the one or the other the power
of thinking. And he endeavours to take advantage of
the admission of his opponent, who attributed sense
[sentiment] to the lower animals, but did not attribute
to them any immaterial substance [164]. He maintains that
liberty and self-consciousness [la consciosité] (p. 408) [165],
and the power of making abstractions (p. 409) [165] can

[159] Cf. Essay, Fraser's ed., vol. ii. p. 240 note.
[160] All the texts give '99,' which seems to be a slip for '399.'
Works (ed. 1823), iv. 463 sqq.; Bohn's ed., ii. 392 sqq.
[161] Works (ed. 1823), iv. 467; Bohn's ed., ii. 395.
[162] The qualitates occultae of the Scholastics. See Introduction,
Part iv. p. 156.
[163] Works (ed. 1823), iv. 463; Bohn's ed., ii. 392. Cf. Essay,
Fraser's ed., vol. ii. p. 194 note.
[164] Works, iv. 466; Bohn's ed., ii. 394.
[165] Works, iv. 468; Bohn's ed., ii. 395.

be given to matter, not as matter, but as enriched by a Divine power. Finally he quotes (p. 434)[166] the observation of a traveller so considerable[167] and judicious as M. de la Loubère[168] that the Pagans of the east recognize the immortality of the soul without being able to comprehend its immateriality.

Regarding all this I will observe, before coming to the statement of my own view, that it is certain that matter is as little capable of producing feeling [*sentiment*] mechanically, as it is of producing reason[169], as our author admits; and that I most certainly recognize that it is not allowable to deny what one does not understand, but I add that we have a right to deny (at least in the order of nature) that which is absolutely neither intelligible nor explicable. I maintain also that substances (material or immaterial) cannot be conceived in their bare essence without any activity, that activity is of the essence of substance in general; and that the conceptions of created beings are not the measure of the power of

[166] *Works*, iv. 485; Bohn's ed., ii. 406.

[167] Locke's word.

[168] Simon de la Loubère, born at Toulouse in 1642, died in 1729. In 1687 Louis XIV entrusted him with a mission to Siam for the purpose of establishing diplomatic and commercial relations between that country and France. As the result of a three months' residence in Siam he published two volumes *Du Royaume de Siam* (1691; Eng. trans. 1693), in which he gives an elaborate account of the Siamese people, their history, customs, and institutions. The book still ranks as an authority on its subject. Locke's quotation is taken from vol. i. ch. 19, § 4.

[169] Cf. *Nouveaux Essais*, bk. iv. ch. 3, § 6 (E. 346 b; G. v. 360): 'The *primary powers* constitute the substances themselves; and the *derivative* powers, or if you like, the faculties, are merely *modes* [*façons d'être*], which must be derived from substances, and they are not derived from matter in so far as it is merely mechanical, that is to say, in so far as by abstraction we take account only of the *incomplete being* of *materia prima*, or that which is entirely passive. And in this I think you will agree with me, sir, that it is not in the power of a mere mechanism to produce perception, sensation, reason.' Cf. Locke, *Essay*, bk. iv. ch. 10, § 10 (Fraser, vol. ii. p. 313); also *Monadology*, § 17.

God, but that their conceptivity, or ability [*force*] to conceive, is the measure of the power of nature: for all that is in accordance with the order of nature can be conceived or understood by some created being [170].

Those who will think out my system will see that I cannot wholly agree with either of these excellent authors, whose controversy, however, is very instructive. But, to explain myself distinctly, it is before all things to be considered that the modifications which can naturally or without miracle belong [171] to a subject [*sujet*] must arise from the limitations or variations of a real genus or an original nature which is constant and absolute [172]. For it is thus that among philosophers the modes of an absolute being are distinguished from the being itself: for instance, we know that size, figure and motion are manifestly limitations and variations of the bodily nature. For [173] it is clear how an extension when limited gives figures, and that the change which takes place in it is nothing but motion. And whenever we find any quality in a subject [*sujet*], we should believe that if we understood the nature of the subject [*sujet*] and of the quality, we should understand [*concevoir*] how the quality can be a result of it [174]. Thus in the order of nature (setting

[170] For Leibniz this would follow *a priori* from the essential unity of nature, shown in the fact that each Monad (and therefore each created being) contains within itself a representation of the whole universe.

[171] E. reads 'come' [*venir*] for *convenir*.

[172] Things do have an 'absolute' original essence of some kind. They are not ultimate bare unities, equally capable of *any* kind of modification.

[173] E. omits 'for.' Cf. Spinoza's *Letters*, 50, § 4.

[174] Cf. *Lettre à Arnauld* (1686) (G. ii. 56): 'Always in every true affirmative proposition, necessary or contingent, universal or singular, the notion of the predicate is in some way comprehended in that of the subject, *praedicatum inest subjecto*: otherwise I know not what truth is. . . . *There must always be some foundation for the connexion of the terms in a proposition and this is to be found in their notions.* That is my great principle, to which I think all philosophers must assent, and of which one of the corollaries is the common axiom,

aside miracles`, God is not arbitrarily free to give to
substances one set of qualities or another indifferently;
and He will never give them any but those which are
natural to them, that is to say, which can be derived
from their nature, as explicable modifications of it. Thus
we may hold that matter will not by nature have the
attraction mentioned above, and will not of itself go in
a curved line, because it is not possible to conceive how
that can happen, that is to say to explain it mechanically;
while that which is according to nature [*naturel*] ought
to be capable of becoming distinctly conceivable, if we
were admitted into the secrets of things. This distinction, between that which is natural and explicable and
that which is inexplicable and miraculous, removes all
difficulties, and to reject it would be to maintain something worse than occult qualities and accordingly to
renounce philosophy and reason, and to provide refuges
for ignorance [175] and idleness by a confused [*sourd*] system
which allows, not only that there are qualities we do not
understand (of which there are only too many), but also
that there are qualities which the greatest mind [*esprit*].
even if God were to give it the widest possible grasp,
could not comprehend, that is to say, qualities which
would either be miraculous or without rhyme or reason;
and that God should usually perform miracles would
certainly be without rhyme or reason. Accordingly this
lazy [176] hypothesis would equally destroy our philosophy,

---

that nothing happens without a reason, which can always be given
why the thing took place so rather than otherwise.' This, of
course, is radically opposed to the view of Locke.

[175] *Asiles de l'ignorance.* Cf. Spinoza, *Ethics*, Part i. Appendix :—
Donec ad Dei voluntatem, hoc est, ignorantiae asylum confugeris (Bruder's
ed., i. 220).

[176] The French is *fainéante*. Leibniz is probably thinking of the
fallacy of ἀργὸς λόγος or *Ignava Ratio*, to which he frequently refers
in the *Théodicée* (cf. E. 470 b; G. vi. 30). The fallacy is that
which counsels doing nothing, because things are fated one way or
another, whatever we do. Leibniz means that the hypothesis of

which seeks reasons, and the Divine wisdom which furnishes them.

Now as to thinking it is certain, and our author more than once allows it, that it cannot be a modification of matter that is intelligible or can be comprehended and explained by matter [177]: that is to say, a feeling or thinking being is not a mechanical thing, like a watch or a mill, so that one might conceive sizes, figures and motions, the mechanical combination of which could produce something thinking and even feeling in a quantity of matter in which there was nothing of this kind—which thinking and feeling would also come to an end in the same way when the mechanism falls into disorder [178]. Accordingly it is not a natural thing for matter to feel and to think, and this can take place in it only in two ways, one of which is, that God should unite with it a substance to which it is natural to think, and the other is, that God should miraculously impart thinking to it. In this matter, then, I am entirely of the opinion of the Cartesians, except that I extend it even to the lower animals, and hold that they have feeling [*sentiment*], and that their souls are immaterial (properly speaking) and no more perishable than are atoms according to Democritus or Gassendi [179]; while the Cartesians, who are without reason perplexed regarding the souls of the lower animals, not knowing what to make of them if there is conservation of them (because it has not occurred to them that there is conservation of the animal itself in a minute form), have been compelled to deny even feeling [*sentiment*] to the lower animals, contrary to all appearance and to the judgment of mankind [180].

which he is speaking is a 'lazy' one, because acceptance of it would imply that it is futile to investigate the 'secrets of things.'

[177] E. omits from 'or can be' to 'matter.'

[178] Cf. *Monadology*, § 17.

[179] Cf. *New System*, § 4.

[180] See *Monadology*, § 14.

But if some one should say that at any rate God can add the faculty of thinking to a mechanism prepared for it, I would answer that, if this took place and God added this faculty to matter, without at the same time putting into matter a substance which should be the subject in which this same faculty (as I conceive it) is inherent (that is to say, without adding to matter an immaterial soul), matter must needs have been miraculously exalted so as to receive a power of which it is not naturally capable: as some Scholastics declare that God exalts fire so as to give it the power directly to burn spirits separated from matter[181], which would be entirely miraculous[182]. And it is enough that we cannot maintain that matter thinks, unless there is attributed to it an imperishable soul or rather a miracle, and that thus the immortality of our souls follows from that which is natural[183]: since we cannot maintain that they are extinguished, unless it be by a miracle, consisting either in the exaltation of matter or in the annihilation of the soul. For we know, of course, that the power of God could make our souls mortal, although they may be quite immaterial (or immortal by nature), since He can annihilate them[184].

---

[181] E. reads 'bodies.'

[182] Cf. *Nouveaux Essais*, bk. iv. ch. 3, § 6 (E. 347 a ; G. v. 360): 'To suppose that God acts otherwise and gives to things accidents, which are not *modes* [*façons d'être*] or modifications derived from substances, is to have recourse to miracles and to what the Schools called *obediential power*, through a kind of supernatural exaltation, as when certain theologians hold that the fire of hell burns "separated" souls. In which case it may even be doubted whether it would be the fire which would do it, and whether God would not Himself produce the effect, acting in place of the fire.' Cardinal Bellarmine (1542–1621) in his *De Purgatorio*, bk. ii. chs. 10-12, expounds a view of this kind, holding that the fire of purgatory is material fire, but nevertheless miraculously burns souls. In this opinion he openly follows Augustine (*De Civitate Dei*, bk. xxi. ch. 10), and a similar view is expressed by Thomas Aquinas (*Summa Theol.* Suppl. P. iii. Q. 70, Art. 3, *conclusio*).

[183] i. e. 'from their nature' or 'from the order of nature.'

[184] Cf. *Monadology*, § 6.

Now this truth of the immateriality of the soul is undoubtedly of importance. For it is infinitely more helpful to religion and morality, especially at the present day (when many people have very little regard for revelation by itself and for miracles) [185], to show that souls are naturally immortal and that it would be a miracle if they were not, than to maintain that our souls would die in the course of nature, and that it is in virtue of a miraculous grace, founded on nothing but the promise of God, that they do not die. Besides it has for some time been generally known [186] that those who have tried to destroy natural religion and to reduce all to revealed religion, as if reason taught us nothing about it, have been counted suspect, and not always without reason [187]. But our author is not of their number. He upholds the demonstration of the existence of God [188], and he attributes *probability* in *the highest degree* to the immateriality of the soul [189], which may accordingly be accounted a *moral certainty*; and consequently it seems to me that, having as much candour as penetration, he could quite well agree with the doctrine I have expounded, which is fundamental in every rational philosophy; for [190] otherwise I do not see how we are to keep from falling back into *fanatical philosophy*, such as the *Mosaic philosophy* of Fludd [191], which

[185] E. omits the passage in brackets.

[186] E. reads ' it has for some time been the case.'

[187] In his *Discours de la Conformité de la Foi avec la Raison* (1710), Leibniz gives, at considerable length, an account of those who insisted on the opposition between reason and revelation, in which he traces the origin of this view to the Averroists. He approves of the condemnation of this position by the fifth Lateran Council, under Leo X, in 1512. (See E. 483 sqq.; G. vi. 56 sqq.) Cf. *Nouveaux Essais*, bk. iv. ch. 17, § 23 (E. 403 a; G. v. 477); also Bayle's *Dictionary*, Appendix (vol. iv. p. 620, IIme *Éclaircissement*).

[188] See *Essay*, bk. iv. ch. 10, § 10 (Fraser, vol. ii. pp. 306 sqq. with notes).

[189] See *Essay*, bk. iv. ch. 3, § 6 (Fraser, vol. ii. p. 194).

[190] E. omits ' for.'

[191] Robert Fludd (*Robertus de Fluctibus*) was born at Milgate, Kent, in 1574 (or 1571), and died at London in 1637. After

finds a ground for all phenomena by attributing them directly and miraculously to God, or into the *barbarous philosophy*, like that of certain philosophers and physicians of the past, who [192] still showed traces of the barbarousness of their time, and who nowadays are rightly contemned, who found a ground for phenomena [*apparences*] by inventing for this purpose occult qualities or faculties, which were pictured as being like little sprites or elves [193],

studying at Oxford he travelled abroad and made acquaintance with the theosophical views of Paracelsus, which he sought to make known in England through his *Philosophia Mosaica* (1638) and his *Historia Macro-et-Micro-Cosmi Metaphysica, Physica et Technica* (1617). In these writings he tries to find a complete philosophy in the Old Testament and more especially in the Pentateuch. His system, if so it can be called, is a combination of Neo-Platonic doctrines with those of the Kabbala, and one of his favourite ideas is that of the analogy between the universe (macrocosm) and the human body (microcosm). Leibniz is here referring to his theory that all things flow directly from God, who continually produces the variations in phenomena by condensation and rarefaction of matter. All things are emanations from God and return into His absolute unity. Gassendi and Kepler wrote against the views of Fludd.

[192] E. reads 'which' [philosophy].

[193] Leibniz is probably referring to the 'elemental spirits' of which Paracelsus (1493-1541) writes in his *De Nymphis, Sylphis, Pygmaeis et Salamandris*. He attributes to the 'nymphs' the phenomena of water, to the 'sylphs' the phenomena of air, to the 'pygmies' the phenomena of earth, and to the 'salamanders' the phenomena of fire. Fludd also adopted this view. Possibly Leibniz may also be thinking of the elder Van Helmont (Johann Baptista Van Helmont, 1577-1644), who was a follower of Paracelsus. In the *Epistola ad Thomasium* (1669), § 11 (E. 52 b; G. i. 23), Leibniz speaks of Van Helmont along with Paracelsus and others as representative of the stupid [*stolida*] form of the reformed philosophy, absolutely rejecting Aristotle. In the same letter he refers to the 'occult philosophy of Agrippa' (Heinrich Cornelius Agrippa von Nettesheim, 1486-1535), 'who ascribes to everything an angel to bring it to birth' [*quasi obstetricatorem*]. 'Thus,' adds Leibniz, 'we return to as many little gods [*deunculi*] as there are substantial forms and we approach the Gentile πολυθεϊσμός.' There may also here be a reference to the *spiritus familiaris* of the Italian physician, philosopher and mathematician, Girolamo Cardano (1501-1575). See his *De Vita Propria*, ch. 47, *Opera* (1663), vol. i. p. 44. On the whole matter, cf. Leibniz's

capable of artlessly doing what is [194] required, as if watches
were to indicate the time of day by a certain horodeictic
faculty without needing wheels, or as if mills were to
crush the grain by a fractive faculty without needing
anything resembling millstones [195]. As to the difficulty
several peoples have had in conceiving an immaterial
substance, it will readily pass away (at any rate in great
part), if it be no longer maintained that there are substances separated from matter, as in fact I do not believe
that there are ever naturally [196] any such substances
among created things.

Antibarbarus Physicus, &c. (G. vii. 337). See also Vaughan's *Hours
with the Mystics*, bk. viii. chs. 4 and 5, and the *Dedication* of Pope's
Rape of the Lock, where the 'nymphs,' &c. are attributed to the
Rosicrucians. Milton speaks of

'Those demons that are found
In fire, air, flood or under ground.'

Il Penseroso, l. 93.

[194] E. reads 'all that is required.'
[195] See Introduction, Part iv. pp. 156 sqq.
[196] i. e. other than miraculously. Cf. *Monadology*, § 72.

PRINCIPLES OF NATURE AND OF GRACE, FOUNDED ON REASON. 1714.

PREFATORY NOTE.

THE *Principles of Nature and of Grace* has much in common with the *Monadology*; and, indeed, it reads like a preliminary study, out of which the *Monadology* has been elaborated. They seem to have been written about the same time; and Gerhardt holds, against the view of previous editors, that the *Principles of Nature and of Grace* is the treatise which was written for Prince Eugene. It has been shown by Gerhardt that when Nicholas Remond wrote to Leibniz from Paris in 1714, asking for a condensed statement of his philosophy, Leibniz sent him a copy of the *Principles of Nature and of Grace*, with a letter in course of which he says: 'I now send you a little discourse on my philosophy, which I have written here for Prince Eugene of Savoy. I hope that this little work will help to make my ideas better understood, when taken in connexion with what I have written in the Journals of Leipzig, Paris and Holland. The Leipzig papers are on the whole in the language of the Scholastics; the others are more in the style of the Cartesians; and in this last writing I have endeavoured to express myself in a way which can be understood by those who are not yet thoroughly accustomed to either of the other styles.' (Letter of Aug. 26, 1714, quoted by Gerhardt vi. 485; E. p. xxvii and p. 704 a.) Kirchmann suggests that probably Leibniz wrote the *Principles of Nature and of Grace* for Prince Eugene, and afterwards, thinking it insufficient, worked it up into the *Monadology*, which he gave to the Prince. The *Principles of Nature and of Grace* was first published in the French journal, *L'Europe Savante*, in November, 1718.

There are three different MSS. of this work. The first of

these, which is the shortest, is divided, not into paragraphs, but into two chapters, the point of division being the end of paragraph 6, where transition is made from 'Physics' to 'Metaphysics.' In the other two MSS. the paragraph division appears, and the text from which the translation is made is that of the last and most complete manuscript. In the *Principles of Nature and of Grace* the arrangement of the matter is much less clear and careful than it is in the *Monadology*. But, following the lines of the division originally made by Leibniz himself, we may say that paragraphs 1-6 inclusive give an account of the created Monads in themselves and in their relations to one another, so far as these can be considered apart from God; while the remaining paragraphs consider the nature of God as ultimate reason of the universe, and the consequences which follow from His perfection in power, wisdom and goodness. Some of the most important points in the *Monadology* are either passed over or very slightly treated in the *Principles of Nature and of Grace*. For instance, in the *Principles of Nature and of Grace* there is nothing to correspond to the passage in the *Monadology* regarding the two great principles of knowledge, and while the pre-established harmony is mentioned, it is not dwelt upon. But the connexion between the two writings, both in treatment and expression, is so close that the annotations to the *Principles of Nature and of Grace* may be comparatively brief.

The *Principles of Nature and of Grace* will be found in E. 714 sqq.; G. vi. 598 sqq.

1. *Substance* is a being capable of action. It is simple or compound. *Simple substance* is that which has no parts. *Compound substance* [1] is the combination of simple substances or *Monads*. *Monas* is a Greek word, which means unity, or that which is one. Compounds or bodies are pluralities [*multitudes*]; and simple substances, lives, souls, spirits, are unities. And everywhere there must be simple substances, for without simple substances there

---

[1] See *Monadology*, note 2. Strictly speaking 'compound substance,' according to Leibniz, is not 'substance' at all. It is not *substantia* but *substantiatum*. Failure to observe this distinction was to some extent the source of Wolff's misinterpretation of Leibniz.

would not be compounds ; and consequently all nature is full of life[2].

2. The Monads, having no parts, can neither be made [*formées*] nor unmade. They can neither come into being nor come to an end by natural means, and consequently they last as long as the universe, which will be changed, but which will not be destroyed. They can have no shape [*figure*]; otherwise they would have parts[3]. Consequently any one Monad in itself and at a particular moment can be distinguished from any other only by internal qualities and activities [*actions*][4], which cannot be other than its *perceptions* (that is to say, the representations of the compound, or of that which is outside[5], in the simple) and its *appetitions* (that is to say, its tendencies to pass from one perception to another), which are the principles of change. For the simplicity of substance is by no means inconsistent with the multiplicity of the modifications which are to be found together in that same simple substance, and these modifications must consist in variety of relations to the things which are outside[6]. It is as in the case of a *centre* or point, in

[2] To say that matter is infinitely divisible is the same as saying that there is compound substance everywhere ; for to be divisible is to be compound. But compound substances are made up of simple substances. Consequently there are simple substances or living beings everywhere.

[3] If they had shape, they would be extended or spatial. But everything extended is divisible, and hence they would not be simple but compound, having parts.

[4] Thus we cannot perceive Monads by means of our senses. What the senses give us is not the substance itself, but merely a *phenomenon bene fundatum*. 'Spirits, souls, and simple substances or Monads in general cannot be known [*comprehendi*] by the senses and imagination, because they have no parts.' *Epistola ad Bierlingium* (1711) (E. 678 a ; G. vii. 501).

[5] The compound, *as* compound, consists of *partes extra partes;* but *as* compound, it is merely phenomenal.

[6] 'The simplicity of a substance is by no means inconsistent with its having within it several modes at one time. There are successive perceptions ; but there are also simultaneous perceptions. For when there is perception of a whole, there are at the same

which, although it is perfectly simple, there is an infinite number of angles formed by the lines which meet in it.

3. All nature is a *plenum*. There are simple substances everywhere [7], which are actually separated from one another by activities of their own [8], and which continually change their relations; and each specially important [*distinguée*] [9] simple substance or Monad, which forms the centre of a compound substance (e. g. of an animal) and the principle of its oneness, is surrounded by a *mass* composed of an infinity of other Monads, which constitute the particular body of this central Monad, and according to the affections of its body [10] the Monad represents, as in a kind of *centre*, the things which are outside of it. This *body* is *organic*, though it forms a kind of automaton or

time perceptions of the actual parts, and even each part has more than one modification; and there is perception at the same time not only of each modification, but also of each part. These multiplied perceptions are different from one another, although our attention cannot always distinguish them, and thus we have confused perceptions, an infinity of which is contained in each distinct perception, because of its relation to everything which is outside. In short, that which is combination of parts in the outside world is represented in the Monad only by combination of its modifications; and without this simple beings could not be internally distinguished from one another, and they would have no relation whatever to external things; and in short, as there are everywhere only simple substances, of which compounds are merely the aggregates, there would be no variation or diversity in things, if there were no internal variation or diversity in simple substances.' *Lettre à Masson* (1716) (G. vi. 628). Cf. *Monadology*, notes 12 and 20.

[7] E. omits *partout*, 'everywhere.'

[8] The idea is that each Monad is separated from every other inasmuch as it has spontaneity, i. e. an activity entirely its own ; for if it had merely an activity like motion, which passes from one thing to another indifferently, it would be united with all other Monads in a *continuum* and would thus cease to be a real, independent unit.

[9] E. omits *distinguée*, reading 'each simple substance.'

[10] Of course, this does not mean that the Monads constituting the body are *really* affected by outside things. Leibniz is here using popular language.

natural machine, which is a machine not only as a whole, but also in the smallest parts of it that can come into observation [11]. Since the world is a *plenum* all things are connected together and each body acts upon every other, more or less, according to their distance, and each, through reaction, is affected by every other. Hence it follows that each Monad is a living mirror, or a mirror endowed with inner activity [12], representative of the universe, according to its point of view, and as subject to rule as is the universe itself. And the perceptions in the Monad are produced one from another according to the laws of desires [*appétits*] or of the *final causes of good and evil*, which consist in observable perceptions, regular or irregular, as, on the other hand, the changes of bodies and external phenomena are produced one from another according to the laws of *efficient causes*, that is to say, of motions [13]. Thus there is a perfect *harmony* between the perceptions of the Monad and the motions of bodies, a harmony pre-established from the beginning between the system of efficient causes and that of final causes. And it is in this way that soul and body are in agreement and are physically united, while it is not possible for the one to change the laws of the other [14].

4. Each Monad, with a particular body, forms a living substance. Thus not only is there everywhere life, accompanied with members or organs, but there is also

---

[11] Cf. *Monadology*, § 64.

[12] 'This "mirror" is a figurative expression ; but it is suitable enough and it has already been employed by theologians and philosophers, when they spoke of a mirror infinitely more perfect, namely, the *mirror of the Deity*, which they made the object of the beatific vision.' *Lettre à Masson* (1716) (G. vi. 626).

[13] Ultimately, motions and desires (*appétits*) are different degrees of the same thing, viz. appetition, or the passage from one conscious or unconscious perception to another. The unconscious appetition is motion or *efficient cause*, not setting before itself an end, while the conscious appetition or desire does set before itself an end of good or evil, i. e. a *final cause*.

[14] Cf. *Monadology*, §§ 78 sqq.

an infinity of degrees in the Monads, one dominating more or less over another. But when the Monad has organs so arranged that they give prominence and sharpness [*du relief et du distingué*] to the impressions they receive, and consequently to the perceptions which represent these (as, for instance, when, by means of the form of the eye's humours, the rays of light are concentrated and act with more force), this may lead to *feeling* [*sentiment*] [15], that is to say, to a perception accompanied by *memory*, in other words, a perception of which a certain echo long remains, so as to make itself heard [16] on occasion. Such a living being is called an *animal*, as its Monad is called a *soul*. And when this soul is raised to *reason*, it is something more sublime and is reckoned among spirits [*esprits*], as will presently be explained. It is true that animals are sometimes in the condition of mere [*simple*] living beings and their souls in the condition of mere Monads [17], namely when their perceptions are not sufficiently sharp [*distingué*] to be remembered, as happens in a deep dreamless sleep or in a swoon. But perceptions which have become completely confused are sure to be developed again in animals [18], for reasons which I shall

[15] The transition from the unconscious to the conscious perception is not by any means made clear. Leibniz is, of course, using ordinary language; but it is difficult to see how he could translate it into the terms of his system, unless he were to content himself with saying that conscious Monads have less confused perceptions than unconscious Monads and have bodies whose organs are differently arranged. For, in Leibniz's view, the action of any one Monad upon another is purely ideal; and there is nothing in the world but Monads. Cf. *Monadology*, § 25.

[16] G. reads *étendre*, which might here be translated 'increase,' for *entendre* [heard], which is E.'s reading. *Entendre* seems more natural.

[17] i. e. unconscious living beings and unconscious Monads.

[18] That is, perceptions (in animals) which have passed into the complete confusion of unconsciousness are sure to pass into consciousness again. Confusion in perceptions is the same thing as envelopment or contraction. (Hence the *petites perceptions* are confused.) On the other hand, clearness in perceptions is the same thing as development or expansion. Cf. note 51 and *New Essays*, Introduction, note 74.

presently mention (§ 12). Thus it is well to make distinction between *perception*, which is the inner state of the Monad representing outer things, and *apperception*, which is *consciousness* or the reflective knowledge of this inner state, and which is not given to all souls nor to the same soul at all times. It is for lack of this distinction that the Cartesians have made the mistake of ignoring perceptions of which we are not conscious [19], as ordinary people ignore imperceptible [*insensible*] bodies [20]. It is this also that has led these same Cartesians to believe that only minds [*esprits*] are Monads, that the lower animals have no soul, and that still less are there other *principles of life* [21]. And as they came into too great conflict with the common opinion of men in denying feeling [*sentiment*] to the lower animals, so on the other hand they conformed too much to the prejudices of the crowd in confounding a *prolonged unconsciousness*, which comes from a great confusion of perceptions, with *absolute death*, in which all perception would cease. This has confirmed the ill-founded opinion that some souls are destroyed, and the bad ideas of some who call themselves free-thinkers [*esprits forts*] and who have disputed the immortality of our soul [22].

---

[19] See *Monadology*, § 14.

[20] 'As in body we hold that there is ἀντιτυπία and figure in general, although we do not know what are the figures of imperceptible bodies; so in the soul we hold that there is perception and appetition, although we do not distinctly know the imperceptible elements of the confused perceptions by which the imperceptible parts of bodies are expressed. . . . You ask whether I believe that there are bodies which do not fall within sight. Why should I not believe it? I think it impossible to doubt it. Through microscopes we see animalculae otherwise imperceptible, and the nerves of these animalculae, and other animalculae, perhaps swimming in the fluid parts of these, cannot be seen. The minuteness [*subtilitas*] of nature goes *ad infinitum*.' *Epistola ad Bierlingium* (1711) (E. 678 a; G. vii. 501).

[21] Leibniz probably means what elsewhere, following Scholastic usage, he calls 'forms.' Cf. Introduction, Part iv. p. 156.

[22] Cf. *Monadology*, § 13.

5. There is a connexion among the perceptions of
animals which has some likeness to reason; but it is
based only on the memory of *facts* or effects[23], and not
at all on the knowledge of *causes*. Thus a dog avoids
the stick with which it has been beaten, because memory
represents to it the pain which this stick has caused it.
And men, in so far as they are empirics, that is to say
in three-fourths of their actions, do not act otherwise
than the lower animals. For instance, we expect that
there will be daylight to-morrow because our experience
has always been so: it is only the astronomer who
rationally foresees it, and even his prediction will ultimately fail when the cause of daylight, which is not
eternal, ceases[24]. But *genuine reasoning* depends upon
necessary or eternal truths, such as those of logic, of
number, of geometry, which produce an indubitable
connexion of ideas and infallible inferences. The animals
in which these inferences do not appear are called the
lower animals [*bêtes*]; but those which know these necessary truths are properly those which are called *rational
animals*, and their souls are called *minds* [*esprits*]. These
souls have the power to perform acts of reflexion and
to observe that which is called ego, substance[25], soul,
mind [*esprit*], in a word, immaterial things and truths.
And this it is which makes science or demonstrative
knowledge possible to us[26].

6. Modern research has taught us, and reason confirms
it, that the living beings whose organs are known to
us[27], that is to say, plants and animals, do not come

[23] G. reads *ou effects* ; E. omits this.

[24] Cf. *Monadology*, §§ 26–28.

[25] E. reads 'Monad' between 'substance' and 'soul'; G. omits it.

[26] Cf. *Monadology*, §§ 29 and 30. In the *Monadology* God is added
as an object of the self-conscious soul.

[27] All Monads have organic bodies, and the series of Monads and
of organisms extends continuously from the lowest of Monads with
the least perceptible of organisms up to the Monad of Monads, God.
At both ends of the scale there are beings whose organs are not
known to us.

from putrefaction or chaos, as the ancients thought, but from *preformed* seeds, and consequently from the transformation of pre-existing living beings. In the seed of large animals there are animalcules which by means of conception obtain a new outward form, which they make their own and which enables them to grow and become larger so as to pass to a greater theatre and to propagate the large animal[28]. It is true that the souls of human spermatic animals are not rational, and that they become so only when conception gives to these animals human nature[29]. And as in general animals are not entirely born in conception or *generation*, no more do they entirely perish in what we call *death*; for it is reasonable that what does not come into being by natural means should not any more come to an end in the course of nature. Thus, throwing off their mask or their tattered covering, they merely return to a more minute theatre, where they may nevertheless be as sensitive [*sensible*] and as well ordered as in the larger theatre[30]. And what has just been said about the large animals applies also to the generation and death[31] of spermatic animals themselves, that is to say, they are growths of other

[28] Cf. *Monadology*, §§ 74, 75.

[29] Cf. *Monadology*, § 82. It would be inconsistent with Leibniz's general principles to suppose that a spermatic animal could have a rational soul (otherwise than in germ, as all souls may be regarded as potentially rational). For the rationality of a soul is merely a very high degree of clearness and distinctness in its perceptions, which again determines its rank as a dominant Monad. But nothing else than its rank as a dominant Monad determines the nature of the body it has. Consequently a rational soul must always have a human body or a body of some higher kind, spiritual or angelic, and the union of a spermatic animal's body with a rational soul is impossible.

[30] Cf. *Monadology*, §§ 73, 76, 77.

[31] E. (manifestly by mistake) omits a clause following these words. A translation of his text would be: 'The generation and death of the smaller spermatic animals in comparison with which they' [*sc.* the large animals] 'may be counted large,' &c. This misses the point of the sentence.

smaller spermatic animals, in comparison with which they in turn may be counted large, for everything in nature proceeds *ad infinitum*[32]. Thus not only souls but also animals are ingenerable and imperishable: they are only developed, enveloped, clothed, unclothed[33], transformed. Souls never put off the whole of their body, and do not pass from one body into another body which is entirely new to them. Accordingly there is no *metempsychosis*, but there is *metamorphosis*. Animals change, take on and put off, parts only[34]. In nutrition this takes place gradually and by little imperceptible [*insensible*] portions, but continually; and on the other hand, in conception or in death, when much[35] is gained or lost all at once, it takes place suddenly and in a way that can be noticed [*notablement*], but rarely.

7. Thus far we have spoken merely as pure *physicists*[36]: now we must rise to *metaphysics*, making use of the *great principle*, usually little employed, which affirms that *nothing takes place without sufficient reason*, that is to say, that nothing happens without its being possible for

---

[32]   'So, naturalists observe, a flea
        Has smaller fleas that on him prey;
        And these have smaller still to bite 'em,
        And so proceed *ad infinitum*.'—Swift, *On Poetry*.
The idea of 'infinities of infinity' is a favourite one with Leibniz, and it is closely connected with the notions underlying his differential calculus. 'For instance, we must conceive (1) the diameter of a small element in a grain of sand, (2) the diameter of the grain of sand itself, (3) that of the globe of the earth, (4) the distance of a fixed star from us, (5) the magnitude of the whole system of fixed stars, as (1) a differential of the second degree, (2) a differential of the first degree, (3) an ordinary assignable line, (4) an infinite line, (5) an infinitely infinite line.' *Lettre à M. d'Angicourt* (1716), Dutens, iii. 500.   Cf. *Monadology*, §§ 65-70.

[33] Cf. 2 Corinthians, v. 4.

[34] Cf. *Monadology*, §§ 71, 72, 77. Aristotle condemns the theory of transmigration of souls in his *De Anima*, i. 3, 407[b] 13.

[35] E. omits *beaucoup* ['much'] and reads, 'all is gained or lost at once.'

[36] i. e. students of nature.

one who should know things sufficiently, to give a reason which is sufficient to determine why things are so and not otherwise. This principle being laid down, the first question we are entitled to put will be—*Why does something exist rather than nothing?* For 'nothing' is simpler and easier [37] than 'something.' Further, granting that things must exist, we must be able to give a reason *why they should exist thus* and not otherwise [38].

8. Now this sufficient reason of the existence of the universe cannot be found in the sequence of contingent things, that is to say, of bodies and their representations in souls: because, matter being in itself indifferent to motion and to rest and to one or another particular motion, we cannot find in it the reason of motion and still less the reason of one particular motion [39]. And although the motion which is at present in matter comes from the preceding motion, and that again from another preceding motion, we are no farther forward, however far we go; for the same question always remains. Thus the sufficient reason, which has no need of any other reason, must needs be outside of this sequence of contingent things and must be in a substance which is the cause of this sequence, or which is a necessary being, bearing in itself the reason of its own existence, otherwise we should not yet have a sufficient reason with which we could stop. And this ultimate reason of things is called God [40].

[37] i. e. more easily brought into existence. But if we can say even this of 'nothing,' must not 'nothing' be 'something'? How can we say of that which is not at all, that it is 'simple' and 'easy' in comparison with other things?

[38] Cf. *Monadology*, § 32.

[39] Motion (which, for Leibniz, is what we should now call an abstraction) is regarded as passing from body to body and as having no definite source in the phenomenal world. The point of view is that which Descartes substituted for the Peripatetic theories, and Leibniz's point is that, while Descartes's view is good so far as it goes, it is insufficient and requires to be supplemented by a deeper explanation.

[40] Cf. *Monadology*, §§ 36-38, and *Ultimate Origination of Things*, p. 338.

9. This primary simple substance must include eminently [41] the perfections contained in the derivative substances which are its effects. Thus it will have power, knowledge and will in perfection, that is to say, it will have supreme [*souveraine*] omnipotence, omniscience and goodness. And as *justice*, taken very [42] generally, is nothing but goodness in conformity with wisdom, there must also be in God supreme justice [43]. The reason which has led to the existence of things through Him makes them also depend upon Him for their continued existence and working; and they continually receive from Him that which makes them have any perfection; but any imperfection that remains in them comes from the essential and original limitation of the created thing [44].

[41] i. e. in a higher degree. See *Monadology*, note 61.

[42] E. omits *fort* [very].

[43] 'There is a great difference between the way in which men are just and the way in which God is just; but it is merely a difference in degree. For God is perfectly and entirely just, and the justice of men is mingled with injustice, faults, and sins because of the imperfection of human nature. The perfections of God are infinite and ours are limited. ... Justice is nothing but that which is in conformity with wisdom and goodness taken together; the end of goodness is the greatest good, but in order to recognize this there is need of wisdom, which is nothing but the knowledge of the good. In the same way, goodness is nothing but the inclination to do good to all and to prevent evil, unless it be necessary in order to secure a greater good or to prevent a greater evil. Thus wisdom is in the understanding and goodness in the will. And consequently justice is in both. Power is another thing; but if it comes into play, it makes the right become actual and causes what ought to be really to exist, so far as the nature of things allows. This is what God does in the world.' *Méditation sur la notion commune de la justice* (Mollat, pp. 60, 62). Cf. *On the Notions of Right and Justice* (1693), p. 283.

[44] Cf. *Monadology*, § 42. This is a brief statement of the main contention of the *Théodicée*, in so far as it endeavours to vindicate the goodness of God in face of the evil in the world. God is the source of the perfections of each Monad, because it is through His choice of the best of all possible worlds that each Monad actually exists and continues in existence. But every Monad has some

10. It follows from the supreme perfection of God that in producing the universe He has chosen the best possible plan, in which there is the greatest variety along with the greatest order; ground, place, time being as well arranged as possible [45]; the greatest effect produced by the simplest ways; the most power, knowledge, happiness and goodness in created things that the universe allowed [46]. For as all possible things in the understanding of God claim existence in proportion to their perfections, the result of all these claims must be the most perfect actual world that is possible. And apart from this it would not be possible to give a reason why things have gone thus rather than otherwise [47].

11. The supreme wisdom of God led Him to choose specially the *laws of motion* which are most fitting and which are most in conformity with abstract or metaphysical reasons. There is conserved the same quantity of total and absolute force, or of activity [*action*], also the same quantity of relative force or of reaction, and finally the same quantity of force of direction [48]. Further,

essential, inalienable imperfection; otherwise it would be indistinguishable from God. And God cannot change the essence of any Monad, as it is in the 'region of ideas,' which is His understanding. He can merely create and support, or withhold His creation and preservation.

[45] Cf. *Ultimate Origination of Things*, pp. 340 sqq.

[46] Cf. *Monadology*, §§ 55–58.   [47] Cf. *Monadology*, §§ 53 and 54.

[48] Every system or aggregate of bodies has a total absolute force, i. e. a total force belonging to the system as a completely independent system—a total force calculated on the supposition that there are no other total forces in relation to it, which might increase or diminish it. The whole matter of the universe is such a system, and consequently its total absolute force remains always the same. But total absolute force is always made up of two partial forces, i. e. forces which belong to the parts of the aggregate or system. These partial forces are (1) 'relative force' or 'force of reaction,' which is the force involved in the mutual action and reaction of the bodies constituting the system or aggregate, i. e. its internal action, and (2) 'force of direction,' which is the force involved in the external action of the system. Cf. Introduction, Part iii. pp. 89 sqq. See also *Explanation of the New System*, note 30.

action is always equal to reaction, and the whole effect is always equivalent to its full cause. And it is remarkable [*surprenant*] that by the sole consideration of *efficient causes* or of matter it was impossible to explain these laws of motion which have been discovered in our time and of which a part has been discovered by myself. For I have found that we must have recourse to *final causes*, and that these laws are dependent not upon the *principle of necessity*, like the truths of logic, arithmetic, and geometry, but upon the *principle of fitness* [*convenance*], that is to say, upon the choice of wisdom. And this is one of the most effective and remarkable proofs of the existence of God for those who can go deeply into these things [49].

12. Again, it follows from the perfection of the Supreme Author not only that the order of the whole universe is the most perfect that can be, but also that each living mirror representing the universe according to its point of view, that is to say, each *Monad*, each substantial centre, must have its perceptions and its desires [*appétits*] as thoroughly well-ordered as is compatible with all the rest. Whence it also follows that *souls*, that is to say, the most dominant Monads, or rather animals themselves [50] cannot fail to awake again

[49] The laws of actual 'concrete' motion cannot be deduced *a priori* under the law of contradiction; but a knowledge of them involves a reference to experience. As a result of this reference to experience we are compelled to conceive body, not as mere externality of parts, indifferent to motion, but as something which always has a *force* of its own. Thus bodies are ultimately or really (as distinct from phenomenally) independent forces (Monads), which differ from one another endlessly but are yet in such harmony that they form one perfectly regular system, the laws of which we can discover and sta*e. Such a system could never have come into existence 'of itself,' by a law of blind necessity, indifferent to good and evil, like the principle of contradiction. An all-wise, all-powerful and infinitely good God must have chosen this system as the best among all possible systems. Cf. *Monadology*, § 51.

[50] E. omits, themselves.'

from the condition of stupor into which death or some other accident may put them [51].

13. For all is regulated in things, once for all, with as much order and mutual connexion as possible, since supreme wisdom and goodness can act only with perfect harmony. The present is big with the future, the future might be read in the past, the distant is expressed in the near. We might get to know the beauty of the universe in each soul, if we could unfold all that is enfolded in it and that is perceptibly developed only through time.

---

[51] Conscious Monads may for a time fall into unconsciousness; but that they should remain permanently in that condition would be against the general order of things. For the tendency of all created Monads is to advance to higher perceptions. In this advance each Monad is essentially limited to some extent; but apart from this *essential* limitation, which is independent of the will of God, no other permanent limitation is imposed. Thus, if a Monad has once been conscious, it may be conscious again, for manifestly it is not *essentially* limited to the unconscious state. And it *must* some day be conscious again, for the world is the best of all possible worlds, not merely on the whole but as regards each of its parts, which is equivalent to saying that the world is so constructed that each of the Monads constituting it shall rise to the highest point of perfection (i. e. of perception and appetition) which its *essential* limitations allow. Leibniz elsewhere speaks of the world in terms which, with slight alteration, he would apply to the individual soul. 'You are right in saying that our globe ought to have been a kind of Paradise, and I add that, if that is so, it can quite well become one yet, and it may have drawn back in order to make a better leap forward.' *Lettre à Bourguet* (1715) (E. 731 a; G. iii. 578). Cf. *Lettre touchant ce qui est indépendant des Sens et de la Matière* (1702) (G. vi. 507): 'Always when we penetrate into the depths of any things, we find in them the most beautiful order that could be desired, even beyond what we imagined, as all those who have gone deeply into the sciences are aware; and accordingly we may hold that the same is the case as regards all other things, and that not only do immaterial substances always continue to exist but their lives, their progress and their changes also are regulated so as to attain a certain end, or rather to approach it more and more, as asymptotes do. And although we sometimes fall back, like lines which have bends in them, advance none the less prevails in the end and gets the victory.' Cf. *New Essays*, Introduction, note 74.

E e 2

But as each distinct perception of the soul includes an infinite number of confused perceptions, which involve the whole universe, the soul itself knows the things of which it has perception, only in so far as it has distinct and heightened [*or* unveiled] [52] perceptions of them ; and it has perfection in proportion to its distinct perceptions. Each soul knows the infinite, knows all, but confusedly ; as when I walk on the sea-shore and hear the great noise the sea makes, I hear the particular sounds which come from the particular waves and which make up the total sound, but I do not discriminate them from one another. Our confused perceptions are the result of the impressions which the whole universe makes upon us.   It is the same with each Monad [53].   God alone has a distinct knowledge of all, for He is the source of all.   It has been very well said that as a centre He is everywhere, but His circumference is nowhere [54], for everything is immediately present to Him without any distance from this centre.

14. As regards the rational soul or *mind* [*l'esprit*], there is in it something more than in the Monads or even in mere [*simple*] souls [55].   It is not only a mirror of the universe of created beings, but also an image of the Deity.   The mind [*l'esprit*] has not merely a perception of the works of God, but it is even capable of producing something which resembles them, although in miniature.   For, to say nothing of the wonders of dreams, in which we

[52] E. reads *relevées*; G. reads *revelées*. *Revelées* (without the usual accents) looks like a slip of the pen and *relevées* is elsewhere used in a similar connexion.   Cf. *Monadology*, § 25.

[53] Cf. *Monadology*, §§ 60 and 61.

[54] 'The world is an infinite sphere, of which the centre is everywhere, the circumference nowhere.'   Pascal, *Pensées*, i. (Havet's ed., p. 1).   Havet traces the phrase to Rabelais (bk. iii. ch. 13), thence to Gerson and Bonaventura, and ultimately to Vincent de Beauvais (early in the thirteenth century) who attributes it to Empedocles. It is not in any writing of Empedocles now known.   See Havet's *Pascal*, pp. 17 sqq.

[55] 'The Monads' here means bare or unconscious Monads, while 'mere souls' means conscious souls, which are not self-conscious.

invent without trouble (but also without willing it) [56] things which, in our waking hours, we should have to think long in order to hit upon, our soul is architectonic also in its voluntary activities and, discovering the scientific principles in accordance with which God has ordered things (*pondere, mensura, numero*, &c.) [57], it imitates, in its own province and in the little world in which it is allowed to act, what God does in the great world [58].

15. It is for this reason that all spirits [*esprits*], whether of men or of angels [*génies*], entering in virtue of reason and of eternal truths into a kind of fellowship with God, are members of the City of God, that is to say, of the most perfect state, formed and governed by the greatest and best of monarchs : in which there is no crime without punishment, no good action without a proportionate reward, and in short as much virtue and happiness as is possible ; and this, not by any interference with the course of nature, as if what God prepares for souls were to disturb the laws of bodies, but by the very order of natural things, in virtue of the harmony pre-established from all time between the realms of nature and of grace, between God as Architect and God as Monarch, so that nature itself [59] leads to grace, and grace, by the use it makes of nature, brings it to perfection [60].

16. Thus although reason cannot make known to us the details of the great future (which are reserved for revelation), we can be assured by this same reason that things are made in a way which exceeds our desires.

[56] E. reads *sans en avoir même la volonté,* 'without even willing it.' G. (from whom I translate) has *mais aussi sans en avoir la volonté.*

[57] *Sed omnia in mensura, et numero et pondere disposuistis.* A quotation (frequently used in Leibniz's time) from the Vulgate, *Book of Wisdom,* ch. 11, v. 21. 'But by measure and number and weight Thou didst order all things' (R. V. ch. 11, v. 20). The phrase *pondere, numero, mensura* occurs in the remains of Ulpian, *Instit.* bk. i, fragment iii.

[58] Cf. *Monadology,* § 82.

[59] E. omits 'itself.'

[60] Cf. *Monadology,* §§ 84–89.

Further, as God is the most perfect and most happy and consequently the most lovable of substances, and as *genuine pure love* [61] consists in the state in which we find pleasure in the perfections and the felicity of the beloved, this love is sure to give us the greatest pleasure of which we are capable, when God is its object.

17. And it is easy to love God as we ought, if we know Him as I have just said [62]. For although God cannot be perceived by our external senses, He is none the less very lovable and He gives very great pleasure. We see how much pleasure honours give to men, although they do not consist in anything that appeals to the external senses. Martyrs and fanatics (though the emotion of the latter is ill-governed) show 'how much influence mental pleasure [*le plaisir de l'esprit*] can have : and, what is more, even the pleasures of sense are really intellectual pleasures confusedly known [63]. Music charms us, although its beauty consists only in the harmonies [*convenances*] of numbers and in the counting (of which we are unconscious but which nevertheless the soul does make) of the beats or vibrations of sounding bodies, which beats or vibrations come together at definite intervals. The pleasure which sight finds in good proportions is of the same nature ; and the pleasures caused by the other senses will be found to amount to much the same thing, although we may not be able to explain it so distinctly [64].

[61] i. e. 'disinterested' love. See *Monadology*, § 90, note 142.

[62] 'God is love [*charitas*], which is known by love [*amor*] and is loved in being known.' Nicholas of Cusa, *Excitationes ex Sermonibus*, 10, 188 b.

[63] For sense is confused perception. Cf. Introduction, Part iii. p. 125.

[64] Leibniz does not mean, as some of his critics (e.g. Kirchmann) seem to have thought, that the pleasure we have in music or in painting is entirely a matter of the senses. What he wants to show is that even the sense-element in artistic pleasure is really of an intellectual kind, and this he does by showing that it depends upon an unrecognized perception of proportion, measure or rhythm. He elsewhere calls it 'a hidden [*occulte*] arithmetic' (G. iv. 551).

18. It may even be said that from this time forth the love of God enables us to enjoy a foretaste of future felicity.   And although this love is disinterested, it constitutes by itself our greatest good and interest, even though we may not seek these in it and though we may consider only the pleasure it gives without regard to the advantage it brings ; for it gives us perfect confidence in the goodness of our Author and Master, which produces real tranquillity of mind, not as in the case of the Stoics, who forcibly school themselves to patience, but through a present content which also assures to us a future happiness [65].   And besides the present pleasure it affords, nothing can be of more advantage for the future than this love of God, for it fulfils our expectations also and leads us in the way of supreme happiness, because in virtue of the perfect order that is established in the universe,

[65] 'There is as much difference between genuine morality [*morale*] and that of the Stoics and Epicureans, as there is between joy and patience ; for their tranquillity was founded only upon necessity, while ours should be founded upon the perfection and the beauty of things, upon our own felicity.' *Théodicée*, § 254 ; E. 580 b ; G. vi. 268. 'What is called *Fatum Stoicum* was not so black as it is painted. It did not keep men from looking after their affairs ; but it tended to give them tranquillity as regard; events, through the consideration of their necessity, which makes our anxieties and regrets useless. . . . The teachings of the Stoics (and perhaps also of some famous philosophers of our own time), being confined to this supposed necessity, can only secure a forced patience ; instead of which our Lord inspires us with more sublime thoughts and teaches us even the way to have content, when He assures us that as God is perfectly good and wise and takes all under His care, so as not even to neglect a hair of our heads our confidence in Him ought to be complete ; so that we should see, if we were able to comprehend it, that it is impossible even to desire anything better (either absolutely or for ourselves) than what He does. It is as if we were to say to men : "Do your duty and be content with what comes of it, not only because you cannot resist Divine providence or the nature of things (which would be enough to make us *tranquil*, but not to make us content) but also because you have to do with a good Master." And this might be called *Fatum Christianum*.' *Théodicée*, Préface, E. 470 b ; G. vi. 30.

everything is done as well as possible both for the
general good and also for the greatest individual good of
those who believe in it and who are satisfied with the
Divine government.   And this belief and satisfaction
must inevitably be the characteristic of those who have
learned to love the Source of all good [66].   It is true that
supreme felicity (by whatever *beatific vision,* or knowledge
of God, it may be accompanied) can never be complete,
because God, being infinite, cannot be entirely known [67].
Thus our happiness will never consist (and it is right
that it should not consist) in complete enjoyment, which
would leave nothing more to be desired and would make
our mind [*esprit*] stupid ; but it must consist in a perpetual progress to new pleasures and new perfections [68].

[66] 'We ought always to be content with the order of the past,
because it is in conformity with the absolute will of God, which
we know through what has come to pass; but we must try to
make the future, so far as it depends upon us, in conformity with
the presumptive will of God or His commandments, to adorn our
Sparta and to labour at doing good, yet without vexing ourselves
when success does not come to us, in the firm belief that God will
be able to find the most fitting season in which to make changes
for the better. Those who are not content with the order of things
cannot flatter themselves that they love God as they ought.'
Lettre à Arnauld (1690) (G. ii. 136; E. 108 a).

[67] According to Leibniz's system, if a Monad were to know God
entirely, it would *be* God and would thus cease to be itself, which
is impossible.   Yet Leibniz regards the relation of men to God as
so close that he calls them 'little gods, subject to the great God.'
Lettre à Arnauld (1687) (G. ii. 125). Cf. Nicholas of Cusa, *Excitationes
ex Sermonibus,* x. 188 a : 'To be able always more and more to
understand (to conform oneself to the Creator) without end, is the
likeness of eternal wisdom.'

[68] 'Felicity is to persons what perfection is to beings.'   Paper
without a title (1686) (G. iv. 462). Cf. *Ultimate Origination of Things,*
pp. 345, 348.

INDEX

—◆—

206; not dependent on the will of God, 57, 242; understanding of God is the region of, 241, 343. See also Truths.

Ethics of Leibniz, 137 sqq.

Eugene, Prince, 215, 405.

Euler's criticism of Leibniz, 255 n.

Evil, origin of, 240 n; problem of, 346 sqq., 416 n; leads to greater good, 349; evil of individuals not to be justified by good of the whole, 348.

Explanation of the New System, 319.

Extension, elements of, 329; not the essence of matter, 28, 94.

Fact and reason, propositions of, 206.

Facultas, 288.

Fatum Stoicum, 423 n.

Feeling an element in every perception, 139.

Fénelon and Bossuet, 270 n.

Fernel, 260 n.

Fichte, 252 n; on the spirituality of the universe, 267 n; influence of Leibniz upon, 178 sqq.; Fichte's Ego and Leibniz's Monad, 180; Fichte and Kant, 178 sqq.

Fitness or choice of the best, 243; degrees of perfection, 247.

Fludd, Robert, 402.

Fluid, perfect, does not exist, 335, 386.

Fontenelle, 309 n.

Force, notion of, 91, 300 n; conservation of, 90 sqq., 327, 417; distinct from Scholastic potency, 91 n; essential to matter, 94; a form of appetition, 226 n; development of Leibniz's views regarding, 351; distinction between absolute and directing force, 328 n; total and partial, &c., 417.

Forces proportional to squares of velocities, 92.

Forms, accidental, 157; substantial, 108 n, 119 n, 156 sqq.; rejected at first by Leibniz, 3; re-introduced by Leibniz, 159,

301; origin and duration of, 259 sqq.; forms in matter, 94 n; indivisible, 302.

Foucher, Simon, 319, 320; Leibniz's comments on his dispute with Hartsoeker, 334 sqq.

Freedom, Leibniz's view of, 141; degrees of, including necessity, 145; freedom and determination, 343; is spontaneity and intelligence, 145; highest freedom accompanied by most perfect knowledge, 146.

Fulgurations of the Divinity, 243.

Galen, 314 n.

Gassendi, 303 n, 319, 352.

Genus, distinction between physical or real and logical or ideal, 394 sqq.

Geometrical relations not merely quantitative, 77.

Geometry, synthetic and analytic, 75; connexion with algebra, 76; analytical geometry of Descartes, 77.

Geulincx, 312 n, 367 n; use of the clocks illustration, 43, 331 n.

God, idea of, in Descartes's system, 161; according to Leibniz and Descartes, 57; inconsistency of Leibniz's account of, 175, 177; proof of His existence, 242; ontological proof, according to Descartes, Spinoza and Leibniz, 274 sqq.; Cosmological proof, 239 n; proof from pre-established harmony, 202, 316, 418; Kant on the proofs, 173; God the ultimate sufficient reason of things, 66, 238, 339, 415; the source both of essences and existences, 241, 343; the ultimate reality, 136; His relation to the world, 257 n, 344, 416; to other Monads, &c., 243 n, 266, 304; God not the only Spirit, 385 n; 'assistance' of God, 43; love of God, 148, 286, 422, 423; His perfection, 240; His antecedent and consequent will, 270, 424 n; His justice compared with human justice,

416 n ; His understanding the region of eternal truths, 66, 241, 343 ; His possibility unlimited, 240 n ; His power, knowledge and will, 244 ; His choice among possible universes, 66, 174 ; His centre everywhere, circumference nowhere, 420 ; without body, 259 ; vision of all things in God, 53 n ; things not modes of God, 137 n ; ethical importance of the idea of God, 293.

Good and evil, relative terms, 146.

Green, T. H., on Leibniz and Kant, 168 n, 172 n.

Grotius, 288, 293 n.

Guhrauer, 37.

Happiness, 287 n ; is a perpetual progress to new perfections, 424 ; nothing more true than, 350.

Hartmann, E., 199.

Hartsoeker, 305 n ; Leibniz's comments on his dispute with Foucher, 334 sqq.

Hegel, 34 ; his solution of the dualism in Leibniz, 186 sqq. ; shows that contradiction presupposes sufficient reason, 187 ; view of self-consciousness, 189, 190 ; his ' notion ' and Leibniz's Monad, 188.

Herbart, 220 n ; his ' reals ' and Leibniz's Monads, 185 ; mathematical methods in psychology, 186.

Herder, 198.

Hermetics, 155 n.

Hermolaus Barbarus. 245.

Hippocrates, 251, 260 n, 373 ; on the indestructibility of animals, 308.

Hobbes, 264 n ; influence upon Leibniz, 7 ; definition of space, 101.

Huygens, 332 n ; intercourse with Leibniz, 6 ; pendulum experiment, 45 n, 332.

Hypotheses, uses of, 325.

Ideas, views of Descartes and Leibniz regarding clear and distinct, 48 ; clearness and distinctness not the sole criteria of truth, 55 sqq. ; innate ideas, 233 n, 360 sqq. ; illustrated by block of veined marble, 131, 366 ; views of Descartes, Locke and Leibniz regarding innate ideas, 125 ; region of ideas in understanding of God, 66, 241, 343 ; symbolizing of ideas, 85.

Identity, principle of, see Contradiction. Identity of the individual, how constituted, 133 n, 373 ; not determined by time and place, 377 n ; physical and moral identity, 258 n.

Ignava ratio, 399 n.

Immortality of the soul, 116, 225 n, 259 sqq., 316, 383, 401 sqq. ; of the rational soul, 116, 307 ; in relation to ethics, 292, 293 n.

Impenetrability, 94 sqq.

Impulse in matter and bodies, 387, 388.

Indeterminism, error of, 143.

Indifference of equilibrium, 375.

Indiscernibles, identity of, 36, 222, 369 n, 377; an application of sufficient reason, 71.

Indivisible elements, how can they form a continuum, 21 sqq.

Inertia of body, 95, 240.

Infinite, different meanings of, 255 n.

Infinitely little, 79.

Infinitesimals, 81 ; a virtual recognition of the principle of Becoming, 82.

Infinity, notion introduced into geometry, 75 ; degrees of, 414 n.

Influxus physicus, 42, 46, 219 n, 333.

Justice, definition of, 148, 283 ; universal, 287 sqq., 294 ; commutative, 287 sqq.; distributive, 287 sqq.; contributive, 289 n ; Aristotle's sub-divisions of particular justice, 287 n ; arithmetical and geometrical equality in justice, 290 n ; Divine and human justice differ only in degree, 291 n, 416 n.

THE END

OXFORD
PRINTED AT THE CLARENDON PRESS
BY HORACE HART, M.A.
PRINTER TO THE UNIVERSITY

WORKS PUBLISHED

AT THE

CLARENDON PRESS, OXFORD.

Bacon. Novum Organum. Edited, with Introduction, Notes, &c., by T. FOWLER, D.D. *Second Edition.* 8vo, 15*s.*

Berkeley. The Works of George Berkeley, D.D., formerly Bishop of Cloyne; including many of his writings hitherto unpublished. With Prefaces, Annotations, and an Account of his Life and Philosophy, by A. CAMPBELL FRASER, Hon. D.C.L. and LL.D. 4 vols. 8vo, £2 18*s.*

The Life, Letters, &c., separately, 16*s.*

—— **Selections.** With Introduction and Notes. For the use of Students in the Universities. By the same Editor. *Fourth Edition.* Crown 8vo, 8*s.* 6*d.*

Bosanquet. Logic; or, The Morphology of Knowledge. By B. BOSANQUET, M.A. 8vo, 21*s.*

British Moralists. Selections from Writers principally of the Eighteenth Century. Edited by L. A. SELBY-BIGGE, M.A. 2 vols. Crown 8vo, 18*s.*

Butler. The Works of Bishop Butler. Edited by the Right Hon. W. E. GLADSTONE. 2 vols. Medium 8vo, £1 8*s.*; or in crown 8vo, 10*s.* 6*d.*

Fowler. The Elements of Deductive Logic, designed mainly for the use of Junior Students in the Universities. By T. FOWLER, D.D. *Tenth Edition,* with a Collection of Examples. Extra fcap. 8vo, 3*s.* 6*d.*

—— **The Elements of Inductive Logic,** designed mainly for the use of Students in the Universities. *Sixth Edition.* Extra fcap. 8vo, 6*s.*

—— **Logic; Deductive and Inductive,** combined in a single volume. Extra fcap. 8vo, 7*s.* 6*d.*

Fowler and Wilson. The Principles of Morals. By T. FOWLER, D.D., and J. M. WILSON, B.D. 8vo, 14*s.*

Green. Prolegomena to Ethics. By T. H. GREEN, M.A. Edited by A. C. BRADLEY, M.A. *Third Edition.* 8vo, 12*s.* 6*d.*

Hegel. The Logic of Hegel; translated from the Encyclopaedia of the Philosophical Sciences. With Prolegomena to the Study of Hegel's Logic and Philosophy. By WILLIAM WALLACE, M.A., LL.D. *Second Edition, Revised and Augmented.* 2 vols. Crown 8vo, 10s. 6d. each.

Hegel's Philosophy of Mind. Translated from the Encyclopaedia of the Philosophical Sciences. With Five Introductory Essays. By WILLIAM WALLACE, M.A., LL.D. Crown 8vo, 10s. 6d.

Hume's Treatise of Human Nature. Reprinted from the Original Edition in Three Volumes, and edited by L. A. SELBY-BIGGE, M.A. *Second Edition.* Crown 8vo, 8s.

—— **Enquiry concerning the Human Understanding,** and an Enquiry concerning the Principles of Morals. Edited by L. A. SELBY-BIGGE, M.A. Crown 8vo, 7s. 6d.

Locke. An Essay concerning Human Understanding. By JOHN LOCKE. Collated and Annotated with Prolegomena, Biographical, Critical, and Historical, by A. CAMPBELL FRASER, Hon. D.C.L. and LL.D. 2 vols. 8vo, £1 12s.

Locke's Conduct of the Understanding. Edited by T. FOWLER, D.D. *Third Edition.* Extra fcap. 8vo, 2s. 6d.

Lotze's Logic, in Three Books; of Thought, of Investigation, and of Knowledge. English Translation; edited by B. BOSANQUET, M.A. *Second Edition.* 2 vols. Crown 8vo, 12s.

—— **Metaphysic,** in Three Books; Ontology, Cosmology, and Psychology. English Translation; edited by B. BOSANQUET, M.A. *Second Edition.* 2 vols. Crown 8vo, 12s.

Martineau. Types of Ethical Theory. By JAMES MARTINEAU, D.D. *Third Edition.* 2 vols. Crown 8vo, 15s.

—— **A Study of Religion: its Sources and Contents.** *Second Edition.* 2 vols. Crown 8vo, 15s.

𝖔𝖷𝖋𝖔𝖗𝖉

AT THE CLARENDON PRESS

LONDON: HENRY FROWDE

OXFORD UNIVERSITY PRESS WAREHOUSE, AMEN CORNER, E.C.

Clarendon Press, Oxford.

SELECT LIST OF STANDARD WORKS.

1. STANDARD LATIN WORKS.

Avianus. *The Fables.* Edited, with Prolegomena, Critical Apparatus, Commentary, &c., by Robinson Ellis, M.A., LL.D. 8vo. 8s. 6d.

Caesar. *De Bello Gallico.* Books I–VII. According to the Text of Emanuel Hoffmann (Vienna, 1890). Edited, with Introduction and Notes, by St. George Stock. Post 8vo, 10s. 6d.

Catulli Veronensis *Liber.* Iterum recognovit, Apparatum Criticum Prolegomena Appendices addidit, R. Ellis, A.M. 8vo. 16s.

Catullus, *a Commentary on.* By Robinson Ellis, M.A. *Second Edition.* 8vo. 18s.

Cicero. *De Oratore Libri Tres.* With Introduction and Notes. By A. S. Wilkins, Litt.D. 8vo. 18s.
Also, separately—
Book I. 7s. 6d.   Book II. 5s.
Book III. 6s.

—— *Pro Milone.* Edited by A. C. Clark, M.A. 8vo. 8s. 6d.

—— *Select Letters.* With English Introductions, Notes, and Appendices. By Albert Watson, M.A. *Fourth Edition.* 8vo. 18s.

Horace. With a Commentary. By E. C. Wickham, D.D. *Two Vols.*
Vol. I. The Odes, Carmen Seculare, and Epodes. *Third Edition.* 8vo. 12s.
Vol. II. The Satires, Epistles, and De Arte Poetica. 8vo. 12s.

Juvenal. *Thirteen Satires.* Edited, with Introduction and Notes, by C. H. Pearson, M.A., and Herbert A. Strong, M.A., LL.D. *Second Edition.* Crown 8vo. 9s.

—— *Ad Satiram Sextam* in Codice Bodl. Canon. XLI Additi versus XXXVI. Exscripsit E. O. Winstedt, Accedit Simulacrum Photographicum. In Wrapper. 1s. net.

Livy. *Book I.* With Introduction, Historical Examination, and Notes. By Sir J. R. Seeley, M.A. *Third Edition.* 8vo. 6s.

Manilius. *Noctes Manilianae;* sive Dissertationes in Astronomica Manilii. Accedunt Coniecturae in Germanici Aratea. Scripsit R. Ellis. Crown 8vo. 6s.

Merry. *Selected Fragments* of Roman Poetry. Edited, with Introduction and Notes, by W. W. Merry, D.D. *Second Edition.* Crown 8vo. 6s. 6d.

Ovid. *P. Ovidii Nasonis Ibis.* Ex Novis Codicibus edidit, Scholia Vetera Commentarium cum Prolegomenis Appendice Indice addidit, R. Ellis, A.M. 8vo. 10s. 6d.

—— *P. Ovidi Nasonis Tristium Libri V.* Recensuit S. G. Owen A.M. 8vo. 16s.

Persius. *The Satires.* With a Translation and Commentary. By John Conington, M.A. Edited by Henry Nettleship, M.A. *Third Edition.* 8vo. 8s. 6d.

Plautus. *Rudens.* Edited, with Critical and Explanatory Notes, by E. A. Sonnenschein, M.A. 8vo. 8s. 6d.

—— *The Codex Turnebi of Plautus.* By W. M. Lindsay, M.A. 8vo, 21s. *net.*

Quintilian. *Institutionis Oratoriae Liber Decimus.* A Revised Text, with Introductory Essays, Critical Notes, &c. By W. Peterson, M.A., LL.D. 8vo. 12s. 6d.

Rushforth. *Latin Historical Inscriptions, illustrating the History of the Early Empire.* By G. McN. Rushforth, M.A. 8vo. 10s. *net.*

Tacitus. *The Annals.* Edited, with Introduction and Notes, by H. Furneaux, M.A. 2 vols. 8vo.
     Vol. I, Books I–VI. *Second Edition.* 18s.
     Vol. II, Books XI–XVI. 20s.

King and **Cookson.** *The Principles of Sound and Inflexion, as illustrated in the Greek and Latin Languages.* By J. E. King, M.A., and Christopher Cookson, M.A. 8vo. 18s.

—— *An Introduction to the Comparative Grammar of Greek and Latin.* Crown 8vo. 5s. 6d.

Lindsay. *The Latin Language.* An Historical Account of Latin Sounds, Stems and Flexions. By W. M. Lindsay, M.A. Demy 8vo. 21s.

Nettleship. *Lectures and Essays on Subjects connected with Latin Scholarship and Literature.*

—— Second Series. Edited by F. J. Haverfield, with Memoir by Mrs. Nettleship. Crown 8vo. 7s. 6d.

Tacitus. *De Germania.* By the same Editor. 8vo. 6s. 6d.

—— *Vita Agricolae.* By the same Editor. 8vo. 6s. 6d.

—— *Dialogus de Oratoribus.* A Revised Text, with Introductory Essays, and Critical and Explanatory Notes. By W. Peterson, M.A., LL.D. 8vo. 10s. 6d.

Velleius Paterculus *ad M. Vinicium Libri Duo.* Ex Amerbachii praecipue Apographo edidit et emendavit R. Ellis, Litterarum Latinarum Professor publicus apud Oxonienses. Crown 8vo, paper boards. 6s.

Virgil. *With an Introduction and Notes.* By T. L. Papillon, M.A., and A. E. Haigh, M.A. 2 vols. Crown 8vo. Cloth, 6s. each; *stiff covers* 3s. 6d. each.

Also sold in parts, as follows—
Bucolics and *Georgics,* 2s. 6d.
Aeneid, in 4 parts, 2s. each.

Nettleship. *Contributions to Latin Lexicography.* 8vo. 21s.

Sellar. *Roman Poets of the Augustan Age.* By W. Y. Sellar, M.A.; viz.
   I. VIRGIL. *New Edition.* Crown 8vo. 9s.
   II. HORACE and the ELEGIAC POETS. With a Memoir of the Author by Andrew Lang, M.A., *Second Edition.* Crown 8vo, 7s. 6d.

—— *Roman Poets of the Republic. Third Edition.* Crown 8vo. 10s.

Wordsworth. *Fragments and Specimens of Early Latin.* With Introductions and Notes. By J. Wordsworth, D.D. 8vo. 18s.

2. STANDARD GREEK WORKS.

Chandler. *A Practical Intro-*
duction to Greek Accentuation, by H. W.
Chandler, M.A. *Second Edition.* 10s.6d.

Farnell. *The Cults of the Greek*
States. With Plates. By L. R. Farnell,
M.A.
    Vols. I and II. 8vo. 32s. *net.*
    Volume III *in Preparation.*

Grenfell. *An Alexandrian*
Erotic Fragment and other Greek Papyri,
chiefly Ptolemaic. Edited by B. P.
Grenfell, M.A. Sm. 4to. 8s. 6d. *net.*

Grenfell and Hunt. *New*
Classical Fragments and other Greek
and Latin Papyri. Edited by B. P.
Grenfell, M.A., and A. S. Hunt,
M.A. With Plates, 12s. 6d. *net.*

—— *Menander's* Γεωργός.
A Revised Text of the Geneva
Fragment. With a Translation
and Notes by the same Editors.
8vo, stiff covers, 1s. 6d.

Grenfell and Mahaffy. *Rev-*
enue Laws of Ptolemy Philadelphus.
2 vols. Text and Plates. 31s. 6d. *net.*

Haigh. *The Attic Theatre.*
A Description of the Stage and
Theatre of the Athenians, and of
the Dramatic Performances at
Athens. By A. E. Haigh, M.A.
Second Edition, Revised and Enlarged.
8vo. 12s. 6d.

—— **The Tragic Drama of**
the Greeks. With Illustrations.
8vo. 12s. 6d.

Head. *Historia Numorum :*
A Manual of Greek Numismatics.
By Barclay V. Head. Royal 8vo,
half-bound, 42s.

Hicks. *A Manual of Greek*
Historical Inscriptions. By E. L.
Hicks, M.A. 8vo. 10s. 6d.

Hill. *Sources for Greek His-*
tory between the Persian and Pelopon-
nesian Wars. Collected and arranged
by G. F. HILL, M.A. 8vo. 10s. 6d.

Kenyon. *The Palaeography*
of Greek Papyri. By Frederic G.
Kenyon, M.A. 8vo, with Twenty
Facsimiles, and a Table of Alphabets.
10s. 6d.

Liddell and Scott. *A Greek-*
English Lexicon, by H. G. Liddell,
D.D., and Robert Scott, D.D. *Eighth*
Edition, Revised. 4to. 36s.

Monro. *Modes of Ancient*
Greek Music. By D. B. Monro, M.A.
8vo. 8s. 6d. *net.*

Paton and Hicks. *The In-*
scriptions of Cos. By W. R. Paton
and E. L. Hicks. Royal 8vo, linen,
with Map, 28s.

Smyth. *The Sounds and*
Inflections of the Greek Dialects (Ionic).
By H. Weir Smyth, Ph. D. 8vo. 24s.

Thompson. *A Glossary of*
Greek Birds. By D'Arcy W. Thompson. 8vo, buckram, 10s. *net.*

Aeschinem et Isocratem, *Scho-*
lia Graeca in. Edidit G. Dindorfius.
8vo. 4s.

Aeschylus. *In Single Plays.*
With Introduction and Notes, by
Arthur Sidgwick, M.A. *New*
Edition. Extra fcap. 8vo. 3s. each.
    I. Agamemnon. II. Choephoroi.
    III. Eumenides.

—— Prometheus Bound. With Introduction and Notes, by A. O.
Prickard, M.A. *Third Edition.* 2s.

Aeschyli *quae supersunt in*
Codice Laurentiano quoad effici potuit et
ad cognitionem necesse est visum typis
descripta edidit R. Merkel. Small
folio. 21s.

Aeschylus : *Tragoediae et*
Fragmenta, ex recensione Guil. Dindorfii. *Second Edition.* 8vo. 5s. 6d.

—— *Annotationes* Guil. Dindorfii. Partes II. 8vo. 10s.

Apsinis et **Longini** *Rhetorica.*
E Codicibus mss. recensuit Joh.
Bakius. 8vo. 3s.

Aristophanes. *A Complete*
Concordance to the Comedies and Frag-
ments. By H. Dunbar, M.D. 4to.
21s.

—— *Comoediae et Fragmenta,*
ex recensione Guil. Dindorfii.
Tomi II. 8vo. 11s.

—— *Annotationes* Guil. Dindorfii. Partes II. 8vo. 11s.

—— *Scholia Graeca* ex Codicibus aucta et emendata a Guil.
Dindorfio. Partes III. 8vo. 20s.

—— *In Single Plays.* Edited,
with English Notes, Introductions,
&c., by W. W. Merry, D.D. Extra
fcap. 8vo.
    TheAcharnians. *Fourth Edition,* 3s.
    The Birds. *Third Edition,* 3s. 6d.
    The Clouds. *Third Edition,* 3s.
    The Frogs. *Third Edition,* 3s.
    The Knights. *Second Edition,* 3s.
    The Peace. 3s. 6d.
    The Wasps. 3s. 6d.

Aristotle. Ex recensione
Im. Bekkeri. Accedunt Indices
Sylburgiani. Tomi XI. 8vo. 2l. 10s.
The volumes (except I and IX) may
be had separately, price 5s. 6d. each.

—— *Ethica Nicomachea,* recognovit brevique Adnotatione
critica instruxit I. Bywater. 8vo. 6s.
Also in crown 8vo, paper cover, 3s. 6d.

—— Contributions to the
Textual Criticism of the Nicomachean Ethics. By I. Bywater. 2s. 6d.

—— Notes on the Nicoma-
chean Ethics. By J. A. Stewart, M.A.
2 vols. 8vo. 32s.

—— *Selecta ex Organo Aris-*
toteleo Capitula. In usum Scho-
larum Academicarum. Crown 8vo,
stiff covers. 3s. 6d.

—— *De Arte Poetica Liber.*
Recognovit Brevique Adnotatione
Critica Instruxit I. Bywater, Litter-
arum Graecarum Professor Regius.
Post 8vo, stiff covers, 1s. 6d.

Aristotle. *The Politics,* with
Introductions, Notes, &c., by W. L.
Newman, M.A. Vols. I and II.
Medium 8vo. 28s.
    Vols. III and IV. [*In the Press.*]

—— *The Politics,* trans-
lated into English, with Introduction, Marginal Analysis, Notes,
and Indices, by B. Jowett, M.A.
Medium 8vo. 2 vols. 21s.

—— *The English Manuscripts*
of the Nicomachean Ethics, described in
relation to Bekker's Manuscripts and
other Sources. By J. A. Stewart,
M.A. (Anecdota Oxon.) Small 4to.
3s. 6d.

—— *Physics.* Book VII.
Collation of various mss. ; with Introduction by R. Shute, M.A. (Anecdota Oxon.) Small 4to. 2s.

Choerobosci *Dictata in Theo-*
dosii Canones, necnon Epimerismi in
Psalmos. E Codicibus mss. edidit
Thomas Gaisford, S.T.P. Tomi III.
8vo. 15s.

Demosthenes. Ex recensione
G. Dindorfii. Tomi IX. 8vo. 46s.
    Separately—
    Text, 21s. Annotations, 15s.
    Scholia, 10s.

Demosthenes and **Aeschines**.
The Orations of Demosthenes and
Aeschines on the Crown. With
Introductory Essays and Notes. By
G. A. Simcox, M.A., and W. H.
Simcox, M.A. 8vo. 12s.

Demosthenes. *Orations*
against Philip. With Introduction
and Notes, by Evelyn Abbott, M.A.,
and P. E. Matheson, M.A.
    Vol. I. Philippic I. Olynthiacs
    I–III. Extra fcap. 8vo. 3s.
    Vol. II. De Pace, Philippic II.
    De Chersoneso, Philippic III.
    Extra fcap. 8vo. 4s. 6d.

Euripides. *Tragoediae et*
Fragmenta, ex recensione Guil. Dindorfii. Tomi II. 8vo. 10s.

Euripides. *Annotationes*
Guil. Dindorfii. Partes II. 8vo.
10s.

—— *Scholia Graeca*, ex Codicibus aucta et emendata a Guil.
Dindorflo. Tomi IV. 8vo. 36s.

Hephaestionis *Enchiridion*,
Terentianus Maurus, Proclus, &c. Edidit
T. Gaisford, S.T.P. Tomi II. 10s.

Heracliti *Ephesii Reliquiae.*
Recensuit I. Bywater, M.A. Appendicis loco additae sunt Diogenis
Laertii Vita Heracliti, Particulae
Hippocratei De Diaeta Lib. I., Epistolae Heracliteae. 8vo. 6s.

Herodotus. *Books V and VI,*
Terpsichore and Erato. Edited,
with Notes and Appendices, by
Evelyn Abbott, M.A., LL.D. 8vo,
with two Maps, 6s.

Homer. *A Complete Concordance to the Odyssey and Hymns of
Homer;* to which is added a Concordance to the Parallel Passages in
the Iliad, Odyssey, and Hymns.
By Henry Dunbar, M.D. 4to.
21s.

—— *A Grammar of the Homeric Dialect.* By D. B. Monro, M.A.
8vo. *Second Edition.* 14s.

—— *Ilias,* ex rec. Guil. Dindorfii. 8vo. 5s. 6d.

—— *Scholia Graeca in
Iliadem.* Edited by W. Dindorf,
after a new collation of the Venetian
mss. by D. B. Monro, M.A. 4 vols.
8vo. 50s.

—— *Scholia Graeca in
Iliadem Townleyana.* Recensuit
Ernestus Maass. 2 vols. 8vo.
36s.

—— *Odyssea,* ex rec. G.
Dindorfii. 8vo. 5s. 6d.

—— *Scholia Graeca in
Odysseam.* Edidit Guil. Dindorfius.
Tomi II. 8vo. 15s. 6d.

Homer. *Odyssey.* Books I–
XII. Edited with English Notes,

Appendices, &c. By W. W. Merry,
D.D., and James Riddell, M.A.
Second Edition. 8vo. 16s.

—— —— Books XIII–
XXIV. By D. B. Monro, M.A.
[*In the Press.*]

—— *Hymni Homerici.* Codicibus denuo collatis recensuit
Alfredus Goodwin. Small folio.
With four Plates. 21s. *net.*

Homeri Opera et Reliquiae.
Monro. Crown 8vo. India Paper.
Cloth, 10s. 6d. *net.*
Also in various leather bindings.

Oratores Attici, ex recensione
Bekkeri:
Vol. III. Isaeus, Aeschines,
Lycurgus, Dinarchus, &c.
8vo. 7s.
[*Vols. I and II are out of print.*]

—— *Index Andocideus, Lycurgeus, Dinarcheus,* confectus a
Ludovico Leaming Forman, Ph.D.
8vo. 7s. 6d.

Paroemiographi Graeci, *quorum pars nunc primum ex Codd. mss.
vulgatur.* Edidit T. Gaisford, S.T.P.
1836. 8vo. 5s. 6d.

Plato. *Apology,* with a revised Text and English Notes, and
a Digest of Platonic Idioms, by
James Riddell, M.A. 8vo. 8s. 6d.

—— *Philebus,* with a revised
Text and English Notes, by Edward
Poste, M.A. 8vo. 7s. 6d.

—— *Republic.* The Greek
Text. Edited, with Notes and
Essays, by B. Jowett, M.A., and
Lewis Campbell, M.A. In three
vols. Medium 8vo. 42s.

—— *Sophistes* and *Politicus,*
with a revised Text and English
Notes, by L. Campbell, M.A. 8vo.
10s. 6d.

—— *Theaetetus,* with a revised Text and English Notes, by
L. Campbell, M.A. *Second Edition.*
8vo. 10s. 6d.

Plato. *The Dialogues*, translated into English, with Analyses and Introductions, by B. Jowett, M.A. *Third Edition.* 5 vols. Medium 8vo. Cloth, 84s.; half-morocco,100s.

—— *The Republic*, translated into English, with Analysis and Introduction, by B. Jowett, M.A. *Third Edition.* Medium 8vo. 12s. 6d.; half-roan, 14s.

—— *With Introduction and* Notes. By St. George Stock, M.A. Extra fcap. 8vo.

　I. The Apology, 2s. 6d.
　II. Crito, 2s. III. Meno, 2s. 6d.

—— *Selections. With Intro-* ductions and Notes. By John Purves, M.A., and Preface by B. Jowett, M.A. *Second Edition.* Extra fcap. 8vo. 5s.

—— *A Selection of Passages* from Plato for English Readers; from the Translation by B. Jowett, M.A. Edited, with Introductions, by M. J. Knight. 2 vols. Crown 8vo, gilt top. 12s.

Plotinus. Edidit F. Creuzer. Tomi III. 4to. 28s.

Polybius. *Selections.* Edited by J. L. Strachan-Davidson, M.A. With Maps. Medium 8vo. 21s.

Plutarchi *Moralia, id est,* Opera, exceptis Vitis, reliqua. Edidit Daniel Wyttenbach. Accedit Index Graecitatis. Tomi VIII. Partes XV. 1795-1830. 8vo, cloth, 70s.

Sophocles. *The Plays and* Fragments. With English Notes and Introductions, by Lewis Campbell, M.A. 2 vols. 8vo, 16s. each.

　Vol. I. Oedipus Tyrannus. Oedipus Coloneus. Antigone.
　Vol. II. Ajax. Electra. Trachiniae. Philoctetes. Fragments.

—— *Tragoediae et Fragmenta,* ex recensione et cum commentariis Guil. Dindorfii. *Third Edition.* 2 vols. Fcap. 8vo. 21s. Each Play separately, limp, 2s. 6d.

Sophocles. *Tragoediae et* Fragmenta cum Annotationibus Guil. Dindorfii. Tomi II. 8vo. 10s. The Text, Vol. I. 5s. 6d. The Notes, Vol. II. 4s. 6d.

Stobaei *Florilegium.* Ad MSS. fidem emendavit et supplevit T.Gaisford,S.T.P. Tomi IV. 8vo. 20s.

—— *Eclogarum Physicarum* et Ethicarum libri duo. Accedit Hieroclis Commentarius in aurea carmina Pythagoreorum. Ad mss. Codd. recensuit T. Gaisford, S.T.P. Tomi II. 8vo. 11s.

Strabo. *Selections*, with an Introduction on Strabo's Life and Works. By H. F. Tozer, M.A., F.R.G.S. 8vo. With Maps and Plans. 12s.

Theodoreti *Graecarum Affec-* tionum Curatio. Ad Codices mss. recensuit T. Gaisford, S.T.P. 8vo. 7s. 6d.

Thucydides. Translated into English, to which is prefixed an Essay on Inscriptions and a Note on the Geography of Thucydides. By B. Jowett, M.A. *Second Edition, Revised.* 2 vols., 8vo, cloth, 15s.

　Vol. I. Essay on Inscriptions and Books I–III.
　Vol. II. Books IV–VIII and Historical Index.

Xenophon. Ex recensione et cum annotationibus L. Dindorfii.

　Historia Graeca. Second Edition. 8vo. 10s. 6d.
　Expeditio Cyri. Second Edition. 8vo. 10s. 6d.
　Institutio Cyri. 8vo. 10s. 6d.
　Memorabilia Socratis. 8vo. 7s. 6d.
　Opuscula Politica Equestria et Venatica cum Arriani Libello de Venatione. 8vo. 10s. 6d.

—— A Commentary, with Introduction and Appendices, on the Hellenica of Xenophon. By G. E. UNDERHILL, M.A. Crown 8vo. 7s. 6d.

3. MISCELLANEOUS STANDARD WORKS.

Arbuthnot. *The Life and Works of John Arbuthnot.* By George A. Aitken. 8vo, cloth extra, with Portrait, 16s.

Bacon. *The Essays.* Edited with Introduction and Illustrative Notes, by S. H. Reynolds, M.A. 8vo, half-bound, 12s. 6d.

Casaubon (Isaac), 1559–1614. By Mark Pattison, late Rector of Lincoln College. *Second Edition.* 8vo. 16s.

Finlay. *A History of Greece from its Conquest by the Romans to the present time,* B.C. 146 to A.D. 1864. By George Finlay, LL.D. A new Edition, revised throughout, and in part re-written, with considerable additions, by the Author, and edited by H. F. Tozer, M.A. 7 vols. 8vo. 70s.

Hodgkin. *Italy and her Invaders.* 8 vols. With Plates and Maps. By Thomas Hodgkin, D.C.L. A.D. 376–744. 8vo. Vols. I and II, *Second Edition,* 42s. Vols. III and IV, *Second Edition,* 36s. Vols. V and VI, 36s. Vols. VII and VIII, 24s.

Hooker, Sir J. D., and B. D. Jackson. *Index Kewensis.* 2 vols. 4to. 210s. *net.*

Ilbert. *The Government of India;* being a Digest of the Statute Law relating thereto. With Historical Introduction and Illustrative Documents. By Sir Courtenay Ilbert, K.C.S.I. 8vo, half-roan, 21s.

Justinian. *Imperatoris Iustiniani Institutionum Libri Quattuor;* with Introductions, Commentary, Excursus and Translation. By J. B. Moyle, D.C.L. *Third Edition.* 2 vols. 8vo. 22s.

Machiavelli. *Il Principe.* Edited by L. Arthur Burd. With an Introduction by Lord Acton. 8vo. 14s.

Pattison. *Essays by the late Mark Pattison,* sometime Rector of Lincoln College. Collected and Arranged by Henry Nettleship, M.A. 2 vols. 8vo. 24s.

Payne. *History of the New World called America.* By E. J. Payne, M.A. 8vo, Vol. I, 18s.; Vol. II, 14s.

Ralegh. *Sir Walter Ralegh.* A Biography. By W. Stebbing. Re-issue. Small Post 8vo. 6s. *net.*
*** *Also in Half-parchment, with List of Authorities separately, post 8vo,* 10s. 6d.

Ramsay. *The Cities and Bishoprics of Phrygia;* being an Essay on the Local History of Phrygia, from the Earliest Times to the Turkish Conquest. By W. M. Ramsay, D.C.L., LL.D. Vol. I. Part I. *The Lycos Valley and South-Western Phrygia.* Royal 8vo, linen, 18s. *net.* Vol. I. Part II. *West and West-Central Phrygia.* Royal 8vo, linen, 21s. *net.*

Rhŷs. *Celtic Folklore, Welsh and Manx.* By John Rhŷs, M.A., D.Litt. 2 Vols. 8vo, 21s.

—— *Studies in the Arthurian Legend.* 8vo, 12s. 6d.

Stokes. *The Anglo-Indian Codes.* By Whitley Stokes, LL.D. Vol. I. Substantive Law. 8vo. 30s. Vol. II. Adjective Law. 8vo. 35s.

Strachey. *Hastings and The Rohilla War.* By Sir John Strachey, G.C.S.I. 8vo, cloth, 10s. 6d.

Woodhouse. *Aetolia; its Geography, Topography, and Antiquities.* By William J. Woodhouse, M.A., F.R.G.S. With Maps and Illustrations. Royal 8vo, linen, 21s. *net.*

London : HENRY FROWDE, Amen Corner, E.C.

4. STANDARD THEOLOGICAL WORKS, &c.

St. Basil: *The Book of St. Basil on the Holy Spirit.* A Revised Text, with Notes and Introduction by C. F. H. Johnston, M.A. Crown 8vo. 7s. 6d.

The Coptic Version of the New Testament, *in the Northern Dialect, otherwise called Memphitic and Bohairic.* With Introduction, Critical Apparatus, and Literal English Translation. The Gospels. 2 vols. 8vo. 42s.

(Vols. III and IV in the Press.)

Bright. *Chapters of Early English Church History.* By W. Bright, D.D. *Third Edition.* 8vo. 12s.

Canons of the First Four General Councils *of Nicaea, Constantinople, Ephesus, and Chalcedon.* With Notes, by W. Bright, D.D. *Second Edition.* Crown 8vo. 7s. 6d.

The Book of Enoch. Translated from Dillmann's Ethiopic Text (emended and revised), and Edited by R. H. Charles, M.A. 8vo. 16s.

Conybeare. *The Key of Truth.* A Manual of the Paulician Church of Armenia. The Armenian Text, edited and translated with illustrative Documents and Introduction by F. C. Conybeare, M.A. 8vo. 15s. net.

Driver. *The Parallel Psalter,* being the Prayer-Book Version of the Psalms and a New Version, arranged in parallel columns. With an Introduction and Glossaries. By the Rev. S. R. Driver, D.D., Litt.D. Extra fcap. 8vo. 6s.

Ecclesiasticus (xxxix. 15—xlix. 11). The Original Hebrew, with Early Versions and English Translations, &c. Edited by A. Cowley, M.A., and Ad. Neubauer, M.A. 4to. 10s. 6d. net.

Ecclesiasticus. *Facsimiles of the Fragments hitherto recovered of the Book of Ecclesiasticus in Hebrew.* 60 leaves, collotype, in a Cloth Box, price 21s. net. (Published jointly by the Oxford and Cambridge University Presses.)

Hatch and Redpath. *A Concordance to the Greek Versions and Apocryphal Books of the Old Testament.* By the late Edwin Hatch, M.A., and H. A. Redpath, M.A. In Six Parts. Imperial 4to. 21s. each.

—— *Supplement,* Fasc. I. Containing a Concordance to the Proper Names occurring in the Septuagint. By H. A. Redpath, M.A. Imperial 4to, 16s.

Ommanney. *A Critical Dissertation on the Athanasian Creed. Its Original Language, Date, Authorship, Titles, Text, Reception, and Use.* By G. D. W. Ommanney, M.A. 8vo. 16s.

Paget. *An Introduction to the Fifth Book of Hooker's Treatise of the Laws of Ecclesiastical Polity.* By the Very Rev. Francis Paget, D.D. Medium 8vo, cloth, 7s. 6d.

Turner. *Ecclesiae Occidentalis Monumenta Iuris Antiquissima:* Canonum et Conciliorum Graecorum Interpretationes Latinae. Edidit Cuthbertus Hamilton Turner, A.M. Fasc. I. pars. I. 4to, stiff covers, 10s. 6d.

Wordsworth and White. *Nouum Testamentum Domini Nostri Iesu Christi Latine,* secundum Editionem Sancti Hieronymi. Ad Codicum Manuscriptorum fidem recensuit Iohannes Wordsworth, S.T.P., Episcopus Sarisburiensis; in operis societatem adsumto Henrico Iuliano White, A.M. 4to. Pars I, buckram, 52s. 6d.

Oxford
176 AT THE CLARENDON PRESS
LONDON: HENRY FROWDE
OXFORD UNIVERSITY PRESS WAREHOUSE, AMEN CORNER, E.C.